Trial of Oscar Slater

Oscar Slater

William Roughead

**TO
THE HONOURABLE LORD GUTHRIE
THIS VOLUME
IS
BY KIND PERMISSION
RESPECTFULLY DEDICATED**

1910

The Hon. Lord Guthrie

INTRODUCTION

THE primary importance of the trial of Oscar Slater for the murder of Miss Marion Gilchrist, and that which well warrants its preservation in such permanent form as the present series affords, is the fact that a conviction was obtained by the Crown upon evidence as to identity based on personal impressions, the corroboration supplied by the circumstantial evidence, though containing elements of strong suspicion, adding nothing conclusive of the prisoner's guilt.

The direct evidence to identification was twofold: firstly, by three witnesses who admittedly saw the supposed murderer leaving the scene of the crime; and secondly, by twelve other witnesses who identified Slater as a man they had seen watching Miss Gilchrist's house for weeks before the murder. Had the identification by the former been clear and unhesitating, the case for the prosecution would have been proved beyond dispute; but as regards the evidence of at least two of them, such was not the fact. The evidence given by those who saw the watcher is also unconvincing in respect of manifest discrepancies as to his dress and personal appearance; while the impossibility of reconciling the conflicting testimony of the various witnesses increases the difficulties which beset the case. That these difficulties were appreciated by the fifteen jurymen is shown by the narrow majority of three votes upon which the verdict turned; and the weight attached to them by the Scottish Secretary and his advisers is apparent in the commutation of the sentence.

The case excited widespread interest at the time, and, by reason of the sensational reports of which it was the occasion, exercised the popular imagination for many months. These rumours, alike hurtful to the memory of the aged victim and prejudicial to the accused, were, happily, dissipated by the evidence adduced at the trial. But apart from these, the case itself contains elements sufficiently strange and suggestive to supply, in an unwonted degree, a legitimate and lasting interest.

A crime of exceptional atrocity, committed in a well-to-do quarter of a great city, not in the dead of night, but at an hour when the streets were yet busy and many people were out of doors; the age and circumstances of the hapless lady; the incredible ruthlessness of the attack; the rapidity with which her murderer effected his fatal purpose; the fact that a witness was literally on the threshold of the tragedy, and heard the deed done; the audacity of the criminal in making good his escape from the very presence of two persons who had frustrated the main object of his design: these are indeed matters of more than common note. The ability with which, in spite of serious obstacles, the Glasgow police ran their man to earth—or rather, to sea—within a week; the extradition proceedings in New York; the trial at Edinburgh, with the curious glimpses it gave of that dark under-world which lies beneath the surface of our modern civilisation; the obvious weakness of certain links in the formidable chain forged by the Crown; the surprising verdict; and, finally, the illogical and unsatisfactory reprieve, combine to merit for this case a conspicuous niche in the gallery of Scottish *causes celèbres*.

In the month of December, 1908, there lived at No. 15 Queen's Terrace, West Princes Street, Glasgow, an unmarried lady named Marion Gilchrist, eighty- two years of age, who had been tenant of the house for upwards of thirty years. Though of independent means and in comfortable circumstances, she kept but one servant; and at the date in question a girl, named Helen Lambie, aged twenty- one, had been in her service for the past three years. The old lady led a very retired life, seeing little of her relatives and less of her neighbours; receiving few visitors other than Mrs. Ferguson, a former servant, with whom she was on intimate terms.

Miss Marion Gilchrist

The house, which is situated in a quiet residential locality in the West End of the city, consists of three public rooms, two bedrooms, bathroom, and kitchen, and forms the first flat of a tenement three storeys in height. The top flat, the only other house upon the same stair, had been unoccupied since the previous Whitsunday; the lower flat, which is entirely separate from those above, having a private entrance, No. 14

Queen's Terrace, opens directly from the street and is what is called in Scotland a maindoor house. Immediately to the left of No. 14 another door, No. 15, gives access to a short passage, locally termed a "close," extending from the street door to the foot of the common stair, which ascends in three short flights to the door of Miss Gilchrist's house and continues to that of the empty house above. The old lady and her servant were thus the only persons living in No. 15. The maindoor house occupies the whole ground floor with the exception of this close, and the dining-room is situated immediately beneath that of Miss Gilchrist. The maindoor and the close door, which are on the same level, are approached from the pavement by four steps and a landing, common to both. Queen's Terrace is the name of a section of West Princes Street, and forms the south side of the east end of that street.

Miss Gilchrist differed from the generality of old ladies of similar habits and condition in one remarkable particular. She had a passion for precious stones, and the collection of jewels which she purchased from time to time, chiefly from a well-known Glasgow firm with whom she had dealt for twenty years, cost her over £3000. As a rule these jewels were kept among her clothes in her wardrobe; but when, as was her custom, she went to the country for a month in summer, they were sent to the jewellers for safe custody until her return. In these circumstances it is not surprising to find that Miss Gilchrist was extremely nervous about burglars, and lived in constant dread of her house being broken into. She was most solicitous as to the fastening of her windows; and the house door, in addition to such securities as the usual lock and chain, had, as further defences, a heavy bolt and two separate patent locks, opened from within by two handles, and from without by two different keys. The street door at the closemouth had only an ordinary latch-key, and was opened from the house by lifting a handle within the hall.

The house below was occupied by a family of the name of Adams. They had merely a slight acquaintance with Miss Gilchrist, and, though they had been neighbours for many years, were not upon visiting terms. She had, however, an understanding with them that if at any time she was alone and required assistance, she should knock upon the floor of her room, and, on hearing this signal, some of them would go up.

At seven o'clock on the evening of Monday, 21st December, the servant Lambie, having finished her housework, went out, as appears to have been her nightly practice, to fetch an evening paper for her mistress, before proceeding to neighbouring shops upon such messages as were required. She left Miss Gilchrist sitting on an ordinary chair at the table in the dining-room, with her back to the fire, reading a magazine, with her spectacles on. She received from her mistress a penny for the paper and a half-sovereign for the messages; the latter she laid on the table, intending to take it when she came back. The dining-room was lit with an incandescent light, the gas in the kitchen was turned down, and that in the hall—a pendant, with a single jet—was half on. The bracket on the landing outside the house door was also lighted. All the windows were fastened except the kitchen window, which was open two or three inches at the top. The girl shut both the house and close doors, taking with her the two keys required to open the former and the latch-key of the latter. It was raining when she left the house. The newspaper shop was situated in St. George's Road at the east end of West Princes Street, and her errand usually occupied less than ten minutes. On this occasion she spoke for a minute or two to a constable of her acquaintance, in plain clothes, whom she met at the corner of St. George's Road, before buying the paper.

At seven o'clock Mr. Arthur Adams and his two sisters were in their dining-room, when they heard "a noise from above, and then a very heavy fall, and then three sharp knocks." Miss Laura Adams at once said to her brother that something must have happened to Miss Gilchrist, and that gentleman instantly left his house to see what was wrong. He found the close door ajar and, running upstairs, observed through the glass panels at the sides of the house door, which was shut, that the lobby was lighted. He rang the bell loudly three times. Listening at the door, he heard a noise which he thought was caused by the servant breaking sticks in the kitchen: "It seemed as if it was some one chopping sticks—not heavy blows." After waiting a minute or two, during which the sounds continued, and being unaware of the servant's absence, Mr. Adams returned to his own house. Miss Adams, meanwhile, had heard further noises from above, but not so distinct as the knocks. She was not satisfied with her brother's account of what was taking place and asked him to go up again. He immediately did so, but by this time the sounds had ceased. He again rang the bell loudly, and had his hand upon the handle when he heard footsteps in the close below, and was joined by Lambie, who was then returning with the newspaper.

The night, as has been said, was wet, and the girl noticed wet footmarks on the lower steps of the inside stair. Whether these were Mr. Adams' does not appear—he was not asked if he had seen them when he first went up. As he had merely to step from the one door to the other, it is unlikely that his feet were wet. Mr. Adams told her that there was a noise in the house, " and that the ceiling was like to crack." She suggested that it was caused by the pulleys in the kitchen (an appliance for drying clothes), which she thought might have fallen down. This explanation did not commend itself to Mr. Adams, who, now knowing that the old lady had been left alone in the house, said there must be something seriously wrong and he would wait to see. Lambie thereupon opened the door with her two keys.

According to the evidence of Mr. Adams, Lambie then entered the house, and made for the kitchen door, in the further left-hand corner of the hall, he himself remaining on the threshold. When she had got past the grandfather's clock upon the left— Lambie states that she was on the door mat beside him all the time—a man appeared from the door of the bedroom, in the right-hand corner at the back of the hall. Keeping along the wall on his left, he passed the hatstand, and quietly approached the front door. There was nothing in his appearance or manner to excite suspicion, and, as he came up " quite pleasantly," Mr. Adams' first impression was that he was a visitor, and was going to speak to him. Having reached the door, however, the man bolted past Mr. Adams and rushed down the stairs "like greased lightning," slamming the close door behind him.

Lambie then entered the kitchen, and next the spare bedroom, the gas in which she found had been lit in her absence, and on Mr. Adams calling to her, "Where is your mistress?" she finally went into the dining-room. Hearing her scream, he quickly joined her. The room at first sight presented its usual appearance, but, lying on her back upon the hearth rug in front of the fireplace, they saw the body of Miss Gilchrist, with a skin rug thrown across the head. A glance showed them what had happened, and they both ran downstairs, Lambie to inform the Adams ladies, who had come out on hearing the rush of feet on the stairs, and Mr. Adams to see if he could overtake the murderer. By the time he reached the street the man had vanished.

Near St. George's Road Mr. Adams met Constable Neil, with whom he returned to the house. They lifted the rug, and found that the old lady had been attacked with horrible ferocity, her head and face being brutally smashed. She was still breathing, and made a movement with her left hand. Mr. Adams then ran across the street for his own medical man, Dr. John Adams, No. 1 Queen's Crescent, and, meeting Constable Brien, informed him of what had occurred. The latter went up to the house, and then proceeded to call the ambulance. Dr. Adams came forthwith, reaching the house at twenty or twenty-five minutes past seven. Ascertaining from an examination of the body that life was extinct, he informed the constables that the ambulance was unnecessary, left the case in their charge, and at once reported the matter by telephone to the Western Police Office. In response to his message Superintendent Douglas, Detective Inspector

Pyper, and Detective Officer M'Vicar promptly arrived upon the scene of the crime, and the body was examined by Dr. Wright, casualty surgeon for the Western District. He found that "nearly every bone in the skull was fractured; the brains were escaping; the head was practically smashed to pulp." The grate, fender, and fire-irons were splashed with blood, but the latter were in their usual places; the coal scuttle was also bloodstained, and the lid was broken. There was no blood except in the immediate vicinity of the head, and the furniture of the room appeared to be undisturbed. Near the head stood the chair upon which the old lady had been sitting; upon the hearth rug beside the body lay the half-sovereign; the open magazine and folded spectacles were upon the table, as she had left them when she rose to meet her sudden doom.

A search of the premises disclosed that a small wooden box, in which the deceased kept her papers in the bedroom, had been wrenched open and its contents scattered upon the floor. In a glass dish on the toilet table were a diamond and two other rings; a gold bracelet and a gold watch and chain lay on the same table; but there was missing from the dish a valuable diamond crescent brooch, which the girl Lambie had seen there the day before. A box of matches, different from those used in the house, and one spent match, with which the murderer had lit the bedroom gas, were the only clues he had left behind. The windows were in exactly the same state as when Lambie went out. No weapon of any kind was found in the house; and Constable Walker, who was put on to watch the premises during the night, searched the back court with his lantern, but discovered nothing. Next day, however, Inspector Rankin found in the court behind the house an auger, having some grey hair adhering to it, which was at first associated by the authorities with the case, but, as will appear later, had no connection with the crime.

The unusual circumstance that two persons had actually seen the supposed murderer leaving the house should have greatly assisted the police in investigating this mysterious affair, but, unfortunately, the description of him which Mr. Adams and Lambie were able to give was of the vaguest—

A man between twenty-five and thirty years of age, 5 feet 8 or 9 inches in height, slim build, dark hair, clean shaven; dressed in light grey overcoat, and dark cloth cap. Cannot be further described.

These particulars were published in the next day's papers; an inventory was taken of the jewels found in the house; and a description of the missing brooch was circulated amongst pawnbrokers, jewellers, and dealers.

The news of the tragedy produced a profound sensation, not only in Glasgow but throughout the country; crowds daily visited West Princes Street to gaze at the ill-fated house; the mysterious and terrible character of the crime formed the sole topic of conversation; while Press and public vied with one another in supplying the authorities with "clues" for the elucidation of the mystery.

On Tuesday, 22nd December, on the instructions of Mr. Hart, Procurator- fiscal for Lanarkshire, Professor Glaister and Dr. Galt visited and inspected the locus. On the following day these gentlemen made a post-mortem examination of the body and the results of their investigations were embodied in reports, which will be found printed in the report of the trial.

On Wednesday, the 23rd, the police were informed of a fresh circumstance of the highest importance. That afternoon Mrs. Barrowman, 9 Seamore Street, met Detective M'Gimpsey, who lived in the same stair, and made a statement to him, as the result of which the evidence of her adopted daughter Mary was taken that night. This little girl of fifteen was in the employment of a bootmaker in Great Western Road. At seven o'clock on the night of the tragedy she was sent to deliver a parcel in Cleveland Street. While passing along West Princes Street, near Miss Gilchrist's house, she saw a man running down the steps from the close of No. 15 Queen's Terrace. He hesitated for a moment on reaching the pavement, looked east to St. George's

Road, and then turned west and ran towards her. She watched him approaching, and he knocked up against her as he passed her. She was standing by a lamp-post at the time and saw him clearly. [The lights in West Princes Street are incandescent.] She followed him for a short distance, but as he turned down West Cumberland Street she stopped and resumed her way. Having gone her errand, she went to a Band of Hope meeting, where, she said, she heard of the murder, and going back to West Princes Street found a crowd assembled in front of the house from the door of which she had seen the man emerge. On her return home that night she told her story to her mother.

Following upon this discovery a more particular description appeared on Friday, the 25th, in the two o'clock editions of the Glasgow evening newspapers—

The man wanted is about twenty-eight or thirty years of age, tall and thin, with his face shaved clear of all hair, while a distinctive feature is that his nose is slightly turned to one side. The witness thinks the twist is to the right side. He wore one of the popular round tweed hats known as Donegal hats, and a fawn-coloured overcoat, which might have been a waterproof, also dark trousers, and brown boots.

The discrepancies between the two descriptions as to colour of coat and kind of headgear should be noted.

At ten minutes past six o'clock that same evening Allan M'Lean, cycle dealer, Glasgow, called at the Central Police Office and informed Superintendent Ord that a man named Oscar Slater, whom he knew at the Sloper Club, 24 India Street, had been trying to dispose in that club of a pawn- ticket for a diamond brooch resembling the missing one, and that he answered to the published description of the wanted man. Accompanied by Detective Powell, M'Lean went to St. George's Road and pointed out the common stair, No. 69, in which he believed Slater lived. Certain inquiries were made in the stair about half-past seven, as the result of which it was found that Slater, under the name of Anderson, was occupying a house on the third flat. Accordingly, at midnight, Detectives Powell, Lyon, and Millican visited the premises for the purpose of apprehending the suspect. The door, which had the name-plate of "Anderson" upon it, was opened by a German servant girl, who denied that any man lived there—"No one but Madame, who was away for a short holiday." They searched the house, which presented the appearance of having been recently vacated, and found, among some papers scattered on the floor of the bedroom, the cover of a registered postal packet, addressed to " Oscar Slater, Esq., c/o A. Anderson, Esq., 69 St. George's Road, Glasgow," bearing to have been sent by Messrs. Dent, watchmakers, London. From the neighbours in the stair they learned that "Anderson," accompanied by a woman, had left the house that night between eight and nine o'clock, their luggage having been previously removed by two porters.

Whether or not it be proved that Slater was in fact the murderer, it is certainly a remarkable circumstance that suspicion was first directed to him by what turned out to be a false clue; for, as we shall afterwards see, the pawned brooch had no more connection with the crime than the fallacious auger, which, it appeared, had been thrown over the wall from a disused factory adjoining the back court.

Next day, Saturday, the 26th, Detective Lieutenant Gordon called at the house 69 St. George's Road, saw the servant, and inquired for "Anderson." She said that Madame and "Anderson" had left the previous night for London. The officer found two German women in the flat, one of whom, named Freedman, said it had been arranged between Slater and her that she should occupy the house while Madame and "Anderson" were in Monte Carlo, and that she had lent him £25 before he went. Detective Gordon called daily thereafter to inquire if any letters had come for Anderson. On the night of the 26th the maid went to London; the two women left on 8th January. The day before they went they handed him a letter with the

American postmark, 29th December, addressed "Oscar Slater, c/o Mr. Anderson, 69 St. George's Road, Glasgow." Written upon the envelope were the words, "If not delivered, return to D. R. Jacobs, 326 Third Avenue, New York, U.S." A copy of this letter is given in the Appendix.

Inquiries made at the railway stations elicited that Slater and his companion had left the Central Station on Christmas night by the 9.5 train for London—whether with London or Liverpool tickets was afterwards disputed; and the London police were instantly advised of the fact. On the 29th the Glasgow authorities received information from Liverpool that the persons wanted had arrived there on the 26th, and had sailed the same day for New York in the "Lusitania," under the names of "Mr. and Mrs. Otto Sando."

On the 31st Mr. Stevenson, Chief Constable of Glasgow, caused a notice to be issued offering £200 reward to any one giving such information as should lead to the apprehension and conviction of the person or persons who committed the crime. The same day Sheriff-Substitute Glegg, on the application of the Procurator-fiscal, granted a warrant for Slater's apprehension, intimation of which was cabled to the New York police.

When these facts became known public interest was redoubled, and news of what would happen when the ship reached port was eagerly awaited.

Early in the morning of Saturday, 2nd January, 1909, the great liner, after a stormy passage, arrived off Sandy Hook. Acting on instructions received from Scotland Yard, six detectives went out in a Revenue cutter, boarded her, and arrested Slater, who, having been taken before Commissioner Shields, of the United States District Court, was remanded to the Tombs Prison, without bail, until 19th January, when the papers in connection with his extradition were expected to be forwarded from Britain. When searching the prisoner the New York police found in his possession a pawn ticket for a diamond crescent brooch, upon which £60 had been lent, issued on 21st December (the date of the murder) by a Glasgow pawnbroker. This brooch, as afterwards appeared, had been originally pledged by Slater for £20, in name of " A. Anderson, 136 Renfrew Street," on 18th November; he raised other £10 on it on 9th December; and at mid-day on the 21st obtained a further advance of £30. The pawned brooch was therefore entirely distinct from that stolen from Miss Gilchrist's house by the murderer; but the coincidence of the dates and articles is a striking example of the adage that "truth is stranger than fiction."

The chief topics of discussion in Glasgow were now the identity of the suspected man, his possible connection -with the crime, the probability of his extradition, and the formalities connected therewith.

The Treaty stipulations between Great Britain and the United States relating to extradition are contained in the tenth article of the Treaty of 1842 and the Conventions of 1889 and 1890, the latter being chiefly important for the extension of the number of extraditable offences; the procedure thereunder involves considerable delay, formal application having to be made through the Foreign Office in London to the United States Government. Meanwhile, the Procurator-fiscal was making arrangements for the despatch of two officers from Glasgow to proceed to New York with the documents necessary to support the application for extradition. The depositions of the witnesses, whose testimony formed the basis of the application, were sworn to in presence of the officers appointed to appear in the American Court, viz., Mr. William Warnock, chief criminal officer of Glasgow Sheriff Court, and Detective Inspector Pyper, of the Western Division of the Glasgow Police Force, two of the most experienced criminal officers in the city. When the arrangements were completed, these officers, accompanied by the three principal witnesses—

Lambie, Adams, and Barrowman—sailed from Liverpool on Wednesday, 13th January, in the White Star liner "Baltic," for New York.

On 19th January, before Mr John A. Shields, U.S. Commissioner for the Southern District of New York, the proceedings were opened "in the matter of the application for the extradition of Otto Sands, alias Oscar Slater, under the Treaty existing between the Kingdom of Great Britain and Ireland and the United States of America." Mr. Charles Fox appeared as counsel for the demanding Government, while the defendant was represented by Mr. Hugh Gordon Miller and Mr. William A. Goodhart. Mr. Fox moved for an adjournment for one week, as the witnesses from Glasgow had not yet arrived; and the Commissioner adjourned the examination till 26th January. On the 25th the witnesses reached New York.

The Court resumed on 26th January. While the witnesses Lambie, Barrowman, and Adams were waiting with Inspector Pyper outside the Court-room before the examination commenced, a dramatic incident occurred. Three men came along the corridor in which they were standing, passed them, and went into the Court; whereupon both of the girls simultaneously said to Mr. Pyper that one of the three was the man they had seen on the night of the murder, Lambie's expression being, "I could nearly swear that is the man!" As this was their real recognition of Slater, the subsequent identification in the Court-room being only that of the man they had already recognised, the incident is of some importance. Slater was being conducted into Court by Messrs. Chamberlain and Pinckney, Deputy United States Marshals, and it was contended by Mr. Miller for the defence that he was obviously in the charge of those officials. He was not, however, handcuffed or otherwise branded as a prisoner, while his companions do not appear to have been in uniform, though one of them wore a badge, which the witnesses said they did not notice, and the other was a very tall man. Both girls denied that they had been prepared to see Slater where they did.

Mr. Warnock was the first witness, and proved a plan of the district in which Miss Gilchrist's house was situated. It was proposed to ask him whether several persons, other than Slater, had not been arrested by the Glasgow police in connection with the crime, but this question was disallowed.

Helen Lambie was next examined. She gave her account of what happened on 21st December at 15 Queen's Terrace. Much difficulty was apparently caused by the absence of a plan of the premises, the structural arrangement of which counsel could not understand, while the meaning of the localism "close" was found to be incommunicable to the American mind. On the other hand, counsel's use of the word "apartment" in the French sense, as referring to the whole house, was equally puzzling to the witness, that term being invariably used in Scotland to describe a single room. When asked if she saw in Court the man she had seen in the hall on the night of the murder, Lambie replied, "One is very suspicious, if anything," and added, "The clothes he had on that night he hasn't got on to-day; but his face I could not tell."

The Commissioner—"What did you say about his face?"

Witness—"I couldn't tell his face; I never saw his face." She then described his dress so far as she recollected—a three-quarter length fawn- coloured coat, "something like a waterproof coat," and a cap which "looked like one of these Donegal caps"; she also gave a representation of the peculiarity in the man's walk, upon which alone she depended for recognising him. Finally she identified the defendant as the man she had seen in the hall of Miss Gilchrist's house. In cross-examination Lambie repeated that she did not see the man's face that night. " I saw the walk; it is not the face I went by, but the walk." She stated that the missing brooch had one row of diamonds, while that pledged by the defendant, which she had been shown in the pawnshop in Glasgow, had three rows. She denied that she had been in any way prompted to recognise the defendant in the corridor, or that she had ever been shown his photograph, in the newspapers or otherwise. [It will be observed that the colour of the coat and character of the hat differ from those given by Lambie in her original description to the police, and are here assimilated to those given by Barrowman.]

The next witness was Mary Barrowman, who recounted how she had seen a man run from the house on the night in question. The "close" difficulty was again in evidence. She described the man as having a slight twist in his nose, and as wearing a fawn-coloured waterproof, a Donegal hat, and brown boots. When asked if she saw the man present in Court, she first said that the defendant was something like him, and then that he was very like him. In cross-examination Barrowman admitted that, before identifying the defendant, she had been shown a photograph of him. She had mentioned the twist in the nose to her mother on the night of the crime, and to the police two days later.

Arthur Montague Adams was then examined, and described what he saw and did on the night of the murder, the "close" and "apartment" being still a cause of stumbling. He said the man in the hall was dressed in a light grey coat, which looked like a waterproof, and dark trousers; his hands were in his pockets, and his head was slightly bowed. Witness thought he wore a hat; he was sharp featured, clean shaven, and " rather a gentlemanly fellow." The defendant was "very much like him." In cross-examination Adams said he had noticed nothing extraordinary about the man's walk, nor did he remark the twist in the nose. He would not go further than that the defendant "resembled him very much." The hearing was then adjourned till 28th January.

When the Court met on that day Mr. Fox offered in evidence depositions of Helen Lambie, Mary Barrowman, Agnes Brown, Allan M'Lean, George Sabin, John Pyper, Arthur Montague Adams, Robert Beveridge, Louise Freedman, Elsie Hoppe, John Ord, and Gordon Henderson; also the depositions and certificates of John Glaister, M.D., and Hugh Galt, M.D.— all of which had been taken in Glasgow, as above narrated. These documents, being duly authenticated in terms of the Act of Congress of 3rd August, 1882, were admitted in evidence; and the hearing was further adjourned till the 29th to allow defendant's counsel to examine the same.

On the resumption of the hearing, Helen Lambie was recalled for further examination by Mr. Miller, and again asked to imitate the characteristic in the man's walk to which she had testified. As this peculiarity consisted in the motion of his legs, which it was obviously impossible for a female witness to illustrate, the girl was subjected to a good deal of useless browbeating. She repeated that she had been shown no photograph of the defendant; and being asked if she could give any reason why none was exhibited to her, as well as to Adams and Barrowman, replied, " Because I couldn't have known it if it had been shown to me." She now gave the man's height as an additional factor in her recognition. She had stated in her original deposition that the man was thin; had deponed, on the same occasion, "I couldn't say whether he had any beard, moustache, or whiskers, or was clean shaven"; and the deposition made no mention of the peculiar walk. With reference to her recognising the defendant in the corridor, she denied that she had been told he was coming, or that Mr. Pyper had described to her the man she was there to identify. She was long and severely questioned as to her relations with Patrick Nugent, a bookmaker of her acquaintance, who had visited her at 15 Queen's Terrace, the suggestion being that, as she admitted having told him her mistress was a rich lady and had a great many jewels, he was therefore concerned in the affair. Mr. Miller closed his examination with the following questions:—"Have your suspicions in this case ever turned towards that gambler [Nugent]? — A. Never. Q. Do you know any other man who would be as familiar with those premises, the wealth of the old lady, her jewellery, and the way to get into those premises as that man?

— *A*. No, sir." The Commissioner then asked, "Was the man you met in that hallway, when you came in from buying the paper, this gambler he speaks of?" to which witness answered, "No, sir." In reply to Mr. Fox, Lambie stated that she had neither seen nor heard anything of Nugent since the beginning of September. [It should be explained that no suspicion whatever now attaches to Nugent in regard to the case.]

Mary Barrowman was recalled by Mr. Miller, and admitted describing in her deposition as tall and thin the man she had seen in West Princes Street. She would describe the defendant in similar terms. Frederick F. Chamberlain, Deputy United States Marshal, gave evidence as to bringing the defendant into Court along with another official, and passing Lambie and Barrowman in the corridor. He was wearing his official badge at the time.

David Jacobs, dealer in diamond jewellery, New York, was next examined. He had known the defendant for eight years, both in London and New York, as a dentist who dealt in jewellery, and he had many dealings with him in diamonds. He knew his handwriting. He had received from the defendant the following letter:—

Glasgow, 29/11/08.

Dear Jacobs,

I have been coming too late to see your wife in London, and I hope that your wife and family are in good health. I expecting to be ready end of January to come over to New York myself. Matters are here very bad. The New York bank affairs have done a lot to it. Now I have found out here in Scotland it would be easy for me to pawn some of your emeralds not only in Glasgow; there are a lot of small towns around Glasgow, also in Ireland. If you like, send me a lot of mounted emeralds over without any diamonds around, special scarf pins, and some loose emeralds; also send me the price list. Don't let me wait too long, because I have only two months time here. The profits I will divide with you. I am bringing the tickets over to you. I have been fourteen days ago in London, and have spoken to Carry. He made some good business. One lot I knowing of from Russia over 7000 pounds. I was offered to buy two lots of loose coloured stones, and only you know I am not a correct judge, and Rogers has advised me not to buy. Bravington in Kings X have spoken to me about your affair, and have told me you would be all right with your affair, only your friends there are the people is all could do the harm. Rogers and I have also seen Blytell, and he sends the best regards to you. I am coming over with Rogers end of January to start some business. Send the kind regards to the two Wrones. In case you don't like to send the stuff, please send answer. Best regards to you and your friends.

OSCAR SLATER.
Care of Anderson,
69 St. George's Road,
Glasgow, Scotland.

[Jacobs' answer to this letter, which reached Glasgow after Slater had left for America, is printed in the Appendix.] Witness saw no peculiarity in defendant's walk. Cross-examined by Mr. Fox, witness said that he had only heard that defendant was a dentist. He never knew his address in London. Beyond dealing with him in jewellery, witness did not know how he made his living. Henry P. Wrone, jeweller, New York, stated that he had known defendant for two or three years, and had dealt in jewellery and diamonds with him. A year and a half before, he had repaired for the defendant a diamond crescent brooch with three rows of stones. Cross-examined by Mr. Fox, witness denied that he had re- set jewellery for the defendant; the latter had never brought him loose diamonds to sell, nor any jewellery the setting of which appeared to have been changed. He had bought no English jewellery from defendant.

Mr. Adams, recalled, said that he had never been asked by the Glasgow police to identify Nugent as the man he had seen in the hall. In reply to Mr. Fox, he stated that he had heard Lambie and Barrowman say, " That is the man," when defendant came along the corridor. He did not observe that the official who accompanied him was wearing a badge. The hearing was then adjourned till 6th February.

When the Court met on that date, Mr. Miller, for the defence, said the defendant's counsel felt that the British Government had not established under the Treaty the case of identity which was necessary; that the defendant was innocent, and his counsel believed him innocent: but rather than have any misapprehension about his connection with Glasgow, the defendant had determined to go back and face any charge that might be made against him. He only asked that the evidence of the witnesses, who testified to his character in New York, should be admitted in the Scottish Court. The Commissioner said that a transcript of the proceedings would be certified as correct for production in Scotland. [This was not, however, laid before the jury at the trial in Edinburgh, where it was only used by the prisoner's counsel for the purpose of cross-examining Lambie, Adams, and Barrowman.]

Mr. Miller then called Sigmund Biber, real estate broker, New York, who stated that he had known defendant for two and a half years, and had bought a diamond ring and a watch from him two years before. He was introduced to him by witness's brother in Germany, and considered him a responsible man in business affairs. He had only one transaction with him. Bruno Wolfram, dealer in live stock, New York, stated that he had known defendant for over two years. His general reputation was that of a reliable man. He had sold him three fox terriers, and knew him as manager of a social club in Sixth Avenue. He had received a postcard from defendant, dated from Glasgow on 25th December, 1908, saying he was returning to the States; witness had left the postcard at home. He had found him trustworthy in his business transactions. In cross- examination, the witness admitted that the sociability of the club consisted in its members playing cards for money. He knew that defendant dealt in jewellery. Mr. Miller then waived further examination, and Mr. Fox moved that the defendant be remanded in the custody of the United States Marshal, to await the action of the Secretary of State. The motion was granted by the Commissioner, and the defendant was remanded accordingly until the warrant for his extradition should be issued by the proper authorities at Washington.

The witnesses Lambie, Adams, and Barrowman having sailed for England in the "Baltic," reached home on 8th February, Mr. Warnock and Inspector Pyper remaining in New York to await the warrant for extradition. This arrived from the State Department in Washington on the 11th; and on the 14th these officers, with their prisoner, sailed direct for Glasgow in the Anchor liner "Columbia," taking with them his luggage, which had been delivered to them sealed with the United States Customs seal. The woman who accompanied Slater to America, and, since his arrest on the "Lusitania," had been detained in the immigrants' quarters on Ellis Island, took her passage in the "Campania" for Liverpool, whence she went to her friends in Paris. Though referred to in the New York proceedings as " Mrs. Slater," she was not married to the prisoner, his wife, from whom he had separated, being still alive. The former was a Frenchwoman, twenty-three years of age, named Andrée Junio Antoine, who had cohabited with him for several years.

Pending the result of the extradition application, the Glasgow police had been busy securing additional evidence in the case. Several persons were found who had seen a man watching Miss Gilchrist's house and haunting the vicinity of West Princes Street for weeks before the murder. The discovery of the auger, the supposed weapon, leaked out, and was duly chronicled in the Press, which daily added to the long list of "Sensational Developments," "Startling Discoveries," "Important New Clues," "Extraordinary Revelations," "Remarkable Evidence," "Interesting Interviews," and "Alleged Confessions," with which the popular mind was persistently inflamed.

Public excitement was intense, and the arrival of the "Columbia" was impatiently awaited. The liner reached the Tail of the Bank, off Greenock, at mid-day on 21st February. Large crowds had assembled on the chance of Slater landing at that port, but the tide being favourable the vessel proceeded up the Clyde towards Glasgow. Near Renfrew, however, she stopped; the officers, with their prisoner and his baggage, were landed, and left for Glasgow in two motor cars, thus evading the great concourse of people who were awaiting the ship's arrival at her berth at Stobcross Quay. After many difficulties and delays, Slater was at length safely in the hands of the authorities, or, in the more eloquent language of a contemporary journalist, "Hurried across the Atlantic in an ocean greyhound, slung ashore at a wayside wharf, and whisked along the last stage of the 4000 mile journey in a motor car: such was his transit."

On the party's arrival at the Central Police Station, the prisoner's baggage, consisting of seven pieces, was unsealed and opened in his presence by Mr. Warnock and Inspector Pyper. In a black leather trunk were found a waterproof coat and a claw-hammer, of which we shall hear further in the sequel. A soft felt hat and two cloth caps were also taken possession of by the police. In a leather case in one of his trunks was found a business card, bearing the printed name and designation, "Oscar Slater, Dealer in Diamonds and Precious Stones, 33 Soho Square, Oxford Street, W.," and an extract certificate of marriage of Oscar Leschziner Slater to Marie Curtis Pryor, dated 12th July, 1902.

On 21st and 22nd February the prisoner was shown to a number of witnesses in the Central Police Station for the purpose of identification by them. What occurred on these occasions we shall have to consider in dealing with the evidence at the trial.

The morning after his arrival the prisoner was brought up at the Central Police Court upon the following charge:—

Oscar Slater, alias Otto Sands, alias Anderson, you are charged with having, on 21st December, 1908, in Marion Gilchrist's house, 15 Queen's Terrace, West Princes Street, Glasgow, assaulted the said Marion Gilchrist, and beaten her and fractured her skull, and murdered her.

Mr. Ewing Speirs, of Messrs. Joseph Shaughnessy & Son, solicitors, Glasgow, appeared for Slater, who was remanded for forty-eight hours. On the 24th he was formally remitted to the Sheriff, before whom, later in the day, he emitted the following declaration:—

My name is Oscar Slater. I am a native of Germany, married, thirty-eight years of age, a dentist, and have no residence at present. I know nothing about the charge of having assaulted Marion Gilchrist and murdering her. I am innocent. All which I declare to be truth.

Thereafter he was removed to Duke Street Prison, to await his trial in the High Court of Justiciary, at Edinburgh.

Meanwhile, on 22nd February, Professors Glaister and Littlejohn had been requested by the authorities to examine and report upon the following articles:—(1) Waterproof coat; (2) hat; (3) hammer, all of which had been found, as above mentioned, in the prisoner's baggage; and (4) auger found in the back court of

Miss Gilchrist's house. The results of their examination were embodied in a report which is printed in the report of the trial.

The preparation of the case for the prosecution entailed an immense amount of labour upon the Crown officials, and the indictment, to which were appended lists of sixty-nine productions and ninety-eight witnesses, was not served on the prisoner until 6th April. It was in these terms?

Oscar Slater, sometime residing at 69 St. George's Road, Glasgow, and presently a prisoner in the prison of Glasgow, you are indicted at the instance of the Right Honourable Alexander Ure, His Majesty's Advocate, and the charge against you is that you did, on 21st December, 1908, in Marion Gilchrist's house, 15 Queen's Terrace, West Princes Street, Glasgow, assault the said Marion Gilchrist, and did beat her with a hammer or other blunt instrument, and fracture her skull, and did murder her.

The trial was appointed to take place before the High Court at Edinburgh on Monday, 3rd May. The pleading diet was held at Glasgow on 20th April, in the Old Court, Jail Square, before Sheriff-Substitute Mackenzie. Mr. Hart, Procurator-fiscal for Lanarkshire, represented the Crown, and Mr. Ewing Speirs appeared for the prisoner. The indictment having been read, the Sheriff put the question, "Are you guilty or not guilty?" to which the prisoner replied, "I am not guilty." He was then formally remitted to the High Court, and was taken back to Duke Street Prison.

In the course of the following week Slater was removed from Glasgow to the Calton Jail, Edinburgh, and there, on 28th April, a consultation was held with Mr. A. L. M'Clure, K.C., Sheriff of Argyll, and Mr. John Mair, advocate, Edinburgh, the counsel retained for the defence. Although over four months had elapsed since the tragedy, public excitement continued unabated, and the result of the impending trial was awaited with intense interest.

The High Court of Justiciary in Edinburgh has been the scene of many a grim and tragic spectacle, the chief actors in which are memorable in the annals of Scottish crime. Among the famous occupants of its historic dock the names of Burke, Madeleine Smith, Pritchard, Chantrelle, Laurie, and Monson are still preserved, as the protagonists of their respective dramas. The man who, in his turn, sat in their seat upon the like awful occasion, was the central figure in a tragedy as strange as any of those by which they are remembered.

Lord Guthrie presided; the prosecution was conducted by the Lord Advocate (Mr. Alexander Ure, K.C.), assisted by Mr. T. B. Morison, K.C., and Mr. Lyon Mackenzie, Advocates-depute; the prisoner, as already mentioned, was defended by Mr. M'Clure and Mr. Mair.

The following record of the trial contains a full report of the evidence, that of every important witness being printed verbatim. The Lord Advocate's address to the jury—than which few more powerful have been heard within those walls— brilliantly presents the case for the prosecution in its strongest light; while that of Mr. M'Clure, though lacking the trenchancy of the Lord Advocate's speech, contains an elaborate criticism of the discrepancies in the Crown case. The weighty and impressive charge of the presiding judge admirably holds the balance of the momentous issue. In view of these advantages, the reader might well be left to a consideration of the evidence as it stands; but, regard being had to its extent and complexity, it may perhaps assist him in its perusal briefly to examine here certain of its more important features.

The evidence adduced for the prosecution was (a) direct and (6) indirect, or circumstantial. By direct evidence the Crown sought to establish from the testimony of eye-witnesses the identity of the prisoner at the bar and (1) a man who before the murder haunted the vicinity of the house, (2) a man seen leaving the house after the murder. By circumstantial evidence the Crown endeavoured to prove, from the behaviour of the prisoner himself, both before and after the crime, and from other relevant facts and circumstances, that his was certainly the hand that did the deed.

Oscar Slater on trial in the High Court of Judiciary, Edinburgh

The accused, as already mentioned, was, on 21st and 22nd February, within the Central Police Station, identified by twelve witnesses as the man they had seen watching the house. Prior to their seeing the man in West Princes Street none of them (excepting Constable Brien) knew him by sight, and none of them had ever seen Slater. Some saw the man five or six times, others once only; some saw him at night, others by day. With regard to the manner of their identification it may be generally observed that all of them had previously seen in the newspapers photographs of Slater, as an obvious foreigner, and had read the alternative descriptions of the wanted man furnished to the police by (1) Adams and Lambie and (2) the girl Barrowman. As the prisoner, in order to identification, was placed among eleven other men, nine being policemen in plain clothes, and two being railway officials, all Scotsmen, none of whom in any way resembled him, it is not too much to say that the task of selecting the suspect was unattended by serious difficulty. All the witnesses picked him out with ease, but the effect of this unanimity was somewhat lessened when, in the witness-box, they had to give the grounds of their belief.

Mrs. M'Haffie lived in the first flat of 16 West Princes Street, on the opposite side from Miss Gilchrist's house, but nearer St. George's Road. She observed from her window, for some weeks before the murder, a man loitering on the other side of the street. She saw him there on five or six occasions, always in the afternoon, and for half an hour at a time. He was dark, had a moustache, and wore a light overcoat (not a waterproof), check trousers, spats, and a black bowler hat. She observed nothing peculiar about his nose.

He did not carry himself well, but slouched along with his hands in his pockets. She last saw him eight or nine days before the murder. The prisoner was the man. He was the only man of foreign appearance who was in the room when she identified him at the Central Police Station.

Margaret Dickson M'Haffie, her daughter, gave similar evidence. On one or two occasions the man was wearing a black morning coat instead of a light overcoat, as well as light check trousers. She admitted that, in March, she had told the agent for the prisoner that she was not then quite sure of the accused being the man, and was only prepared to say there was some resemblance; but she had been thinking it over, and had come to the conclusion that he was the man.

Annie Rankin M'Haffie, another daughter, said that four weeks before the murder, between seven and eight at night, a man rang the bell of their front door, which bore the name " Mr. M'Haffie " on a brass plate, and asked her if any one named Anderson lived there. She said " No," and he turned and walked downstairs. The bell rang again within a minute, and she found her cousin Madge at the door, who said she had met a man on the stair. That was the only time she saw the man. The prisoner was like him. In reply to the judge, witness did not notice anything about the man's accent; he did not appear to be a foreigner. [It is to be noted that Slater speaks broken English, and that his accent is unmistakably foreign.]

Madge M'Haffie spoke to calling at her aunt's house on the occasion in question, and meeting a peculiar-looking man on the stair. He was dark, and had a moustache. His nose did not attract her attention. He wore black check trousers, a fawn overcoat, a black bowler hat, and fawn gaiters. A few days later she saw from her aunt's window the same man walking up and down. On leaving the house she passed him in St. George's Road. He walked with a shuffling gait. The prisoner was fairly like the man in general appearance.

Constable Brien knew the prisoner by sight, having seen him several times in St. George's Road for seven weeks before the murder. One night, a week before 21st December, he saw him, at half-past nine, standing against the railings in West Princes Street, a few yards from the corner of St. George's Road. Witness thought he was drunk, and took a good look at him, but saw he was sober. He had on a light coat and a hat. When witness identified the prisoner the other men present were constables in undress and detectives. [It may be mentioned, with general reference to the evidence of these witnesses, that the distance between Slater's house in St. George's Road and West Princes Street is less than a quarter of a mile.]

Constable Walker, who was on night duty in the beginning of December, at a quarter to six o'clock on 1st December saw a man standing on the edge of the pavement opposite 15 Queen's Terrace. He thought he recognised him as Mr. Paradise (a Crown witness), whom he knew, and waved to him across the street. He saw he was mistaken. Three nights later he met the same man, at the same hour, further down the street, walking towards Queen's Terrace. On 17th or 18th December he again saw the man, at a quarter to seven, standing at the east end of West Princes Street, near St. George's Road. On each occasion witness was on the opposite side of the street. When he identified the prisoner as the man, he knew the man he was to identify was a person of foreign appearance. The other men there were policemen and detectives.

Euphemia Cunningham, employed in St. George's Road, was going home for dinner about one o'clock on Monday, 14th December, through West Princes Street, when she saw a man standing at the corner of Queen's Crescent looking towards Miss Gilchrist's house. On 15th, 16th, and 17th December she saw the same man at the same time and place. On each occasion, when she passed again about two o'clock, the man had gone. He was of foreign appearance, very dark, with a sallow complexion, and heavy-featured. He was clean shaven. She saw no peculiarity about his nose. He wore a dark tweed coat and a green cap with a peak. She only saw the side of his face and the back of his head. She identified the prisoner in the police office as the man, where he was shown to her in a green cap, which did not belong to him. She had previously recognised him from a photograph of his full face, with a moustache. When she identified the prisoner the other men present were obviously policemen.

William Campbell accompanied the witness Cunningham on 15th, 16th, and 17th December, and corroborated her statement. He had a better opportunity of seeing the man than she had, because he passed next to him. There was a general resemblance between the prisoner and the man, but he could not positively identify him.

Alexander Gillies resided in a flat at 46 West Princes Street, directly opposite Miss Gilchrist's house. On the evening of the Wednesday, Thursday, or Friday before the murder, on returning home at a quarter to six o'clock, he found a man standing at the foot of the common stair at the back of the close, the door of which was open. The man turned his back and blocked the passage; witness asked him to let him pass, but the man went up to the second flight, and still stood on the stair. Witness had again to ask leave to pass, passed him, and entered his own house. The man's face was then towards him. He was sallow, dark-haired, and clean shaven; and wore a long fawn-coloured coat and a cap. The prisoner resembled him, but witness could not say he was the same man.

Robert Brown Bryson was walking from Queen's Crescent into West Princes Street at 7.40 p.m. on Sunday, 20th December, accompanied by his wife. He observed a man standing at the top of the steps leading to the close 58 West Princes Street, a little to the west of Miss Gilchrist's house, on the opposite side, staring up at her windows, which were lighted. When the man saw witness looking at him he came down the steps, met witness about four feet from the close, and passed him on the left, walking slowly westward. Witness turned round and watched him as he walked away. The walk did not attract his notice, further than that it was not smart. The man wore a black coat (or jacket) and vest, and a black bowler hat, but no overcoat. He had a black moustache with a slight droop, was sallow, and of foreign appearance. Witness identified the prisoner as the man, first from a photograph of Slater shown him by a detective, afterwards at the police station, and then in Court. He had drawn his wife's attention to the man at the time, but she did not recollect his making any remark on the subject. [She was not called as a witness at the trial.] Witness was unable to describe what the accused was wearing when he, along with the other witnesses, identified him at the police office.

Andrew Nairn, at a quarter-past nine o'clock the same night (Sunday, 20th December), was passing across West Princes Street from Queen's Crescent on his way home. His wife and children were following some distance behind. On the north side of West Princes Street, about one hundred and twenty yards from Miss Gilchrist's house, he waited for them to join him. While doing so he noticed a man thirteen yards away on the same side standing at the corner of the gardens in the middle of the pavement, with his back to the witness, looking towards 15 Queen's Terrace. Witness did not see his face. He had broad shoulders, a longish neck, and black hair. He wore a motor cap with the flaps up and a light overcoat reaching below the knees. Witness watched him for five minutes till his wife came up, and pointed him out to her, when they left him standing in the same place. [His wife was not called as a witness at the trial.] Nairn had already identified prisoner in the Central Police Station as the man; and being asked by the Lord Advocate if the accused was the man, witness said to the prisoner, " You might turn your back. Yes, I am certain that is the man I saw." Pressed by Mr. M'Clure as to how he could be so positive in his identification of a man he had seen but once, seeing only his back, at a distance of thirteen yards, at 9.15 on a December night, that man being upon his trial for murder, witness replied, " Oh, I will not swear in fact, but I am certain that he is the man I saw; but I will not swear," adding that, not having seen the man's face, he would not go the length of being positive. [The relative positions of this witness and the man are indicated by the numbers 8 and 7 upon the enlarged plan of West Princes Street.]

No attempt was made by the defence to prove an alibi with respect to any one of the occasions spoken to by the first nine witnesses above mentioned. But, in regard to the testimony of the two last, Bryson and Nairn, it was contended that the prisoner could not have been the man they had seen, as he was not out of his own house that night. Antoine, his mistress, and Schmalz, his maid-servant, swore that Slater, during the time he was in Glasgow, always remained indoors the whole day every Sunday; and that, in particular, he was never out of the house at all on Sunday, the 20th. They further stated that a friend of his, named Samuel Reid, dined with them at 69 St. George's Road that evening, coming about six o'clock and remaining until 10.30 or 10.45. Reid deponed that he dined with Slater at seven o'clock that night. He went at six and stayed till 10.30. He had one of his children with him. Slater never left the house during his visit. He had spent every Sunday evening with Slater while in Glasgow, and remembered the 20th, as it was the last time he saw him, witness going to Belfast next day. On the night in question Slater's moustache was growing, and was very noticeable, his hair being very black. No one could have mistaken him for a clean-shaven man.

At the trial the learned judge, with general reference to Antoine's evidence, alluded to the " tremendous motives " which she had for standing by the prisoner. In the case of Schmalz these would not operate, as her connection with the Slater menage had terminated on 26th December. The Lord Advocate elicited from Keid, in cross-examination, that he was a bookmaker; but this fact does not necessarily infer a proneness to commit perjury, and in other respects his evidence was unshaken.

The last witness to identify Slater as the watcher in the street was Mrs. Liddell, a married sister of the witness Adams. On Monday, 21st December, the night of the murder, this lady called at her brother's house in Queen's Terrace at five minutes to seven. She approached from the direction of St. George's Road. Before reaching the door she saw a man leaning with his arm on the railing under the eastmost window of her brother's dining-room. She stared at him "almost rudely." She only saw the left side of his face. She was much struck by the peculiarity of his nose. He had a very clear complexion, not sallow; was very dark, and was clean shaven. He wore a low-down collar, an ordinary cap of brownish tweed, and a heavy coat, also of brownish tweed, the collar of which had a hemmed edge. It was a thick coat, of different material from the waterproof produced. After she passed "he glided from the railings and disappeared." She did not mention having seen the man till the following Wednesday—two days after the murder. When she identified Slater at the police station she was surprised at his robust figure; the man at the railing had the appearance of a delicate man, "rather drawn together." Finally, witness said she believed the prisoner was the man.

We now come to the three crucial witnesses for the Crown— Lambie, Adams, and Barrowman—with whose evidence, as given at the extradition proceedings in New York, we have-already dealt. The substance of the evidence of Lambie and Adams forms the foregoing account of what occurred on the night of the murder in the hall of Miss Gilchrist's house. In reply to the Lord Advocate, Lambie repeated, with some variations, the story she had told in America. She looked at the clock before she went out—it was just seven. She saw no one in West Princes Street except her friend the constable. She was away from the house about ten minutes altogether. She still maintained that she had not entered the house when the man appeared in the hall and passed Adams on the threshold. Adams stood behind her while she unlocked the door. When she did so, and saw the man, she stepped back. "The man when he passed me was very close to me. I noticed that he held his head down. I turned round to look at him, and I got a good look at him. I heard him going down the stairs. He did not go down rapidly; he went deliberately. I went instantly into the house. The man, when I saw him first, was coming from the direction of Miss Gilchrist's bedroom. He had nothing in his hand. He was wearing a dark cap, a fawn overcoat, and dark trousers. His coat was open. No. 43 of the productions is the coat that he wore."

It is to be observed that, had Lambie been standing in the doorway, she would have seen the man as he descended the stairs; if, as Adams states, she was in the act of entering the kitchen at the time, she could only hear him doing so. Her version of the scene should be compared with that of Adams, the next witness mentioned.

In cross-examination, Lambie was asked by Mr. M'Clure what enabled her to identify the waterproof produced as the very coat the man was wearing, to which her only reply was, "That is the coat"—an instance of her mental capacity to which Lord Guthrie referred in his charge to the jury. As she stated in her examination-in-chief that she had seen the man's face, and identified it as the prisoner's, Mr. M'Clure made effective use of her reiterated statement in America that she never saw the face, but went by the walk alone. She now said what she then meant was that she did not see the full face, but only the side; she saw it when he was going down the stair. The man was clean shaven. She did not notice the man coming out of the bedroom door; he was past the door before she saw him. When he passed her and Adams, "they were both on the door mat." [Had this been so, Lambie must have seen the man face to face as he emerged from the bedroom door. If, as Adams swears, she was then about to enter the kitchen, her back was towards the bedroom door; which her own expression, "I turned round to look at him," confirms.]

Arthur Montague Adams deponed to the facts as already narrated. The man was a little taller than witness, a little broader in the shoulders, not a well- built man, but well featured and clean shaven. He had on dark trousers, and a light overcoat; whether fawn or grey witness could not say, and was not sure as to the kind of hat, but it was not a cap.

He seemed gentlemanly and well dressed. He had nothing in his hands. Witness saw nothing special about his nose, and did not notice anything about his way of walking. When Lambie unlocked the door there was no one in the hall. She made straight for the kitchen, had got as far as the hall clock, some eight or ten steps in, and was just going to enter the kitchen, when the man appeared from the bedroom. She was thoroughly taken aback; "she stood and stared, and did not open her mouth." Witness had no doubt at all that he had a better opportunity of seeing the man than Lambie, because he met him face to face. The lobby was well lit. The man "walked quite coolly, as if the house belonged to him," till he got up to witness, and then darted down the stair "like greased lightning, and banged the door at the foot of the close." Witness had pointed out Slater in the Commissioner's room in New York, but did not say that he was the man; he said he closely resembled the man. He went by the general appearance only. In cross-examination, Mr. Adams, quite fairly, admitted that, before indicating Slater on that occasion, he had seen him identified by Lambie and Barrowman. Even after all he had heard, witness did not give an absolutely confident opinion that the prisoner was the man; "it was too serious a charge for him to say from a passing glance." [In justice to Mr. Adams, it has to be borne in mind that he said he was somewhat short-sighted, and had not on his spectacles when he saw the man in the hall.]

Had the Crown relied solely upon the testimony of Lambie and Adams to identify the accused as the murderer, they could hardly have expected a verdict; but the prosecution was able to produce a witness of a different calibre, who saw the murderer flying from the house. This was Mary Barrowman, the message girl of fifteen, who had identified the prisoner in the corridor and in the Commissioner's room at New York, as already mentioned, and also at the police station in Glasgow. She repeated how, at the lamp-post, she saw the man run from the close and down the steps. He came towards her very fast, ran up against her, and on towards West Cumberland Street, down which he turned. She got a good look at him, both as he was coming up to her and when he knocked up against her. When he passed her, she turned to look after him. It was quite bright near the lamp-post. The man was tall and broad-shouldered, and " had a slight twist in his nose." He was clean shaven and dark haired. "He had a Donegal hat on, and was wearing it down on his face." He wore a fawn overcoat, a dark suit of clothes, and dark brown boots. She then told how she turned back, and followed the man as far as the next lamp-post, until she saw him run round the corner into West Cumberland Street, when she resumed her way. She had picked out the prisoner, both in America and at the police station, without any difficulty. On the latter occasion he was shown to her wearing the waterproof No. 43 of the productions, and the hat No. 44; both were very like the articles worn by the man on the night of the murder. She had asked prisoner to pull the hat down further, and then recognised it as she had seen it that night. In answer to the Lord Advocate's final question, "Look at the prisoner: is that the man?" she replied, "Yes, that is the man who knocked against me that night." In cross-examination, Barrowman said that the man came down from the close two steps at a time; when he passed her, he was running at the top of his speed. His hat was pulled down "just about as far as his eyes." His coat was not buttoned; he was holding it up as he ran, with his hands in the pockets. When she followed the man, she thought he was running for a car. [The nearest car lines are in Great Western Road and St. George's Road, the opposite direction to that in which the man was then running.] She did not see his face for more than a couple of seconds. Slater had a moustache when she recognised him in America and in Glasgow; and the three photographs by which, in New York, she had identified him as the man, also showed him with a moustache. She had recognised him in all the photographs, although Inspector Pyper, who was present at the time, said she failed to do so in any of them. The nose of the man was twisted to the right side. She and Lambie occupied the same cabin for twelve days on the voyage out, but they never mentioned the object of their journey, nor discussed the appearance of the man. Lambie had pointed Slater out in the Court-room before she (witness) identified him. When she recognised Slater in the corridor at New York she did not see that he was in charge of the two men, between whom he walked. In reply to the judge, no one had told her not to talk to Lambie about the case. In re-examination, she had now seen Slater several times, and had no doubt he was the man.

The main objections to which the strong evidence of this witness is open are her youth (she was not fifteen till January, 1909); the improbability of her being able to describe, with so great minuteness, the appearance of a man rushing past her at top speed, shortly after seven o'clock on a December night; the fact that the hat No. 44 was not a Donegal or tweed hat, but a soft, black felt hat; and the obvious difficulty in believing that two girls of fifteen and twenty-one, in such unusual circumstances as a voyage across the Atlantic for the purpose of identifying a murderer, never spoke of the matter at all. On the other hand, it has to be kept in view that Barrowman told her mother what she had seen on her return home that night, and then said she would know the man again if she saw him; that, on 23rd December, two nights later, she described the man to two detectives; and that she never varied her original description, but stuck to her story throughout.

The name of Agnes Brown, teacher, 48 Grant Street, Glasgow, stands No. 46 on the list of witnesses for the prosecution. This witness, though in attendance at the trial, was not called either by the Crown or the defence; but her testimony was embodied in a deposition which, among others, had, as already mentioned, been admitted in evidence by the Commissioner at the extradition proceedings in New York, and thus, though not before the jury at the trial, it forms part of the case against the prisoner. A copy of the deposition will be found in the Appendix. This lady stated to Mr. Speirs, the agent for the defence, that, on the evening of 21st December, she was going from her house in Grant Street to an evening class in Dunard Street. Leaving shortly after seven o'clock, she had reached the corner of West Cumberland Street and West Princes Street at 7.10, when two men came running westward along the pavement of that street from the direction of St. George's Road, one of whom collided with her, and nearly knocked her down. The men continued to run along West Princes Street as far as Carrington Street, when they left the pavement and ran on in the middle of the road. They then ran across the road, and turned down Rupert Street to the right. They were well-dressed men, and she wondered why they were running in that manner, When one of them collided with her she obtained a profile view of both their faces; she also had a back view of them as they passed her. The man next her, and who collided with her, was dressed in a winter overcoat of a medium grey, three-quarters length, reaching past his knees. He had a close-fitting, dark cloth cap, with a scoop in front. It was a plain cap, with plain sides and no double brim, and had no buttons. He had on dark trousers. She was not sure whether his boots were black or brown. His coat was buttoned close up, and he had his hands in his pockets. He was a dark man, neither tall nor short. He had neither beard nor whiskers. She could not be positive whether he had a moustache or not. She saw nothing peculiar about his nose. He would be about 5 feet 8 inches or 5 feet 9 inches in height. The other man was about the same height. He had dark hair. He had neither beard nor whiskers. She was inclined to think he was clean shaven. He had no hat on, and he was not carrying any hat in his hand, so far as she saw. He had on a navy blue Melton coat, with a dark velvet collar. His coat was open. He had on a dark pair of trousers and black boots. The man with the blue coat had on a spotless collar. It looked almost new. She did not see anything peculiar about his nose. This man had his right arm hanging by his side, and seemed to be holding something in his hand. He had his left hand at his side as he passed her; but, after passing her, he seemed to carry whatever he was carrying a little in front of him. She saw no man running away by himself, clad in a waterproof coat and a Donegal hat. She heard of the murder on her return home, at ten o'clock, and told her sisters about the men she had seen. The same week she made a statement to two detectives. She was interviewed later by Superintendent Douglas; Mr. Stevenson, the chief constable; and Mr. Hart, the Procurator-fiscal. She was also at the Western Police Office for the purpose of identifying several suspects, but recognised none as being either of the men she had seen. On 21st February she was shown Slater, among twelve to fifteen other men, in the Central Police Station. She could recognise none of them by their front face view. Having seen them in right profile and also in back view, she pointed out Slater as the further away from her of the two men who passed her on the night of the murder. What led her to point out Slater was his black hair, and the fact that his ears stuck out somewhat from his head and were rather low down on the side of his head, his rather short neck, and his square shoulders. He also had rather a square jaw, and appeared to her to be about the same height. The back view and the profile view made her come to the conclusion that he was very like the man she had seen. [This statement should be compared with the sworn deposition printed in the Appendix.]

It is, of course, to be kept in view that the importance of Miss Brown's statement might have been materially affected by cross-examination in the witness-box; taken as it stands it only deepens the mystery, and affords a further example of the difficulties attending evidence of identity based on personal impressions.

Two witnesses remain who recognised the accused in circumstances alleged by the Crown to connect him with the murderer. Annie Armour, booking clerk, was on the night in question attending to her duties in the ticket office at the Kelvinbridge station of the Glasgow District Subway, when, between half past seven and eight o'clock, a man rushed through the turnstile, flung down a penny, and, without waiting for his ticket, ran down the stair to the platform. He stumbled on the stair and caught hold of the railing. He looked so excited, and gave witness such a fright that she cried out. He was of medium height, dark, clean shaven, and wore a light overcoat— she did not know whether he had on a hat or a cap. She saw his face. She had no difficulty in pointing out Slater at the police station; the prisoner was the man. In cross- examination she stated that the man's coat was a shade darker than the waterproof produced, but was otherwise similar to it. She did not notice the man's nose, but was quite certain he had no moustache. She had seen Slater's photograph and read the description before identifying him. The time could not have been later than a quarter to eight.

Oscar Slater

William Sancroft, car conductor, stated that on Wednesday, 23rd December, at 6.5 p.m., a man boarded his car at the end of Union Street, near Argyle Street, and took his seat on the top. The man was in a hurry. When witness went upstairs to collect the fares near West George Street the man had a penny in his hand and received a ticket. Witness asked a boy who was reading an evening paper on the opposite seat if there was any clue to the murderer. The boy replied, "No, there is not any clue yet, and I don't think there is any likelihood of getting one." The man then jumped up and, pushing past them, ran downstairs. Witness followed him, and saw him running full speed across to Garscadden Street. He left the car before reaching the halfpenny station. The prisoner was the man. He had been unable to trace the boy, who at that time was a regular traveller on his car.

Having dealt in some detail, as befits its importance, with the evidence of all the witnesses who identified Slater either as the supposed murderer or as the watcher in the street, we have now briefly to examine the circumstantial evidence adduced by the Crown in its support.

The main facts, so far as these were ascertained, of Slater's life in Glasgow during the months of November and December, 1908, were not in dispute, and may, for the reader's convenience, here be shortly narrated in the order in which they occurred from the evidence of the witnesses who spoke to them at the trial. The inferences to be drawn therefrom formed the question at issue.

Oscar Slater (whose real surname appears to be Leschziner), a German Jew, thirty-eight years of age, who described himself indifferently on his visiting card as "dentist" or "dealer in diamonds and precious stones," arrived in Glasgow from London on or about 26th October, and put up at the Central Hotel. He had been in Glasgow on at least two previous occasions, viz., for some nine months in 1901, the year of the Glasgow Exhibition, and again, for what period is not stated, in 1905. On 3rd November he pledged for £5 with J. L. Bryce, pawnbroker, two gold rings, three pearl studs, and other articles in the name of "Oscar Slater, Central Station Hotel." On the 4th he was joined by Andrée Junio Antoine (who in London was known as Madame Junio) and her servant, Schmalz. The three then took lodgings for a week at 136 Renfrew Street. That day Slater called on Stuart & Stuart, house furnishers, St. George's Road, saw the manager, Isaac Paradise, and asked their terms for furnishing a house on the instalment system. He gave his name as "Mr. Anderson." Following upon the above interview, Slater, as A. Anderson, dentist, 36 Albemarle Street, Piccadilly," called on J. S. Marr, house agent, and proposed to take a flat at 69 St. George's Road. On the 6th Mr. Marr, being satisfied with the references given—Robert Rogers and Davenport & Co., both of London—let the flat to Slater from 28th November till 28th May, 1909, at a rent of £42 per annum. Slater again called on Stuart & Stuart, and selected furniture for his house to the value of £178 16s. 6d., paid £10 as a deposit, and agreed to pay the balance by monthly instalments of £4. On the 9th he ordered from W. Lyon, stationer, fresh visiting cards in name of "A. Anderson, 69 St. George's Road, Charing Cross, Glasgow, three up, right," and, on the 10th, bought from Hepburn & Marshall a set of household tools, consisting of a hammer, screwdriver, pliers, &c., on a card for 2s. 6d. The furniture having been delivered, Slater, "Madame," and Schmalz then removed to the flat in St. George's Road, the door of which bore the name of "Anderson." Antoine explained the false name as a device to evade his wife, who had previously interfered with them.

During Slater's stay there his daily habits, according to the evidence of Schmalz, were as follows:—he rose about 9.30, and generally went out in the forenoon, returning for lunch; went out in the afternoon, and always dined at home, the dinner hour being seven o'clock—though Schmalz had seen it as late as eight. He was never out of the house on Sundays. No dentistry business was carried on in the house, and, so far as she knew, her master had no occupation.

It appears from the evidence that Slater's chief friends, while in Glasgow, were the witnesses Cameron and Rattman, with whom he was in company nearly every day. They frequented Gall's public-house, Cowcaddens; the Crown Hall billiard rooms, 98 Sauchiehall Street; Johnston's billiard rooms, 126 Renfield Street; the Motor Club, 26 India Street; and the M.O.S.C. or Sloper Club, 24 India Street, of which Slater afterwards became a member. The two last named were gambling clubs.

On the 12th November Slater opened a Post Office Savings Bank account in name of "Adolf Anderson," and next day made, through the bank, a purchase of Consols in that name. He also redeemed the articles he had pledged with Bryce. On the 14th he pledged with A. J. Liddell, pawnbroker, a diamond scarfpin for £5 in name of "Anderson." On the same day he called at the shop of Jacob Jackson and offered to sell him a diamond ring, as he was hard up. Jackson refused to buy the ring, but offered him employment as a canvasser, which he declined. He did not give his name or address. On the 16th Slater called at the shop of R.S. Bamber, hairdresser, Charing Cross, and was shaved by the witness Nichols. He then had a moustache. Nichols observed a peculiarity about his nose—it was not a twisted nose, but a nose that had been broken. He made some purchases there in the name of "Anderson" that day; deposited his own shaving materials; and continued regularly to call to be shaved, several times a week, till 25th December. On the 17th he pledged with Liddell a gold purse, fountain pen, three pearl studs, and a ring for £6, and on the following day he obtained an advance of £20 upon a diamond crescent brooch, giving his address as "136 Renfrew Street." Between 21st November and 1st December Slater, in Bamber's shop, offered to sell to Nichols, who was shaving him, some blankets, curtains, and kitchen furniture, which he said were quite new.

About 23rd November (four weeks before the murder), according to the witness Rattman, Slater, in Gall's public-house, wanted to sell him a ring. The witness Aumann made an offer for it, which Slater would not accept. About 24th or 25th November Slater called at the Motor Club and asked for the witness Cameron, who came out and took him upstairs. About 30th November, the witness Barr met Slater in the Sloper Club in the company of Cameron, who asked him to propose Slater as a member. Barr demurred to doing so, as Slater's reputation was not good, but ultimately agreed to put his name up.

On 1st December Slater was elected a member of the Sloper Club, his address being given as " Renfrew Street." About the 4th Slater mentioned to Nichols, who was shaving him, that he had lost a diamond pin. Nichols advised him to communicate with the police, but he replied it was best to leave them alone as much as one could. About this date Slater spoke to Aumann of his intention to go to America. He said he would go so soon as he got rid of his house, and mentioned a letter which he had received from San Francisco. On 6th December Slater was seen in the Motor Club with Cameron by the witness Henderson. He then wore a black bowler hat and a Melton coat. On the 7th Slater pledged with Bryce a pair of binocular glasses for £2 10s. About this date Slater told Cameron of his intention to go abroad. Between this time and 21st December Slater was seen by the witness M'Lean every second or third night playing cards at the Sloper Club.

On the 9th Slater sent his watch to Dent, watchmaker, London, for repair, giving his name as "Anderson," and requesting its return to him at 69 St. George's Road not later than 30th December. The same day he obtained from Liddell a further advance of £10 upon the diamond brooch. About this date Aumann, by Slater's desire, inspected the flat and furniture at 69 St. George's Road, with a view to his taking them over. Aumann, however, declined to do so, and Slater said he would look out for some one else. On the 10th Slater, in name of "Anderson," paid £4 to Stuart & Stuart as an instalment to account of the price of the furniture supplied by them. About 11th December Slater showed Cameron a letter he had received from San Francisco, advising him to come out, as business was good. Slater said he intended to go, and gave Cameron his address there.

About ten days or a fortnight before Christmas (11th or 15th December), when Slater called at Bamber's to be shaved as usual, Nichols remarked that his moustache had been taken off, and that day he shaved Slater's upper lip for the first and only time. Slater told him he was a dentist, and was waiting for his partner to join him. He mentioned several places—Queensland and San Francisco. About the middle of December, Cameron noticed that Slater had shaved his moustache; he commented on the fact, and Slater explained that it was "getting a bit scraggy."

About 15th December (ten days before Christmas), Slater showed Rattman a letter, which he had received from San Francisco, and said he intended going there so soon as he could arrange for his house being taken over. On the 17th, Slater deposited £5 in the Post Office Savings Bank—the last deposit he made. On the 18th or 19th, Cameron says he saw Slater for the last time before the murder, and, on one or other of those nights, the witness Barr met Slater at the Sloper Club. He generally saw him there once or twice a week. Slater was always well dressed. He never saw him wearing a drab or fawn- coloured waterproof.

Between one and three o'clock, on the morning of Sunday or Monday, 20th or 21st December, the witness M'Lean, who subsequently gave information to the police, saw Slater at the Sloper Club playing "poker." He was then clean shaven, or had a very small growth on his upper lip. He wore a dark suit, a fawn overcoat, and a dark cap. On that occasion M'Lean left the club with a friend, and walked home some ten yards behind Slater and another member. He saw Slater enter the close in St. George's Road. Till then he had not known where Slater lived.

The divergent accounts of how Slater was occupied on Sunday, the 20th, we have already noticed.

Before considering the evidence relating to the eventful Monday, 21st December, the day of the murder, it may be convenient to mention here the statements of Cameron and Rattman as to Slater's ordinary habits and appearance. Cameron said that he saw Slater frequently. Slater had no occupation, and was seldom out until mid-day; he was a gambler, and frequented the Motor, Sloper, and other clubs. He and Slater, when in company, filled in the time by going to the skating rink in Victoria Road in the afternoons, to a music hall in the evenings, and from thence to the Sloper Club, where cards were played till well on in the morning. He never saw Slater dressed in check trousers or light-coloured spats at any time during November or December. As a rule, his clothes, with the exception of the waterproof, were dark. He had seen him wearing a hat like production No. 44, but never saw him with a cloth hat with a rim round it and without a split in the centre. He had seen him in the cap produced, No. 46, but Slater generally wore a black bowler hat.

Rattman said that he met Slater, while in Glasgow, almost daily, in Gall's public-house and Johnston's billiard rooms during the day, and at various clubs at night. He never saw Slater wearing light-check trousers or light-coloured gaiters. Once or twice he had seen him in brown boots. He never saw him with a Donegal hat, but had seen him wearing a cap with the sides up. His clothes were generally dark or brown. When he last saw him, on Thursday, 24th December, Slater was wearing a dark suit and a bowler hat.

On Monday, the 21st, according to the evidence of Antoine and Schmalz, Slater received, by the morning post, two letters: one from his friend Rogers in London (who was not called as a witness), saying Slater's wife was still bothering him (Rogers) for money, the other from his partner Devoto in San Francisco, asking Slater to join him. These letters were not produced. There had been a previous letter from Devoto on the subject. In consequence of these letters, Antoine said, Slater decided to go to San Francisco, which he had intended doing since the beginning of the month. At 12.30 p.m. Slater called at Liddell's pawnshop, and raised £30 more upon the diamond brooch, making £60 in all. He also redeemed the gold purse, fountain pen, pearl studs, and ring, which he had pawned on 17th November, paying £6 4s. After lunch, at two o'clock, Slater gave Schmalz notice, and said she could return to London on the following Saturday. Schmalz overheard Slater and Antoine say they were going to San Francisco. In the afternoon Slater offered the pawn ticket for the brooch to a friend of the witness M'Lean, named Anderson, in the Sloper Club. At 4.30 Slater came into Gall's public-house and offered the pawn ticket for £4 to Rattman, who had seen the brooch. Rattman refused, and suggested that Aumann, who was present, should buy it; but the latter said the pawnbroker had already advanced too much on it. Slater then left.

At 5 p.m., as appears from the postmark on the envelope, a letter, written by Slater, was posted to the Post Office Savings Bank, West Kensington, London, asking that his money be sent at once, if possible by wire, as he had an urgent call to America because his wife was ill. At 6.12 a telegram, in the handwriting of Slater, was despatched from the Central Station, addressed to Dent, London, in these terms—"If possible send watch at once."

According to the evidence of Rattman and Aumann they, along with a third man whom they did not know, were just finishing a game of three hundred up, in Johnston's billiard rooms, Renfield Street, when Slater came in about 6.20. Rattman asked him whether he had succeeded in selling the pawn ticket, and he replied that he had not. Slater said he was going home to dinner; and on Rattman observing that he was going later to the Palace Music Hall, Slater remarked, "Very likely I will come and see you." Slater then left, having remained for about ten minutes. The game was finished two or three minutes after Slater's departure— Rattman says at 6.35; Aumann, at 6.40. Johnston, the proprietor of the saloon, and Gibb, the marker, proved that the table, upon which these men usually played, was engaged that day from 5.8 to 6.40. Johnston had gone out for tea at the time, and Gibb did not recollect who were playing there that afternoon. Neither Rattman nor Aumann could remember how Slater was then dressed, but Rattman said he had a moustache about a quarter of an inch long which, being dark, was quite noticeable. Rattman would never have taken him for a clean-shaven man that day.

Antoine and Schmalz swore that Slater dined at home that evening as usual at seven o'clock. The murder, as we know, was committed between seven and ten minutes past seven; and the man believed by Mrs. Liddell to be Slater was standing at the railing in Queen's Terrace at five minutes to seven.

About 9.45 that night the door bell of the Motor Club, 24 India Street, rang, and on the witness Henderson (the clubmaster) opening the door, he found Slater, who stepped into the hall. He was not a member of the club, but Henderson knew him by sight, having twice seen him there with Cameron. Slater asked Henderson if he had any money in the club, and said, "Give me what you have and I will give you a cheque." Henderson replied that his committee did not allow him to lend money, and suggested that Slater should go "next door" (the Sloper Club), and ask Cameron for it. Remarking that Cameron was " no use," Slater then left; he did not go into the club next door, but turned to the right, to Elmbank Crescent. He was not in the hall for more than four or five minutes. He had a short moustache "like stubble," and was wearing a waterproof like that produced (No. 43), and a Donegal hat, of different colour and make from hat No. 44. Henderson saw no discomposure about his dress; but he seemed to be excited, and witness thought he had been losing money at cards somewhere, and wanted to continue play. It will be remembered that at 12.30 that day Slater had received £30 from Liddell on the brooch.

With reference to the incident spoken to by Henderson, there was produced at the trial a letter, written by Slater to his friend, Hugh Cameron in Glasgow, on 2nd January, from the Tombs Prison, New York, a copy of which will be found in the Appendix. He writes—

I don't deney I have been in his [Henderson's] place asking him for mony because I went brocke in the Sloper Club. He would not mind to get me hangt, and I will try to prove that from a gambling point, I am right to ask for some money. The dirty caracter was trying to make the police believe I done the murder, was excitet, asking for mony to hop off.— I must have a good lawyer, and after I can proof my innocents befor having a trial, because I will prove with five people where I have been when the murder was committed.

On Tuesday, 22nd December, the day after the murder, Slater called at four o'clock at Bryce's pawnshop, saw the witness Kempton, and redeemed a pair of prism binocular glasses, which he had pledged on the 7th. He mentioned that he was going to America, and asked witness about the Anchor Line. He was then dressed in a dark overcoat and a hard hat, and had a slight, stubbly moustache. On Tuesday or Wednesday, 22nd or 23rd December, Slater called at Bamber's shop and was shaved by Nichols, who stated that Slater' told him he was going to Queensland on the following Wednesday (the 30th). Slater said that his wife was not going with him, as the weather was too cold, but she was to follow in the summer. He showed no sign of excitement. On one or other of these dates Cameron met Slater, who gave him the pawn ticket for the brooch, and asked him to dispose of it among his friends for £10. Cameron tried to sell the ticket to two people, but was unsuccessful, and returned it to Slater.

On Wednesday, 23rd, Slater received from the Glasgow branch of the Post Office Savings Bank the amount standing at the credit of his account, £39 18s. 3d. At 12.1 noon he despatched from Charing Cross Post Office a telegram to Dent, London, in the following terms:—"Must have watch, leaving to- morrow night for the Continent." Between four and five in the afternoon, Slater called at Cooks' tourist office, Buchanan Street, saw the witness Bain, and inquired for a second class two-berth cabin for himself and his wife by the "Lusitania," from Liverpool, on Saturday, 26th. He gave his name and address as "Oscar Slater, c/o Anderson, 69 St. George's Road, Glasgow." He was asked to call back next day, when the agent should have heard from the Cunard Company, with whom he was to communicate. That evening, between ten and eleven o'clock, as Rattman and Aumann were playing billiards in Johnston's billiard rooms, Slater and Cameron came in and sat watching the game. Johnston, the proprietor, asked them if they wanted a game, but Slater said that they would not play that night. His upper lip, said Johnston, was then a little dark, he had not much to show, but he was not exactly clean shaven. Gibb, the marker, remembered seeing Slater on this occasion, but not Cameron. Slater's moustache was, he said, quite noticeable from the other end of the room, sixteen feet distant. He had about a fortnight's growth on his upper lip; no one could have taken him for a clean-shaven man. When the game was finished at 11.20, Slater, Cameron, and Rattman left together, Cameron saying good-night to the others at the corner of Cambridge Street and Sauchiehall Street, while Rattman went on with Slater, and parted with him at his house in St. George's Road.

On Thursday, 24th December, Slater received at the Glasgow branch of the Post Office Savings Bank the proceeds of the 2£ per cent. Consols, which had been sold on his instructions, the amount paid to him being £49 7s. 2d. Rattman said that on this date he saw Slater for the last time before he left. Slater asked him to come and see him in his house next day (Christmas Day), but Rattman did not do so. Slater said nothing to him on this Thursday as to his intention of sailing on the following Saturday. About four o'clock the same afternoon Slater called at Cooks' office in Buchanan Street, and again saw the witness Bain, who had heard from the Cunard Company offering room E76, at £12 rate, by the " Lusitania," sailing on Saturday, 26th December. Bain showed Slater the room on the ship's plan, but the latter said he preferred an outside cabin, and could do better in Liverpool. Bain said if he booked the one offered then he could adjust matters in Liverpool, and Slater said he would call back next day. He did not do so, and that day (Friday, 25th) Bain wrote to the Cunard Company asking them to release the cabin, and to let him know if "Mr. and Mrs. Slater" booked with them on Saturday.

Cameron stated that shortly after four o'clock on Thursday, the 24th, at the corner of Gordon Street and Renfield Street he met Slater, who said he was looking for the Cunard Line shipping office, in Jamaica Street, to make inquiry as to the sailings to America. Cameron accompanied him there; Slater went into the Cunard office and got a pamphlet. When he came out he remarked to Cameron, who had been waiting for him outside, that perhaps the "Campania," sailing on Saturday week (2nd January, 1909), might suit him. He then asked Cameron to get a Bank of England £5 note for five Scotch £1 notes, as he wanted the note to send to his people in Germany, which he had done, he said, almost every Christmas. Cameron having failed to get it in the Cunard office, they tried the booking office at the Central Station, the Central Station Hotel, and Forsyth's shop, all without success. Finally, at the Grosvenor Restaurant, they got the note, which Slater enclosed in an addressed envelope, and registered at Hope Street Post Office. Having had tea at Cranston's tea-rooms in Sauchiehall Street, they parted shortly before six o'clock, Cameron arranging to call for Slater after dinner. This was the last time Cameron saw him. That day Slater had, as described by Cameron, "a very stubbly moustache," which was quite noticeable. Cameron called at Slater's house as arranged about eight o'clock, but was told by the servant Schmalz that he had gone out half an hour before with a gentleman. As a matter of fact, Slater was in at the time, but had instructed Schmalz to tell Cameron he was out.

On the morning of Friday, 25th December, as stated by Antoine and Schmalz, Slater received a postcard from Mrs. Freedman, who had come from London in pursuance of an arrangement whereby she should take over the flat and furniture, intimating her arrival at the Alexandra Hotel, Bath Street. Antoine sent Schmalz to bring her to the house, and Mrs. Freedman came at 12.30 p.m. She found Antoine crying; and Slater, who was busy packing his luggage, explained the reason was that he would not take her with him. He asked and obtained from Mrs. Freedman a loan of £25. [It will be remembered that Mrs. Freedman, who was not called as a witness, stated to Detective Lieutenant Gordon, on 26th December, that she understood their destination to be Monte Carlo.] Antoine said that Slater wanted her to go to her people in Paris, but, in the end, he agreed to let her accompany him.

Later in the day Slater called at Bamber's shop, and was shaved, for the last time, by Nichols, according to whom he then had a moustache " a quarter of an inch or five-sixteenths long." It had been growing for about ten days or a fortnight. Slater told Nichols he was leaving Glasgow that night, and was sailing next day by the "Lusitania." When Slater left the shop he removed the shaving materials which he had previously deposited there for his own use. During the last week of his visits Nichols observed no difference in his appearance, except that he was wearing a peculiar vest. He had seen Slater in various suits, and wearing a dark blue overcoat, but not a light fawn-coloured overcoat.

That afternoon (Christmas Day) the description of the supposed murderer, given by the girl Barrowman, appeared, by the authority of the police, in the two o'clock editions of the Glasgow evening newspapers— *Times*, *News*, and *Citizen*.

At 6 p.m. Slater again went out. Between six and seven o'clock John Cameron, city porter, said that a man, whom he identified as Slater, spoke to him at the Central Station, and told him to call at 69 St. George's Road for some luggage "at the back of eight o'clock." He gave the name of "Anderson." Along with another porter (Mackay) Cameron went to the house as directed, but, by mistake, called first at the top flat instead of the third. At the latter he saw the man who had engaged him, and two women. He removed ten articles of luggage on his barrow to the Central Station for the 9.5 train for London and Liverpool. Slater met him at the station and paid him. Cameron could not say whether he was then clean shaven or not.

Margaret and Isabella Fowlis, who lived in the flat above Slater, and knew him by sight as "Anderson," remembered the porter calling at their door for luggage. They told him that "Anderson" occupied the house below; and, looking over the stairs while the luggage was being removed, saw Slater handing it out. The time was about 8.30. Slater was then dressed in a blue overcoat, a hat, and patent boots. They said he had no moustache. They were sure his upper lip was clean shaven, because he looked up at them, and saw them watching him. He left the house on foot, followed by the two women. Ruby Russell, a servant in the same stair, also witnessed the removal of the luggage, and saw from her window the departure of Slater, Antoine, and Schmalz. They walked a few yards together, and Slater went away by himself. Antoine and Schmalz said that they all walked together to Charing Cross, where they entered a cab and drove to the Central Station.

On arriving there at 8.45 the cab door was opened by James Tracey, railway porter, who was waiting with the porter Cameron and the luggage. Slater and the two women got out. Slater told Tracey to have the luggage labelled for Liverpool by the 9.5 train; and, ""his having been done, Tracey, by order of the guard, put it into the rear brake van. He did not know what tickets Slater had. Only one of the two women travelled with him. Tracey said Slater that night had a moustache. It was quite noticeable. He had no difficulty in identifying Slater, but failed to recognise either Antoine or Schmalz. John Brown, booking clerk, Central Station, said there were few people travelling by that train, being Christmas night. Among the tickets which he issued by the 9.5 were two third class singles to London and two third class singles to Liverpool. He recollected selling the two London tickets to a man with a slight moustache, who was very like Slater, but he could not swear to it. The Liverpool tickets, so far as he remembered, were issued separately to two different persons. It was a regular practice to travel with a London ticket, and break the journey at Liverpool.

On 26th December, about 12.30 p.m., a man wearing a soft hat and a blue overcoat entered the offices of the Cunard Company in Liverpool, saw John Forsyth, manager of the second class department, and asked for accommodation for a gentleman and his wife by the "Lusitania," sailing that day. Strangely enough, Forsyth offered him room E76, the very cabin which Slater had refused in Glasgow. The man said, "No, I do not like that, it is inside; it was offered me by your agents in Glasgow." He appeared to regret having made the remark, and said no more. He seemed, to witness, somewhat nervous, and, while he was talking, looked at the door as if expecting some one. Forsyth asked him what he required, and he replied that he wanted an outside room. After some discussion, an outside cabin was agreed upon, and £28 in Scotch notes paid for the two tickets. Forsyth asked the man's name, and he said, "Otto Sando." He spelt it, "S-a-n-d-o," remarking, "It is not Sandow, the strong man." He then filled up the requisite application form, giving, inter alia, his destination and American address as " Chicago, 30 Staate Street." Slater was undoubtedly the man, and, said Forsyth, "he can recognise me, too."

While in Liverpool Slater wrote from the London & North-Western Station Hotel a letter in German to his friend Rattman, a translation of which will be found in the Appendix, giving as his reason for not saying good-bye, his "absolutely suddenly" leaving Glasgow, "Freedman's girl" having taken over his flat; and, further, stating, "My French girl leaves for Paris from here." Their arrangements concluded, and the duties of friendship thus discharged, "Mr. and Mrs. Otto Sando" sailed the same day in the "Lusitania" for New York.

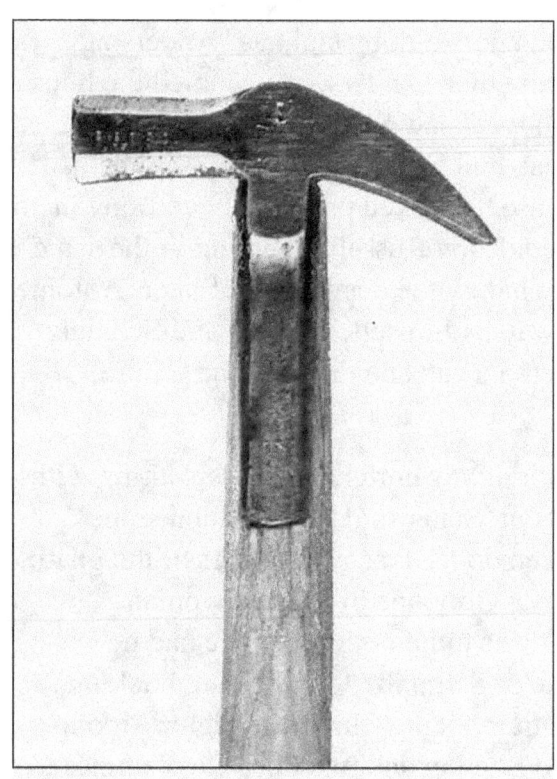

Head of Hammer (duplicate) produced in court.

Whether or not Slater's departure from Glasgow was, in the words of the Lord Advocate, "a flight from justice," or, as Mr. M'Clure put it, an act in which "nothing suggesting subterfuge occurs until the tickets were taken at Liverpool in the name of Otto Sando," was a question for the jury; and they determined it against the prisoner. The explanation given by Antoine of Slater's concealment of his destination was, in the first place, because of his wife, and, secondly, in case of the landlord of the house and the furniture company bothering, Mrs. Freedman about the flat. This does not, however, explain why he failed to disclose the date of his departure to his intimate friends Cameron and Rattman.

Having recorded the facts with regard to Slater's behaviour, as disclosed in the proof, we have now only to consider the purport of the medical evidence adduced. It will be remembered that the police, when searching Slater's luggage on his return from New York, found in one of his trunks a hammer, which he had bought on 10th November, as before mentioned. With this weapon the Crown undertook to prove that the murder had been committed. Professor Glaister deponed that he did not find in the dining-room of 15 Queen's Terrace any implement that looked as if it had been used for the purpose of murdering Miss Gilchrist. He was clear, from the spattering of blood in the neighbourhood, that the injuries had been produced practically at the point where the body was found, within an area bounded by a radius of three feet from the head; and, from his experience, his view was that the assailant knelt on the woman's chest, and, kneeling upon the chest, struck violently at the head with the implement that he employed. From the nature of the injuries inflicted witness inferred that the weapon was not uniformly the same at the striking part; the wounds were of different sizes and shapes, and the left eyeball, in a burst condition, was driven into the brain. That indicated that the weapon must have been of a pointed character, because a larger weapon, that would have been likely to have caused the larger wounds, could not have entered the orbit. The hammer, No. 47, could, in his opinion, in the hands of a strong man and forcibly wielded (plus the kneeling on the chest), have produced the injuries found on the body. That instrument accounted most easily for the different classes of wounds, particularly the eye mischief. In cross-examination the witness could not say positively that the hammer was used. His view of the course of the assault was that the woman was on her feet, facing her assailant, when she received a blow with something and was knocked down on the floor; the assailant instantly pounced on her and knelt on her, fracturing her ribs and breast bone during the act of the repeated blows; and that the instrument, whatever it was, produced those frightful injuries upon her head and face. To give a rough guess, judging from the wounds and the size of them, between twenty and forty blows must have been inflicted, with almost lightning rapidity. It must have been a furious, continuous assault before the assailant rose to do anything further. The man who applied the violence in the way he (witness) thought he did would have his clothing to a fairly large extent bespattered with blood. His hands could not escape, nor the implement he employed. It was one of the most brutally smashed heads witness had ever seen in his experience.

Dr. Hugh Galt, who, in conjunction with Professor Glaister, had made the post-mortem examination, concurred. The number of blows struck must have been very great, certainly not under fifty or sixty, probably a good many more. The smashing in this case was most extensive. The hammer, No. 47, could produce the injuries witness saw. In cross-examination witness admitted that, a priori, he would have expected a heavier weapon. It was impossible to say exactly what instrument had been employed; it was a weapon of some weight, and with sharp edges. In reply to the judge, the injury to the eye was the only wound that could not have been produced by a weapon of greater diameter than the hammer in question.

Professor Glaister also deponed to the result of his examination of the four articles submitted to him as before mentioned, viz., (1) waterproof, (2) hat, (3) hammer, and (4) auger. With regard to the waterproof, he found twenty small stains, externally and internally, some of which, after treatment and on microscopic examination, showed corpuscular bodies, resembling in general appearances mammalian red blood corpuscles; but, by reason of the small amount of material at disposal, confirmatory tests for blood could not be employed. The stains appeared to have been subjected to the influence of water. No stains were found upon the hat. The hammer, from the head to halfway down the shaft, had the appearance of having been scrubbed, the surface of the wood being roughened and bleached. Yellowish stains were found on both sides of the head and on the flanges, which, on examination, showed corpuscular bodies, resembling red blood corpuscles of the mammalian type. For the reason already adduced, witness was unable to state positively that these were red blood corpuscles. The auger, on examination, gave no indication of the presence of blood. In cross-examination witness said that in his first report to the police, dated 22nd December, it was stated, "On examination we found that adhering to the metal of the instrument [the auger] were several grey hairs, and, in addition, what seemed to be blood." Witness had examined twenty stains in all on the waterproof, and only in some of them did he find the corpuscular bodies referred to. He found no stains in the pockets of the waterproof. Witness could not positively prove that any article found in the possession of the accused contained blood. In reply to the judge, if it were not a case of murder, but some commercial question, judging from his very long experience of examination of such stains, witness would without hesitation say that, in his view, to the best of his knowledge and belief, these were red blood corpuscles.

Professor Harvey Littlejohn, who, in conjunction with Professor Glaister, had examined the articles, concurred.

For the defence, Dr. W. G. Aitchison Robertson deponed that, looking to the extent and multiplicity of the wounds, he considered the hammer produced a very unlikely weapon. He had examined the hammer for blood stains, but found no sign of blood about it, and he saw no appearance of the handle having been washed or scraped. The man who committed the murder as described would, in the opinion of witness, be more or less covered with blood. Witness had examined the waterproof coat and found no signs of blood whatever upon it. In cross- examination witness said that his evidence was given on the facts as disclosed in Professor Glaister's report. The wound whereby the left eyeball was driven in was 2 inches by ¾ inch, which was much larger than the head of the hammer. Witness thought a heavy poker or crowbar more likely to have produced the injuries, by beating and thrusting with it. He could not see how the spindle-shaped wounds could have been produced by the hammer. He made no tests for the purpose of ascertaining the presence of blood.

Dr. Alexander Veitch, who had also examined the hammer and coat, found absolutely no appearance of blood. He considered the hammer produced an unlikely instrument to inflict the injuries described; a blunt instrument, such as a piece of railing, a crowbar, or a larger hammer, would be more likely. The assailant could not escape getting a good deal of blood on his own person. Had the hammer produced been used by the assailant, it would necessarily have had a lot of blood about its head, and probably all over it. His hands would probably be bloody, and witness would have expected to see some sign of that on the lower part of the handle. There was no sign of scraping or scrubbing. In cross- examination, witness had never seen a case where there was such an amount of mauling. The weapon used would, in his opinion, be twice as large as the hammer produced. Had the latter been used, he would have expected a class of fracture which was not present, i.e., a depressed fracture, penetrating, and of comparatively small size. He made no analysis of the stains found on either of the articles.

With reference to the failure of Drs. Aitchison Robertson and Veitch to discover blood stains on the waterproof, it may be remarked that twenty-five suspected portions had been cut out of it by Professor Glaister prior to its being examined by them. It is also to be observed, as a point of interest, that neither at the instance of the prosecution nor of the defence was the metal head of the hammer removed from its soft white wood shaft. Had this been done the question at issue would probably, to that extent at least, have been settled.

The condition of the hammer and waterproof was of vital importance to the Crown case, for these were the only links between Slater and the murder. Apart from them, nothing incriminating was found in his possession. In the seven trunks belonging to him the police discovered neither Donegal hat, light- coloured cloth overcoat, check trousers, fawn spats, nor brown boots. No proof was offered that he had any knowledge of the existence of Miss Gilchrist or of her jewels; none of the deceased's property was traced to him, and nothing proved to be his was found in her house. With the exception of the disputable stains on the waterproof, no article of clothing belonging to him was bloodstained.

In this connection it may be mentioned that both Antoine and Schmalz swore that, so far as they knew, none of Slater's clothes were washed, burned, or otherwise destroyed during their last week in Glasgow. With regard to the hammer, they stated that it was solely used by Schmalz for breaking coals. It was kept in the drawer of the hatstand in the hall—not, one would think, the most convenient receptacle; it was never out of the house, and, to their knowledge, was neither washed nor scraped. The Lord Advocate, with tact and good taste, waived his right to cross-examine the girl Antoine, whose position as a witness in the case was plainly indicated by Lord Guthrie in his charge to the jury. Schmalz, however, was subjected to a trenchant cross-examination, from which ordeal she emerged comparatively unscathed, either because she told the truth and knew nothing to incriminate Slater, or because she was a match for her learned adversary.

A fact most damaging to the prisoner's character was elicited by the Lord Advocate from the witness Schmalz. She admitted that Antoine, obviously with Slater's concurrence, had led, both in London and Glasgow, an immoral life. From the witness Cameron the Lord Advocate had already learned that Slater supplemented his gains as a gambler by the proceeds of prostitution, and that, in Lord Guthrie's striking phrase, "He had maintained himself by the ruin of men and on the ruin of women, living for many years past in a way that many blackguards would scorn to live." Of this fact the Lord Advocate made deadly use in his address to the jury, going so far as to say that it removed the one serious difficulty which confronted them—the difficulty of conceiving that there was in existence a human being capable of doing such a dastardly deed. " That difficulty removed," proceeded the learned Advocate, "I say, without hesitation, that the man in the dock is capable of having committed this dastardly outrage, and the question for you to consider is, whether or not the evidence has brought it home to him." With reference to this point the exception taken thereto by Mr. Speirs, the agent for the defence, in his introductory note to the memorial prepared by him on the prisoner's behalf as after mentioned, may be quoted—

That evidence against his character was before the jury, and strongly commented upon by the counsel for the prosecution; and while the jury was afterwards told by the counsel for the prosecution and the presiding judge not to allow the evidence against Slater's character to influence them against him, there is a very strong general opinion to the effect that it must have influenced the jury. As the accused did not plead good character, his character should not, according to the law of Scotland, have been attacked.

It must, however, be observed that no objection was taken by counsel for the prisoner to any of the Lord Advocate's questions as to Slater's means of livelihood. His false assumption of the designation of dentist made it clearly competent for the Lord Advocate to ask the witnesses for the defence how the prisoner maintained himself. If the defence desired to exclude the evidence objected to in Mr. Speirs' memorial, they should not have examined either Cameron or Schmalz.

The case for the defence closed with the examination of the two medical men, and, contrary to expectation, the prisoner did not avail himself of his right to enter the witness-box. No reference to this fact was made either by judge or counsel; but there can be little doubt that it told heavily against him with the jury. His agent, in the memorial before referred to, with respect to this circumstance, states—

It is only fair to the prisoner to point out that he was all along anxious to give evidence on his own behalf. He was advised by his counsel not to do so, but not from any knowledge of guilt. He had undergone the strain of a four days' trial. He speaks rather broken English—although quite intelligibly— with a foreign accent, and he had been in custody since January.

Apart from this, however, the prisoner, in view of his manner of life, might well have hesitated, for reasons best known to himself, to expose his whole past career to the scrutiny of the Lord Advocate.

The total number of witnesses examined at the trial was seventy-four, sixty being called by the Crown, and fourteen by the defence.

At eleven o'clock on the morning of the fourth day of the trial the Lord Advocate rose to address the jury for the prosecution. To those who were present his speech was, perhaps, the most impressive episode in this remarkable case. Out of doors the day was one of brilliant spring sunshine; and past the drawn blinds that screened the windows of the Courtroom there streamed three shafts of light, one of which fell upon the strong features of the Lord Advocate, as he stood in front of the dock, facing the jury. He used no ornaments of rhetoric, made no impassioned appeal; but sternly, almost relentlessly, marshalled, one by one, his facts and inferences, crushing the while his handkerchief in his clenched right hand, as though it were a symbol of the prisoner's fate. He spoke for an hour and fifty minutes; and the opinion was generally expressed that no more masterly address had been delivered in that place since the historic speech of the late Lord President Inglis, when, as Dean of Faculty, he successfully defended Madeleine Smith. The impression was heightened by the fact that the learned Advocate referred neither to notes nor documents; but, by a gift of memory, in the circumstances little short of marvellous, wove into a coherent pattern the complex web of the Crown case. That he was convinced of the justice of his cause was manifest; but in one or two points his argument would seem to go somewhat further than was warranted by the evidence. It is noteworthy that the address contained no reference to the witnesses Reid, Antoine, or Schmalz. In an early passage the promise, "We shall see in the sequel how it was that the prisoner came to know that she [Miss Gilchrist] was possessed of these jewels," appears rather to beg the question, for upon that point no evidence whatever was led, nor did the speaker again refer to it. With regard to the statement that " there is not a single human being in this case who, having once seen the prisoner, has failed to know him at once, so striking, so peculiarly distinctive is his face," it has to be observed that the instances given of those who admittedly saw Slater, were of persons who, though seeing him but once, all spoke to him and heard him speak. Further, the Lord Advocate was mistaken in stating, which he did more than once, as a reason for the prisoner hastening his departure, that Slater's name, as well as the description given by Barrowman, appeared in the newspapers of 25th December. As a matter of fact, the name of Slater was first published in the Glasgow Herald of 2nd January. On the conclusion of his address, the Lord Advocate left the Court, to which he did not return.

At half-past one Mr. M'Clure commenced his speech for the defence, occupying exactly the same time as his learned opponent. His address obviously suffered in comparison with that for the Crown, its chief concern being to refute seriatim the arguments of the Lord Advocate. It would therefore be unfair to contrast the speakers from the oratorical standpoint. Mr. M'Clure opened with a strong protest against the newspaper campaign, of which, he said, his client had been the victim, and referred to the prejudice created by the false reports set afloat concerning the case. In view of what afterwards happened, it is curious to note his warning to the jury, that, if they convicted the prisoner, " there was no possibility of a commutation of the capital penalty." While one may have difficulty in assenting to his proposition, that, as regards the behaviour of Slater before and after the murder, "in the main facts there is nothing suspicious," the skill with which he analysed the evidence of the identifying witnesses, and made the most of the many points telling in the prisoner's favour, is worthy of all praise. His examination of the evidence was at once careful and exhaustive; and the case for the defence was adequately presented. He called the jury's attention to the fact that Slater was first suspected upon grounds, one of which was false, and the other innocent, viz., because he had pawned a brooch which was supposed to have belonged to Miss Gilchrist, and because, when he was looked for, it was found that he had left Glasgow. Mr. M'Clure made effective use of the American evidence, as showing the obvious inconsistencies of Lambie's testimony, and satisfactorily disposed of the Crown theory that Slater fled as the result of the description published in the newspapers. The excellent point, too, was made that Slater, if he were, in fact, the watcher seen by the witnesses, had been so careful as to destroy the clothes spoken to by them, while preserving the very garment in which he did the deed. Upon the vexed question of the murderer's moustache, the following summary was given:—

The man wanted is alleged to have been clean shaven by Mrs. Liddell, Helen Lambie, Barrowman, Adams, and Armour. It is, on the contrary, proved that Slater had a moustache by Rattman, Aumann, Cameron, Reid, Nichols, the barber; Gibb, the billiard man; Kempton, and Tracey.

In conclusion, Mr. M'Clure made a legitimate and telling reference to the notorious case of Adolf Beck, as showing the dangers attending evidence of identity based on personal impressions.

Lord Guthrie began his charge to the jury at five minutes to four o'clock. His lordship suggested that the man who entered Miss Gilchrist's house did so with the intention only to rob her of her jewels, and was not contemplating murder. When she resisted, and attempted to raise an alarm by knocking on the floor, then arose the necessity to silence her— "Dead men (and dead women) tell no tales." His lordship then proceeded to explain to the jury the nature and relative value of the evidence, direct and circumstantial. He described the evidence with regard to the prisoner's character and financial circumstances as double-edged; and told the jury that, if they decided to convict him, they ought to be able to say they had disregarded it, and had convicted him irrespective of it. Referring to the mystery, of which the prisoner was the key, his lordship said that he never knew a case like the present, either in his own experience or from reading. As to the question of identification, his lordship held that it would be unsafe to convict on mere evidence of personal impression of his identity on the part of strangers, without reference to any marked personality or personal peculiarity. It was for them to consider whether some of that evidence was not given by persons who had an opportunity of familiarising themselves with the individual identified. One fact, his lordship said, was quite clear—the prisoner resembled the murderer. But it was to be kept in view that the witnesses to identification were all Scotch, while the prisoner was patently a foreigner; therefore the mere fact that a witness thought the prisoner the same as a man he had seen, because both had a foreign appearance, went for very little, if it went for anything at all. With these general observations, his lordship then proceeded to review the evidence on this part of the case, and having done so, observed—

The questions for you are—and they are purely jury questions—so far as identification is concerned, first, has the prisoner such a marked personality, and had the witnesses Lambie, Adams, and Barrowman such an opportunity to observe the man leaving Miss Gilchrist's house, and are they sufficiently credible witnesses, to enable you to hold it proved that the prisoner is the same man? Second, has the prisoner such a marked personality, and had the eleven or twelve witnesses above referred to such opportunities for seeing the man who haunted the street, as to enable you to hold it proved that the prisoner was the same man— I assume — but again it is for you to say — that there can be no reasonable doubt as to the identity of the man haunting the street and the murderer. Lastly, is there corroboration, in other parts of the evidence, of the personal impression given you by these witnesses, assuming that they are strangers, and assuming that there is no such marked personality or personal peculiarity as would add weight to the mere personal impression?

His lordship then examined the purely circumstantial evidence, and commented on the fact that nothing was found in the prisoner's possession on which the jury could rely as being connected necessarily with the murder. With regard to the telegram said to have been despatched by Slater from the Central Station at 6.12 on the night of the crime, there was no evidence that, although it was in his handwriting, he personally handed it to the telegraph clerk. [Curiously enough, there was no evidence even that it was in Slater's handwriting.] The jury would consider whether, even accepting the evidence of Aumann and Rattman, the prisoner had not plenty of time to walk from Johnston's billiard rooms to West Princes Street and to arrive at the scene of the murder by seven o'clock. With regard to the evidence of Antoine and Schmalz they would also judge whether, in a disreputable house such as Slater's, they were, without evidence, to credit the statement that hours were so punctual and so regular that the inmates always dined at seven o'clock. As to the alleged flight from Glasgow, his lordship did not think it could be suggested that Slater was not intending at some time or other to go to America. It was for the jury to say whether, in the circumstances they had heard detailed, there was a hastening of that intention, which was suggestive, if it did not prove, that he had a new and very serious motive for expediting his departure. His lordship noted that Antoine, who must have known, was not asked by counsel for the defence to say that the tickets were taken for Liverpool, and not for London. After some observations on what constituted reasonable doubt, his lordship concluded his impressive and impartial charge as follows:—

Gentlemen, I suppose you all think that the prisoner possibly is the murderer; you may very likely all think that he probably is the murderer. That, however, will not entitle you to convict him. The Crown have undertaken to prove, not that he is possibly or probably the murderer, but that he is the murderer. That is the question you have to consider. If you think there is no reasonable doubt about it, you will do your duty and convict him; if you think there is, you will acquit him.

The jury retired to consider their verdict at 4.55 p.m. Contrary to the usual practice, the prisoner, it is understood by his own desire, did not leave the dock to await their decision in the cells below the Court-room. It was obvious from the demeanour of those in Court that a verdict adverse to the accused was not at first expected; but as the time wore on, and the jury did not return, this anticipation visibly decreased. The general restlessness communicated itself to the prisoner, until the ringing of the jury bell at 6.5, announcing that his fate had been decided, was succeeded by intense silence. The jury, having returned to the box, and Lord Guthrie having taken his seat, the foreman, in reply to the Clerk of Justiciary, announced their verdict as follows:—"The jury, by a majority, find the panel guilty of murder as libelled." Mr. Morison, K.C., in the absence of the Lord Advocate, then formally moved for sentence.

It is not too much to say that the verdict came with a shock of surprise to most of the auditors in the crowded Court-room. Upon none, however, did the blow fall with such fearful effect as on the man in the dock. He had been, it appears, throughout the trial, confident of acquittal, and had borne himself from day to day with inflexible composure. The recording of the verdict and sentence, which followed upon the jury's finding, occupied an actual seven minutes; but the tense stillness, broken only by the sound of the official pen, seemed interminable. It proved too much for the prisoner's iron nerve. He rose in the dock, and, labouring under strong emotion, made an incoherent effort to address the judge. Lord Guthrie informed Mr. M'Clure that he should advise the prisoner to reserve anything he had to say for the Crown authorities; but Slater commenced another hysterical appeal, which his lordship mercifully terminated by pronouncing the inevitable sentence, adjudging the prisoner to be hanged in Glasgow on 27th May. A scene more painful it is fortunately the lot of few to witness, and none who did so on this occasion is likely to forget it. The prisoner was then removed, and the Court rose.

It is satisfactory to note that, as the result of what occurred upon this trial, an Act of Adjournal was passed on 1st June, 1909, abolishing the unnecessary and cruel delay between the declaration of a verdict of guilty and the pronouncing of the capital sentence. A copy of the Act of Adjournal will be found in the Appendix.

The votes of the fifteen jurymen were, it is understood, given as follows:—Nine for "guilty," five for "not proven," and one for "not guilty." It is noteworthy that, had two of the majority voted differently, Slater would have been set free.

In England, of course, a conviction in such circumstances could not have been obtained, and a new trial would have resulted.

On the night of the last day of the trial, Thursday, 6th May, it was stated in the Press that the prisoner, on being taken to the cells below the dock, exclaimed to the detectives, "I am not the only guilty party"; but this alleged confession was afterwards emphatically denied by Mr. Speirs, the agent for the defence, in a letter to the newspapers.

The verdict was variously received by the Press. One newspaper stated that, at the conclusion of Lord Guthrie's charge, it appeared impossible for the prisoner to escape; while another, taking exactly the opposite view, declared that the judge's summing up made it impossible for the jury to convict! Perhaps the more general view was that a verdict of "not proven" would, in the circumstances, have been a safer finding. Arrangements were made forthwith for the presentation of a public petition for commutation of the death sentence, to be forwarded to the Secretary of State for Scotland, the grounds being (1) that the evidence led against the prisoner was insufficient to justify the jury finding him guilty of the charge, there being, in the petitioners' opinion, insufficient evidence to identify the prisoner with the murderer; and (2) that the question of the prisoner's immoral character was brought before the jury and, in the petitioners' view, must have influenced their judgment. This was duly prepared, and having been signed, it is stated, by over twenty thousand members of the public, was forwarded to the Scottish Secretary, Lord Pentland, together with a memorial in Slater's behalf prepared by Mr. Speirs, on Monday, 17th May, ten days before the date fixed for the execution. A copy of this memorial, which ably embodies in lucid and succinct form, the arguments on the evidence against the verdict, will be found in the Appendix. With the exception of the statement of Agnes Brown, to which we have before referred, no new facts are given; nor does the memorial contain any further information regarding Slater's movements on the night of the crime. If, as is alleged in the memorial, the prisoner " was all along anxious to give evidence on his own behalf," and only refrained from entering the witness-box on his counsel's advice, it is difficult to understand why, when he had an opportunity of telling his own story to the Scottish Secretary, his lips remained sealed.

Meanwhile the "campaign" in the Press, against which Mr. M'Clure had protested at the trial as prejudicial to his client, was conducted more vigorously than ever; but on this occasion in favour of the condemned man. To such lengths was this crusade of sentiment carried, that one respectable Glasgow journal actually despatched an emissary to an obscure mining village in Upper Silesia, for the purpose of interviewing the convict's parents; and for some days improved its readers with anecdotes of "Oscar's Youth," and harrowing accounts of "How the News of the Verdict Reached Them," and "The Mother's Judgment: 'If he has done that he deserves to die.'"

As time went on, and no word reached Glasgow from London, the authorities proceeded with the necessary arrangements for carrying out the sentence on 27th May. Not till seven o'clock on the evening of the 25th was the following telegram received from the Scottish Office:—

To the Lord Provost of Glasgow, City Chambers, Glasgow.—Case of Oscar Slater. Execution of sentence of death is respited until further signification of His Majesty's pleasure.

UNDER-SECRETARY FOR SCOTLAND.

The news was at once communicated by the magistrates to the prisoner in the condemned cell. The next morning the Lord Provost received the following letter in confirmation:—

Scottish Office, Whitehall, May 25th, 1909.

My Lord Provost,—
I am to signify to you the King's command that the execution of the sentence of death passed on Oscar Slater, presently in His Majesty's prison at Duke Street, Glasgow, be respited with a view to its

commutation to penal servitude for life.—I am, my Lord Provost, your obedient servant,
PENTLAND.

The Hon. the Lord Provost of Glasgow, City Chambers, Glasgow.

It is understood that Lord Pentland, in arriving at his decision, had the assistance of the Lord Chancellor and Mr. Muldane, Minister for War; and that Lord Guthrie, as the judge presiding at the trial, was also consulted. On 8th June the following questions with reference to the respite were asked in the House of Commons:—

Sir J. H. Dalziel (L., Kirkcaldy Burghs) asked the Lord Advocate whether he would state the grounds on which he advised that the extreme penalty of the law should not be carried out in the case of Oscar Slater, convicted of murder, and now detained in Glasgow prison, and on what grounds the said prisoner was now detained in custody.

The Lord Advocate (Mr. Ure)—The Lord Advocate does not advise the Crown in regard to the exercise of the prerogative of mercy, and it would be contrary to practice to state the grounds on which the prerogative of mercy is exercised in any particular case. Oscar Slater is detained in custody on the ground that he has been convicted of the crime of murder.

Sir J. H. Dalziel—Was the Secretary for Scotland in possession of the right hon. gentleman's views before any decision was taken with regard to the matter? and, further, if Slater is detained in custody for the crime of murder, why was he not called upon to suffer the extreme penalty for this brutal crime?

The Lord Advocate—The Secretary for Scotland was in possession of my views before the decision was taken; but I think the House will agree that it is entirely contrary to practice and to public policy to state the grounds on which the Secretary for Scotland exercised the- prerogative of mercy.

Sir J. H. Dalziel—Are we to understand from that, the view of the Government is that Oscar Slater was guilty of this brutal crime?

The Lord Advocate—I am afraid that is only asking in another form a question which I have declined to answer.

On 8th July, Slater, along with seven other convicts, was removed from Duke Street Prison, Glasgow, to the Convict Prison at Peterhead, there to undergo his commuted sentence of penal servitude for life.

The reward of £200, offered by the Crown authorities for information which would lead to a conviction, was ultimately apportioned as follows:—Mary Barrowman, £100; John Forsyth, £40; Allan M'Lean, £40; and Gordon Henderson, £20, all of whom were witnesses at the trial.

Of the many mysteries which the four days' inquiry failed to elucidate two remained not only unsolved, but, as regards one of them, even unnoticed—(1) How did Slater (or the murderer) acquire his knowledge of the existence of Miss Gilchrist's jewels? and (2) by what means did he obtain entrance to her house?

As regards the first point, the witness Mrs. Walker, a former servant, was asked if Miss Gilchrist's jewels formed a subject of conversation in the neighbourhood, but she stated that she had only heard it remarked among the tradespeople that her mistress was well dressed and wore some jewellery. Lambie swore that, so far as she knew, no one in the neighbourhood was aware of the existence of the jewels except a girl friend of hers, whom she had informed of the fact; and that she had also mentioned the matter to her admirer,

Nugent, a year before the murder. These are the only references to the subject which the evidence contains. The members of the Adams family, who had resided in the hue house below for many years, were not asked, when examined, if any report of the old lady's jewels had reached them.

With regard to the second point, no reference to it was made by either of the counsel or by the presiding judge. No doubt exists of the fact that the murderer did somehow obtain access to the house; but the manner of his entrance was not alluded to. It is clear that he did not do so by the windows, for these, as we have seen, were, with the exception of the kitchen window, all fastened when Lambie went out, and were in tile same condition when she returned. The height of the flat from the ground, in the absence of a ladder, further precludes this theory. That the murderer was not concealed in the stair leading to the empty house above, but entered from the street after Lambie's departure, is also indicated by the wet footmarks noticed by her on the lower steps of the stair, to which attention has been drawn. If the evidence of Lambie be accepted, there is no question that both the house and close doors were securely closed when she left, and could only be opened either by keys from without or by Miss Gilchrist from within. The conjecture that the murderer used false keys is unlikely; the close door could, no doubt, be readily opened either by a knife or a common latch-key, but the house door, as we have seen, was guarded by two separate patent locks which required two different keys. The murderer, therefore, probably rang the street door bell. Mr. Adams stated that he generally, but not invariably, heard Miss Gilchrist's bell when rung; he did riot do so that night.

It is in evidence that Miss Gilchrist was apprehensive of attacks upon her property, and it seems, at first sight, unlikely that she would voluntarily admit a stranger, or would not, at least, have opened the door upon the chain, till she had ascertained his business. But, as she kept only one servant, she must frequently (as on the servant's night out) have had occasion to answer the door herself, being alone in the house. No question was put to Lambie as to her mistress's practice in this regard, nor was she asked if, when she went upon her nightly errand for the paper, she had not, on some former occasions, forgotten to take the keys.

Assuming that this had happened before, it is possible that the murderer (who had presumably studied the habits of the inmates), being on the watch in one of the adjacent closes, rang the street bell immediately after Lambie left the house. The close door is opened by raising a handle within the hall, just outside the dining-room door. The old lady, thinking that Lambie had forgotten the keys, may have removed her spectacles, laid them (as they were found) beside her magazine, and, rising from her chair, have gone to the hall and lifted the handle. She may then have opened the house door, and at once have returned to the dining-room, the door of which immediately adjoins, and is at right angles to, the front door in the hall. That she did so is more probable than that she waited at the door to see if it were Lambie, as, even if the difference of tread did not apprise her that it was not the maid, she could have seen a stranger coming up the stairs in time to close the door.

That no struggle occurred in the hall or in the dining-room, and that Miss Gilchrist was felled as she stood on the hearth rug, near her chair, would appear for three reasons—(1) There was no indication of such in the position of the furniture of either the hall or dining-room; (2) the first sound heard by the Adams family was the fall of a heavy body; and (3) the evidence of Professor Glaister proves that the deed was done on the spot where the body was found.

It is therefore likely, in view of the medical evidence, that the old lady had regained her chair, when she realised that the footsteps approaching were not those of Lambie. She turned, and took a step or two towards the door as the murderer entered the room. With one swift blow she was struck down, her head crashing against the lid of the coal scuttle (which, we know, was broken and bloody) on the right hand side of the fireplace; she rolled or was dragged on to the hearth rug; and, voluntarily or involuntarily, gave, probably with her heels, the three knocks upon the floor. Her assailant may then, furious at what he perceived to be a signal for help, have snatched up the skin rug, which lay in front of the sideboard, and using it partly to stifle her cries, partly as a screen for himself, have, kneeling upon her chest, completed his ghastly task.

The meaningless ferocity of the assault may have been due to the fury of fear; for it is to be remembered that, early in the attack, the three " rude rings " of Mr. Adams rang through the house. That these gave the murderer pause is shown by Mr. Adams' statement that he "had been standing at the door for half a minute or so" before he heard the gruesome sound which he described. On his second visit to the door, two or three minutes later, the sounds had ceased; the murderer was then in the bedroom.

Apart from such hypotheses, one fact, however, is clearly proved: the murderer's hands were clean. The deed done, he hurried to the bedroom. The match-box he had brought with him, the match he struck, the gas bracket he lighted, the box he broke open, the papers therein which he scattered on the floor, the glass dish on the toilet table from which he took the brooch, each handled by him in turn, were all free from blood. It is remarkable that, if the murderer knew nothing of the house, he made straight for the spare bedroom in which the jewels were kept, passing the door of Miss Gilchrist's bedroom on his way, and entering, as appears, none of the other rooms. He was certainly in the house for less than ten minutes, yet had time not only to deliver the blows—" not under fifty or sixty, probably a good many more "—which silenced his victim, but to ascertain in which of the six apartments the jewels were secreted, to light the gas, to open and examine the contents of the box, to secure the brooch, and to walk leisurely past Lambie and Adams, so soon as they unlocked the door.

The question of time brings us to the consideration of another point. The murder, according to the Lord Advocate's theory, was committed by a man who had thoroughly familiarised himself with the movements and habits of the inmates by "careful, prolonged, and steady watching with a skilled eye." That being so, why did he select for his purpose the shorter period of the maid's nightly errand to the newsagent's (which, she said, never exceeded ten minutes), rather than her necessarily longer absence for the messages later in the evening, or, better still, her weekly night out? It may be that he had already attempted to gain admission to the house on one or other of these occasions, but found that Miss Gilchrist would not then open the door. Even assuming that his original design was robbery, and did not embrace the possibility of incidental murder, he must have expected that to obtain the jewels would require a search, more or less protracted, during which their owner might raise the alarm, unless, indeed, he thought she would give them up at once. But, with deference to the suggestion of the learned judge upon this point, it may -well be that not only did the intruder contemplate the murder of Miss Gilchrist from the first, but chose his time with reference to the maid's short absence; so that, had she returned, as usual, alone, she might have shared the fate of her mistress, thus leaving him free to search the premises at his leisure.

In this connection mention may be made of the case of John Paul Foster, recorded by Feuerbach, the eminent jurist, in his admirable studies of German criminal trials,* which presents some striking points of resemblance to the present case.

Narratives of Remarkable Criminal Trials Translated from the German of Anselm Ritter von Feuerbach by Lady Duff Gordon. London: John Murray, 1846.

This miscreant was, on 22nd July, 1821, convicted of the murder of Christopher Baumler, a corn chandler of Nürnberg, and his maid-servant, Anna Katherina Schutz, in the following circumstances:—Baumler, who was reputed a wealthy man, lived above his shop, the only other occupant of the house being the servant, a girl of twenty-three. His ordinary business included the right of selling brandy. On the night of 20th September, certain citizens who had been drinking in the shop left together at nine o'clock, leaving there one customer, a stranger to them, drinking by himself. The shop was usually closed at 11 p.m. At 9.45, the maid called at the baker's, "a hundred steps" distant, and purchased two rolls. This errand could not have occupied above five minutes. About the same hour, an opposite neighbour noticed, to his surprise, that Baumler's shop was closed. Next morning, as the shop remained shut after its usual hour, the neighbours effected an entrance by an upper window, when it was found that the whole house had been ransacked, and two bags of money, as well as some clothing, stolen. In the parlour, behind the shop, the corpse of Baumler was discovered lying on its back between the stove and the table, beside the stool upon which he had sat. smoking his pipe; while behind the shop door lay the dead body of the maid, with the two rolls beside her. The injuries inflicted upon the old man and the girl were identical, and, by a strange coincidence, closely resemble those disclosed on the post-mortem examination in the present case. Both heads had been shattered, in the opinion of the surgeons, "with a heavy instrument, having a flat surface, with sharp edges, probably the back of a hatchet." In each case the sternum and ribs were fractured, it was thought by stamping on the bodies. At the trial it was proved that Foster had been seen, for several days before the murder, walking about the street in a suspicious manner, watching the house; he was identified as the man who had outstayed the other customers, one of whom had spoken to him casually, and it is instructive to note that the witnesses, who identified him, described him as wearing a blue coat, when, in fact, its colour was brown. The brown great-coat which he wore on the night of the murder and had disposed of, was recovered, "much stained and in some places soaked with blood"; an axe, bearing unequivocal traces of the deed, was found concealed in his house; and, finally, some of his victim's property was traced to his possession. Having studied the habits of the household, Foster had entered the shop and ordered a glass of brandy. Immediately upon the maid's departure, he had, in the parlour, felled Baumler with the axe, which he carried hidden under his great-coat, closed the shop, lay in wait for the girl behind the street door, opened it for her, end attacked her as she returned from her errand. In spite of the strong circumstantial evidence adduced against him, Foster escaped capital punishment for the singular reasons that there were no eye-witnesses to the murder, and that no confession could be extorted from him! He was accordingly condemned to imprisonment in chains for life.

The statement of Agnes Brown before referred to raises the additional question, was the murder and robbery at 15 Queen's Terrace the work of a single hand? This question is also suggested by the evidence led at the trial. For instance, the man seen by Mrs. Liddell at five minutes to seven, standing at the railings outside the house, and minutely described by her, was obviously a man quite differently dressed from the man seen and described by Lambie, Adams, and Barrowman. It would be unprofitable to pursue the surmise that the murderer had an accomplice further than to remark that, if he had, and one of somewhat similar appearance to himself, it might go far to reconcile the otherwise conflicting testimony of the witnesses who describe the watcher and the man leaving the house. That the man seen by Lambie, Adams, and Barrowman bore no visible traces of blood is certain; and it is conceivable that the actual murderer had made his escape between Mr. Adams' visits to the door, while his more callous associate lingered to secure the jewels.

It appears from the evidence of all the medical witnesses that the murderer, using the short hammer as alleged by the Crown, would be more or less bloodstained. Upon this point the theory of Dr. John Adams, 1 Queen's Crescent, the first medical man to see the body, but who was not called as a witness at the trial, is of interest. Dr. Adams, it is understood, had, when returning home at about 11 p.m. from his professional duties, observed, on six or eight occasions shortly before the murder, a man hanging about the corner of Queen's Crescent, outside his own house. The man walked with a slouching, rolling gait, and had his hands in the pockets of a fawn-coloured overcoat. Dr. Adams mentioned the matter, some time before the murder, to the policeman on the beat, who said that he had not seen the man. It will be remembered that Dr. Adams was summoned by Mr. Arthur Adams immediately after the discovery of the murder, and visited the scene of the crime at 7.20 or 7.25. He found Miss Gilchrist lying on her back on the hearth rug, with the skin rug across her face. Close to the head, and facing it, stood an ordinary chair. Having examined the body and ascertained that life was extinct, Dr. Adams' attention was attracted by the condition of this chair. He observed that the left back leg, furthest from the head, was soaked with blood, and that the inner aspect of each front leg was spotted with blood. The back leg, in his opinion, had evidently been in contact with the wounds. With this instrument, in his view, the injuries to the head had been inflicted. In addition to the appearance of the chair, he inferred that it had been so used from the character of the injuries, the comparatively small quantity of blood near the head, and the restricted area of the blood stains. In the opinion of Dr. Adams the assault was committed by a few heavy, swinging blows from the back leg of this chair, the assailant, while wielding it, stamping upon the body, and thereby fracturing the ribs. The hands of the assailant would thus be clean, and the seat of the chair would be interposed between his person and the spurting blood at the moment of impact. With reference to the condition of the chair, it is to be kept in view that the locus was not inspected by Professor Glaister and Dr. Galt until the following day, when the appearance it presented may not then have been marked.

We may close our account of the salient features of this mysterious and perplexing case by quoting the dictum of Lord Collins from the Report of the Royal Commission appointed in 1904 to inquire into the affair of Adolf Beck, prevising that no parallel between the two cases is here suggested. His lordship observed—"Evidence as to identity based on personal impressions, however bona fide, is perhaps of all classes of evidence the least to be relied upon, and therefore, unless supported by other facts, an unsafe basis for the verdict of a jury."

FIRST DAY — MONDAY, 3rd MAY, 1909

The Court met at Ten o'clock.

Judge Presiding—
LORD GUTHRIE.

Counsel for the Crown—
THE LORD ADVOCATE (Mr. Alexander Ure, K.C.).
Mr. T.B. MORISON, K.C., and Mr. W. LYON MACKENZIE, *Advocates-Depute*

Agent—
Mr. W.S. HALDANE, W.S., Edinburgh.

Counsel for the Panel—
Mr. A.L. M'CLURE, K.C., and Mr. JOHN MAIR, *Advocate.*

Agent—
Mr. EWING SPEIRS, of Messrs. Joseph Shaughnessy & Sons, Solicitors, Glasgow.

The panel was placed at the bar, charged with the crime of murder, as set forth in the following indictment against him, at the instance of His Majesty's Advocate:—

OSCAR SLATER, sometime residing at 69 Saint George's Road, Glasgow, and presently a prisoner in the prison of Glasgow, you are indicted at the instance of the Right Honourable ALEXANDER URE, His Majesty's Advocate, and the charge against you is that you did, on 21st December, 1908, in Marion Gilchrist's house, at No. 15 Queen's Terrace, West Princes Street, Glasgow, assault the said Marion Gilchrist, and did beat her with a hammer or other blunt instrument, and fracture her skull, and did murder her.

T.B. MORISON, A.D.

LIST OF PRODUCTIONS FOR THE PROSECUTION.

- 1. Declaration of accused.

- 2. Joint report by John Glaister, M.D., &c., Glasgow, and Hugh Galt, B.Sc, M.B., &c., Glasgow, dated 22nd December, 1908.

- 3. Joint report of a post-mortem examination by the said John Glaister and Hugh Galt, dated 23rd December, 1908.

- 4. Report by Harvey Littlejohn, M.B., Professor of Medical Jurisprudence in the University of Edinburgh, and the said John Glaister, dated 11th March, 1909.

- 5. Photographs of said house and street at 15 Queen's Terrace.

- 6. Plan of the said Marion Gilchrist's house and stair.

- 7. Plan of streets in Glasgow, with enlarged section of part of West Princes Street.

- 8. Cabinet photograph of deceased with small stamp photograph on back.

- Label No. 9. Half-set false teeth.

- Label No. 10. Pair spectacles, case, and catch thereof.

- Label No. 11. Purse containing return half railway ticket, excess luggage ticket, and one halfpenny stamp.

- Label No. 12. One half-sovereign and one halfpenny.

- Label No. 13. Three keys.

- Label No. 14. Body clothes, consisting of combinations, chemise, stays, stockings and garters, white flannelette petticoat, maroon petticoat, black lustre petticoat, black dress, small knitted shawl.

- Label No. 15. Coal scuttle.

- Label No. 16. Hearth rug.

- Label No. 17. Skin rug.

- Label No. 18. Box of matches and spent match.

- Label No. 19. Bundle of papers.

- Label No. 20. Box.

- Label No. 21. Two accounts (1 for gas and 1 for inhabited house duty) for 15 Queen's Terrace, receipted of date 21st December, 1908.

- 22. Inventory and valuation of household furniture, &c.

- 23. List of jewellery.

- 24. Two designs of diamond crescent brooch.

- Label No. 25. Iron auger and quantity of hair.

- 26. Letter, Oscar Slater to Max Rattman, dated 26th December, 1908, in envelope.

- Label No. 27. Letter, D. R. Jacobs to Oscar Slater, dated 28th December, 1908, and envelope.

- Label No. 28. Torn paper wrapper addressed to Oscar Slater, c/o Anderson, 69 St. George's Road, Glasgow.

- Label No. 29. Letter from Shanghai to Frau L. Freedman, with small label attached, bearing name and address of Oscar Slater.

- Label No. 30. Nine cash slips (3 from Messrs. Hepburn & Marshall, and 6 Messrs. Stuart & Stuart).

- 31. Sale note from Messrs. Hepburn & Marshall, of date 10th November, 1908.

- Label No. 32. Box containing 2 visiting cards of "A. Anderson."

- Label No. 33. Ten visiting cards of do.

- 34. Missive of let of house at 69 St. George's Road, to A. Anderson, with visiting card of A. Anderson attached.

- 35. Account of Messrs. Stuart & Stuart, house furnishers, to A. Anderson, amounting to £176 16s. 6d.

- 36. File of telegrams passing between Oscar Slater and Dent, London, dated 21st and 23rd December, 1908, and letter from Slater to Dent, dated 9th December, also card of Oscar Slater with addresses thereon.

- 37. File of letters, &c., containing (1) letter, Messrs. Thomas Cook & Son to Cunard Line, Liverpool, 23rd December; (2) telegram from Cunard Line to Messrs. Cook, 24th December; (3) letter, Thomas Cook & Son to Cunard Line, Liverpool, dated 24th December; (4) letter from Messrs. Cook & Son to Cunard Line, dated 25th December, 1908; (5) application form to Cunard Company for contract tickets; also (6) a contract ticket for two berths from Cunard Company in name of Mr. and Mrs. Otto Sando.

- 38. *Evening Times* of 25th December, 1908 (first edition).

- 39. *Evening News* of 13th January, 1909.

- 40. *Glasgow News* of 25th December, 1908 (two o'clock edition).

- 41. *Evening Citizen* of 25th December, 1908 (fourth edition).

- 42. *Police Gazette* of 15th January, 1909.

- Label No. 43. Waterproof overcoat.

- Label No. 44. Felt or woollen hat.

- Label No. 45. Lady's waterproof coat.

- Label No. 46. Two cloth caps.

- Label No. 47. Hammer.

- Label No. 48. (1) Screw driver; (2) pair pliers; (3) gimlet; (4) bradawl.

- Label No. 49. Trunk or travelling case with rope and seal attached.

- Label No. 50. Dark grey overcoat with blue velvet collar.

- Label No. 51. Diamond crescent 3-row brooch.

- 52. Pawn ticket for same.

- 53. Letter, Oscar Slater, Tombs Prison, New York, to Hugh Cameron, Glasgow, dated 2nd February, 1909.

- 54. Photograph of a woman.

- 55. Extract from Register of Births of birth of Mary Jane Gilmour Sword (otherwise Mary Barrowman).

- 56. *News of the World* newspaper, dated 27th December, 1908.

- Label No. 57. Photograph of Oscar Slater.

- 58. Card bearing name and address, "Oscar Slater, dealer in diamonds and precious stones, 33 Soho Square, Oxford Street, W."

- 59. Account, Oscar Slater to D.R. Jacobs, New York, dated 29th February, 1908.

- 60. Extract certificate of marriage, Oscar Leschziner Slater to Marie Curtis Pryor, dated 12th July, 1902.

- 61. Account, Oscar Slater, Glasgow, to M. F. Dent, London, amounting to 13s. 6d.

- 62. Extract registered trust disposition and settlement by the deceased Miss Marion Gilchrist, 28th May, 1908, with codicil thereto appended.

- Label No. 63. A tram car ticket.

- Label No. 64. A quantity of grey hair.

- 65. Tramway way-bill, 22nd December, 1908.

- Label No. 66. A leather hat case with rope and seal attached.

- 67. Letter, Robert Rogers, London, to J. S. Marr, Glasgow, dated 5th October, 1908.

- 68. Letter. Davenport & Co., London, to J. S. Marr, Glasgow, dated 5th November, 1908.

- 69. Balance book kept by John Brown, Caledonian Railway Central Station, Glasgow, for 25th December," 1908.

- T.B. MORISON, A.D.

LIST OF WITNESSES FOR THE PROSECUTION

- 1. Jane Duff or Walker, 3 Carrickarden Street, New City Road, Glasgow.

- 2. Maggie Galbraith or Ferguson, wife of and residing with David Ferguson, railway guard, 86 Kilgour Terrace, Bonnytown Road, Kilmarnock.

- 3. James Macdonald, writer, 2 Buckingham Street, Hillhead, Glasgow.

- 4. David Dick, 4 Maitland Avenue, Langside, Glasgow.

- 5. William Sorley, jeweller, St. Vincent Street, Glasgow.

- 6. John Stewart, 2 Kelvin Drive, Kelvinside, Glasgow.

- 7. Robert Perry, M.D., 11 Queen's Terrace, West Princes Street, Glasgow.

- 8/11. (8) William Moodie, detective lieutenant, (9) John Mowatt, detective officer, (10) James Stuart, sergeant, and (11) George Robson, police inspector — all Edinburgh Police Force.

- 12. Ada Louisa Payne, flat 2, No. 45 Newman Street, London, W.

- 13. William Kempton, 889 Argyle Street, Glasgow.

- 14. John S. Marr, C.A., Brookfield Cottage, Kilbarchan.

- 15. Isaac Paradise, 9 Dunearn Street, Glasgow.

- 16. John Ruthven, c/o Sinclair, 70 Renfrew Street, Glasgow.

- 17. Jacob Jackson, 116 South Portland Street, South Side, Glasgow.

- 18. Max Brooks, c/o Samuel Shaw, Suffolk Street, Glasgow.

- 19. Max Rattman, c/o Fox, 23 Cromwell Street, New City Road, Glasgow.

- 20. Hugh Cameron, jun., 140 Cambridge Street, Glasgow.

- 21. John Crawford, dairyman, 33 West Cumberland Street, Glasgow.

- 22. Peter Johnston, 94 Hill Street, Garnethill, Glasgow.

- 23. Adam Gibb, c/o Ritchie, 12 Rutherford Lane, Glasgow.

- 24/25. (24) Margaret Dickson or M'Haffie and (25) Margaret Dickson M'Haffie — both residing at 16 West Princes Street, Glasgow.

- 26. Madge M'Haffie, 79 West End Park Street, Glasgow.

- 27. Annie R. M'Haffie, 16 West Princes Street, Glasgow.

- 28. Christopher Walker, constable, 78 B Division, Glasgow Police.

- 29. James Johnston, sergeant. Western District, Glasgow Police.

- 30. Euphemia Cunningham, 114 South Woodside Road, Glasgow.

- 31. William Campbell, photographer, 40 Napiershall Street, Glasgow.

- 32. Robert Brown Bryson, 17 Somerville Drive, Mount Florida, Glasgow.

- 33. Andrew Nairn, 4 Stanley Street, Woodlands Road, Glasgow.

- 34. Elizabeth Donaldson, 46 West Princes Street, Glasgow.

- 35. Frederick Nichols, 10 Leyden Gardens, Bilsland Drive, Glasgow.

- 36. Elizabeth M'Intosh, 1 Queen's Crescent, Glasgow.

- 37. Josef Aumann, diamond dealer, 309 Hope Street, Glasgow.

- 38. Helen Lambie, domestic servant, 3 Nelson's Land, Main Street, Holytown.

- 39. Ellen Swanson, 89 Elderslie Street. Glasgow.

- 40. Arthur Montague Adams, 51 West Princes Street (14 Queen's Terrace), Glasgow.

- 41. Laura E. Adams, 51 West Princes Street, Glasgow.

- 42. Rowena Adams or Liddell, wife of and residing with George Liddell, teacher, 63 Elmbank Street, Glasgow.

- 43. Mary Jane Gilmour Sword, otherwise Mary Barrowman, 9 Seamore Street, Glasgow.

- 44. Barbara Macdonald or Barrowman, wife of and residing with Robert Barrowman, moulder, 9 Seamore Street, Glasgow.

- 45. James Howatt, clerk, 36 Cleveland Street, Glasgow.

- 46. Agnes Brown, teacher, 48 Grant Street, Glasgow.

- 47/48. (47) William Neill and (48) Francis Brien— both constables, Western District, Glasgow Police.

- 49. Annie Armour. 393 Dumbarton Road, Partick.

- 50/53. (50) John Pyper, detective inspector, (51) James Dornan, detective sergeant, (52) William Douglas, superintendent, (53) Alexander Rankin, inspector, all Western District, Glasgow Police.

- 54. Annie Gillies, saleswoman, 6 Brooklyn Place, Govan.

- 55. John M'Gimpsey, detective officer, Northern District, Glasgow Police.

- 56. John Wright, M.B., casualty surgeon, Western District, Glasgow Police.

- 57. The said John Glaister.

- 58. The said Hugh Galt.

- 59. The said Harvey Littlejohn.

- 60. Peter Crawford M'Laren, pawnbroker's manager, residing at 1109 Argyle Street, Glasgow.

- 61. James Barr, 12 Douglas Street, Glasgow.

- 62. Gordon Henderson, club master, 26 India Street, Glasgow.

- 63. William Bancroft, 22 Huntershill Street, Springburn, Glasgow.

- 64. John Bain, 5 Shaftesbury Cottages, Whiteinch, Partick.

- 65. Allan M'Lean, cycle dealer, 100 Agnes Street, Maryhill, Glasgow.

- 66. Catherine Schmalz, general servant, 72 Charlotte Street, London.

- 67/68. (67) Isabella Fowlis and (68) Margaret Fowlis, both at 69 St. George's Road, Glasgow.

- 69. Ruby Russell, domestic servant, 69 St. George's Road, Glasgow.

- 70. John Cameron, porter, 7 Park Place, Stockwell Street, Glasgow.

- 71. John M'Kay, porter, 22 James Watt Street, Glasgow.

- 72. John Brown, clerk, 80 South Cromwell Road, Queen's Park, Glasgow.

- 73/74. (73) John Millican, detective constable, and (74) David Lyon, detective sergeant, both Central District, Glasgow Police.

- 75. John Thomson Trench, detective officer, Central District, Glasgow Police.

- 76. John Forsyth, 73 Highfield Road. Rock Ferry, Cheshire.

- 77. John H. Chadwick, 19 Holland Road, Liscard, Cheshire.

- 78. Francis Newcombe, porter, 17 Bankburn Road, Tuebrook. Liverpool.

- 79. James A. Latham, porter, 109 Spencer Street, Liverpool.

- 80. William Warnock, Sheriff criminal officer, County Buildings, Glasgow.

- 81. Alexander Cameron, detective officer. Central District, Glasgow Police.

- 82. Patrick Nugent, commission agent, Campsie View, Carfin, Motherwell.

- 83. John Ord, superintendent. Criminal Investigation Department, Glasgow Police.

- 84. Reginald George Tuckett, 2 Manor Cottage, Merton Park, Merton, Surrey.

- 85. R.W. Horn, A.R.I.B.A., 40 Cranworth Street, Glasgow.

- 86. George Bell, photographer, 326 Sauchiehall Street, Glasgow.

- 87. Mary Anderson M'Murdo, 13 Hayburn Street, Partick.

- 88. Frederica Caroline Lang, c/o Cameron, 248 Sauchiehall Street, Glasgow.

- 89. George Findlay, Barnsheen, Troon.

- 90. Alexander Gillies, 46 West Princes Street, Glasgow.

- 91. James Jupp, 308 Dumbarton Road, Partick.

- 92. John Logan, 44 Gloucester Street, South Side, Glasgow.

- 93. William Gordon, lieutenant. Central District, Glasgow Police.

- 94/95. (94) George D. Balfour, keeper, and (95) Robert D. Gray, assistant keeper — both of Register of Deeds, &c., H.M. General Register House, Edinburgh.

- 95. James Neil Hart, Procurator-fiscal of Lanarkshire, Glasgow.

- 97. Andrew Currie, 77 Marlborough Avenue, Broomhill, Partick.

- 98. Marion Carson, 40 Grove Street, Glasgow.

- T.B. MORISON, A.D.

LIST OF ASSIZE.

For the Sitting of the High Court of Justiciary at Edinburgh, on the 3rd day of May, 1909.

- CITY OF EDINBURGH.

- *Special Jurors.*

- 1. Alexander Garden Sinclair, artist, 18 Ann Street.

- 2. George Beevers, engineer, 156 Brunton Gardens.

- 3. James Robert Scott, retired farmer, 21 Willowbrae Avenue.

- 4. James Drummond Shiels, photographer, 13 Cumin Place.

- 5. William Perry, merchant, 8 Leopold Place.

- 6. James Ritchie, watchmaker, 6 Brunton Place.

- 7. George Brown, M.A., teacher, 5 Willowbrae Avenue.

- 8. John Waldie, woollen warehouseman, 20 Thirlestane Road.

- 9. George Proudfoot, picture dealer, 68 Spottiswoode Street.

- *Common Jurors.*

- 10. William Wallace, spirit merchant, 27 Howe Street.

- 11. George Pennycook Blyth, estate factor, 38 Cowan Road.

- 12. Alexander Arnott, cellarman, 13 Roxburgh Street.

- 13. John West, tinsmith, 18 Tay Street.

- 14. Laurence Smith Blanche, grocer, 19 Bruntsfield Avenue.

- 15. Peter Redpath Logan, clerk, 18 Briarbank Terrace.

- 16. James Morrison Duncan, commercial traveller, 4 Queen's Bay Crescent, Joppa.

- 17. Alexander Purves Boyes, assistant clothier, 154 Craiglea Drive.

- 18. James Dickson, clerk, Bellevue Crescent.

- 19. Thomas Harkness, schoolmaster, 21 Wellington Street.

- 20. Robert Wallace, builder, 60 Bath Street, Portobello.

- 21. Henry Jobson Bell, artist, 27 Greenhill Gardens.

- 22. John Sanderson, brewery manager, Meadowfield, Willowbrae Road.

- 23. Robert William Findlater, architect. 30 Buckingham Terrace.

- 24. Neil James Stewart, traveller, 15 Queen's Bay Crescent, Joppa.

- 25. William Ross, compositor, 233 Dalkeith Road.

- 26. George Arnott, clerk, 32 Morningside Road.

- 27. George Inglis Alexander, grocer, 77 Cumberland Street.

- 28. James William Caie, clothier, 1 St. Giles' Street.

-

- BURGH OF LEITH.

- *Special Juror.*

- 29. John Smith, merchant, 1 East Restalrig Terrace, Leith.

- *Common Jurors.*

- 30. James Ferguson Milne, insurance agent, 70 Cornhill Terrace, Leith.

- 31. William Dawson, shipmaster, 48 Albany Street, Leith.

- 32. Robert M'Cabe, tailor's cutter, 35 Darnell Road, Leith.

-

- COUNTY OF EDINBURGH.

- *Special Jurors.*

- 33 William John Gulland, farmer, Monktonhall, Inveresk.

- 34. Patrick Alexander Guthrie, C.A., The Loan, Colinton.

- *Common Jurors.*

- 35. William Terras, junior, gardener. Quality Street, Davidson's Mains.

- 36. John Dalling, blacksmith, Kaimes, Liberton.

- 37. Henry Baillie, contractor, Cramond.

-

- COUNTY OF LINLITHGOW.

- *Special Juror.*

- 38. Andrew A. Ralston, factor, Philipstoun House, Philipstoun.

- *Common Jurors.*

- 39. George Thomson, dairyman, Old Town, Broxburn.

- 40. David Kennedy, quarryman, Bridge Street, Fauldhouse.

- 41. William Nicol, contractor, Hawthorn Place, Uphall.

-

- COUNTY OF HADDINGTON

- *Special Juror.*

- 42. Walter R. Munzo, Soapmaker, Prestonpans.
- *Common Juror.*
- 43 William 3ardie, blacksmith, Cockenzie.
-
- COUNTY OF PEEBLES.
- *Special Juror.*
- 44. James P. Ketchen, farmer, Nether Horsburgh, by Peebles.
- *Common Juror.*
- 45. Thomas Graham, shepherd. Carirona Mains, by Peebles.

LIST OF PRODUCTIONS FOR THE PANEL, OSCAR SLATER.

- 1. Stenographer's minutes, taken before Commissioner Shields, during the extradition proceedings (in two pieces).
- 2. Card containing hammer and other tools, marked "Set, useful household tools."
- 3. Copy, envelope with post office mark "Glasgow, 5 p.m., December 21, '08," addressed to "The Controller, Post Office Savings Bank, Blythe Road, West Kensington, London, W."
- 4. Copy of the letter contained in said envelope, dated "Glasgow, 20th/11/1908" and signed "Adolph Anderson."
- 5. Copy of the reply to above letter, dated 22nd December, 1908, and signed "H. Davies, Controller."
- 6. House agreement dated 28th May, 1908, by Peter de Silvestri, in favour of Oscar Slater and John Devoto, co-partners.
- 7. Letter dated 12th October, 1908, from the Excelsior Bank, New York, to Oscar Slater.
- 8. Copy of letter, William A. Goodhart, attorney, New York, to Ewing Speirs, writer, 190 West George Street, Glasgow.

LIST OF WITNESSES FOR THE PANEL, OSCAR SLATER.

- 1. Andrée Junio Antoine, 25 Rue des 3 Frères. Paris.
- 2. Hugh Murphy, Cherryhill View, Larkhall.
- 5. James Tracey, 21 Robson Street, Govanhill, Glasgow.
- 4. Samuel Reid, Clarence Hotel, Dublin.
- 5. James T. Makins, surveyor, 116 Elderslie Street, Glasgow.
- 6. [...] Freedman, Coventry Club, London.

- 7. Robert Rogers, 56 Albemarle Street, London, West.

- 8. Official from the Post Office to prove Numbers 3, 4, and 5 of the productions for the panel.

- 9. William Kempton, 889 Argyle Street, Glasgow.

- 10. Peter Crawford M'Laren, pawnbroker's manager, residing 1109 Argyle Street, Glasgow.

- 11. Catherine Schmalz, 72 Charlotte Street, London.

- 12. Ewing Speirs, writer, 190 West George Street, Glasgow.

- 13. Dr. Alexander Veitch, 12 Gilmore Place, Edinburgh.

PLEA OF PANEL TO INDICTMENT

The following is a transcript of the procedure at the Sheriff Court diet, as endorsed on the record copy of the indictment, viz.:—

At Glasgow, the twentieth day of April, nineteen hundred and nine, the said Oscar Slater, having been called on to plead to the following indictment, pleaded not guilty.

A.O.M. MACKENZIE.

LIST OF JURY

The panel was remitted to an assize, and the following jurors were all duly balloted for, viz.:—

- George Proudfoot, picture dealer, 68 Spottiswoode Street.

- James Robert Scott, retired farmer, 21 Willowbrae Avenue.

- John Waldie, woollen warehouseman, 20 Thirlestane Road.

- George Brown, M.A., teacher, 5 Willowbrae Road.

- James Ritchie, watchmaker, 6 Brunton Place.

- James William Caie, clothier, 1 St. Giles' Street.

- Lawrence Smith Blanche, grocer, 19 Bruntsfield Avenue.

- William Ross, compositor, 233 Dalkeith Road.

- Peter Redpath Logan, clerk, 18 Briarbank Terrace.

- John West, tinsmith, 18 Tay Street.

- Neil James Stewart, traveller, 15 Queen's Bay Crescent, Joppa.

- William Wallace, spirit merchant, 27 Howe Street.

- James Morrison Duncan, commercial traveller, Queen's Bay Crescent, Joppa.

- James Ferguson Milne, insurance agent, 70 Cornhill Terrace, Leith.

- Henry Jobson Bell, artist, 27 Greenhill Gardens.

The Clerk of Court having read over to the jury the charge against the panel, they were all lawfully sworn to try the present libel.

APPOINTMENT OF SHORTHAND WRITERS

Of consent of parties, the Court appointed the evidence to be taken down in shorthand, and appointed Messrs. Harry Hodge, Robert Hislop, and Thomas Cowan, 8 North Bank Street, Edinburgh, to take the said evidence in shorthand, and the declaration *de fideli* was administered to each of them.

The trial then proceeded.

EVIDENCE FOR THE PROSECUTION.

ROBERT WILLIAM HORNE, examined by the LORD ADVOCATE — Proved two plans made by him, one of Miss Gilchrist's house, 15 Queen's Terrace, and one of West Princes Street, and adjacent streets, being respectively Nos. 6 and 7 of the productions for the Crown.

GEORGE BELL, examined by the LORD ADVOCATE — Proved eight photographs of the late Miss Gilchrist's house and of part of West Princes Street, being No. 5 of the productions for the Crown.

DAVID DICK, examined by the LORD ADVOCATE — I made an inventory and valuation of the household furniture, electro-plate, and jewellery at the late Miss Gilchrist's house. No. 22 of the productions is the inventory and valuation which I made. I found jewellery in the house to the value of £1382 12s. If bought in shops they would cost at least twice as much. We found jewels scattered all over the wardrobe; some were laid between dresses, and some were in an old, detachable pocket with a string on it for tying round the waist. I made a very careful examination for a brooch which I was told was missing. I am quite satisfied that it was not in the house. I was shown a sketch of that brooch. The brooch was shaped like a horse-shoe, crescent- shaped, with a double row of diamonds. Judging from the sketch the value would be between £40 and £50.

Cross-examined by Mr. M'CLURE — Have you not made a mistake? You were shown a sketch of the stolen brooch. Has not that a single row of diamonds? — Yes.

And not a double row? — That is so. I have made a mistake.

You never heard in connection with this case of any double row of diamonds brooch? — No.

No one was searching for that at all? — No.

The missing brooch was one with a single row of diamonds? — Yes.

And none such has been found? — No.

WILLIAM SORLET, examined by the LORD ADVOCATE — I am a partner of the firm of R. & W. Sorley, jewellers, Glasgow. I knew the late Miss Gilchrist. She had been a customer of my firm for about twenty years or more. About the beginning of January a detective called at my firm's premises and asked if I could give a sketch of a diamond crescent brooch which I knew that Miss Gilchrist had possessed. I then cut from one of our catalogues a print of a brooch of a similar kind and gave it to the officer. No. 24 of the productions is the sketch that I cut out. I later on furnished a sketch of the brooch. The last occasion on which that brooch was in my possession was in March, 1908, when we had it for cleaning. So far as I am aware that was the only diamond crescent brooch that she had.

Cross-examined by Mr. M'CLURE — How long after 21st December, the date of this murder, was it that the police first made inquiries at you regarding brooches? — I think it would be early in January.

Did the police produce to you a diamond crescent brooch and ask you to identify it if you could? — Yes.

How many rows of diamonds had the brooch the police produced to you? — Three rows.

Were you informed then that it was one which had been pawned by Slater? — I think I was.

Do you know when it had been pawned? — No, I did not.

It was no brooch of Miss Gilchrist's at all? — No.

Did you know that it had been lying in the pawnbroker's shop for two months before the murder? — No, I did not.

Re-examined by the LORD ADVOCATE — Did you at once tell the police that that was not her brooch? — I told the officers that were there with the brooch that it was not her brooch.

Mrs. JANE DUFF or WALKER, examined by the LORD ADVOCATE — I knew the late Miss Gilchrist well. I had been a servant with her for about five years. I left about eight years ago or more. I visited Miss Gilchrist several times after I left her service. She was not accustomed to wear her jewels always; she always wore some jewellery, but she had special ones for special occasions. She was quite well known in the locality round about where she lived. She had lived there for about thirty years. I could not say whether it was known that she had a great deal of jewellery. I never spoke much about it to any one. I found in talking to other people that that was known, but the information did not come through me. She had not very many friends visiting her. She had very few men friends. I am not quite sure about the last time that I visited her, but it was towards the end of October, 1908. I recollect her saying something about the house above being empty. She said occasionally that it was much nicer to have the people away, as the stair was always clean, and then she said that she would rather have these people there than be alone, as it was too quiet. That was all I remember her saying about that. Before that time she spoke to me about an arrangement she had made with her neighbour, Mr. Adams, downstairs. She told me that she had arranged with Mr. Adams that when she was left alone if she wanted him she would knock down to him. Mr. Adams' sitting-room was below her dining-room. The old lady was afraid of her house being broken into. She was never afraid of any one doing any personal injury to her, but she had a great fear of the house being broken into. I do not know why that was, but perhaps she felt that she was an old lady, and she was always very careful to leave the place in charge of the policeman when the house was shut up.

Do you think that the jewels had anything to do with it? — They were never in the house when she was away. They were always left with Mr. Sorley when we went to the coast or the country. When we were at home she took the jewels out for a special occasion, and they usually remained in the house till we went away again. She kept them in a small box in the wardrobe. They were all kept in the one box. She was a lady of about eighty-three years of age, I think.

Cross-examined by Mr. M'CLURE — Were you told that she had jewellery to the value of £1383, or what would cost about twice that to buy? — I cannot tell you that, because I do not know the value of jewellery.

Did she keep all that stuff in her house? — She had it in the box, and it was kept there till we went to the coast, and then she put it into Mr. Sorley's hands.

How long had the girl Nellie Lambie been there in December last? — Three years.

Have there been a great many rumours in connection with this case? — Yes.

Have you heard that Miss Gilchrist was a resetter? — Yes.

She was not? — No.

Did she have unset stones in the house? — I never saw them.

You have heard that rumour also? — Yes.

Have you heard that she was the mother of Nellie Lambie? — No, I did not hear that, but I heard that she was the mother of Mrs. Ferguson.

Did you hear that she was the mother of Slater? — No, I did not hear that.

In point of act, Nellie Lambie was twenty-one years of age, and the old lady was over eighty? — Yes.

You said that from conversation with people in the neighbourhood you thought that they were aware that she had a lot of jewellery? — It has been sometimes remarked to me in shops when I was shopping.

What was said? — I cannot remember the words exactly, except that Miss Gilchrist dressed very well and wore some jewellery — it is a long time since.

Did she wear anything except a brooch and a couple of bracelets? — Not every day, except that and three rings.

And she wore gloves? — Yes.

So that the visible jewellery that this lady would carry would be two bracelets? — Yes; she was particular that her jewellery was not visible.

What leads you to say that there was a rumour that she was a wealthy lady? — I do not think it was a very special remark, further than the people speaking to me in the shop that she dressed well. That was all.

Did you ever tell people outside that she was a lady possessed of a great deal of jewellery? — No.

And you never heard that said outside? — No.

It was only that she was a well-dressed lady? — Yes, and wore jewellery.

She must have kept herself pretty much aloof from her neighbours? — Yes, she did.

Did you have many visitors when you were there? — A few.

Did Miss Gilchrist lay down any rules about your visitors? — No, not particularly. She did not like me to have too many visitors, but she always allowed me visitors.

Did you have a night out? — Yes, Thursday night.

Do you know whether Nellie Lambie had the same night out? — I think she told me that it was Wednesday night, but I am not sure, and I could not say.

By the COURT — Was that case in which the jewels were kept in the wardrobe locked? — The wardrobe and the case were always locked.

Who kept the keys? — She always carried the keys in her pocket.

Did she ever give you the keys? — Never, except when she sent me to open the case.

Did she live comfortably in the way of food and anything else? — Not extravagantly. She was comfortable, but not extravagant.

What wages did you get? — £12 when I went, and £16 when I left.

JOHN SINCLAIR MARR, examined by the LORD ADVOCATE — I am a house factor in Glasgow. In the beginning of November last I had a telephone message from Stuart & Stuart, in St. George's Road, that a man was inquiring about a house to let in Woodlands Road. I telephoned to Stuart & Stuart that I had a house to let at 69 St. George's Road on the third floor, and on that day, or on the following day, I had a call from a man, who gave me a visiting card. (Shown production No. 34.) That is the card he gave me. The words "A. Anderson, dentist, 36 Albemarle Street, Piccadilly." were printed on the card, and the words "136 Renfrew Street, 2 up," were in pencil. He told me that his purpose was to start business with some one else as a dentist in Glasgow. He agreed to take the house. I asked him for references, and he noted the names which he gave me on the back of his calling card. On the same day I wrote to the persons whose addresses he gave me, and I received replies which were satisfactory. On 6th November Anderson again called, and I told him that I was satisfied with the references, and let him the house No. 69 St. George's Road at a rent of £42. He took the house for eighteen months — from 2Sth November till 2Sth May a year afterwards. (Shown production No. 34.) That is the missive. The quarter's rent was due on 2nd February. There was nothing paid. Shortly after Christmas I learned that the police were keeping an eye on my premises 69 St. George's Road, and I gave up to the police the letters and references and the visiting card. On 10th March last I went to Duke Street Prison, Glasgow, to see a prisoner there, and I identified him as the man who took the house 69 St. George's Road, giving the name of Anderson, a dentist. (Shown the prisoner.) That is the man.

Cross-examined by Mr. M'CLURE — When did you first know that he had gone away? — Just about Christmas.

Did you go personally to the premises? — No.

Then is your information entirely hearsay from the police or other people as to the fact of him being away? — Yes.

Were there any other people in the house? — I have heard that there were others in the house.

After he left? — Yes, I was told that he had gone, and that a subtenant was in the house.

ISAAC PARADISE, examined by the LORD ADVOCATE — I am manager for Messrs. Stuart & Stuart, house furnishers, in Glasgow, at 65 St. George's Road. On 4th November last a man called at our premises in St. George's Road and asked about our terms for furnishing. He gave me his name as Anderson. I explained the terms to him. He told me that he was looking after a house just above our shop, and I believe he asked me about the rent. I ascertained the rent of the house. I believe I told him the rent. A day or two later Anderson returned to our premises, and I saw him. He selected furniture that day to the value of £170 odds. He was to pay £4 a month, and give £10 as the first deposit. That is what we call the hire system. The goods were delivered at his house, and he paid the £10 at the time he selected the furniture. He signed an agreement of hire. Anderson got and paid for a few extra things after the first lot was delivered — £2 worth. On 10th December he paid £4 as an instalment to account. I saw Anderson two or three times after that in our warehouse. We got the money that was paid — £16 in all, but the balance does not remain unpaid; we took the furniture back. I went to the Central Police Office in Glasgow in February. I was shown a prisoner there, and I identified him as the man who gave the name of Anderson. (Shown prisoner.) That is the man. (Shown production No. 35 of process.) That is the account for the goods which I furnished to Anderson.

Do you recollect whether he sent you a message that he was going away, and that you might have the furniture back or not? — I got no message, but after I heard that he was arrested I went up to the house, and there were two ladies there. They told me that Mr. Anderson had left word with them that they were to stay on, and that if he did not return they were to continue paying £4 on the 10th of each month, and if they were to leave the house they were to return the furniture to us. When the ladies went away they gave up the keys, and we removed the furniture. That was the first I heard of his going away — when he was arrested.

Cross-examined by Mr. M'CLURE — Can you remember how long these ladies were in the house No. 69 St. George's Road? — I believe they were there somewhere about three days before they left — from the time I got to know.

Do you know the date that they handed over the keys? — It was the same day that they left Glasgow — I do not remember the date.

By the COURT — Can you tell me the month? — No, but it was the same day that the ladies left the house.

Cross-examination continued — Slater left the house about 25th December, I understand, and did the ladies come then? — I cannot say.

Then all you know is that Slater left some time in December? — I do not know when he left.

JOHN RUTHVEN, examined by the LORD ADVOCATE — Gave evidence of taking an order for visiting cards from a man who signed his name "A. Anderson," and afterwards identified the prisoner in the Central Police Office as the man who ordered the cards.

JACOB JACKSON, examined by the LORD ADVOCATE — I am a general warehouseman in South Portland Street, Glasgow. I am a German. About the middle of November last I recollect of a man coming to my shop. He wanted to sell me a diamond ring. I said to him that I did not buy any diamonds in that shop. I asked him how it was that he came to me with the ring. He told me that he was sent to me as a countryman of his — a German.

Did you ask him in German why he wanted to sell the ring? — Immediately he spoke I could tell he was a foreigner, and we Germans have a sort of mutual understanding that if we want to know whether the party we are speaking to is a German or not we do not generally ask him if he is a German, but begin just to speak German immediately. I asked him why he wanted to sell the ring, and he would put in other words that he was hard up and required the money. I think he told me he came from Hanover. I said, "If you are hard tip, I do not see there is any necessity for you to sell an article of that description, but I can give you a job to do, to travel for me, to canvass for me." He refused; he said he did not think he would be suitable for that kind of employment. He did not tell me his name or address; I did not ask him. I would say the value of the ring was about £15. I have never seen him since. I recollect seeing in the *Evening Times* of the 22nd February last a profile photograph of a man named Slater, who had been arrested in connection with the murder of Miss Gilchrist. When I saw that I wrote at once to the detective department in Glasgow to the effect that I thought I could recognise from the photograph the man who had called at my shop. In consequence I was asked to attend at the Central Police Office on Tuesday, 23rd February last. I was shown a good few men — not prisoners, but men — and I recognised the man who is in the dock just now as the man. The prisoner is the man that I recognised immediately.

Cross-examined by Mr. M'CLURE? All this happened between six and seven weeks before Miss Gilchrist was murdered? — Yes.

Constable FRANCIS BRIEN, examined by Mr. MORISON — I am a constable in the Western District of the Glasgow Police. I was on night duty in the week beginning the 20th December, 1908. I had been on night duty for a fortnight before that. My district included the south side of West Princes Street, in which Queen's Terrace is situated. I went on duty at 6 p.m. I remained on duty till two in the morning. During that period I passed Miss Gilchrist's house in West Princes Street about every half-hour. My beat embraces also part of St. George's Road, part of Woodlands Road, and West Cumberland Street. As a rule I go on duty with William Neill. He is a police constable also. When I am out from six to two he is out from six to nine; he is on the day-shift when I am on the night-shift. When I go on duty Neill and I walk together along St. George's Road, past West Princes Street, and then along Great Western Road to Rupert Street, through Rupert Street to West Princes Street, and eastwards along that street to St. George's Road again. That was my regular routine of duty during the fortnight I have been speaking about.

Are there many people or much traffic in West Princes Street? — No, not a great many people. It is particularly quiet at night, about seven o'clock. I sometimes went through it and met nobody. (Shown prisoner.) I knew him by sight. I saw him one night standing just a few yards from the corner of West Princes Street and St. George's Road. Roughly, that would be about 80 yards from Miss Gilchrist's house. I saw him on the occasion I am speaking to just now the week before the murder. I cannot give any date. It was about half- past nine at night when I saw him. He was standing there. I did not notice what direction he was looking in. He was alone. I left him standing. He was standing against the railings, and I thought he was a drunk man. I took a good look at him when passing him; I thought he might have been a drunk man; as a rule, we get them lying against the railings when drunk. I took a good look at the man. I saw he was quite sober. When I first saw him I was just coming round the corner of St. George's Road, about 8 yards off from him, and then I passed him. I did not look round, but he was standing in the same place when I came round the corner that he was when I passed him. (Shown photograph No. 5 of productions.) No. 6 marks the point where I saw him that night — just about No. 6. That was the second week of the night-shift, and the week before the murder. That was the last time I saw the prisoner before the murder.

Had you seen the prisoner before that? — I had seen him several times.

Within that locality? — On St. George's Road. I cannot exactly say which way he was going. He was always alone. I should say the first time that I saw him would be about seven weeks before the murder, so far as I can remember. I saw him occasionally in or about St. George's Road between that time and the week before the murder.

Was it always at night when you saw him? — I saw him in the afternoon.

In the late afternoon? — Late afternoon, and early too. I saw the prisoner in West Princes Street only on that one night. The other times were in St. George's Road. On 21st December I passed along West Princes Street at night. It would be half-past six, I suppose, when I passed from West Princes Street into St. George's Road. We came round West Princes Street again, and passed by the house again about ten minutes to seven. On neither of these occasions was there any person in the street. When I passed at ten minutes to seven rain was falling. I passed along, and there was nothing that attracted my attention at ten minutes to seven.

When did you pass it the next time? — The next time I went to get Neill's cape, as it was raining, and I came back about twenty minutes past seven. In consequence of a statement which a gentleman made to me, I went to Miss Gilchrist's house, and I then learned of the murder. I entered Miss Gilchrist's house. I saw the old lady lying on her back near the fireplace in the dining-room. There was a quantity of blood about her face and below her head. She made a movement with her left hand. Her body was on the hearth rug. I saw that her head was battered. I did not touch the body. I went for the ambulance, and I returned to the house. I found that the body had not been interfered with till the police came. It was lying, when the police stretcher came and the detectives, in the same position as when I found it.

You saw the girl Lambie when you went to call the ambulance? — No, I went to pass word for the superior, and I met the girl Lambie at Blythswood Drive; she had been up at some friends of Miss Gilchrist. On the 22nd of February I identified the prisoner from a number of men in the police office. (Shown prisoner.) That is the man.

Cross-examined by Mr. M'CLURE — How many other people were in the room with the prisoner when you identified him? — Three or four.

Were there any foreign-looking gentlemen? — No.

Was there just what you would call police constables in undress? — Yes.

And detective officers? — Yes.

Can you tell us who were present when you identified the prisoner? — I did not know them all.

There were four or five altogether? — Yes.

Who was it that asked you to look at him and see if he was like the man? — Superintendent Douglas.

You say that the only occasion when you saw the prisoner in or about West Princes Street was the week before Miss Gilchrist was murdered? — Yes.

And he was just at the corner of the street? — He was about 8 or 9 yards round the corner.

Against the railings? — Yes.

How was he dressed? — He had a light coat on and a hat.

What kind of hat? — I cannot say for the hat.

Can you tell us anything more? — Well, I know that I passed him by; I thought myself I had seen him before; I had seen him previous to that.

You say he was leaning against the railings? — Yes.

And you thought he was a drunk man? — Yes.

Did you speak to him? — No, I passed him by.

What made you think he was drunk? — Because we very often get a half-drunk lying there, turning into St. George's Road; it seems to be a convenient place for them.

Was that the only reason you had to suppose he was drunk? — Yes.

Then what was it that convinced you afterwards he was not drunk? — I had a good look at him.

Did you walk up to him close and peer into his face? — Yes.

And he never said a word? — No, he never said a word.

And you cannot say what hat he had on? — No.

Can you say what trousers he had on? — No.

Or what boots he had on? — No.

How long did you stop to examine him? — Just a passing look; but that is the man.

Was he doing anything of a suspicious character? — Just standing leaning against the railings.

That is not suspicious? — No.

Was he looking about him? — I did not notice him looking about him.

Had he his head hanging down? — No.

Was his head up in the air? — Well, just in the ordinary way; it was not up in the air exactly.

Have you told us everything you have got to say about this incident? — Yes, that night.

Is that corner you have spoken of a place where nuisance is committed sometimes? — No.

Re-examined by Mr. MORISON (Shown production No. 43) — Was it a coat like that which the man who was leaning against the railings was wearing at the time? — Yes, it was like that.

Of course, you just took a passing glance at his figure? — Yes.

And you looked at his face in passing? — Yes.

You wanted to ascertain whether he was drunk or sober? — Yes.

Mrs. MARGARET DICKSON or M'HAFFIE, examined by the Lord Advocate — I am the wife of Alexander Rankin M'Haffie, horseshoer, and I live at 16 West Princes Street. Our house is one stair up, and is on the opposite side of the street from that of the late Miss Gilchrist's. It will be about 30 yards from her house. We have a good view of her house from our windows. For some weeks before the murder of Miss Gilchrist my attention was directed to a man loitering about on the opposite side of the street. He was not always there at the same time, but it was always in the afternoon that I saw him. He appeared to be a dark man, and he had a moustache; he was not very tall, and I would say he was close on forty. Two or three times I saw him with a light overcoat, check trousers, spats, and a black bowler hat. I should think that I saw him five or six times before the murder.

Were your suspicions aroused by seeing him? — Yes, I thought it very strange to see him, and I called my daughter's attention to it. I saw him walk on the opposite side of the street from the corner, up the street a little. He would have time to go as far as Miss Gilchrist's house, but I never looked. I watched him from our window.

Where did he look? Did he look at the windows, or at what?

Mr. M'CLURE — I think you should ask what the witness saw him doing.

The COURT — She may be asked if he was looking anywhere, in what direction he was looking.

Examination resumed — He was just looking about him. Sometimes he looked up towards our windows, and when he saw us looking he put down his head and moved away. I observed a photograph in an evening newspaper something similar to production 39. The photograph seemed to me to be like the man I had seen. I think the last time that I saw him was about eight or nine days before the night of the murder. On 21st February I went to the Central Police Office and I saw there the man that I had seen loitering in front of my window. I identify the prisoner as the man. When I went to the police office there was a number of other men in the room. I had no difficulty in identifying the man. I would see him moving back and forward on the street for perhaps close on half an hour at a time. As regards his walk, he did not carry himself very well — he slouched along, with his hands in his pockets sometimes. I would think that he caught sight of us watching him because of the way he put down his head. He put down his head very quick and moved away.

Cross-examined by Mr. M'CLURE — You say this man was about five or six times altogether on the street? — I saw him that number of times.

And with a light overcoat, check trousers, and light-coloured spats? — Yes.

What kind of hat? — A black bowler hat.

Was he always on the opposite side of the street? — I always saw him there.

How far is it across the street? — Not very far.

Was the coat a waterproof coat or not? — I do not think it was a waterproof. It was just a light-coloured coat. It might perhaps be shower- proof.

It was not like No. 43 of the productions? — No.

What is the difference between it and that coat? — It was scarcely the same colour as that. It seemed to be softer looking in appearance.

What did you see the man do? — He just walked about.

He passed back and forward on the opposite side of the street? — Yes.

You say you do not know how far up the street he went, because you did not look? — I did not look.

What was it you said was suspicious in his appearance? — It was very strange to see him hanging about there several times, seemingly with no intention of doing anything.

I do not follow you. If you see any person walking back and forward upon a pavement do you suspect that person of anything? — Not always.

What made you suspect this man? — I thought him rather peculiar.

You thought him peculiar? — I thought it was very peculiar — always about the same time.

How long did his visits to the street last? — He would be there about half an hour at a time.

Just with his head down and strolling? — Yes, and looking about him.

I again ask you, is there anything in that which occurs to you as suspicious; and what did you suspect? — I suspected he was not after any good walking about there.

Did you see nothing more in his appearance than you have told us now? — No, I did not.

It was in broad daylight all the time? — Yes.

Can you tell us anything about what sort of tie he had on? — No, I could not say. I never took notice.

Did you take very much notice of him altogether? — As I glanced from the window, as far as I could see, I could see him quite plain.

Across the street? — Yes. He would stand perhaps ten minutes or so and then move away.

Did you see anything peculiar about his nose? — No, I did not.

The man who was described in the newspapers was said to have a twisted nose? — I heard so.

You saw nothing of that kind about the person who walked about in front of your house? — I could not see very well.

Is it not the fact that you were not exactly certain of the man, and are only prepared to say that he resembles him? — He is the man who was loitering about West Princes Street.

Did you say he resembled him? — I said that he was the man.

You had seen a photograph of the prisoner in the papers, had you not? — Yes.

What kind of man did you expect to see when you went down to the police office? — I expected to see the man I had seen loitering about. It was not the papers I was going by.

The photograph in the papers was something like the man? — It was like him.

And the man that you saw in the police office was something like him, too? — Yes.

When you got to the police office how many men were in the room you were put? — There were a good many — I could not say the exact number.

By the COURT — Would there be half a dozen? — I am sure there were over a dozen.

Cross-examination resumed — Were there any foreign-looking gentlemen there? — None but himself.

Were the rest of the people who were in the room policemen? — I do not know what they were.

Did you not look at their boots? — No. They were sitting.

And the only man in any way having a foreign appearance, when you went down to identify the man, was the prisoner? — Yes.

When you were down at the police office who else were there for the purpose of identifying? — There were a good many.

Can you tell me who any of them were? Were there any of your own acquaintance? — My two daughters and my niece. That is all I know.

Those that went down with you were Madge M'Haffie, your niece, Annie M'Haffie, and Margaret Dickson M'Haffie? — Yes.

Did you go in singly to the room where this man was? — Yes.

Re-examined by the LORD ADVOCATE — Were you house-cleaning for nine or ten days before the murder? — Yes.

And you were not looking out of the window? — Not so much then at the front.

Is West Princes Street a very quiet street? — Yes.

Was there any object that occurred to your mind that the man could have in loitering, moving back and forward there? — I thought at first it might be robbery.

That was the only object? — Yes.

Was there any place special to go to up the street? — There was no place.

Had you the smallest difficulty in identifying the man? — I had not.

Is the accused the man? — Yes.

You recognise him quite easily? — Yes.

MARGARET DICKSON M'HAFFIE, examined by the LORD ADVOCATE — I reside with my mother at 16 West Princes Street, one stair up. I remember several weeks before the murder of Miss Gilchrist seeing a man loitering about the street. I just saw him walking up and down, and he would stand for a minute or two. I would see him for about half an horn* each time walking slowly up and down and standing. I did not see him look at anything particular. I could see from our house the whole way up to Miss Gilchrist's house. I observed that the man walked further than Miss Gilchrist's house, but I did not take any notice how far he walked up the street. I know the corner of West Cumberland Street. I cannot see as far as that from our window. The man sometimes walked so far westwards that we could not see him from our windows. I would then see him walk back again. I did not observe whether he ever saw me watch him. No reason occurred to me why the man should be walking back and forward in front of our house. I identify the accused as the man that I saw. When I saw him he had light check trousers and a light overcoat, and I think I saw him once or twice with a black morning coat. I would see him about six times altogether. The last time I saw him before the murder was about a fortnight before it took place. We were house-cleaning about nine or ten days before the murder, and were not looking out of the window so much, as we were busy indoors. I went down to the police office on 21st February last to see a man. I was taken into a room where there were ten or twelve men I think, and I identified the man I had seen loitering about. I could do that quite well.

Cross-examined by Mr. M'CLURE — Were you down at the police office for purposes of identification on the same day as your mother? — Yes.

How many foreign-looking people were there in the room when you went in? — He was the only one.

And he was like a photograph you had seen? — I was not going by the photograph at all.

But was he like the photograph you had seen? — Yes.

Had you read of his description in the papers? — Yes.

Is it your evidence that the man is like and resembles the person you saw in West Princes Street? — No; he is the man I saw loitering in West Princes Street.

Is it not the case you were not prepared to swear to him at first? — Yes, but I thought over what I said to the Crown, and I still adhere to what I said.

Why were you not prepared at one time to swear to his being the man? — I did not think it was necessary at that time. I was not on my oath at the time.

By the COURT — But tell us what was your impression at the first? — I was asked if he was the man that was loitering about, if I was prepared to swear when I was in Edinburgh that he was the man, and I said I did not know, I was not quite sure at the time.

Cross-examination resumed — When were you not quite sure? — When I was interviewed by Mr. Speirs.

Can you tell us when that was? — I think it would be in March.

As I understand it, that would be about three months after you had seen the man in West Princes Street? — Yes, fully.

And you were not prepared then to say he was the man; you were only prepared to say there was some resemblance? — Yes.

What has made you change your mind since the middle of March? — I said to the Crown that he was the man, and I say he is the man still.

But that is not the point. Seeing you were unable to say in the month of March that this was the man, what has enabled you to change your mind and say now that he is the man? — I have been thinking it over, and I have come to the conclusion that he is the man I saw loitering about.

Did you discuss the matter with your mother? — No, not very much.

Had your mother a strong view that he was the man? — Yes.

And had that any influence on your mind? — No.

I ask you once again what was it that led you to change your opinion between March and now? — The more I thought of it the more I was convinced that he was the man.

The further you get away from the month of December your impression of the man's appearance becomes less distinct? — Yes, but, of course, I had seen him between that time.

Did you see him between the month of March and to-day? — No.

So, while in the month of March you were uncertain of his being the man, and never saw him again till to-day, you have changed your view? — No, I still say he is the man.

Which you would not say in March? — I did not need to say to Mr. Speirs that he was the man at the time.

Can you give us any other explanation? — No.

How often have you been seen by the police since March? — Not at all. Or by the fiscal? — No.

Did you notice any striking peculiarity about the man's nose? — No.

Would you have described his nose as a twisted nose? — No, I did not take any notice of it.

You saw him across the street? — Yes.

Were you at any time suspicious of him? — When I saw him loitering about I wondered what he was loitering about for. That was all.

Surely you do not suspect people who merely walk up and down the street? — But seeing him so often, and about the same time.

What did you suspect him of in broad daylight, walking up and down the street? — I did not suspect him. I just wondered what he was doing there.

You do not mean that you had arrived at the state of suspicion? — Yes.

Were you suspicious of anything? — I was not suspicious of him doing anything at the time.

Anything he was doing there seemed quite harmless? — Yes.

Might he have been waiting for a friend? — He might.

Did he see you at the window? — I do not know.

Did you see him do anything peculiar? — No.

Did you see him do anything which would lead you to suppose he was afraid of being seen? — No.

Did you communicate with the police, or did they come to you first? — They came to us first.

How long after the murder was it that the police called on you? — I think it was after the New Year; I think it was in January.

Re-examined by the LORD ADVOCATE — Did you ever see him meeting a friend? — No.

Did you ever before or since see any man loitering back and forward for half an hour at a time? — No.

When you went to the police office on 21st February did you identify the man without any difficulty? — Yes.

And did you tell the fiscal that that was the man? — Yes.

Then in March were you spoken to by Mr. Speirs? — Yes.

Did he ask you whether you were prepared to go to Edinburgh and swear that that was the man? — Yes.

What did you tell him? — I said I did not know.

You did not know what? — Whether I was prepared to swear at the time or not.

Had you any doubt that was the man? — No.

MADGE M'HAFFIE, examined by the LORD ADVOCATE — I reside at 79 West- End Park Street, Glasgow. I am the niece of Mrs. M'Haffie. I frequently called at her house at 16 West Princes Street. I recollect being there on two occasions two weeks or so before the murder. The first of these two occasions was about seven o'clock in the evening. When I was going up stairs I met a man. I had never seen him before. He was coming down the steps. He wore black- checked trousers, a fawn over-coat, a black bowler hat, and fawn gaiters. I saw that man a few days afterwards in West Princes Street in the afternoon. I was in Mrs. M'Haffie's house, and he was on the street, passing her house. He was walking slowly. I saw him pass the house, and I saw him coming back. I do not know how often he passed and repassed. I called my aunt's attention to him. I do not know how long he would be there, but he might be about half an hour. I went down stairs, but I was not going home then. I was going towards Charing Cross; that would be east from West Princes Street. I passed the same man walking towards Charing Cross. It was in St. George's Road that I passed him — that is, down to the place where St. George's Road joins Sauchiehall Street. He was walking slowly in that direction. I noticed that he was walking with a shuffling gait. On 21st February last I went down to the Central Police Office, and I was taken into a room where a number of men were.

Were you able to pick out anybody in that room that was like the man whom you say you saw in West Princes Street? — Yes, he was like the man.

Were you quite sure about him, or not? — No, he was just like him.

Look at the prisoner; is that the man? — He is like the man.

Cross-examined by Mr. M'CLURE — When you saw him from the window of your aunt's house, who was with you? — My aunt.

Did she pass any remark on the man at the time? — I do not remember.

Had you any suspicions about the man at all? — No.

At the time you saw him from your aunt's window, was there anything suspicious about what he was doing, or was he just walking up and down the street? — I think so.

Then may I take it that till after the murder was committed in the neighbourhood, and when you were thinking back upon it, you had any suspicions in your mind, or had you any suspicions at all? — What about?

About the man who was there? — I wondered what he was doing there.

Is that all? — Yes.

I think you went home after the time you had been in your aunt's house, and you came back on 3rd January? — Yes.

Do you remember seeing your aunt then, and that she had to remind you that there had been a man? — Yes.

You had really forgotten all about it? — I had never thought about it.

Do you remember what the date was when you were taken down to the police office in order to identify the man? — It was in February.

About two months after the occurrence? — I think so.

When you went into the room was there any person at all like the prisoner — was there any other dark-haired, dark-complexioned man in the place at all? — I do not know.

Did you notice from your aunt's window, or when you were passing the man in St. George's Road, whether he was a man who had a twisted nose? — No.

May I take it that you never saw any one who answered that description walking about West Princes Street? — I never saw a man with a twisted nose.

Was this person who was walking up and down in West Princes Street a person whose nose did not attract your attention at all? — I was not attracted by his features. I did not see them properly.

If you did not see his features at all what was it that led you to say that he resembled the person you had seen in West Princes Street? — He was fairly like the man in general appearance. In the general look of him, although you cannot mention any particulars? — Yes.

Were you talking over this matter with your aunt some time since the occurrence? — Yes.

Did you find her stronger than you -were as to the identity? — Yes.

And did your cousins also discuss the matter in your presence with your aunt? — Yes.

Re-examined by the LORD ADVOCATE — When you went upstairs did your cousin Annie open the door to you on the occasion when you met the man coming downstairs? — I cannot remember who opened the door.

Do you remember anything passing between you and your cousin Annie? — Yes.

Will you tell us what passed between you? — I said, "I met a peculiar-looking man on the stairs."

What did she say in answer? — She said that he had been at the door.

By the COURT — You told us that you met a man on the stairs, and afterwards you saw a man walking up and down; was that the same man? — Yes.

Then you told us you saw a man walking along the street, and you noticed that he was shuffling; was that the same man as you had met on the stairs? — Yes.

Are you sure about that? — Yes.

And you think that the prisoner is like that man, but you cannot swear? — Yes.

Could you say whether the man you saw was dark or fair? — I thought that he was dark.

Could you say whether he had a moustache or not? — Yes, he had a moustache.

To that extent you saw his features? — Yes.

ANNIE RANKIN M'HAFFIE, examined by the LORD ADVOCATE — I am the daughter of Mrs. M'Haffie, and I live at 16 West Princes Street, Glasgow. I recollect one day four weeks before the murder that a man called at our door and rang the bell. That was between seven and eight o'clock at night. I opened the door. Our name, "Mr. M'Haffie," is on the door in large letters on a brass plate. When I opened the door the man asked if any person of the name of Anderson lived there, and I said "No." I could not understand at the time how anybody could ask for Anderson at our house with "Mr. M'Haffie" on the door. When I said "No" the man turned and walked downstairs again. Within a minute or so afterwards some one came to our door. I thought that it was the same man coming back again. I opened the door, and it was my cousin, the last witness. I asked her if she had met a man on the stair, and she said "Yes." I do not remember what I said to her. I never saw that man again. I went to the Central Police Office on 21st February last with my mother and sister, and I was taken into a room where there was a number of men.

Did you see anybody in the room who was like the man to whom you opened the door? — I pointed out a man as like the man who was at the door.

You were not quite certain? — No.

Is the prisoner like the man to whom you opened the door? — He is like the man. As far as I know, that was the only time I had ever seen him, when he came to the door.

Cross-examined by Mr. M'CLURE — I suppose the question about Anderson might be put by anybody who was asking for a lodger in the house? — Yes.

Is there anything peculiar about that question? — No, I do not think so.

By the COURT — Did you notice anything about the man's accent? — No, I did not.

He did not appear to be a foreigner? — No, I do not think so.

What kind of a light was there on the stair at your house? — There is a light below our door.

Gas? — Yes.

One jet? — Yes, below our door, further down the stair.

There is no light above your door? — No.

Was there any light in your lobby that would come out into the entrance? — Yes.

Was the light good or bad? — It was not good.

East end of West Princes Street (looking towards St. George's Road), Queen's Terrace (right).

JOHN THOMSON TRENCH, examined by Mr. MORISON — I am a detective officer in the Central District of Glasgow Police. On Sunday, 218t February, I, along with Detective Alexander Cameron, went to Renfrew in a motor car and met the prisoner. He was in charge of the witnesses Warnock and Pyper. I accompanied them to the Central Police Station at Glasgow. I had charge of the arrangements under which certain of the witnesses were to identify, if they could, the prisoner.

What arrangements were made for securing that the test of identification was a fair one? — The prisoner was placed along with eleven other men in a row in the detective office, and the witnesses were brought in one by one. The other men were mostly police officials, all in plain clothes. There were also two railway officials there. Two of the men had what I would call peculiar noses. The twelve men were made to stand up in a row, and the prisoner was allowed to take up any position in the row that he pleased.

Was every precaution taken so that the witnesses should not have an opportunity of seeing Slater before they saw him along with the other men? — Yes; there was every precaution taken to avoid that. Slater was taken to the doctor's room, where he got his tea, and during that time the witnesses were all collecting in the office, and he was taken by me from the doctor's room through the lieutenant's bar and through the telephone room and through the detective office into the officers' room at the back, where he could not be seen by any of the witnesses.

And accordingly in point of fact he was not seen by any of the witnesses before they saw him amongst the twelve people? — Not as far as I saw; I do not think they could see him. The witnesses were also taken in singly, and precautions were taken to prevent the witnesses from meeting each other after they had been in the room where the prisoner was. No witness was brought into the room for identification purposes who had an opportunity of speaking with any other witness; they were put into another room. The witness Mrs. M'Haffie was brought in; she was the first witness to see him. She was brought into the room by me, and I asked her if she could point out the man that was referred to in her statement which she had previously given, and she pointed to the accused. I said, "Now, go forward and point out your man; do not be afraid," and she went forward and put her hand on his coat sleeve. The other M'Haffies also identified him in the same way, one after the other. I brought in the witness Bryson. As he came in at the door he glanced along the row of men, and without hesitation he went right forward to the accused and put his hand on the man, and said, "This is the man." I did not take in the witness Mary Barrowman. It was Sergeant Dornan of the Western District who brought her in, but I saw her brought in. At the time she was brought in the accused was dressed in a light fawn overcoat, which was found in one of his trunks, and a soft split hat. She stood and looked at him, and she said, "Pull it down a little further — further yet"; then she said, "That's it, that is the way you were dressed when I saw you."

By the COURT — Pull what down? — His hat.

Examination continued — It was principally the witnesses in the Central District that I had charge of, but I did not have charge of the Western District. On the 2nd of January of this year I, in company with Superintendent Douglas, went to the prisoner's house at 69 St. George's Road. It is three stairs up, and consists of four rooms and a scullery and kitchen. There were two German women in the house. I did not ask where the prisoner had gone, but the woman Freedman made a statement as to the prisoner. I searched the house. (Shown production No. 33.) These are ten visiting cards that I found in the house. These visiting cards bear the name and address, "A. Anderson, 69 St. George's Road." I found these in the house. (Shown account and invoice for furniture, production No. 35.) I got these in the house also. I took them to the Police Office, and labelled them. I have been at the locus of the murder. I examined the close No. 46 West Princes Street. The close is what is called here an entry, but in the west it is called a close. The close No. 46 West Princes Street is on the opposite side of the street from the close leading into Miss Gilchrist's house, directly opposite. The stair leading to the houses there begins immediately behind the close door, and takes a turn. It is a spiral one, and is continuous until the first flat is reached. About six steps down from that landing there is a staircase window fronting West Princes Street, and the sill of that window is about 6 feet from the steps of the stair. By getting up to the landing at the first flat you can see through this window, and you can see to the door of the close of Miss Gilchrist's house. When I went up the second flat I found a staircase window there. That staircase window is only 2| to 3 feet above the stair. That window' looks directly into the room of the house where Miss Gilchrist was murdered. If the blinds of Miss Gilchrist's room were up I believe you could see into the room. When I was there the blinds were down. There is a gas on that stair. If one were looking through the window at night the gaslight would not interfere with one's view — not the gas on the stair.

Is there a gaslight that might interfere with it? — No, the gas is on the first flat; this window I refer to is one and a half stairs up — half way on the road to the second flat. The stair begins just immediately from the door, and if the door is pushed back there is a recess formed between the outside wall and the door. The recess is of considerable size, and a man could quite easily stand behind it. I did not notice the same in connection with Miss Gilchrist's door. I did not go in to see.

Cross-examined by Mr. M'CLURE — You met the prisoner at Renfrew, and motored him into Glasgow? — Yes.

Can you tell me whether the arrival of your motor with the prisoner in it could be seen through a glass door of the room in which all the witnesses were — in the lobby? — There were none of the witnesses present when he arrived in the motor for two hours afterwards.

From the room in which the witnesses were congregated is there a glass door which looks into the lobby? — There is.

And if the witnesses had been there upon the arrival of the prisoner could they have seen him? — Some of them could.

You say they were not there? — Not to my knowledge; they were not there till four o'clock, and he arrived at two.

Do you say that in point of fact at the time of his arrival you know that none of the witnesses had arrived? — Not so far as I know; I did not see any of them.

The prisoner was placed in a row with eleven men; was there any foreign- looking man amongst them? — No; they were all Scotsmen, I think.

No person of dark complexion and foreign appearance? — There were some of them of dark complexion.

And foreign appearance? — No; not foreign appearance.

So that anybody looking for a foreigner would, of course, go straight to the prisoner? — Possibly, yes.

That is an irregular way of conducting an identification, is it not? — I do not think so.

I understood that when you were going to identify a person in connection with any alleged crime you attempted to get him placed amongst men who were more or less like him; is not that so? — No, it is not.

Is that not your practice in Glasgow? — No, it is not.

Just as a matter of ordinary fairness, do you not think that that would be a proper practice to observe? — It might be the fairest way, but it is not the practice in Glasgow.

So that you had two railway officials and eleven policemen? — There were eleven including the railway officials, and the prisoner.

Nine policemen and two railway officials? — Yes.

And you cannot mention any one who resembled Slater? — Oh, none of them resembled Slater.

Slater's photograph, as an obvious foreigner, had been published in the Glasgow evening papers before that? — Yes.

So that any person who had seen his photograph would look for a foreigner, and could not escape singling out Slater at your identification? — I do not think they could very well.

You said two of the men had peculiar noses? — Yes.

Were you looking for a man at this time who had a twisted nose? — No. It happened that two men who were selected had peculiar noses.

What were the peculiarities? — One of them has a little hump on his nose, and the other has a kind of flattish nose; they were not noses like Slater's at all.

Then I may take it that there was no person in the room who had a nose the least like Slater's? — No, I should think it is very difficult to find one like it.

Had you anything to do with the description which was published in the papers after this crime had been committed? — No, I had nothing to do with that.

Do you describe Slater's nose as a twisted nose? — No, I would not describe it as a twisted nose.

Was that not the way it was described by the girl Barrowman? — I could not say; there were so many rumours and stories that I did not pay attention to them.

Has the Glasgow public not gone pretty nearly mad over this case? — I would not like to say they have gone mad; it has certainly caused a lot of sensation and talk.

Have you heard that old Miss Gilchrist was a resetter? — I have heard that frequently.

And that she kept uncut diamonds in her house, which she had got from thieves? — Yes, I have heard that too.

Not a word of truth in it? — Not a word of truth in it, as far as I know.

Have you heard within the last fortnight a rumour to the effect that people have been back at her house tearing up the floors and throwing uncut diamonds, which were found under the floors, into the street? — No, I have never heard that story.

Have you heard that she was the mother of the servant girl Lambie? — No.

But of another? — Yes.

Have you heard that she was the mother of Slater? — No.

May I take it that the case has given rise to extreme excitement amongst the Glasgow public, and to no end of unfounded rumours? — There is no doubt of that — all sorts of rumours.

Have other men been in custody in connection with this case besides Slater? — I believe there were several men arrested shortly after the murder, but I had no connection with them at all.

And a number of witnesses failed to identify these men? — Yes.

Have a number of witnesses failed to identify Slater? — Oh, there have been a number of people who have seen him who did not know him at all.

You say that Mrs. M'Haffie pointed out Slater? — She did.

Do you say that all the other M'Haffies did the same? — They did.

Is it your evidence they were all quite sure of him? — Every one of them was absolutely certain of him.

Do you say that Madge M'Haffie absolutely identified the man? — I do; I took them all in myself, and every one of them was sure of the man.

Do you say that Annie M'Haffie absolutely identified the man? — She did.

When the witness Barrowman was brought in you say you were present? — Yes.

That is the girl who was in the street, some distance from the doorway out of which the man rushed, just after the murder? — Yes.

When the girl Barrowman came in to identify Slater this was after her visit to America? — Yes.

And do you say that she did not identify him until a hat had been pulled down over his nose; did the girl Barrowman, when he was dressed in the office with an overcoat and a soft split hat, say, as regards the cap, "Pull it down"? — She did— "Pull it down more."

And was it after the cap had been pulled further down that she said, "That's it"? — "That is the way you had it when I saw you," referring to his hat.

Do you say she was doubtful about the identification to start with? — No, I do not say that.

The hat which you put on Slater you called a soft split hat? — Yes, a soft kind of tweed hat.

Could you tell me the hat it was? — I could if I saw it.

(Shown production No. 44) — Is that what you call a Donegal hat? — No.

Are you aware that in the first information given by Barrowman to the police she said that the man who came rushing out of the close had a Donegal hat? — No; but I have heard the Donegal hat mentioned several times.

And as being the thing which was characteristic of the man who came out of the close? — Yes, that is so.

That (production No. 44) is not a Donegal hat? — No.

Then what was the purpose of dressing the man up to Barrowman with this hat, which was not the kind of hat which he was supposed to be wearing at the time he came out of the close? — That was the only hat which was found in his box.

In point of fact, there was no Donegal hat found in the box? — No.

What is a Donegal hat? — I iunderstand a Donegal hat to be a soft tweed hat of round shape, with a brim all the way round.

And certainly not this at all? — No.

Did you see the boxes of clothes? — Yes, I saw them opened.

Have you produced in this case all the articles of clothing which you suppose would assist the prosecution towards an identification? — Yes.

Did you find any checked trousers? — I could not say; I was present when the boxes were opened and searched, but I really could not say whether there were checked trousers or not.

Were there any light-coloured fawn spats found? — I could not say.

But you went through the boxes? — I was there when the boxes were examined.

Were you looking? — The men who particularly examined the boxes were Mr. Warnock and Detective Inspector Pyper.

And, as far as you know, no fawn-coloured spats were found? — Not as far as I know.

And no Donegal hat was found? — No.

Were any brown boots found? — No, I do not think so; I did not see any brown boots; there were some lady's boots — I think a pair of lady's brown boots.

Then I may take it this way: if the man who came out of Miss Gilchrist's house had a Donegal hat on and brown boots you found nothing in the contents of the prisoner's boxes which would support the view that he is the murderer? — No, they were not there; I did not see anything of that kind.

And if the prisoner is supposed to have walked up and down West Princes Street with checked trousers on and fawn-coloured spats, you found nothing in his boxes which would support the charge against him? — I did not see anything like that found in the boxes.

Did you find any light, soft overcoat? — No, we did not find a light, soft overcoat.

The only light coat is this waterproof (production No. 43)? — Yes.

Did you show that at any time to Mrs. M'Haffie? — No, I did not.

Supposing Mrs. M'Haffie says that the prisoner was wearing a light, soft overcoat, which was not a waterproof, you found nothing in his boxes which would support that? — No, there was not a light cloth coat found at all that I saw.

How many boxes of clothes or bags did this man have? — There were seven trunks altogether.

And did the police go carefully over them all? — Yes.

By the COURT — Were they all full? — They were all full.

Cross-examination continued — He had a great many suits of clothes? — He had a lot of clothing — good clothing.

By the COURT — And amongst them there were old clothes; they were not all new clothes? — No, they were not all new clothes; a lot of them had been worn.

Cross-examination continued — You went into a close, as I understand, called No. 46 West Princes Street and looked across from it towards Miss Gilchrist's house? — Going up the stair, one and a half stairs up, at the staircase window, when you were standing on the stair looking through the window you saw right into the window of the room in which Miss Gilchrist was murdered.

You never actually had an opportunity of trying whether you could or not? — No, the blinds were down.

Re-examined by Mr. MORISON — It was not part of your duty to examine the boxes? — No.

And the examination was really conducted by two other witnesses who are on the Crown list? — That is so.

And, of course, you do not know the details of what was found in the boxes? — No.

But did you see that there was a large variety of clothes? — Yes, there was a large variety of clothes.

And was there a considerable number of overcoats? — Yes, there were several overcoats.

Can you tell me when the boxes were opened and examined? — Immediately on his arrival at the Central Police Office on the Sunday, 21st February.

Of course, Slater had been out of Glasgow from the 25th of December? — Yes, from Christmas night.

By the COURT — Was there any name on the boxes? — The letters "O.S." were on several of them.

CHRISTOPHER WALKER, examined by the LORD ADVOCATE — I am a constable in the Glasgow Police Force. I was on duty in the end of December, 1908, on the north side of West Princes Street. I was on day duty in the beginning of December. I recollect passing along the north side of West Princes Street in the direction of St. George's Road on 1st December about a quarter to six o'clock. I saw a man standing on the edge of the pavement. I know 15 Queen's Terrace. The man was opposite that, standing on the opposite side. I took a good look at the man. I thought I knew the man, and I waved to him. I saw he was not the man I knew, and I passed right on to St. George's Road, leaving the man standing still on the pavement. He was looking in a slanting direction towards 15 Queen's Terrace. I thought he was waiting for some party to meet him. About three nights after that I met the same man in West Princes Street 40 or 50 yards further down towards St. George's Road, on the north side of West Princes Street. On that occasion he was walking leisurely up the street, towards Queen's Crescent. That was about a quarter to six o'clock. I did not look after him. I simply recognised him as the man I had mistaken the previous night. I did not see him again that night. The next time I saw him was about a fortnight after that, on 17th or 18th December, about a quarter to seven o'clock, standing at the foot of West Princes Street, near St. George's Road, opposite the chemist's door. He was on the south side of West Princes Street. I stood for several minutes, and he stood all the time, and I went away and left him standing. I was on the opposite side of the street. When I left I went in the direction of St. George's Cross. Those were the only three occasions on which I saw the man in West Princes Street. I am not aware that I had ever seen him before. On Monday night, 22nd February, I saw the man in the Central Police Office, Glasgow. I recognised him at once as the man I had met in West Princes Street. I had no difficulty in recognising him at all. I was put on to watch Miss Gilchrist's house after the murder, about 9.30 p.m. I was at the close on the street until five o'clock in the morning. There were very few people going about, and I thought I would look and see if I could find the weapon with which the deed had been done. I went with my lamp to the back green and searched to see if anything had been thrown from the house. I did not find anything at all.

Did you search very carefully? — In a hurry. I searched with my lamp. The accused is the man I identified at the Police Office.

Cross-examined by Mr. M'CLURE — Of course, you are quite certain that is the man you saw in the Police Office? — Yes, and in West Princes Street also.

On each occasion when you saw the man in West Princes Street you were on the opposite side of the street? — From 15 Queen's Terrace.

Do I understand that you saw the man on the other side of the street? — The opposite side from Queen's Terrace.

And you took him for your friend? — Yes, for a gentleman that I knew.

Who was the gentleman? — He is in Court here.

So much the better. What is his name? — Mr. Paradise.

That was a gentleman who gave evidence, and who sold furniture? — Yes, the very same.

He is a foreign-looking gentleman, is he not? — Yes.

Of dark complexion, and with a moustache? — Yes.

How long have you known him? — About twelve months.

You waved your hand to a man you thought to be Mr. Paradise? — Yes. Before I came up to him I raised my hand, but as I reached him I saw it was not him.

What was he doing, the man you took for Mr. Paradise? — Simply standing on the pavement and glancing about the street.

I suppose you did not think there was anything suspicious in his actions? — I saw nothing suspicious about him.

Was he strolling about? — He was standing on the edge of the pavement.

You say that you saw him on 1st December, at a quarter to six? — Yes.

When was the next time you saw him? — Three or four days after that. Where was he then? — Forty or fifty yards further down the street.

On the same side? — Yes.

That is to say, on the north side? — Yes.

Where was he the next time? — The foot of West Princes Street, the opposite side.

What was he doing on these later occasions? — Simply as if he was standing waiting for some person.

There was nothing to attract your attention? — No.

You said you thought he was waiting for somebody? — That was the opinion I formed seeing him standing there.

You did not think he was watching any house in particular? — I could not say that I thought that. He was simply looking in the direction of 15 Queen's Terrace.

You passed behind him? — Yes.

And on the other occasions? — I met him coming up on the second occasion, and on the third occasion he was standing on the opposite side of the street.

Would you undertake to identify positively a man standing on the opposite side of West Princes Street in December, at or about seven o'clock? — There is a chemist's shop at the corner, and they have a door to West Princes Street which is well lighted up. He was standing facing this door, and I was on the opposite side.

He was facing the door of the shop? — He was right in a line with the door.

Was his back towards you? — No, his face was towards me.

The chemist's shop would only light up his back? — Yes.

That would make it a little more difficult. Do you say under these circumstances you have confidence in your identification of the man standing on the opposite side of the street? — Yes, I have every confidence. There is an electric lamp in St. George's Road at that corner, which throws a very bright light.

On the second occasion he was further down the street than on the first occasion. How far was he from St. George's Road? — About 50 yards.

The electric light would not help you very much there? — No.

Would you say that, on the second occasion, you could positively identify the man? — Yes, because there was a lamp on the opposite side of the street.

What did you identify him by? — I just thought he resembled this man. That is all.

You thought he was a foreign-looking person with a darkish moustache, something like Mr. Paradise? — Yes.

Is that all you can say about him? — Yes.

You never saw this man again until 22nd February? — No, not until 22nd February.

By that time the newspapers had been full of photographs, had they not? — Yes, there were lots of photographs.

And you knew the person you were to identify was the person of foreign appearance? — I daresay I did.

Who was at the Police Office when you arrived there? — I could not say. There were a number of detectives.

Was there any person of a foreign appearance except the prisoner? — Mr. Paradise himself was there.

You would not mistake him, of course? — No.

Was there any person of a foreign appearance except the prisoner? — — Not that I saw.

Was he there among detectives and policemen? — Yes. Did they go through the farce of asking you if you saw any one like the man? — They asked if I saw any one that I recognised, and I went to him.

You at once went to him? — Yes.

As I understand, you knew the other people in the room to be either detectives or Mr. Paradise? — I did not know that they were. Mr. Paradise was not in the room, he was in some other room.

When you went down, do I understand that the only person of foreign appearance in the room into which you went was the prisoner? — Yes. And the others were detectives? — I do not know what they were. I thought you said before that they were detectives? — Some of them were, but I do not know whether they were all detectives. Who were the other people? — I do not know. None had a foreign appearance? — No.

So you were able to identify a foreigner at once? — I did not go there to identify a foreigner at all.

There was an auger found in the back green that you searched with a light? — I am told there was.

You had looked the whole place with your lamp on the night after the death of Miss Gilchrist? — Yes.

What is the extent of the back green? — It is a pretty large-sized back green.

Did you make a thorough search? — Yes.

If there was an auger found in the back green next day, do you think it had come into the back green between the time of your search and the time of its being found? — There were some parts of the back green where there was long grass, and although I made, as I thought, a careful examination, I did not look for so small a weapon as an auger, and I might have passed it.

It was just under the kitchen window? — Yes.

Was there long grass or short grass there? — There were long weeds lying about where this auger was found.

You did not see it found? — This is the first time I have seen it.

Re-examined by the LORD ADVOCATE — Look at photograph No. 1 of No. 5 of the productions. Do you see a No. 4 on the photograph? — Yes.

Was that near the place where you saw the man the first time? — It was further round than that.

You mean nearer St. George's Road? — Yes.

A foot or two? — A yard or two.

And nearer Miss Gilchrist's house? — Yes.

Do you see a No. 6 on that photograph? — Yes.

Was that about the place where you saw the man the third time? — Yes, that is about the place.

Do you see a No. 2 on the photograph? — Yes.

Is that near the place where you saw the man the second time when he was walking westwards? — Yes.

Are the lights in West Princes Street incandescent? — Yes.

And is it electric light that you have in St. George's Road? — Yes.

In the middle of the road or at the sides? — The sides.

Was there an electric light in St. George's Road near the comer, near No. 6? — Immediately opposite, on the St. George's Road, right in the centre of West Princes Street.

It throws a powerful light on that corner where you see No. 6? — Yes.

EUPHEMIA CUNNINGHAM, examined by the LORD ADVOCATE — I live at 114 South Woodside Road, Glasgow. I am in the employment of a photographer at 167 St. George's Road. My dinner hour is from one to two, and I go home daily at that hour by West Princes Street and Queen's Crescent. That is a very quiet district and a quiet street. On Monday, 14th December last, when I was going home for my dinner, I observed a man standing at the comer of Queen's Crescent and West Princes Street. I had never seen him before. He was looking towards Miss Gilchrist's house. I should think that he would be about 60 feet away from the house, and just at the comer of Queen's Crescent. I returned again about two o'clock, but the man was not there. On the following day I went for my dinner at the same hour. I saw the man again standing at the same place. On Wednesday, the 16th, I went for my dinner at the same hour. I saw the same man standing at the same place. On Thursday, the 17th, when going for my dinner at the same hour, I saw him again standing at the same place and looking towards Miss Gilchrist's house. William Campbell was with me, and I said to him, "There is that man again." It occurred to me as odd, and I wondered what took the man there. I never saw him on any occasion when I was coming back from my dinner. I thought his appearance was foreign, and he was very dark, with a sallow complexion, and was rather a heavy-featured man. I thought he was clean shaven, but, of course, I did not get a very good view of the front face; it was the side face that I always saw. He had a dark tweed coat on, and a green cap with a peak. He was on the same pavement as I was on on each occasion, but Mr. Campbell was nearer to him than I was. I do not recollect seeing the man before 11th December. I saw him at the Central Police Office in February. I was taken into a room where there were a lot of men, and I saw there the man I had seen on these different occasions in West Princes Street. The accused is the man that I saw in the police office and on the street.

Cross-examined by Mr. M'CLURE — Have you been shown the green cap that the man was wearing since? — Yes.

Was it a green cap with a peak? — Yes, a dark green cap.

I show you one of the caps under label 46? — That is not the cap.

Is the other one the cap? — No.

Is No. 44 the cap? — No. This cap that I see is more like it.

That is a cap that is obviously of black cloth? — Yes.

Do you say that is the cap that the man was wearing? — No, there seemed to be more green in it.

Who was it that showed you the green cap that you identified? — Mr. Hart, the fiscal.

You were not told that the cap belonged to Slater? — No.

It comes to this, that you say that Slater was wearing a green cap which has not been shown to you here? — That is so.

Can you give me the date when you identified the prisoner in the police office? — About 28th February.

That is fully two months after you had seen the man? — Yes.

Did you notice any peculiarity about his nose? — No, I did not.

That is not part of the identification? — No. It was the left side that I always saw.

The nose did not appear to you to be in any way striking? — No.

Did you ever see him front face? — No.

When you say the man was standing in a set attitude day after day looking towards Miss Gilchrist's house, what makes you say that he was looking towards her house? — Because his face was turned in that direction.

But equally well, I suppose, the man might have been looking down towards St. George's Road? — His face would have been more front if he had been looking that way.

He was doing nothing at all? — No.

Did he seem to be anxious to escape your observation? — No. He had the collar of his coat up.

Did he seem to you to be hiding in any way? — No. I thought he was waiting for some one or looking for some one.

It was always at one o'clock that you saw him, and he was always away by two o'clock? — Yes.

Did you say that he was quite clean shaven? — Yes, I thought so.

I mean with no moustache at all? — I could not say very well, because the collar of his coat was up.

Do you suggest now that on every occasion when you passed the man he had his upper lip buried in his coat collar? — I do not say that, but I did not get a very good view of the front face. It was more the back of the head and the side of the face that I saw.

Suppose if any gentleman of sallow complexion and clean shaven, with dark hair and of foreign appearance, had been shown you in the police office, you would have been quite ready to say that he was the man? — No.

You had seen this man's photograph in the papers? — Yes, I saw one.

And did you think you recognised him from that? — I did at once.

The man in the photograph in the papers had a considerable moustache? — No, a slight moustache.

Was that the photograph that you saw (shown No. 39 of the productions)? — Yes.

There is a very distinct moustache there? — Yes.

If the man you saw at the comer was clean shaven, how did you recognise at once a man with a heavy moustache as being the same? — It was more the side of the face and the back of the head that I recognised, not the front of the face.

There is no doubt if you saw the side of his face you would see one-half of his moustache? — I did not notice that he had a moustache.

That is exactly what I am suggesting. My point is this, if the man whom you saw, as you say, at the corner of Queen's Crescent had no moustache on the 14th, 15tli, 16th, and l7th December, how did you come to recognise in the paper of 15th January a man with a noticeable moustache as the same person? — He was quite easily recognised. I would not forget the side of the face.

But it is a front face that is shown in the paper? — Yes.

Can you explain how it was if, on the 14th, 15th, 16th, and 17th December, you saw a clean-shaven man, side face, standing in West Princes Street, you came to identify the photograph of a man full face towards you and with a considerable moustache as the person whom you saw? — It is not only the photograph I am going by. I was shown the man down in the police office.

But you first identified him from the photograph alone? — Yes, I did.

Can you understand how you failed to notice the moustache? — No, not any more than it was not very prominent. He had the collar of his coat up, and it was always this side of the face and the back of the head that I saw.

Can you have a very confident identification from the back of his head? — Yes.

What was peculiar about the back of his head? — The ears were sticking out slightly.

Did you ever see a man with ears sticking out before? — Yes, many a man.

It is not very characteristic, you know? — Then there was the side of the face, the heavy jaw bones.

Surely the jaw bone would also be under the coat collar? — Yes, it was a little.

Why did you identify a jaw bone which you never saw? I am only suggesting to you that you may have been a little hasty in your identification. — I don't think so.

The cap you saw is not here? — No.

Are there any other details of the clothes that you noticed? — The dark coat.

Anything else? — That was all, and the green cap.

Had he checked trousers or fawn spats? — I did not notice.

You cannot tell anything about his boots or his trousers? — No.

Do you say that his jaw was set right down in his coat collar? — No. it was not buried right down, but the collar of his coat was up.

Over his jaw? — Not right over, but I did not get a very good view of the front face. What I saw was more the side and the back of the head and the neck.

Do you not think that if the man was clean-shaved you ought not to have identified a man with a moustache as being the same? — I think it is very like the man I saw.

When you went down to the police office to identify this man later on, on 28th February, how many people were in the room? — I could not tell. I did not count them.

How many were with Slater? — I should fancy about a dozen.

Were there any men there like Slater? — No, I could not say that.

Was there any foreign-looking man in the room except Slater? — No.

In point of fact, Slater had then a moustache, had he not? — Yes.

So he was like the photograph which you had seen before? — Yes.

When you went into the room where Slater was, was it not perfectly obvious to you that the rest of the men who were in the room were all detectives and policemen? — They certainly looked like it.

Did you observe their boots? — No.

When you saw Slater in the police office what kind of boots had he? — I did not look at his boots.

What kind of coat had he on that day? — The first time I saw him he had on a blue coat.

How often did you see him in the police office? — Twice.

Re-examined by the LORD ADVOCATE — Did you pass within 2 or 3 feet of him on the pavement? — Yes.

Had you a clear view of him each time? — Yes, I had.

Are you sure the accused is the very man you saw? — Yes.

Was it raining when he had up his coat collar? — No, but it was cold.

By the COURT — On each occasion were his clothes, including his cap and his greatcoat, the same? — Yes, they were always the same clothes.

WILLIAM CAMPBELL, examined by the LORD ADVOCATE — I am a photographer in Glasgow. On Tuesday, Wednesday, and Thursday, 15th, 16th, and 17th December last, I was walking home at the mid-day meal hour, one o'clock. I was going up West Princes Street, which is invariably a very quiet street. One seldom or never sees anybody hanging about there. On Tuesday, 15th, when I was going home that way, I observed a man who was standing at the corner of West Princes Street and Queen's Crescent. He was looking towards Mr. Adams' house on the other side of the street. That was the door next Miss Gilchrist's house. The last witness was with me at the time. I did not observe anything particular about the man. When I came back I did not notice him. On the two succeeding days, Wednesday and Thursday, I passed the same place about the same hour and I saw the same man. He was standing on the same spot looking over in the same direction. I remember Miss Cunningham saying, "There is that same man again; I wonder what he is doing there." I do not know whether he heard what she said. We were pretty close to him at the time, and as we were passing he turned round and turned away his head, but that was all. I formed no opinion as to why ho should be there. I have never seen the man standing there since. I have never seen any one standing there since, except in the week following the murder, when there were crowds standing there. After the murder I saw the photograph of a man Oscar Slater in the *Evening News*, and I thought there was something similar between the features in the photograph and the man I had seen at the comer. I went down on Sunday afternoon, 21st February, to the police office, and I was taken into a room where there were a number of men. There was a man there who bore a general resemblance to the one I saw. I did not identify him positively, but there was a general resemblance to the man I had seen. (Shown prisoner.) That is very like the man I saw.

Cross-examined by Mr. M'CLURE — You do not go the length of saying that there is more than a general resemblance? — No,

I think you had fully as good an opportunity of seeing him as Miss Cunningham, had you not? — Even better.

Why? — I was next him. I was between Miss Cunningham and him.

At the time you saw him was there anything in what the man was doing or not doing that occurred to you as casting some suspicion upon him? — Nothing further than that the man was standing there day after day at the same spot, where I never saw a man standing — it is such a quiet locality.

But he certainly was not screening himself from public observation? — Not so far as I observed.

He was there to be seen by anybody who passed down the street? — That is so.

ROBERT BROWN BRYSON, examined by the LORD ADVOCATE — I am a cabinetmaker and live at Somerville Drive, Mount Florida. For a number of years I was in the employment of Mr. Bruce Martin, cabinet-maker and upholsterer, at Charing Cross, Glasgow. While there I was frequently employed in going to the houses in West Princes Street and the district and doing work. I have been in the house now occupied by Mr. Adams, and I have also been in Miss Gilchrist's house, but it is twenty years ago. I was frequently in West Princes Street in the course of my work and going to and from my work. It is a very quiet street. I have seen the old lady several times at her window; I do not know that I have seen her moving about. It is probably eight or ten years ago, more or less, since I was in the way of going about there. She was living there then. On Sunday, 20th December last, my wife and I were on our way from Mount Street, off the New City Road, to Glassford Street to get a car, and we had occasion to pass through Queen's Crescent into West Princes Street. The time was about 7.40 or 7.43 p.m. About that hour I was in West Princes Street, almost opposite Miss Gilchrist's house. I had occasion to pass it. When there I observed a man standing in an entry or close, on the stone part of the close at the front of the front door. That close has a front door, and this man was standing on the stone area which is the entrance to the close door. He was standing almost directly opposite Miss Gilchrist's house — not exactly, but at a slight angle from Miss Gilchrist's house or Adams' house. (Shown photograph No. 1, looking towards St. George's Road.) This man was standing at the close where the board is out, which is at a slight angle from Adams' house or Miss Gilchrist's house. He was not standing against the door of the close; he was standing, roughly speaking, 2 or 3 feet from the close door on the stonework above the area. He was looking slightly towards the left — towards the east. It was his looking at the windows of Miss Gilchrist's house that attracted my attention. He was staring up at the windows, and I thought that probably he was looking for some one or waiting on somebody. That was the whole idea I took from it.

Did his position and attitude excite your suspicion? — I naturally looked at him and stared at him, because he was staring up at the windows, and I thought that he was waiting for somebody, or that there was something peculiar about it. I did not exactly think that there was anything further than that. I accordingly took a very good look at him. I could see him quite well. He saw me looking at him, and he took about two or three paces and stepped off and passed me to my left, going westward. The close door was closed. I looked after him as he walked away westward, and I turned round and looked at him till he was perhaps half a dozen paces past me.

Did it appear to you that he moved off because he saw you taking a good look at him? — I thought that it was the fact of my staring at him that made him go down from the step. I wondered at him coming down from the step. I stared at him intensely. There was a light in Miss Gilchrist's house at the time. She had Venetian blinds, and they were down. The two windows furthest east were lit. There is a large square lamp at the corner of Queen's Crescent and a very small lamp above Dr. Adams' door. The lamp at the corner is an incandescent lamp, which gives a big light. It was a very clear, decent night — not a wet night. I saw how the man was dressed. He was dressed in a black coat and vest, as far as I could see, and I think that he had on older trousers than the coat and vest, and he had a black boat hat. He had a slight moustache with a slight droop, and not pointed or turned up. Otherwise he was shaven. His gait or walk did not attract me particularly. I did not think that he had a smart walk. He walked past very slowly and sluggishly. I was shown a photograph of two men by Detective M'Gimpsey (No. 57). That is a photograph of two men. M'Gimpsey came down and handed me that photograph, and he said, "Which of these two men, or, rather, are either of the two men the least like the man you saw in West Princes Street?" I looked at the photograph and I said, "Yes, that is the man I saw in West Princes Street."

Had you any difficulty in identifying him? — That is exactly what I am telling you. On that Sunday night, 21st February, I went to the Central Police Office in Glasgow, and was taken into a room where there were a number of men. I was asked to point out a man whom I saw on the step. I was asked if I could point out the man, or if any of these men was the least like the man I had seen, and I pointed out the man whom I saw in West Princes Street. I pointed him out as the man I saw there. (Shown prisoner.) That is the man I saw in West Princes Street on the Sunday night.

Cross-examined by Mr. M'CLURE — I think Mrs. Bryson was along with you? — Yes.

I think you spoke to her about the man? — I do not know whether I said anything particular.

Is it the case that, in the statement you made, you made a remark specially as to his appearance? — I do not think I made any remark about his appearance, but I think I said that he was looking for a lady love or something. His intentions were not particularly good. I think I said something like that. As to his appearance, I do not think I mentioned that.

I do not like to make suggestions, but did he look to you as if he might be a man hanging about waiting for his sweetheart? — He looked to me as I have explained, and I think the remark I passed to Mrs. Bryson was that he was after a sweetheart, or after no good intentions.

But which did you think? — I think the latter was the more likely — that he was after no good intentions.

Why do you say that? — Because he seemed taken when I stared at him to such an extent. It was from the fact of me staring at him. He walked down and walked away as if he took guilt to himself. That is the only answer I can give you.

Guilt of waiting for a girl or what? — I cannot tell you what was in the man's mind, but I think he was after no good intentions.

You thought that he looked ashamed of himself? — I do. I think he was taken — whatever he was after I do not know.

Is it the case that you recalled this remark to Mrs. Bryson, and she could not say any such thing? — I do not think she paid any attention, because I spoke to her and she could not recollect what I said to her.

Is it the fact that Mrs. Bryson has no recollection of having passed a man at this place, and has no recollection of you having made a remark to her about it? — She has no recollection. I do not think she has any recollection particularly about me having passed any remark regarding the man.

Or having seen the man at all? — I never asked her upon that point.

Is it not the fact that she does not remember any man being there? — I do not know whether she remembers any man being there or not. I spoke to her casually, but I do not think she could recall anything about it.

Is it the case that she says that she does not remember any man being there? — It is the case thus far, that she does not remember me having said anything about it at all. It is quite out of her memory.

But you see the further point I am making? — Yes.

Did she not say that she did not remember passing any man at all? — No, she does not remember distinctly about me passing any remark.

Do you say that she does remember passing this man? — I say that she does not remember anything about that remark being passed.

Nor about the man being there? — I do not say that.

But is it not the fact that the mental position of your wife on this subject is that she does not remember a man being passed, and she does not remember you making any remark? — She does not remember particularly me passing any remark regarding the man or anything else. She has taken no notice of my remark seemingly.

Nor of the man? — Well, according to that, if you put it in that fashion, I say that she does not remember me passing any remark.

Can I not get you past that? — No, I do not think so.

Had you ever seen the man before? — Never in my life.

How long did it take you to pass him? — Probably six paces — three on either side of him.

You did not observe the man till you were three paces on? — No, I was six paces from the corner of Queen's Crescent.

Is it the case that you did not see him till you were about 3 yards from him? — No, it would be the corner of Queen's Crescent, and it is about six paces or fully that from the corner. I observed him four or five paces from that. I was walking slowly.

The man came down and walked to meet you; did he meet you before you had reached the close from which he emerged? — About a pace or so. I met him about 4 feet from the close.

May I take it that what happened is this, that when you were about four paces off him he immediately came down from the step and passed you? — About four paces before I came to the close I stared at him, and by the time I got one pace he was coming down during that time, and I was staring at him all the time.

The man was only standing on the step inside the railings when you saw him? — No, he was standing on the sandstone, the plat of the entrance, which is about 7 feet in from the area. The area bridge is the phrase, I understand.

Whom did you first communicate with about this? — I mentioned it in the place where I am employed.

At what date? — On the Tuesday after the Sunday it happened.

Did you observe that the man had a foreign appearance? — Yes, it struck me that he had a slightly foreign appearance.

Was that what struck you? — Yes, his sallow complexion and his peculiar appearance, and his staring up at the windows.

Would you have thought anything about it if he had not been staring at the windows? — No, I do not think I would.

Was it because there had been a murder at Miss Gilchrist's that you were suspicious that a man should have been looking at the windows? — I merely mentioned the fact when I heard about the thing.

You suspected him of nothing except of intense staring, which might have been directed to any other house? — The intense staring was at that house.

Which windows was he looking at? — The windows furthest east, which were lit. The Venetian blinds were down, and one could see a glimmer of light through the Venetian blinds.

Did you observe that as you came round Queen's Crescent? — No, when I saw him staring I looked at what he was staring at. I stared at him, looked up at the windows, and then looked at him.

And at that time was he coming down? — Yes.

Are there six windows facing the street in Miss Gilchrist's house? — I never counted them, but I think there will be six or so. These are the two windows furthest away from Adams' house — past the close, next to the other tenement.

But had you time, in the glance which you gave across the street, to take stock of the fact that there were only lights in two windows out of six? — I had.

And while you were making this observation your attention was directed from the man standing on the street? — Just a glance as I looked back.

Do you remember the appearance of anybody you passed on the street going home that night? — Do you mean in West Princes Street?

Any street — do you remember the appearance of any of the passers- by? — Yes.

Is that somebody you knew? — No.

Did you pass a number of people that night? — I must have passed a considerable number. One does not pass along a street without passing people.

But do you recollect the appearance of any of these people? — Yes, I recollect the appearance of one man I passed in West Princes Street.

Do you mean the one you were talking of? — No, you were asking me about other people. It was a little gentleman that I met — the only party that I passed after I passed the close. He was another man, who was out taking a smoke.

Was he observing any windows? — No, he was away down at the foot of West Princes Street, near St. George's Road.

Would you recognise him again? — I would.

Do you remember what his clothes were like? — Yes.

Is that the only man you remember? — The only man in West Princes Street.

Do you say that you have an accurate recollection of the people you meet on the street, and can describe them by having seen them with a rapid glance? — It is not a very difficult thing, passing down the street the length of West Princes Street and not another living soul in it except myself and my wife, when you meet a man, or see a man standing in a close, and taking a thorough good look at that man — I do not think it is very difficult; and if you only meet another man between that and the end of West Princes Street you can remember him.

But do you say that innocent passers-by become photographed in your brain so as to enable you to describe their clothes and walk afterwards? — I do not photograph anybody particularly in my brain, nor am I an expert of what people wear or do not wear; but I am talking of this particular person and as to how I saw him. I do not say that I would come out of West Princes Street and go into St. George's Road and state what the first fifty men I meet wear. I would not pay particular attention in an ordinary thoroughfare; but it was in such a quiet street that it was almost impossible for me or any other person to pass a man or woman without noticing them, particularly if they were taking up their attention with any particular object.

And you take in the details of the dress? — There is not much detail necessary to tell whether a man has a black coat and a hat.

Any boots? — I never looked at his boots.

But you were sure that it was a black coat and vest? Was it a tail coat or a jacket? — I do not know - whether it was a tail coat or a jacket — I would not swear to that.

Was there an overcoat? — No, there was no overcoat.

Now, when you went on to the police office you knew the purpose for which you had gone was to identify Slater as the man you had seen in West Princes Street? — Yes, I was asked to come down on the Sabbath night.

And you had seen Slater's photograph, shown you by M'Gimpsey, before that? — Yes.

What was the date on which he showed you the photograph? — I could not tell you. I never paid any attention to it.

By the COURT — About how long before you went down to the police office was it? — I think about a fortnight.

Cross-examination continued — Can you tell when you went to the police office? — No, I do not remember the date.

When you went down were you shown into a room where there was a number of men? — I was shown into a large room where there was a number of men.

Were you told that the man was there that you were to look for among them? — No, I was not told that he was amongst them, but I naturally expected he would be.

What did the policeman say to you? — The detective officer said, "Look amongst these men there and see if you can recognise anybody the least like the man you saw in West Princes Street."

Were you down on the same day as any of the other witnesses who have been here? — Yes, on the Sunday. There were several witnesses.

Was Mrs. M'Haffie there? — I don't know them by name, but there were several witnesses.

Among the people in the room when you were asked to look round were there any of foreign appearance except Slater? — I do not know how many men there would be.

Were any of them of foreign appearance except Slater? — Yes, there were some of them of foreign appearance.

How many foreigners? — I do not know whether you call it foreign appearance, but some of them had the same sort of way. I saw various types of sallow complexion, and black moustaches, and broken noses.

Were there any policemen amongst the men whom you inspected? — If there were they were not much credit to the force. I think they were all small- looking persons. They were not policemen.

I want to ask you — do you say that there were policemen amongst them or not? — Do you think that I would know whether they were policemen or not?

By the COURT — Did you know a number of them or any of them were policemen? — No, I did not. I do not know who the men were at all.

Cross-examination continued — How many men in the room were of foreign appearance? — I think, out of the number of men I saw, I am quite sure there would be three or four with sallow complexions and black moustaches. I do not say they were of foreign appearance.

Were any of the people except Slater people of foreign appearance, or were any of the people the least like Slater? — Yes, there were one or two not unlike him.

Had you any trouble in identifying him? — None whatever.

Although they were like him? — None whatever, although they were very like him.

How many were very like him? — Those four that had sallow faces and black moustaches. I would say that there were at least four.

You were able, however, to discard the four people that you have mentioned, and to select Slater. What enabled you to do that? — The man's face was so vividly printed on my mind from the Sabbath night — that was it.

That is all you can say? — That is how I identified him.

Can you tell me when you saw these four men what clothes they had on? — The whole of the men were dressed in plain civilian clothes.

Light or dark? — I think they were, most of them, in dark clothes. I do not say that they were, but as far as my memory serves me the bulk of the men that I saw were all in dark clothing.

Was Slater in dark clothing? — He was.

Can you tell me what he was wearing on the night you identified him? — I think he had on a black coat and vest.

Are you sure? — The garments that he had on were dark. It was not the man's clothing that I was taken to identify; it was his face.

Had he a tail coat or a jacket? — That I won't swear to.

What trousers had he on on the Sunday night? — That I won't swear to. It was the man's face; I never looked at his garments. He had a dark garment, but whether it was a coat or jacket I cannot say.

How is it if you cannot remember what clothes were worn by Slater when you saw him in February, after he came back from America, that you were so positive as to the clothes he was wearing when you saw him for a few seconds on the Sunday night? — I am not going to commit myself by swearing that he had a coat and vest the night that I identified him, but he had on a dark coat or jacket. I did not pay any attention to what he had on in the police office because I had no occasion. It was the man's face that I was taken to identify.

Was the light in the police office when you went to identify him much better than the light in West Princes Street, and should you not have had a better view? — Yes, but you do not take such a look at a man's coat as to whether it is a coat or a jacket. It is in my mind that it was a coat on the Sunday night, but I won't swear to it. I won't commit myself.

If your recollection is so vivid as to the clothes worn by a man on 20th December, why should you forget the details of the clothing of a person that you saw in a better light in the end of February, when you had longer time for observation? — That is one way of putting it, why I should forget. I was not so much interested in the coat or jacket. It was a dark garment that he had on, and that is all I can say. I won't swear to whether it is a coat or a jacket.—

By the COURT — Had the man that you saw on the platform anything in his hand? — No, he had nothing. He was standing with his hands at his back.

ANDREW NAIRN, examined by the LORD ADVOCATE — I am a provision merchant in Glasgow. On Sunday, 20th December last, I was returning home by Queen's Crescent from visiting some friends. My wife and children were following at some good distance behind. It was a quarter past nine o'clock. When I entered Queen's Crescent I proceeded westwards to West Princes Street, and I stood there for fully five minutes to wait for my wife and children coming up. I would be about 120 yards from Miss Gilchrist's house. I was on the right hand side of West Princes Street coming down. That was on the opposite side from Miss Gilchrist's house. When I was standing there my attention was attracted by a man standing at the corner of the gardens, in the middle of the pavement, with his back to me, looking in the direction of Miss Gilchrist's house. The man was in West Princes Street. I just saw his back at that time. He was on the north side of West Princes Street too. He seemed to be waiting for somebody. I did not see his face.

Did you see whether he kept his face away from you or not? — His face was directed in the one position the whole time, standing a little on the angle, looking that way (witness illustrated by turning sideways). I did not see any part of his face. He was about 13 yards away from me. There was a good light. He had on a light coat, about 2 inches underneath the knee at the back. He was broad shouldered, and a little long in the neck, and had black hair. He had what I would call a motor cap, with the flaps up, and a broad back. I stood observing him for some time, till my wife and children came up. That was about five minutes. During that time the man continued standing and looking in the direction of Miss Gilchrist's house.

Could you tell whether he had observed you or not? — No, he could not. When my wife and children came up I went on my way. I made a remark to my wife, pointing my finger. I said, "There's a man standing there watching."

Did it occur to you that there was anything suspicious about him? — What caused me to suspect the man was that we had had one or two cases of housebreaking round about our district a fortnight before, and it was that which caused me to stand and look. I afterwards pointed out the place where I saw this man standing to Detective Pyper and to Detective Dornan. I think that was about three weeks or so afterwards; it might be fully that. I could see Miss Gilchrist's house from the spot. I had a grand view of the house; there is a lamp-post nearly opposite Miss Gilchrist's entrance, and there is a brass plate — Mr. Adams' brass plate — on the other side, and the reflection of the light strikes the brass plate, and it meets and throws the reflection down, which causes a good light at Miss Gilchrist's door.

Did you notice whether that was the best spot from which to observe Miss Gilchrist's house? — Yes, it was a splendid view of the place — a grand view. I moved on when my wife and children came up. When I went away, the man was still standing there, and at the corner of Cumberland Street I turned round, and he was still standing in the same place and looking in the same direction. On Monday, 22nd February last, I went to the Central Police Office, and I there identified the man; I am certain that he is the man that I saw that night. There were a good number of officials here and there about the room when I identified him.

But you pointed out the man? — Yes.

Will you look at the prisoner. Is that the man you saw? (To accused)— You might turn your back. Yes, I am certain that that is the man I saw.

Cross-examined by Mr. M'CLURE — Do you call that a long-necked man (pointing to accused)? — I don't mean exactly a man with an ordinary neck.

You said a longish neck? — Yes.

Has this man got a longish neck? — He has got the average man's neck.

When you spoke of a longish neck, did you mean something longer than the average? — No.

Have most men got longish necks? — No; I did not mean a short neck.

You mean one that was not the average, which was on the long side of the average? — It depends very much on the collar that the man wears.

Name us anything else by which you identify this man who stood with his back to you? — Broad shoulders, black hair.

Anything else? — No, that was all.

Do I take it, then, that if you see a broad-shouldered man with a longish neck, at 9.15 on a December evening, at a distance of 13 yards, without seeing his face at all, you are able to be positive about his identification? — It was a frosty, clear night, and the light round about is fairly good; there are two lamp-posts within a radius of 13 or 14 yards with incandescent light, which give a very fair light.

You heard the question I put. Are you positive of your identification of a man whom you only saw once, he being a man you had never seen before, and you only saw his back at a distance of 13 yards, on a December night, at 9.15, that man, being upon his trial for murder. I want you to be fair. — Well, I am certain that it is the same man that I saw.

And that is because he has broad shoulders, a neck of the description you have given, and black hair? — Being suspicious, I certainly gave the man a good look.

Suspicious of what? — We had numbers of oases of housebreaking round about our district, I think three or four in the fortnight before that, and that was what caused me to look at the man.

Do you consider you are quite fair in swearing positively to the man, when you never saw whether his eyes were blue or brown, and whether he had any hair on his face? — I cannot swear about his face, not having seen his face.

Have you ever gone up behind a man in the street, thinking he was a person you knew, and clapped him on the shoulder, and then discovered you had made a mistake? — Not to my knowledge, but I know it has happened.

And the only way of knowing whether it is a man's friend or not is to see his face. How can you, on the face of that, swear positively to a man in a murder trial whose face you have never seen at all? — Oh, I will not swear in fact, but I am certain that he was the man I saw; but I will not swear.

If you are upon your oath, and state you are certain it is the man, are you not aware you are swearing to it? — Yes, to a certain extent, but I will not swear, not seeing the man's face, that he is the man.

Then, do I understand now that, after all you have said, your identification is not positive? — Oh, well, I would not go that length. You will not go the length of being positive? — No.

ELIZABETH DONALDSON, examined by the LORD ADVOCATE — I am house- keeper to Mr. Edward Gillies, a stockbroker, at 46 West Princes Street, Glasgow. The house is up one stair, and it is directly opposite the house of Miss Gilchrist. I recollect on several occasions before the night of Miss Gilchrist's murder the stair gas at the landing at our door was turned out. It had been done before several times. On the night of the murder, 21st December, I found the gas turned off. I re-lit the gas.

Cross-examined by Mr. M'CLURE — As I understand, all you can say is that on the night of the 21st December the gas on the stair was out at 6.50? — Yes.

And on the 13th of February it was out again? — Yes.

Who put it out on either occasion you do not know? — I do not knoW'.

Do you know whether it was lighted on either occasion first? — No.

ALEXANDER GILLIES, examined by the LORD ADVOCATE — I am a manufacturer in Glasgow, and reside at 46 West Princes Street. My house is directly opposite where Miss Gilchrist lived. It is one flight up. On Wednesday, Thursday, or Friday of the week before the murder I was returning home about a quarter to six. As I was about to enter the close I observed a man standing there, at the back of the close, at the foot of the stair. The close door was open at the time.

Was the man standing in the middle of the passage, about half-way up to the first flight? — He walked up there after I entered the close. He was a stranger to the close. I tried to get past him. When I did so he rather blocked my passage. He turned his back to me, and instead of allowing me to pass, he sort of blocked the passage, and the stair not being wide enough, I had to ask him to allow me to pass. Instead of allowing me to pass he walked up the second flight of stairs, and again blocked my passage in the same fashion, and at that time I had again to ask him to allow me to pass, and I got past then. When I got up to my own landing, the man was still. standing on the steps. His face was towards me. "When I put my latch key in the door and opened it he was still standing. I have not seen him again since that night, to my knowledge. He had a long fawn-coloured coat on, and a cap; otherwise I really cannot say anything about him. He was sallow, and had dark hair. He was about 5 feet 8 inches in height. He was clean shaven. On the 1st of March I went to Duke Street Prison and I saw the prisoner there. He resembled the man I saw on the stair, but I cannot say it was the same man. (Shown prisoner.)

Is that like the man? — He resembles the man, but I cannot say it is the same man. I had observed the gas on the stair turned off several times before the murder. On one or two occasions shortly after the murder I have observed that, and during the last fortnight it has occurred several times.

Cross-examined by Mr. M'CLURE — Of course, as regards the later occasions you do not suspect the prisoner at the bar; he has been in jail. — I cannot suspect him at all.

Who turned out the gas you have no notion? — I have not; I did not see it turned out; I have seen the gas out when I came in, when it should have been in.

FREDERICK NICHOLS, examined by Mr. MORISON — I was a hairdresser with R.S. Bamber, hairdresser at Charing Cross, Glasgow, at the end of last year. I remember on the 16th of November last a German coming to get shaved. He did not say at the time where he belonged to; he said he came from America, as I understood. He bought some things at our place. I asked his name in order to put it on the bottles, and he wrote it on himself; he put on Mr. Anderson. He did not give any address. At that time he had a moustache. After the 16th of November he came in several times a week, up till the 25th of December. On these occasions he was shaved by me. The last time that I shaved him was on Christmas Day. On that date he left, taking with him his bottles and his shaving utensils. He did not give me any address.

On Christmas Day when he came to you what like was his upper lip, was there any sign of a moustache there? — Yes, a very short moustache. I should say it had been growing for about a fortnight — a little more than a fortnight. It was about ¼ inch or 5-16ths long.

About a fortnight before Christmas, on one occasion when he came into your premises, had you noticed whether he had made any change in his appearance from the time you had seen him just before? — Yes. He had had his moustache shaved off. That was about a fortnight before Christmas as near as I could say. When he came in I passed some jocular remark about him having his moustache off, and I said he looked rather comical with it off, and that was all the remark that I passed. I shaved his upper lip that day. That was the only occasion I shaved it; I did not take his moustache off; it was off previous to him coming in that morning. I had shaved him before that, although I had never touched his moustache. I had a talk with him upon what line of business he was in. He said he was a dentist. He said he was expecting to start business, but he was waiting for his partner coming.

From where? — Well, he mentioned several places. He mentioned Queensland and San Francisco, and I understood he was expecting one coming from either the one or the other of these two places. On one occasion, I should say from about three weeks to a month before Christmas, he wanted to sell me some blankets, curtains, and kitchen furniture. He said they were quite new. I remember him calling on one occasion, either on the 22nd or the 23rd of December, to get shaved. He said that he was going away to Queensland. I understood him to say in that week, on the Wednesday, that was somewhere about Wednesday, the 30th. He did not say anything as to his taking his passage, but I understood he was to sail on the following Wednesday. I asked if his wife was going. He said not at the present time; the weather was too cold, and she was going to follow in the summer time.

Did he mention anything about the Sloper Club to you on one occasion? — Yes.

What did he say about that? — He was talking about being able to get a shave on Sundays, and I understood him to say he could get one there or at the Central Hotel. I did not know what the Sloper Club was or where it was. On another occasion, in the first week of December, he mentioned that he had lost a diamond pin. He said he was sorry that he had lost it, and I advised him to go to the police about it, and he said it was best to leave them alone as much as you could.

Could you give me a description of the man? — I would say he was a well-built man with broad shoulders, about 5 feet 8 inches or 5 feet 8½ inches in height. There was a peculiarity about his nose. I would not describe it as a twisted nose; I would describe it as a nose that had been broken.

Were you shown the prisoner in Glasgow Police Office on 21st February? — I would not say what date; it was the day he arrived back from New York.

You can take it from me it was the 21st of February; could you identify him as the man you have been talking of in your evidence? — Yes, Mr. Anderson. I had no doubt about it. The prisoner is the man.

Cross-examined by Mr. M'CLURE — I think you have got a better reason for knowing that the prisoner is the man. Did he not tell you that he was going abroad on the 25th of December? — He came in on the 25th of December and said he was going by the "Lusitania."

He told you he was leaving Glasgow that night? — Yes.

On the 25th of December, and that he was going to travel to New York by the "Lusitania"? — Yes.

Of course, you know that the "Lusitania" does not go to Queensland, do you not? — Yes.

It is for New York? — Yes.

Must you not have gathered that his destination was not Queensland, but New York? — Yes, I knew that on the Friday, on the Christmas Day, when, he told me he was sailing on the Saturday.

It was on the 22nd or 23rd that he mentioned Queensland? — Yes. He said he had a partner there that he had written for, and that he was going to start business. He mentioned about San Francisco also.

Did you know that he was going to San Francisco and not to Queensland when he spoke to you on the 22nd or the 23rd? — I did not know which place he was going to; he mentioned both of them.

Do you think you cannot have been mistaken about that? — No, I do not think I can; he mentioned both places distinctly.

On the 22nd or 23rd, did he mention San Francisco? — Yes, about that date he did.

And then he told you on the Friday, the 25th, that he was travelling by the "Lusitania," and leaving Glasgow that night? — Yes.

For Liverpool? — He did not say for where, but he was travelling by the "Lusitania."

And that day he lifted his materials from your shop? — Yes.

Tell me what apparatus he had? — His shaving brush, soap, sponge, pot, and hair brush.

Does it come to this, that in the earlier days of his acquaintance you sold him a full shaving equipment? — No, he had it with him. I sold him two bottles, one for his hair and one for his face.

Then he deposited his own shaving equipment at your shop? — He brought it from his house a week or so later.

As he was leaving on the Friday for Liverpool he got them all back again? — He took everything with him.

Was the moustache which he had when you saw him during that week quite noticeable? — Well, it was quite noticeable to me.

His hair is very black? — Yes, rather black.

And grows speedily? — Yes, it grows very quickly about the chin — not so quickly about the upper lip. I had a good opportunity of seeing him.

Then do I take it that your evidence is that about a fortnight before Miss Gilchrist was murdered he had had his upper lip shaved? — Yes.

But that from that date it had grown? — He had it shaved at night, and I shaved it the next day, and it was growing after that.

And the time you shaved it was about a fortnight before the 25th of December? — About ten days or a fortnight.

Before that week which we have been discussing had Slater informed you that he was going abroad, without mentioning his destination? — He had mentioned that business in Glasgow was very quiet; he thought that he would clear out of it, that he could do better elsewhere.

Can you tell me how long it was before the 25th December that he said that? — Probably about a month before.

By the COURT — What kind of business did you understand him to refer to? — A dentist's.

Cross-examination continued — When he said he was going away to New York by the "Lusitania," did he speak to you quite freely? — Yes.

Did you see during that week when he was attending your shop, on the 22nd or 23rd, and again on the 25th, any sign of excitement about him? — None in the least.

Did you see any difference in him from the previous time he had been in your shop being shaved? — Only as regards his dress.

What was that? — He had a peculiar kind of vest on that I had never seen on before; bar that there was nothing else.

Re-examined by Mr. MORISON — What sort of dress did he usually wear when he came to your place? — Generally a full suit.

Did he come in different suits sometimes? — Yes.

Did he sometimes have an overcoat and sometimes not? — Yes.

Have you seen him wearing a light fawn-coloured overcoat? — No, not to my knowledge.

Have you seen him wearing a dark blue overcoat? — Yes.

When he told you he was going on the "Lusitania" on Christmas Day, was that the first you had heard of his going away by the "Lusitania"? — Yes.

And was it when he was getting his shaving things from you that he gave you that explanation, or when was it? — During the time that I was shaving him.

Did he give any reason why he was going by the "Lusitania"? — No.

Can you tell us just what he said about that? — He just said that he was going away that night, that there was nothing in Glasgow, there was no money stirring in Glasgow, and he was going away that night to go by the "Lusitania" on the Saturday.

Did you ask him where he was going to? — Not that I know of.

Did you know where he was going to? — Not that I know of; I had no knowledge.

Re-cross-examined by Mr. M'CLURE — Except to New York, by the "Lusitania"? — I did not know he was going to New York; I knew he was going by the "Lusitania," but I did not know his destination.

By the COURT — Can you tell me how near the time of the murder it was that you saw the prisoner? The murder was on Monday, 21st December? — Yes.

How near can you come to the date before that when you saw him? — About the Friday.

The 18th or so? — Yes; about that time.

Then, after 21st December, Monday, what was the next? — Well, I would not be sure whether it was the Tuesday or Wednesday; it was one or other of these two days.

Did you see the photographs in the papers of Oscar Slater? — I saw the photograph after I had given my evidence.

Front of houses, 15 and 14 Queen's Terrace
Showing close door of Miss Gilchrist's house (left); main door of Mr. Adams' house (right)
The windows of the dining-room are the two above the close door.

HELEN LAMBIE, examined by the LORD ADVOCATE — I am a domestic servant. I was in the service of Miss Gilchrist for three years and two months before the date of her murder. She and I were the only occupants of the house. The house was one of six apartments and a kitchen, the apartments being a dining-room, a drawing-room, parlour, and two bedrooms. Both the bedrooms look to the back court, and one of them is a larger room than the other. The dining- room and the drawing-room look out on West Princes Street. Miss Gilchrist had not very many visitors. There were some business gentlemen who came to the house. The most frequent visitor was Mrs. Ferguson, an old servant. Miss Gilchrist always slept alone. I know that she had a great many jewels. (Shown production No. 20.) Miss Gilchrist did not keep jewels in that box; she kept papers and accounts there. She had that box (No. 20) on the dressing table in one of her bedrooms. She kept her jewels in her wardrobe in her bedroom. She wore jewels every day, usually a ring and a brooch. She sometimes wore more than one ring. When she went out to tea and to dinner she wore more jewels. It was the usual practice for me to go out errands in the evening. I usually went out on my errands about six o'clock, and sometimes a little later. The house is one storey up, and the outer door is on the stair landing. The door on the stair landing is secured by a common lock, a patent lock, and a Chubb. When I went out on my errands I left the door on these two locks, and I took the keys with me. The locks I left the door on were the two upper locks. These two upper locks are shown in the photograph No. 5. There is a door to the entrance to the close, and that was usually kept closed on a check lock. The entrance to the close is about four or five steps up from the level of the pavement. The door at the entrance of the close is opened by raising a handle inside the house. There was no one living above us at the time of Miss Gilchrist's murder; we were the only people inside the close. On 21st December a girl friend of mine paid a visit to the house; she was the only visitor that day. Miss Gilchrist rose out of bed that day about twelve o'clock, and she was out of doors in the afternoon and returned about 4.30. I went out for a newspaper that night, and I had some other messages to do after that. Miss Gilchrist gave me Id. for the newspaper and 10s. for the other messages. I looked at the kitchen clock just before I went out and I saw that it was just seven o'clock. I intended to go for the newspaper first and come back to the house, and then go out again for my other messages; I had done that before. I went to St. George's Road for the newspaper. Before leaving the house I saw Miss Gilchrist sitting on a chair at the dining-room table, with her back to the fire. She had her spectacles on and was reading. There was an incandescent light lit in the dining-room, and there was a light lit in the lobby. There was no light in the bedroom. I went into the dining-room and saw Miss Gilchrist just before I left, and it was then that she gave me the money. I recollect laying down the half-sovereign on the dining-room table before I left. I intended to get it when I came back with the paper. I had to go to St. George's Road for the newspaper. It would take me about three minutes to walk from the house to the newspaper shop in St. George's Road. It usually took me ten minutes from the time I left the house till I got back with the newspaper. Miss Gilchrist knew that that was my practice. I noticed the light in the lobby as I left. When I went out I closed the door on the two locks and took the two checks with me. I closed the door at the stair foot. It was raining when I went out. When I left the house I did not go straight to the newspaper shop in St. George's Road. I spoke for a minute or two to a constable in plain clothes whom I met at the corner of West Princes Street and St. George's Road. When I bought the newspaper I went straight back to the house. I would be away from the house about ten minutes altogether. I did not see anybody except the constable in West Princes Street when I walked along to St. George's Road. West Princes Street is a very quiet street. When I got back to the house I noticed that the door at the close mouth was open, and was not as I had left it. I went upstairs. I did not have to use my check to open the door. I saw a wet footmark on two of the steps when I got inside the door. I had not observed that when I was coming down before. The footmark was on the two steps nearest the close. When I got up to the landing I found Mr. Adams there, a neighbour who lived down below. He was never a visitor at the house, and I was astonished to find him there. He said to me that there was a noise in our house, and that the ceiling was like to crack. The house door was locked. I unlocked it with my keys. I said to Mr. Adams before I went in, "Oh, it would be the pulleys." By the pulleys I meant the clothes-lines in the kitchen. We had an arrangement for drying the clothes in the kitchen, consisting of lines and pulleys. Mr. Adams said that he would wait and see if everything was all right. When I unlocked the door I saw a man coming, and I stepped back. The man was coming from the direction of the spare bedroom. I saw that the light was lit in the spare bedroom. It was not lit when I left the house. The light in the lobby was still lit. The man came through the hall and passed me, and went downstairs. I then went into the kitchen and saw that everything was right there. I -went into the bedroom. It was all right there. Then I went into the dining-room and saw Miss Gilchrist lying on the rug in front of the fire. The rug was over her head. I did not see her face. I went out and told Mr. Adams that something was wrong, that the man had done something to Miss Gilchrist. Mr. Adams had stood behind me when I unlocked the door. The man, when he passed me, was very close to me. I noticed that he held his head down. When he passed me I turned round to look at him, and I got a good look at him. I heard him going down the stairs. He did not go down rapidly; he went deliberately. I went instantly into the house. The man, when I saw him first, was coming from the direction of Miss Gilchrist's bedroom. He had nothing in his hand. He was wearing a dark cap, a fawn overcoat, and dark trousers. I did not notice what else he was wearing. His coat was open. He was about 5 feet 7 or 5 feet 8 high. No. 43 of the productions is the coat that he wore. I am not sure about the cap he wore, but it was dark. He did not say anything as he passed. I noticed his walk; he was forward a little. I noticed a peculiarity about his walk; it was a little shaky. When I saw my mistress lying on the floor with the rug over her, I ran downstairs, and then I stood on the steps when I got down. Mr. Adams also ran downstairs, and then he went in the direction of Queen's Crescent. I saw Mr. Adams' sisters come out, and I told them what had happened. I did not see any trace of the man when I got downstairs. When I returned to the house I saw Constable Neill there. I did not go straight back to the house; I went and told Miss Birrell, a niece of Miss Gilchrist's, what had happened. Dr. Adams was summoned. There were several people in the house when I got back. Later in the evening Detective Pyper asked me to go into the dining-room, and I then saw my mistress's body exactly as I had seen it when I first went in. Her head was near the fender and her feet were towards the door. She was quite dead. Next day I identified her body in presence of Dr. Glaister and Dr. Galt. I did not find anything out of its place in the dining-room. After going into the dining-room I went into the spare bedroom, and I saw the box there with the papers. The papers had been taken out of the box and were scattered about on the floor. I never saw anybody visiting the house the least like the man who came out of the bedroom when I opened the door that night. That night I missed a brooch that belonged to Miss Gilchrist. The brooch was usually kept in a small open dish on a dressing table in the bedroom. It was a diamond crescent brooch, and about the size of half a crown. I saw it in the dish on the Sunday, the day before the murder. I saw beside it a gold and diamond ring which was left, while the brooch was taken. I mentioned to the detectives that night that I had observed that the brooch had disappeared. Miss Gilchrist had that brooch all the time I was in her service, and she sometimes wore it during the day. On 12th January I left Glasgow along with Mr. Adams, a girl Barrowman, Mr. Warnock, and Detective-Inspector Pyper. We sailed by the S.S. "Baltic" for New York, and we arrived there on 25th January. On 26th January I attended at the Law Courts, along with Detective- Inspector Pyper, Mr. Adams, Mr. Warnock, and the girl Barrowman. I remember standing in a corridor there along with Detective-Inspector Pyper, Mr. Adams, the girl Barrowman, and Mr. Warnock.

Do you remember whether Mr. Warnock and Mr. Adams went into the Court- room before you? — I think Mr. Warnock went in, but I could not say for Mr. Adams. The girl Barrowman and Detective-Inspector Pyper remained with me. When I was standing in the corridor, and before I went into the Court, I saw three men coming along the corridor. I had a good view of them. They passed me.

Did you say anything to Inspector Pyper when you saw the three men? — No.

When they passed you did you say anything to him? — Yes. I said, "There is the man that passed me in the hall." He was one of the three men. I recognised him by his height and his walk. When I saw him he had a dark overcoat and a bowler hat on, different from the hat and coat that he wore when I saw him in the lobby. I saw part of his face in Glasgow, on 21st December, immediately after he passed me and when I turned round, just before he went down the stairs. I recognised the man in the corridor as the man I had seen in the lobby of the house. He was the middle one of the three men. I recognised his walk. No one had asked me to point him out at the time when the three men walked up the corridor and passed me. I just pointed him out myself. I was not told that he was coming or anything of that kind. I just recognised him as one of the three that passed me. No one asked me any question about it when I spoke to Detective-Inspector Pyper. That was the only chance I had of seeing him before I went into the Court-room. After the three men passed me, Detective- Inspector Pyper, the girl Barrowman, and I went into the Court-room. The two men who were with the man that I recognised were in plain clothes. I do not know who they were; they were strangers to me. When I went into the Courtroom I found a number of people there. I sat in a chair. I saw the man in the room that I had seen in the lobby of the house. I recognised him and I identified him. He was sitting on my left side, about a yard away. Beside him were sitting Mr. Goodhart and Mr. Miller. Mr. Goodhart was between him and me, but I had no difficulty in pointing him out in the Court in New York. I had to look round the back of Mr. Goodhart to see him, and I did that; and when I looked round I pointed him out. There were a number of other people in the room besides these three. I had no difficulty in pointing him out as the man. I had never seen any photographs of him before. There were in the room at the time Mr. Warnock, Detective-Inspector Pyper, the girl Barrowman, and Mr. Adams. Where I was sitting I had to lean round to see the man. I came home a day or two afterwards. On Monday night, 22nd February, I went down to the Central Police Office, and was taken to a room where there were a number of men. I pointed out in that room the man I had seen in the lobby, the same man as I had seen in New York. I had no difficulty in recognising -him. When I first went into the room at the Central Police Station the man was dressed in a dark suit. About fifteen minutes afterwards I was again shown the man dressed in the coat No. 43 of productions. He had not either of the caps under label No. 46, nor had he the hat No. 44. It was a lighter cap than No. 44.

Look at No. 46 again? — It was neither of these caps. I recognised the coat No. 43 as the coat he was wearing the night I saw him in the lobby. The cap that he was wearing the night I saw him in the lobby was a dark cap, and something of the shape of a Donegal hat.

Is No. 44 what you call a Donegal? — Yes, something of that shape.

By the COURT — The cap he had on when I saw him at the Central Police Office was a light green cap. When I saw him in the lobby he had a dark cap on. I am not sure what was the difference between it and the one I am shown now.

Examination resumed — You are not sure that that is the cap? — No. I think it was more like the light one in No. 46 as regards shape. I was in West Princes Street on the Sunday night before the murder, between six and a quarter to seven. I saw a man passing back and forward on the street on the same side as I was on. I did not take any particular notice of him. I could not very well recognise the man I saw that Sunday night. He had a dark overcoat on and a bowler hat. I could not say whether he was clean shaven or not. He had a sallow complexion. The prisoner is the man I saw in the lobby, and he is also the man I saw at New York and in the Central Police Office.

Cross-examined by Mr. M'CLURE — You say that you could not recognise the man that you saw in the street on the Sunday? — Yes.

And so little did you think of that that you did not mention it to any one at all till the 12th of March? — Yes.

You had been in America in between, and you had been examined by the fiscal different times, but you never thought of the man walking on the street on 20th December till 12th March? — No.

You said that you could not recognise him? — Not the one that I saw on the Sunday night.

As regards the identification of the man who was in the lobby that night, I wish to ask you a few questions When you left the house that night you have told us that the dining-room gas was lit? — Yes.

And the lobby gas? — Yes.

How was the lobby gas lit? — Half -on.

By the COURT — Was it incandescent? — No.

Cross-examination continued — An ordinary burner? — Yes.

Has not the lamp a burner inside the glass? — Yes.

What kind of glass is it? — Stained glass.

Is it thick stained glass? — Yes.

What are the colours? — Blue colour.

When you saw the man in the lobby how far was he from the door? — About 6 yards.

The whole lobby is not 18 feet long, is it? — I think it is.

When you saw him first was he standing or walking? — Walking.

And coming out of the door at the far end of the lobby? — I did not notice him coming out of that door; he was past the door a little.

He had only about 3 or 4 yards to walk to you and go out? — I think it was about that.

You have told us that you did not recognise any of the caps here as being the cap that he was wearing that night? — I am not sure.

You said something about a Donegal hat, but it is not a thing split in two like that? — You can split it in two.

Is it not an ordinary cloth cap with a rim right round about it? — Yes, and that is one with a rim like it.

Can you say that it was a Donegal hat, or is it just thinking back that the idea has come to you? — No.

Is that only an impression? — No, I am sure of that.

Next, I am going to ask you about the coat; what is it that made you use the expression that not only was the coat one which was like that, but that that was the very coat? — That is the coat.

The same sort of coat? — That is the coat.

Do you say that he wore a coat like that? — Yes.

But that is all? — Yes.

And dark trousers? — I am sure he had dark trousers.

I wish to ask you this — what did you recognise in him which enabled you to identify him afterwards in America? — By his walk and height, his dark hair, and the side of his face.

Was it only his walk and his height and dark hair? — Yes, and the side of his face.

Is it not the fact that you were not quite sure of him to begin with, when you saw him in America? — Yes, I was quite sure.

I wish you to be careful about this. In America when you were asked if you saw the man present you said first, "One is very suspicious, if anything"? — That is a mistake.

These were your words? — Yes, I quite believe it.

When the question was put to you you said, "One is very suspicious, if anything"? — Yes, because he walked up and down.

That was after you had seen the man walking. You were asked, "Now, do you see the man here you saw that night," you said, "One is very suspicious, if anything"? — It was the way it was put. It was what Miller meant. That was the expression he used.

But you used these words in America. The question was put, "Now, do you see the man here you saw that night?" and your first answer was, "One is very suspicious, if anything"; what did you mean by that? — Because it was the same man.

Why did you say that you were suspicious? — It was a mistake.

You mean that you did not say what you intended to say? — Yes, I did not intend to say that.

I suggest to you that you were not quite sure of him then? — Yes.

Why did you say that you were only suspicious? — It was a mistake.

You have told us to-day that you recognised him by his face? — The side of his face.

I will read the question again that was put in America, "Now, will you describe, please, this man that you saw on that night that passed you at that doorway, the height if you can tell, the clothes if you can tell, or such other description of him that would in any way identify him to anybody else?" and your answer is, "The clothes that he had on that night he has not got on to- day, but his face I could not tell" — did you say that? — Not the broad face, but the side.

The Commissioner said, "What did you say about his face?" and your answer is, "I could not tell his face; I never saw his face." Now, when you said these things in America and stated on two different occasions that you never saw his face, why do you go back upon that now and say that you saw the man's face and recognised him? — I did see his face.

Why did you say that you did not see it? — There has been a bit left out.

Did you say in America that you did see his face? — I do not remember.

Why do you say that a bit has been left out? — If I did not say it there I could not say it here.

If you had never seen it in the lobby, why did you say "I could not tell his face: I never saw his face"? — I did not see the broad face. He held down his head, and it was only the side of his face.

But you did not say that? — I know that I can say that.

You are speaking now at a distance of many months — four months and more — since you saw the man in the lobby when your recollection was fresh, on the 26th of January, just a month after the occurrence, and you said that you had never seen his face at all. How do you explain that? — Because he did not look at me, but I saw it when he was going down the stair.

Why did you not say so? — I am saying it now.

Why did you not say it then in America, when you were asked? — (No answer).

The question was put to you repeatedly, and you gave that answer? — That was what I meant, but he did not look at me, and I did not see the broad of it.

Here is another question I wish to ask you about — what did you mean in America by saying that you could not tell the man's face, that you never saw his face, if, in point of fact, you did see it, so as to help you to recognise it — what do you mean by that? — Nothing.

You meant nothing by it, and that is the statement that you made within a month of the occurrence — why do you contradict it four months afterwards? — It is not four months since I said that. It is less than that.

It is three months then, is it? — Yes.

February, March, April — why do you contradict three months after you made the statement in America the actual words that you then used, that you could not identify the man by his face? What are you going on now? — I am going on his face now.

I do not understand that. Listen to this question. You were asked by Mr. Miller in America, "Did you not state a moment ago that you did not see the man's face?" and your answer was, "Neither I did. I saw the walk. It is not the face I went by, but the walk"? — Yes, I said that.

Is that correct? — Yes, quite correct.

What do you mean by saying that it is his face if it was his walk that you spoke to in America? — I saw his face — the side of his face.

You said in America that you were going on nothing but his walk, and you did not see his face. Do you contradict that now? — Yes.

What has led you to change your evidence from what you gave in America? — Nothing has led me.

Was the thing fresher in your recollection when you were examined in America, just one month after the occurrence? — Not one bit fresher.

Why did you say in America, confidently, that you never saw the man's face, and that you did not go by his face, and only by his walk, if, in point of fact, you had seen his face, and you recognised him? — It was the side of the face. That is all I saw.

Why did you not say in America that you saw the side of his face? — I could say it if I went to America now, but I was excited the first day.

And then you would give different evidence? — No, it would be the same.

I ask you again, can you give any explanation at all? — None.

Why did you say that it was his walk and not by his face, and that you had never seen his face, if, as a matter of fact, you did see his face — can you explain why you said so? — No.

You were examined twice over in America. You were taken back the second day, and asked some more questions? — Yes.

You were asked again on the second day whether you had seen his face, and you said, "No, sir." Q. The photograph was not shown to you at all? — A. No. Q. And you never saw any? — A. No. Q. The photograph of defendant before you came into Court? — A. No, sir. Q. And you had never seen his face?

— *A*. No sir." On the second day you made the same statement; that you never saw his face. Why did you repeat the same mistake on the second day, if, in point of fact, you had recognised the man by his face all along? Have you not been talking too much about this thing. Miss Lambie? — I had the side of his face.

By the COURT — Why did you not say in America that you saw part of his face — that is the question? — I cannot say anything for myself for saying that, but I know that I did see the side of his face.

Cross-examination continued — Did you say that the man was clean shaven? — Yes. I saw that from the side.

No hair about his face at all? — No.

You say that you identified the man by his walk? — Yes.

What is the peculiarity of the walk to which you allude? — He shakes forward a little.

What do you mean by shaking forward? — There is a peculiarity about his walk.

You might name what it is, because I wish to know — do you mean that he bends forward? — A little.

Is that all you mean by shaking forward? — No.

What else do you mean? — That is what I mean.

You say that he bends forward — is it his head that is bent forward? — A little.

Anything else? — His walk.

What about his walk? — Nothing about his walk, but I identified him by his walk.

But there is nothing peculiar about it? — Yes.

There is nothing peculiar about his walk, but you identified him by it? — There is a peculiarity about his walk.

What peculiarity? — I identified him by his walk. I cannot tell you. His head bends forward, and he shakes himself a little.

How does he shake himself? — His shoulders.

What does he do? Does he jog them up and down like this (showing)? — Yes, but not so much as that.

As I understand, this peculiarity in the walk, by which alone you were able to identify him in America, you only saw while the man walked 3 or 4 yards along the lobby, which was dimly lighted. Is that so? — It was not dimly lighted.

I thought you said that the gas was half on? — Yes, if you put it full on it goes up in a blaze.

It was quite a good blaze? — Yes.

I wish to read another passage from the American evidence which sums it up. The question is put to you, "And all that you remember about the difference in his walk from other men's walk is what you have shown us here when you were standing up?" and you say, "Yes, sir." Did you give them an exhibition of how it was done? — Yes.

" And that is all you have to identify this man as the man you saw in the hallway?" and you say, "Yes." That is another passage in which you refer to the walk as the only means of identification — "why did you on all these occasions say that it was the walk only that you have in your mind — that you had not seen his face, and could not recognise him by that? — It was quite a good identification.

The walk? — Yes.

Why did you not mention this appearance of the man's face in America when you had three or four different opportunities of doing so? Can you give any explanation? — Because when I saw him with his own coat on I was surer than when I saw him without it.

When? — On the Monday night.

But why did you not on four different occasions in America answer that his face had something to do with the identification? — If I had seen him with his own clothes on — the clothes that he had on that night — I could have done so.

How did that alter his face? — It made a big difference.

Now when you saw him walking down the corridor in America, the man was walking down between the assistant marshal of the United States Court and a man with a large badge? — Yes.

And you were do-mi there for the purpose of identifying the man? — No.

What were you there for? — I do not know what we were standing there for.

Did you not know that you were going to see the man Slater at the Courts? — No, I did not know.

What did you go to do? — To identify a man.

The man Slater? — Yes.

And when you went there did you know that he was the party that you went to identify? — Yes.

When he was being brought down the corridor did you know that that was the man who was coming? — I picked him out myself.

But you knew that he was coming? — No, I did not know that he was coming.

You knew that the man was coming down, or a man who was being brought for identification? — No, I picked him out myself.

And you said that that was like the man who was in the Court? — Yes.

Of course, -when you came back ix) this country, you had no difficulty in recognising the man who was shown you at the Central Police Station as the man you had seen in America? — Yes.

You knew before you went down that you were going to see him again? — Yes.

You did all the identification you had to do in America, and you saw that it was the same man at the Central Police Station and the same man who was here? — Yes.

I want to know, when you were standing at the door with Mr. Adams, and had opened the door, is it not the case that you went in towards the kitchen at the time the man was coming forward? — The first time I was standing at the door.

Had you not gone inside? — No.

Where was Adams? — Behind.

Is it not the case that you turned round to go to the kitchen, and that the man passed by when you were inside by the kitchen door? — No.

How close did the man pass to Adams? — A little further than the distance that he passed me, because he was further back than I was.

Was Adams not standing right in the doorway, and the man who passed him almost touching? — Not when I was there.

But you were both there together? — Yes.

Is it not the case that what happened was that you opened the door and passed in towards the kitchen, and that the man walked down and came right past Adams, who was still on the door mat? — Yes.

So that the man passed Adams as Adams was standing on the door mat? — Yes; we were both on the door mat.

Was Miss Gilchrist in the habit of going out with jewellery on her? — Yes.

What did she wear when she was out? — If she was going to her tea she put on more jewellery.

But what would she wear if she was going to tea? — A better brooch and more rings.

Did anybody in the neighbourhood know that she was a person who kept jewellery in her house? — Some may.

But do you know of any? — Yes.

Who? — A girl friend of mine whom I told that Miss Gilchrist had a lot of jewellery.

But except for that girl you have no notion of anybody who knew? — No.

Did you yourself inform a man named Nugent that she had jewellery? — Yes.

How long ago was that? — Shortly after the New Year.

Last New Year? — The year before.

When you went out, were all the windows snibbed except the kitchen window? — Yes.

And the kitchen window was slightly down — 2 or 3 inches at the top? — Yes.

When you got back to the house were the windows in exactly the same position as when you left them? — Yes.

Did Miss Gilchrist use to have a dog? — Yes; an Irish terrier.

What happened to it? — It got poisoned.

When was it poisoned? — I think on the 7th or 8th of September.

Was that thought to be done by somebody? — I did not think it, because I thought that it might have eaten something; but Miss Gilchrist thought it was poisoned by somebody.

Intentionally to kill the watch dog — was that the idea? — She did not say.

What did she say? — She thought it was a shame of anybody to do such a thing to a dog.

Was that all that passed? — Yes.

There is one thing I wish to ask you also — did you, when you saw the man coming down the corridor in New York, say this, "Oh, I could nearly swear that was the man"? — Yes.

If that was your state of mind, do you mean to suggest now that you had no doubt of any kind? — Yes.

Why did you say that you could nearly swear it was the man? — It was from the distance. I thought that it was the man; I knew that it was him.

Re-examined by the LORD ADVOCATE — Did you just get a glimpse of him as he was coming down the corridor? — Yes; he was walking on.

And you recognised the gait in the corridor? — Yes.

Do you recollect whether anybody asked you any questions about him when he was coming down the corridor? — No.

Did you know that he was to come that way? — No.

Do you recollect whether you saw his face in the corridor? — Yes.

As he passed you? — Yes; he looked at me when he passed me.

Is it the case that when you opened the door that night, when you just caught sight of him, he had his head down? — Yes.

And as he came across the lobby did he keep his head down the whole time? — Yes.

So that you could not see his full face? — No.

Was that what you meant in New York when you said that you did not see his face? — Yes.

Is it the case that when you turned round after he had passed you, you got a glimpse of his side face then? — Yes.

Did you have a better opportunity of seeing his gait, the way he walked, than you had of seeing his face? — Yes.

Did you look at him till he disappeared? — Yes.

As he walked across the landing? — Yes.

Did Nugent visit you at Miss Gilchrist's house? — Yes.

Did he, on one occasion at least, have a meal in the house? — Yes; dinner.

And did Miss Gilchrist know that he came into the house, and was she quite pleased that he should? — Yes.

Is Nugent the least like the prisoner? — Not the least like.

When did you last see him? — Last September.

Where does he live? — Carfin.

Were you a good deal excited and agitated over at New York? — Yes.

You were asked a great many questions in the two days? — Yes.

Did you get a better chance of looking at the man when you were in the room than you had in the corridor? — Yes.

Had you any doubt about him when you saw him in the room? — No.

Look at No. 5; that is the photograph which you now have before you, showing very well the outside door and landing? — Yes.

Now, does it show the mat on which you were standing when the man passed you? — Yes.

And was Adams standing immediately behind you? — Yes.

Does the door open inwards? — Yes.

And did the man come from your right hand? — Yes.

When you opened the door did he come out of the bedroom, or did you see him coming out of the bedroom? — No; he had come out.

Was he near the bedroom door when you first saw him coming towards the door? — He was on the other side of the door that goes into the bedroom.

Can you see in that photograph the bedroom door? — No.

Look at this other photograph. Does that show the bedroom door? — No.

Will you tell me what is the room we see into in that photograph? — The dining-room.

What is the door on the right-hand side? — The kitchen door.

When you are looking at the photographs are you standing as it were on the same side as the bedroom door? — No.

What door is opposite the bedroom door? — There is another bedroom opposite the bedroom door.

Look at No. 5/5. You see the bedroom door? — The side of it.

Which of the two doors is it? — The second one in.

Is that the door from which the man came? — Yes.

Do you see the top of the lobby light there? — Yes.

At the bottom of the light is there a coloured light quite open? — Quite open.

And was the light, such as it was, at its best? — No.

Could you have made it better? — Yes, by screwing it higher.

Quite sufficient to enable you to see the man? — Yes, quite sufficient.

By Mr. M'CLURE — You saw the man's walk in the corridor in America? — Yes.

Now, after he went into the room you saw him, but you saw him sitting down? — Yes.

Was that the only time you saw him walking as he came down the corridor? — Yes.

How far did you see him walking down the corridor? — 12 yards.

And inside, while you saw him close at hand, you did not see him walking? — I saw him walking into the room, coming through the corridor.

But after he was in the room you did not see him walking? — No; he was sitting all the time.

The Court adjourned at half-past six o'clock.

SECOND DAY — TUESDAY, 4TH MAY, 1909.

The Court met at ten o'clock.

JOHN PYPER, examined by the LORD ADVOCATE — I am a detective inspector in the Western District of the Police, Glasgow. About twenty minutes to eight on Monday, 21st December, while I was in the Western Police Office, a telephone message came from Dr. Adams, of No. 10 Queen's Crescent, to the effect that a lady had been murdered at 15 Queen's Terrace. Along with Detective M'Vicar I immediately went to the house, and arrived there about five minutes to eight. I went upstairs and found Constables Neil and Brian in charge. The house consists of six rooms and kitchen on one floor, and there is only one other house upstairs to which the stair gives access, that house being unoccupied. The lobby of Miss Gilchrist's house is about 18 feet long and about 10 feet wide. Entering from the door the dining-room is immediately on the left hand side. The dining-room is about 21 feet long by 15 feet wide. I observed that the handle for opening the door at the stairfoot was just inside the lobby, between the dining-room door and the door leading to the house. I entered the dining-room, and I found the deceased lady lying on her back in front of the fireplace, with her feet stretched out towards the door. Her right hand was stretched out, and her left hand was partly on her breast. Her face and head were smashed and very much disfigured. I saw a set of false teeth lying on the rug just opposite her head. There were sparks of blood on the grate, on the fire-irons, and on the coal scuttle. I saw a half-sovereign on the rug beside her left hand. Constable Neil picked up that half-sovereign and put it on the mantelpiece. I searched the house carefully to see if there were any implements left which had caused the injuries, but I found nothing. The poker and tonga in the dining-room were lying on the fender in their usual place. (Shown plan No. 6 of the productions.) The red mark indicates where the deceased lady was lying. (Shown photograph i/o of productions.) In that photograph I see the handle by which the door at the foot of the close is opened. It is shown in the corner between the door of the house and the door of the dining-room. Although the poker and tongs bore sparks of blood upon them, there was nothing to indicate that they had been used to maul the old lady. They certainly had not been used. When I was in the house the servant, Helen Lambie, searched it to see if anything was amissing, and she reported to me that she missed a crescent brooch in the bedroom, and nothing else. She pointed to a wooden box on the floor of the bedroom, that box being label No. 20. She also pointed out a number of letters and papers scattered on the floor.

By the COURT — Helen Lambie was a little excited, but not much, considering the position of matters.

Examination resumed — Label No. 19 contains the letters and papers that were scattered on the floor of the bedroom. (Shown plan No. 6 of 62 the productions.) The bedroom where these papers and the box were found is the room in the top right hand corner. The servant Lambie told me that these papers and letters used to be kept in the box. There was a diamond ring and there were two other rings in. a little glass dish on the toilet table. Helen Lambie told me that the missing brooch used to lie on that same table. There were also on the table a gold bracelet in a case and a gold watch and chain. Nothing else in that room or in the other rooms had been interfered with. None of the furniture was displaced. The hearth rug was very much stained with blood. Constable Neil informed me that he had found a skin rug lying on the top of the deceased's body when he went in. When I went in that skin rug was lying beside her head. (Shown labels No. 16 and 17.) No. 16 is the hearth rug and No. 17 is the skin rug that was lying on the top of the deceased. On the dining-room table I found a magazine and the lady's spectacles lying beside it. Her spectacle case was attached to her dress. The outer door of the house is secured by a Chubb lock, a patent lock, and a common lock. I saw that the common lock was used for securing the door at night, while the patent and Chubb locks were used by day. It required two keys to open the door. I instructed Inspector Rankin to search the back green the following morning as soon as daylight came in. When the back green was searched a piece of an old broken auger was found; that was the only thing that was found. (Shown production No. 25.) That is what was found in the back green. I took possession of the two rugs, the coal scuttle, and the deceased lady's spectacles. I superintended the removal of the body to the Royal Infirmary. It had been previously identified in presence of Professor Glaister and Dr. Galt. A description of the missing brooch was circulated amongst pawnbrokers and jewellers and dealers. (Shown production No. 42.) That is the description of the brooch. I was present on several occasions between 24th December and 7th January in the house at 15 Queen's Ten-ace, when a large quantity of jewels were found. A list was made by Mr. Dick, and it is correct; I saw it and went over it carefully. On 22nd December, 1908, I saw a purse containing a number of tickets, and so on, found in the pocket of the late Miss Gilchrist when the body was undressed. I took possession of it and of the half- sovereign. Superintendent Douglas took possession of a box of matches and a spent match which were found in the bedroom. (Shown production No. 18.) These were found in the bedroom. The servant girl said that these matches did not belong to the house. On the morning of 24th December I saw the girl Mary Barrowman, and she described to me a man she said she had seen running out of Miss Gilchrist's close on the night of the murder. On the same day I forwarded that description to Superintendent Ord at the Central Police Office, and on the following day, 25th December, the description appeared in the newspapers. (Shown productions Nos. 38, 40, and 41.) These are the newspapers containing the description. These would appear in the five o'clock edition of the evening papers of 25th December.

Did you cause inquiry to be made that night at the house, 69 St. George's Road, at which Anderson, a dentist, was said to live? — No, I did not cause inquiry to be made, but I learned that inquiry was made. I learned that Anderson, the dentist, disappeared that night. On the 12th of January, 1909, I was instructed to accompany Mr. Warnock and the witnesses Lambie, Barrowman, and Adams to New York, and I accompanied them. I arrived in New York on the 25th of January, 1909. On the following day I went to the

Court there with the witnesses. The examination was conducted in Mr. Commissioner Shield's room. Before the examination commenced I was standing in a corridor leading to the room. The girls Lambie and Barrowman were with me. They were standing beside me.

Will you describe to us in your own words what happened when you and the two girls were standing in the corridor? — I was looking along to see if Mr. Fox, the Crown agent, was coming along, when both of the girls touched me on the shoulder at the same time and said, "Oh! there's the man away into the Court." I did not see the man to whom they referred; there were quite a number of people there; I could not distinguish one from another. I knew that some men had passed me; there were quite a number of people going out and in to the Court. The girls identified some man — both at the same time. I had not told them to expect the man to come along the corridor; I told them nothing. I had not asked them any question. That came entirely from themselves. I then went into the room. The girls went in also. I did not myself see Slater enter the room. When I went into the room there were a number of people there. There were about forty, I should say, altogether. I think there was one woman, at any rate, besides the two female witnesses. Some of them were sitting; some of them were standing. It was a comparatively email room. It was crowded all round about. I and the two witnesses stood at the window near the Commissioner's desk. He was seated at a table with a desk on it. Slater was seated on a chair alongside one of the marshals behind his two agents, Mr. Goodhart and Mr. Miller. He was not handcuffed or distinguished in any way. The girl who was giving evidence had a seat, but the others were standing. I was present when the girl Helen Lambie gave her evidence. In my presence she was asked to identify the man she saw on the night of the murder. She stood up and looked round the Court, and Mr. Goodhart, who was immediately in front of the accused, also stood up and spread out his frock coat, and, after looking round for a little bit, she looked over his shoulder and pointed to the accused. She had not any hesitation about him. She had to lean over to get a sight of him. I was present when the girl Barrowman was examined. She pointed him out also, and said that he was very like the man. She had no hesitation. I cannot tell myself whether it was the same man that they had seen going in; I did not see him going in. I was present when Mr. Adams was examined; he said he was very like the man, but he was not too confident, or something to that effect. Adams was examined when there were a number of men in the Court-room too. No assistance of any kind was given to him. He was just asked to look round to find the man that he had seen that night. In Adams' case, as in the case of the two girls, Slater was seated, but he was told to stand up afterwards. I took possession of all Slater's luggage in New York. Each parcel was sealed with the Government seal. There were seven packages. They were portmanteaus and bags. There were initials on some of them — "O.S." They were brought to this country in the same ship that I and the prisoner and Mr. Warnock came back in. I arrived in Glasgow on the 21st of February, 1909. I came home in the same ship as Slater. The witnesses came in a different ship. I was in charge along with Mr. Warnock. When we arrived the accused claimed all the baggage, and I opened and searched it. In a black leather trunk I found a fawn-coloured waterproof coat. (Shown label 43.) That is the coat. Slater claimed it as his property. I found in the same black leather trunk a hammer. (Shown label 47.) That is the hammer. Slater claimed that as his property. I examined the coat and hammer. I found several dark stains on the coat, in front, mostly on the shoulders. The polish appears to have been removed from the handle of the hammer, particularly towards the bottom end of the handle. It seems to be scraped from the middle to the head. I further found in the baggage a soft hat. (Shown label 44.) That is the hat. Slater claimed that hat. I also found two cloth caps. (Shown label 46.) These are the caps. Slater claimed these caps. There was a large quantity of clothes in the baggage — overcoats, coats, and other things of all descriptions. I saw no dentist's apparatus. Mr. Warnock and I went over the baggage very minutely. On 21st and 22nd February the accused was shown to a number of witnesses. He was placed among other eleven men, all in plain clothes. Some of these men were railway men and the others were police officials, but all in plain clothes. The accused was allowed to take up any position among them that he pleased. I was present when a few of the witnesses identified the accused. I was present when Adams, Barrowman, Armour, and several others identified him — I forget their names. These witnesses had no difficulty in identifying him. They were not assisted in any way. On 23rd February I met the witnesses Barrowman, Bryson, and Nairn in West Princes Street. They pointed out to me the places in the street on which they said they had seen the accused. I observed that from all these places there was a good view of Miss Gilchrist's house obtained. I remember in particular the position that Nairn pointed out. He pointed out the corner of Queen's Crescent and West Princes Street, and said that he was standing just at the corner of the turning looking towards the house, and from there a good view could be obtained of the house. There is a lamp 8 yards from the entrance with a very good incandescent light. There is a good view obtained of the house from the stair opposite. That is the place where Bryson pointed out that the man was standing. When the witnesses were asked to identify Slater he was dressed in a dark suit with a dark overcoat and bowler hat. He was afterwards shown to some of the witnesses with a fawn coat and the soft hat (label 44). All the other men had their hats on — bowler hats. I recollect of Slater's dress being changed when the witness Barrowman was asked to identify him in the Central Police Office. She asked that his hat should be put down a little, and he did so. Then she said, "A little further, please, pull it down a little further," and he did so. Then she said, "That is how it was on that night" or "That is it." The hat that he had on was the soft felt hat (label No. 44). (The witness showed how the hat was placed on the head.) The witness Annie Armour identified the accused with the dark clothes and the bowler hat. The witness Euphemia Cunningham also picked him out. The witness William Campbell seemed to have a doubt about him. He said he was like him, but he seemed to hesitate a little. The accused was dressed in the fawn-coloured coat for Helen Lambie to identify him, and she did so without any difficulty. There is a gas jet at the top of the first flight of stairs, that being the first jet that you come to. Then there is another jet at the deceased's door, and there are two on the top flat. The jet at the door is close by the door, projecting from the wall. In the lobby of the house there is a pendant hanging from the ceiling in about the middle of the hall with one burner. It is open below. I have on several occasions seen the light on the wall of the stair just outside the door lit, and the light in the lobby lit with the door open. There is quite a good light. Photograph No. 5/7 shows the jet immediately outside the door of which I have spoken. Photograph No. 5/6 shows the jet in the lobby. If the dining-room door was open and the gas lit there that would make the light in the lobby stronger. I have tried the light. I have seen the light at the door on the stair lit with the light in the lobby half-on. There is quite a good light. The light in the pendant when it is half- full on is quite strong enough for usual service. I had an opportunity on the night of the murder immediately after I came to the house of seeing the lights as I have described them.

By the COURT — When I say that the light is quite good I mean that by it one could read ordinary print.

Examination resumed — If the girl was standing just at the entrance from the door into the house and looking in, I should say that she should have quite a good view of a man coming out of the bedroom towards her. The full length of the lobby is 18 feet. From the entrance door to the door of the bedroom which was lit, and where I saw the box and the papers scattered, the distance is 12 feet, I should say. If, as the man passed, the girl turned round to look at him, she should see him quite well on the stair with the gas lit. West Princes Street is a very quiet street in a quiet residential locality. If the man ran from Miss Gilchrist's house to Kelvingrove Subway station his direct course would be along this quiet street and turning to the right at the end, that being rather less than half a mile. I have walked the distance; it takes seven and a half minutes. From end to end there is very little traffic either of foot passengers or otherwise.

It is very seldom you see any one there except an odd passer-by. Kelvinbridge Subway station is not the nearest subway station to the place where the murder was committed. There is one at St. George's Cross, which would be nearer, but in order to get to that station one would require to pass through more traffic and to get into a busy thoroughfare.

Cross-examined by Mr. M'CLURE — Are you detective inspector? — Yes.

And may we take it you are the person who had charge of this case? — Yes, I believe I have made the greatest inquiry in connection with the matter, but not altogether.

Had you charge of the arrangements under which the witnesses attended to identify the accused? — No.

Who had charge of that? — Superintendent Ord.

You said it was about ten minutes to eight when you arrived at the house on the night of the 21st? — About five minutes to eight.

And you examined the witness Lambie that night, or got a statement, at any rate, from her? — Yes.

You said you were also present in America when Lambie made a statement? — I was.

Now, in the boat over did you have any conversation at all with the witnesses? — None whatever relative to the case.

About the crime? — None.

Were the witnesses Lambie and Barrowman companions during the voyage? — They were.

Were there just you three and Mr. Adams on board the boat of a party? — And Mr. Warnock.

By the COURT — Did Lambie and Barrowman occupy the same cabin? — Yes, Lambie and Barrowman occupied the same cabin.

Cross-examination continued — Did you and Warnock occupy the same cabin? — And Adams; we occupied a cabin of a different class.

You had spoken, of course, to Adams about what he had seen on the night of the 21st? — Oh, yes.

Did you revert to that in any way on the way across? — No.

You never mentioned at all the purpose of the voyage on the way over? — They knew the purpose of the voyage; they were being sent there to see if they could recognise the man as the murderer — as the man they had seen that night.

When you got across to America I think a man called Mr. Fox was attending to the Crown's interests? — That is so.

And on the day when the man Slater was to be exhibited to the girls for identification Barrowman had first of all an interview with Mr. Fox in his office? — Yes, I understand she had.

At which two photographs were submitted to her? — Photographs of newspaper cuttings.

Why did you show the photographs in America? — I did not show the photographs; it was Mr. Fox who showed them.

You were present at the time? — I was present.

Were these shown as the photographs of the suspected man? — Yes.

And did they show a dark complexioned man with a dark moustache? — Well, I could not take it as that; they were very defective photographs.

Did they show the general appearance of Slater? — I presume they did, but they were very bad photographs; no person, to my mind, could recognise any person from them.

Do you say that they were not the least like the man? — Yes, I say they are not the least like the man.

Were they recognised in your presence by Barrowman as being the man? — She could not recognise the photographs.

You say so? — I say so.

Now, when you were out in the passage and this man was brought down a corridor, as I understand, you did not see him come down the corridor at* all? — I did not.

The two girls were standing together? — They were standing together.

And what view could they have; for how far could they see the man walking down the hall if they were looking? — Well, it depended on where they had seen him first; he might have been close up to them before they observed him, or he might have been 20 yards away from them; it is a long passage.

What were you attending to when the girls were looking? — I was looking in the opposite direction; they were standing at my back.

And the first thing that attracted your attention was when you heard one say—? — Both touched me on the arm at the same time.

Both on the same arm and at the same time? — Yes. And both spoke at once? — Both spoke at once. And both said the same thing? — Both said the same thing. What did they say? — They said, "Oh, there's the man away into the Court"; I looked into the Court, but I could not distinguish any person.

Is it not curious that the girls used the same words at exactly the same time and clapped you on the shoulder? — It may seem curious, but it is the fact all the same.

Did you hear the girl Lambie say, "I could almost swear that's the man"? — I cannot say that I heard her say that.

Did you hear her make any remark at all till the remark you have quoted to us? — No, that was the first.

Are you prepared to say there was no remark made till the one quoted by you? — Yes, there was no remark made.

So that if the girl Lambie says, "I could almost swear that's the man," are you in a position to contradict that? — She may have said it after that, but not before that.

I am talking of before. — She did not say that to me before; I did not hear her say so.

Do you mean that the remark was never made, or that you did not hear it? — I did not hear it.

Is that all you can say? — That is all I can say.

Did the girl Lambie tell you how she recognised him? — She said in the Court-room from his walk.

Was that the first you heard about it? — Yes. In the Court did he walk at all? — He did not.

So that if she recognised him by his walk it must have been only from having walked down the passage outside the Court when you were looking the other way? — I presume so.

Did she say she could not recognise him by anything else? — No, I did not hear her say that.

Were you in the Court? — I was.

I mean you give that now as your accurate testimony? — Yes. "When she was in the Court, do you say that she positively identified the man at the first attempt? — No, I do not think she did; I think she said, "That is very like the man," or some words to that effect.

Did she use the words when she was asked, "*Q*. Now, do you see the man here you saw that night? — *A*. One is very suspicious, if anything"? — Yes, she made a remark something to that effect.

And that was the first remark she made? — After the accused was in the Court.

That was the first remark she made under examination by Mr. Fox? — I think it was. "I am not quite sure, but I think it is"; I did not hear all that she said, but I remember hearing that remark.

I mean, one would like to know how much you heard and how much you did not; were you present during the whole examination of Lambie. and are you prepared to tell us what she said? — I am not prepared to tell you all she said.

But you remember this, however, that the first remark she made was that she was suspicious, if anything? — Yes.

Now, later did you hear her say that "The clothes he had on that night he has not got on to-day, but his face I could not tell"; did you hear her say that? — I did not.

How can you account for missing that? — Well, there was a big noise going on, bustling about, and you could not hear all that she said, and she spoke very low; I was some little distance from her, and I could not hear all she said, but it is quite possible she said that.

By the COURT — How far would you be away from her? — About 8 yards, I would say.

Cross-examination continued — I want to ask you this; I think you said that she identified the man without hesitation? — Commissioner Shields asked her to look round the Court-room and see if she could point to the man that she had seen in the hall that night, and she, as I have already described, looked round and pointed out the accused.

Do you say it was without hesitation when she began by intimating that she was very suspicious, if anything? — Well, it depends on how you put it.

Well, it is a great deal in this case how it is put; would you tell me whether you call that unhesitating identification? — Certainly it was hesitating.

Not confident? — There seemed to be a want of confidence to speak straight out, or stupidity, I could not say which; she seemed a bit excited.

She was stupid and excited? — There is no doubt she was.

And hesitating? — Yes, a little.

What did she say about his walk which identified him? — Well, she was asked to exhibit the manner in which he walked, and she tried to do so.

Was there anything very characteristic? — No, I could not see very much about it.

You saw nothing very peculiar in it? — No.

Nothing to distinguish the walk from the walk of many other men? — Well, the only thing that I have seen about his walk is that his left foot is a little in-toed.

Is that the only thing you have observed? — That is the only thing I have observed.

What is the thing called a shaking of the shoulders which is mentioned by Lambie? — I should fancy a rocking gait.

Have you observed a rocking gait also? — Slightly.

Why did you not tell us that just now when you told us all you observed was a hen-toe? — That is all; he shoves his shoulders forward a little.

And you have told us you have seen nothing characteristic except the hen- toe? — It is not very conspicuous.

Do you say that an identification from Slater's walk would be one that would impress you? — Not from his walk altogether.

Suppose you had nothing but the walk to go upon, would you have any confidence in your identification? — No, not quite absolute.

By the COURT — Is there anything characteristic in his walk at all, and, if so, what? — Well, he is a little in-toed in the left foot, and when he lifts his foot to walk he throws out his knee a little; you require to look minutely at him before you observe it.

Nothing that would attract your attention specially? — No, I do not think I would take any particular notice of it, except if I was asked to do so or taking particular notice.

Cross-examination continued — Did you hear the girl Lambie say over in America in answer to a question this — the question is "Q. Didn't you state a moment ago that you did not see the man's face? — A. Neither I did, I saw him walk; it is not the face I went by, but the walk"; did you hear her say that? — Yes.

And you say now that the walk is not one that would attract your attention? — It is not very conspicuous, except if you are looking carefully at the person.

Is it a thing that you would expect to be picked out in a walk of some 3 yards across a lobby? — It depends entirely upon how you are looking at it; one might observe it and another might not.

But you would have no great confidence in that being picked out? — No.

By the COURT — The period of observation would be something under two seconds? — Yes.

Cross-examination continued — Do you not think that the attention of the people, if they were looking at a man who was in the lobby, would be mainly directed to his face? — I should think so, but it is not for me to say; I do not know how they were looking.

If you saw a stranger in the lobby you would not look to see if he had a hen -toe at first? — No.

Did the woman Lambie tell you he was a clean-shaven man? — She told me he was clean shaven that night.

If she never saw his face could you understand that? — Well, it is difficult.

Now, I may take it, I suppose, from you who were present time after time in the examination in America, Lambie was asked by what she identified him, and she said consistently that she did not see his face, and it was by his walk alone? — That is so.

The girl called Barrowman was examined in America also in your presence? — Yes.

Did you say that when she was first examined in America her identification was confident? — She picked out the man. She was asked to point him out.

Did she say, "That is the man"? — She pointed out the accused.

But did she say that that was the man? — She said that he was very like the man at first, and then she said that he was the man.

Do you remember her being asked whether the man was there, and she replied, "That man here is very like him"? — Yes.

Then the two lawyers got talking, the one saying, "The man here is something like it," while Mr. Fox said, "Very like it," and the witness said, "I said something like him the first time, and then very like him after I had said something like him"? — Yes, I remember that.

Would you call that a confident identification? — No, I would not.

That identification by both of these women which I have put to you just now is after the remark outside the Court which you say you heard? — That is so.

And in the case of Barrowman, at least, it was after she had seen the photograph of the man? — Yes, quite so.

Can you tell me if there was anything special about the man by which the girl Barrowman claimed to identify him? — She identified his nose principally.

Was not that the only thing she professed to go by? — Yes, by the face.

And her previous opportunity of seeing that had been, I think, while the man was running past' her on the street on 21st December in the vicinity of a lamp? — Yes.

She described it, I think, as a twisted nose? — Yes, or turned a little to the right side.

I ask the accused to stand up. Does that man's nose turn any way to the side when you regard his front face? — No, I do not see much twist in it. It is somewhat peculiar, but otherwise there is no twist in it.

The profile creates an impression which the front face does not? — That is so.

By the COURT — Did the witness Barrowman say for about what distance she had had the man in view? — She explained to me at the time that when he came down the stair he stood at the bottom step leading to the pavement for a little, hesitating, looking to the right, and then he turned towards her and ran past her while she was standing under the lamp post.

Cross-examination resumed — Now, after this identification in America the girls were brought back? — Yes.

And, of course, when they were taken into the police office to identify Slater they were looking for the man they had seen in America? — I presume they were.

May I take it that when they looked for the man they had seen in America among these policemen at the police office and the two railway officials there was no person who bore a foreign appearance or was the least like Slater except himself? — That is so.

I wish to ask you this — I have already asked detective Trench — have you considered that to be a fair way of conducting an identification, to have the only man that they hope to identify in the presence of a number of others who do not bear to him the least resemblance? — I do not know that it is for me to say whether it is fair or not. It is a matter over which I had no control.

What you mean is that you do not want to criticise your superior officer? — I do not.

When you said that Slater was allowed to take up any position he chose in the police office that was really no use, was it? He was the only man the least like Slater there? — Yes, he was the only man like Slater.

Did he ask to be allowed to take up any special position? — No.

He allowed you to show him off to these people in any position you chose? — Yes,

Did you march them and make them turn their heads, and so on, and Slater never objected? — That is so.

Were you present when Miss Cunningham was down to identify the man? — Yes.

Had she been shown a photograph before? — I cannot tell.

During the process of identification did you put any coat upon the accused that was not his own? — Yes.

Whose coat did you put on? — I cannot tell you. I did not put it on, but I saw one put on.

Was he identified in that coat? — Yes.

By whom? — The girl Barrowman.

Did the coat differ from the waterproof coat? — No, it was exactly the same pattern and colour.

Was it a different length? — No, it was the same length.

Why did you not put on his own coat? — It was not available at the time.

Was the coat you put on a short coat? — I did not put it on.

Did you see it put on? — I saw him with a coat on, but I do not know where it came from.

Was it down to his knees? — It was below his knees a little.

In America you took possession of the man's luggage? — Yes.

Have you been through the whole of his luggage? — Along with Mr. Warnock I went through it all. I did not take an inventory.

You went through it with the express purpose of finding garments in his baggage which would tally with the descriptions you had got? — Yes.

And also with the purpose, I suppose, of looking for blood stains? — Yes.

How many suits had he? — A great number.

May I take it that there is no coat, waistcoat, or pair of trousers found in his baggage which bears the slightest appearance of blood? — I saw no blood on any of his garments.

And you searched for it? — Yes.

Did you find among his baggage anywhere a pair of brown boots? — No, I did not see them.

If you had found them you would have produced them. Did you find other boots? — Yes. I think there was another pair of boots and some slippers.

Do you mean there was only one other pair of boots? — Yes. There may have been more, but I do not remember of there being more.

But were you not searching? — I looked over them; I looked simply for garments that he was described as having been seen wearing, or I was looking for blood stains.

You searched for brown boots and you got none? — I did not see any brown boots.

Did you get what is commonly called a Donegal hat anywhere? — The hats that have been produced are the only ones I found.

Were there not a great many hats and caps in the man's baggage? — I did not see a great many.

There were more than those that have been produced? — I do not remember seeing any more hats.

I put it to you there were about seven or eight hats and caps in his baggage? — That is possible. I did not see them.

Who would see them? — Mr. Warnock may have seen them.

There is none that you would describe as a Donegal, and you did not find brown boots. Did you find any checked trousers? — No, I do not think so. There were some striped trousers.

Any fawn-coloured spats? — No, no spats at all. I saw none.

A great many coats? — Yes.

And they were all minutely examined? — Yes. Now, with regard to the coat which is produced, what did you find on it? Anything of an incriminating nature? — I cannot say what that is. There were several dark stains, but what these are I do not know.

Are they very minute? — They are not very distinct, but they are visible.

Did you see the room and the body lying in it? — Yes.

Was there not a good deal of blood splashed about? — Yes.

Were the fire-irons not merely covered with mere sparks, but with a great deal of blood? — Quite a number of sparks.

Does not the coal scuttle show lots of blood? — Yes, quite a number of sparks.

Are there not splashes running right down it? — Yes.

There are signs on it of blood having run down the whole length of the coal scuttle? — Yes.

There were bits of the woman's brain found on the rug? — Yes.

And a great deal of blood on the carpet? — Yes.

There was a rug over the top of her? — Yes.

Had not that rug blood on both sides? — Yes.

Did it bear the appearance of having been put over her to cover her after she was dead? — Yes.

There was blood on the top side of the rug as it lay over her. I show you label No. 17, the second rug. Was not the hairy side of that rug covered with blood — was there not a lot of blood on it? — Yes.

Was not the end doubled back over the woman? — It was lying flat, I think.

Was it not doubled back over the woman? — Yes, it was lying right over her body. That may have been caused by the constable who lifted it before I went there. He lifted it and saw the body.

Was she lying upon this rug to any extent? — No, she was not on it at all. She was lying on the other rug.

This second rug was on top of her? — Yes.

With the hairy side on the top of her body? — Yes.

If that be so, how would the blood which appears on the other side have come there? — The place was smeared with blood, and throwing it off and throwing it down blood may have gone on to the other side in that way.

Would it not have come from the weapons or from the clothes of the murderer? — It might have come from the clothing or from the other rug. It could have got there in different ways.

From the condition in which you found the room, and from the amount of blood that was spread about, can you conceive of the man having executed that murder without having splashed himself a good deal with blood? — I would fancy he would have stains of blood over his clothing.

And a lot of it? — Yes, I should say a good deal of it.

Would you expect more than the doubtful spots you found upon that waterproof? — Yes.

By the COURT — Why? Was there any mark of blood behind the chair? — No.

Suppose the old lady was hit from behind, would the person so hitting her, do you expect, bear any mark of blood if no blood was found behind the chair? — I cannot say; the blood might have been on the clothes or it might not. It depends on how the blow was given.

There was no blood on the table? — No.

Cross-examination resumed — Was not the chair set in to the table as if the old lady had been reading at the table? — Yes.

And her back was rather towards the door? — She was lying on her back.

Must not the murderer have dealt considerably with her body, because was not her chest found completely collapsed? — I cannot tell.

The ribs were all broken? — The doctors will be able to speak to that.

Do you not know that? — No.

Was not her head all smashed to pieces? — Yes, I saw that.

Do you not think that the probabilities are that the person who achieved all that upon the body of the woman would exhibit blood stains on himself? — It depended on how the sparks of blood went and how the woman was struck.

By the COURT — But you assent to the probabilities? — Yes.

Cross-examination resumed — The probability is that there would be a great deal more blood than was found on that coat? — I should fancy that there would be some sparks of blood.

By the COURT — Do you know where that red rug usually lay? — It usually lay in front of a sideboard, on the other side of the room altogether from where the lady was sitting. It had evidently been lifted from there and thrown over.

That would all increase the probability of the man getting some blood on him? — (No answer.)

Cross-examination resumed — Now, about the hammer (label No. 47). Take it that the head of the woman was extensively smashed so that the brains were out in portions and the head had deep holes in. it and the ribs were smashed, is that weapon that you have in your hand the least likely to have caused injuries to that extent? — It would certainly have required great force to do it.

Is it in the least likely to be a weapon to do it? — I would not say it is not.

But would you say that it was? — I would not like to say.

Would it not give the man a great deal of trouble and an immense deal of labour to smash the woman up in that way with a hammer like that? — It would require a great deal of force.

Would you not have thought that a hammer with a larger surface would have been necessary for the extensive smashing that there was in this case? — I would not say so.

That is a light hammer? — Yes, but if it was used with force it would have bad effects-.

Show me where the blood stains are on that hammer? — I do not say that there are any.

Is it your theory that that hammer has been scraped? — It seems to me to have been scraped.

Is it your theory that the hammer was originally varnished or anything of that kind? — You can see that it has been tampered with in some way. Something has been done in the way of cleaning it up.

Do you see coal dust at the top of the stick where it joins the hammer head? — Yes.

Towards the lower part of the shaft, where there is a difference between it and the upper part of the shaft, does not that look as if a dirty hand had grasped the hammer? — It is possible.

Is there, in your opinion, any more difference between the top and the bottom of that hammer than what you would expect if the hammer had a plain wooden handle and a dirty hand had been in the habit of grasping it at the foot? — It is rough at the top as if it had been rubbed with something.

Look at that new hammer which we have produced. Is that an exact replica of the hammer (label No. 47)? — Yes.

The same size exactly? — Yes.

Has it not got the same kind of handle? — Yes.

Is there any more signs of scraping on the one than on the other? — The one is new and the other has been used.

But is there any sign on either of scraping up towards the hammer head? — Yes, the new hammer is all the same, whereas the other is smooth at the top and the bottom half is rough.

I show you label No. 48. Did you find in Slater's box four different implements exactly corresponding to the four implements which I show you on this card? — Yes.

Were these recovered? — I did not recover these.

Suppose somebody with a hand covered with coal dust gripped this new hammer, would you expect that the clean hammer would become exactly like that after a little use? — It might.

Do you persist at all that there has been obvious scraping? — I cannot say what it has been. I simply say there has been some rubbing. Whether it has been tear and wear I do not know.

You mean rubbing at the lower part? — Yes.

But there is nothing like scraping at the other part? — You call it the upper part.

(The hammers were handed to the jury for inspection.)

You said at the end of your examination — I do not know why you emphasised it — that it took seven and a half minutes' walking to go from the door of Miss Gilchrist's house to a Subway station. Which Subway station? — The station in South Woodside Road.

Is that by Kelvinbridge? — By West Princes Street. It is near Kelvinbridge, and is called the Kelvinbridge station.

Was the person who was supposed to have committed this crime seen at the Kelvinbridge station, or reported to have been seen there? — Yes.

Somebody answering to the description? — Yes.

At what hour? — I do not know. I did not take the statement from the person who spoke to that.

At what hour do you take it that this crime was committed? — It must have been between 7 and 7.15, or between 7 and 7.30.

So a direct run by the murderer — if it was he — on the route you have mentioned should have brought him up there, I suppose, by something about twenty minutes past seven? — Yes.

A walk would have taken him there just after twenty minutes past seven? — Yes.

Then there is another thing I want to ask you; was anybody seen running in the direction you have spoken of? — The girl Barrowman described that the man was running west along West Princes Street.

How far? — As far as West Cumberland Street she took notice of him, she said.

I mean, he did not run straight along to this Subway, but turned to the left along West Cumberland Street? — Yes.

Was anybody else seen running along there? — A Miss Brown speaks of two men running along this direction.

That is two other men entirely separate? — They were two together.

I mean, they were not Slater; they were not the men who went down West Cumberland Street? — Well, I do not know whether it was or not; you will get that from the witnesses.

At any rate, running straight down in the direction of the Subway, there were two men seen running? — Yes, Miss Brown speaks to that.

And then Barrowman says there was a single man seen running, who turned to his left down West Cumberland Street? — Yes.

And was that at or about the same time — both of them? — Well, near the same time.

Is Miss Brown coming? — She is here to-day.

Re-examined by the LORD ADVOCATE — Were there a number of men who were clean shaven in the Court-house at New York? — Oh, quite a number.

Were there a number of clean-shaven men in the Central Office in Glasgow? — There were.

Were all the men different — just ordinary types of men that you see in the streets? — That is so.

Did either of the girls ever point to anybody in the room, either in New York or in the Central Office, except Slater? — Except the one man, no.

Did they ever hesitate between him and somebody else? — Never.

Do you recollect that the girl Barrowman in your presence was asked the question in New York, "Did you see the man here you saw that night?" and then the accused's agent said, "I think she ought to be asked to describe him"? — Yes.

And then she described him? — She described him.

And then do you recollect the Commissioner said, "Is the man in this room among all these men here that you saw that night"? and Barrowman answered, "That man here is very like him"? — These are her words.

And then do you recollect that the accused's agent, Mr. Miller, said, "The man here is something like him"? — Yes.

And Mr. Fox, for the Crown, said, "She said very like him"? — Yes.

And is it not the fact that the girl Barrowman said, "He is very like him"? — Yes.

And then do you recollect the witness saying, "I said 'something like him' the first time, and then 'very like' after I had said 'something like him'"? — Yes.

Now, did she take a careful look at the man? — She did.

It was not a mere casual glance? — No.

She looked carefully at him? — Yes, he was asked to stand up.

And when she had looked carefully at him did she then say he was very like him? — Yes.

And then do you recollect the Commissioner said, "Point the man out," and did she point him out? — She pointed him out.

Without hesitation? — Without hesitation.

Now, do you say the same of the witness Helen Lambie, that she never hesitated between this man and anybody else? — Never.

Did you see anything in his gait apart from the way in which he turned in his left foot; did you see anything in his gait when he moved along which is peculiar? — He puts his shoulders forward as he steps along in a rocking gait, slightly.

Suppose you saw him walking, taking both this rolling movement you have described and this turn of his left foot, would that strike you as peculiar? — Putting everything together it is noticeable, I should fancy; it is observable if you were looking at the person minutely.

And with such light as you saw, and the distance from the room out to the stair, would there be sufficient opportunity for the girl to see his way of walking? — Yes, if she looked to see — if she was looking at his feet.

Or his shoulders? — Yes.

Did you hear her say in New York that the man held down his head as he came out? — Yes.

By the COURT — Did you recover Slater's luggage from the boat? — No, we recovered it from the Government stores in New York — sealed.

You do not know where the box containing the coat and the hammer was during the voyage — whether it was down in the hold or whether it was under Slater's control? — It was down in the hold, and Mr. Warnock had the keys of all the boxes.

Do you know whether, at the time that the warrant was issued for Slater's apprehension, it was known that the diamond brooch which he had pawned was not the same as that which was amissing? — It was known from the very start that it was not the same.

ARTHUR MONTAGUE ADAMS, examined by the LORD ADVOCATE — I live at 51 West Princes Street, Glasgow. It was called 14 Queen's Terrace. It is next door to No. 15, Miss Gilchrist's house, immediately to the west. My house is on the ground floor. It is entered by a front door up six steps from the pavement. My door is on the same level as the door of the closemouth leading to Miss Gilchrist's house. Her dining-room is just over my dining-room. I knew Miss Gilchrist as a neighbour only. I did not visit. My mother and five sisters live in the same house with me. On Monday night, 21st December last, I was in my house after six o'clock. About seven o'clock I was sitting in the dining-room with my two sisters, Laura and Rowena. When I was sitting there I heard a sound like a thud, and three distinct knocks, as if wanting assistance, up above in Miss Gilchrist's dining-room. My sister Laura drew my attention to it.

Did she suggest that you should go up and see if anything was wrong? — She sent me up instantly. The door at the closemouth was ajar. I did not require to ring; it was open. I went right upstairs to Miss Gilchrist's door. I rang the bell three times for certain. I rang it hard — rude rings. Her house door was apparently locked. There is a glass panel on each side of the door. Looking through it I could see quite distinctly that the lobby gas was lit. I listened for any sounds inside the house. After I had been standing at the door for half a minute or so I heard what I thought was the .servant breaking sticks in the kitchen; I could not say what it was; that was only my surmise. It seemed as if it was some one chopping sticks — not heavy blows. At that time I did not know whether Miss Gilchrist's maid-servant was out or not; I imagined that she was in. I know her by sight quite well. I waited fully a minute or a minute and a half at the door.

Did you hear any further sound? — I just heard what I thought was the girl breaking sticks.

Afterwards? — While I was at the door.

But did you hear it going on and then stopping, and then resuming again, or was it continuous? — I formed the opinion that the girl was doing up her kitchen, and that she was not going to open the door. I could not really properly explain it. After waiting for a minute or two I went downstairs again and entered my own house. I left the door at the close-mouth ajar just as I had found it. I went into the dining-room again. I told my sisters the house was all lit up, and I did not think there was anything wrong; I thought it was the girl. My sister Laura thought otherwise. She made me go back again. She thought there must be something wrong. Without sitting down or waiting any time I returned upstairs to Miss Gilchrist's door. I gave the door bell an ordinary good pull. I did not hear any sound the second time. I stood, after pulling the bell; I had my hand on the door bell when I heard footsteps in the close. This was the servant girl, Helen Lambie. When the girl came up I told her I thought there was something wrong, or something seriously wrong; I cannot give you the exact words. She told me that it was the pulleys in the kitchen that I had heard.

Outer side of house door, 15 Queen's Terrace, showing portion of common stair.

Did the girl put two keys into the locks and open the doors? — She opened the door, but I cannot say whether there were two keys or not. I was standing at the back of her. I said I would wait. She opened the door.

Will you now tell us what happened in your own words? — Well, there is a bedroom over there (pointing to the right); say, that is the bedroom, and there is the drawing-room, this is the door where I am standing now. The dining- room is on the left-hand side, and then there is an old-fashioned grandfather's clock between that, and just over on that side of the kitchen. I stood at the door on the threshold, half in and half out, and just when the girl had got past the clock to go into the kitchen a well-dressed man appeared. I did not suspect him, and she said nothing, and he came up to me quite pleasantly. I did not suspect anything wrong for a minute. I thought the man was going to speak to me, till he got past me, and then I suspected something wrong, and by that time the girl ran into the kitchen and put the gas up, and said it was all right, meaning her pulleys. I said, "Where is your mistress?" and she went into the dining-room. She said, "Oh, come here"; I just went in and saw the horrible spectacle, and I said, "Go to the closemouth and stand there till I come back." I went down to St. George's Road, and I could see no people there, but I could see up to Park Road, and could see people in the distance, and I made after him as hard as I could go, but it was no use.

Did you see the man go downstairs? — I saw the man walk quite coolly till he got up to me, and then he went down quickly, like greased lightning, and that aroused my suspicions. He walked coolly till he got past me, and then he went down quickly and banged the door at the foot of the close. I heard him going rapidly down the stair.

Will you describe the man you saw to the best of your ability? — Well, it was a passing view I got of him. He was a man a little taller than me, a little broader in the shoulders; not a well-built man, but well featured and clean shaven, and I cannot exactly swear to his moustache, but if he had any it was very little. He was leather a commercial traveller's type, or perhaps a clerk, and I did not know but what he might be some of her friends. He had on dark trousers and a light overcoat; whether it was fawn or grey I could not really say. I do not recollect what sort of hat he had; I am not sure on that point. He seemed gentlemanly and well dressed. He had nothing in his hand so far as I could tell. I did not notice anything about his way of walking at all.

Did you see him at all after he passed you; did you look round to see him disappear down the stairs? — I got a good view; I saw him run down the stair, but he was too quick for me. I mean he darted down immediately he had passed me.

By the COURT — He left the house door open.

Examination continued — Could you tell he was coming from the direction of the large bedroom? — Yes, now that I know where the bedroom is. I just took a look into the dining-room before I went down the stairs. I saw Miss Gilchrist lying covered up with a rug. with her feet towards the door and her head towards the fireplace, but I did not touch her; I thought my best plan was to make after the man as quickly as possible. When I failed to get on his track I came back to the house. I then found the servant and a constable in it. The constable and I entered the dining-room together. We uncovered the body and found she had been battered to death, but she was breathing — just breathing. I went for Dr. Adams as hard as I could go. I brought another constable, and I 'phoned to the police office. I myself waited in the house for the police; I waited there till eleven o'clock. I had not on my spectacles at the time.

Did you form any sort of idea about the age of the man? — Well, I said in my deposition he was between twenty five and thirty, I thought. I did not hear any sound as of Miss Gilchrist's bell being rung that night. I noticed her bell being rung, but I did not notice it that night. I might miss that. I was occupied at the time in the dining-room. I was tying up a parcel for a young lady to send away some groceries. I do not always notice when her bell is rung. I did not see the girl go out for a newspaper; I got the girl in the close. I did not know at the time that there was nobody in the house except Miss Gilchrist; I know that there were just her and a maid living there — that there were just the two of them. I went to America with Warnock and Pyper, and with the two female witnesses Lambie and Barrowman. When I arrived there I recollect that before going to the Court-house I was shown a photograph in Mr. Fox's office. That was a newspaper cutting.

Was it a good photograph or a bad one as far as you could judge? — I really could not judge from the photograph at all. When we were being examined we were all together in the Commissioner's room in New York. There were a number of people in the room. I did not see Slater come into the room. He was in the room before I came in. When he came in I was standing up against the wall. There were a number of men in the room. I think I sat on a chair when I was being examined. I was asked to point out among the men present the man that I had seen that night. I pointed out Slater, but I did not say that he was the man. I said he closely resembled the man. Slater was the only man I did point out as closely resembling him.

Had you any difficulty between him and the other men there? — The general appearance of the man was all I went by.

Was he the only man amongst all the men pointed out? — Yes, as resembling the man that came out of that house.

From what was it that you judged that he was like the man or resembled the man you saw? — His general appearance.

Did you notice if there were other clean-shaven men there? — Oh, there were all sorts of men. The room was pretty full; there were a good few people there.

Was he handcuffed or was there anything distinctive about his appearance? — I thought he had rather a superior appearance.

By the COURT — There was nothing to mark him out as a prisoner. He was just sitting twiddling his thumbs like that. (Illustrating.)

Examination continued — I came home from America after being examined in New York. I was examined twice in New York, on two successive days, but on the second day there was nothing asked hardly; it was only a word or two. The first day was the day of examination for identification. After I came back to this country I saw Slater again in the Central Police Office. I am not sure of the date, but it was in February some time. I should think there would be a dozen men any way — perhaps more — in the room at the Central Police Office. I pointed out Slater again. I said of him in the Central Police Office the same as I said in New York. I had no difficulty in pointing him out from all the other men in the room in Glasgow, as in New York. I did not hesitate between him and somebody else.

And was it again just from your general recollection and the general appearance of the man? — That is so.

Cross-examined by Mr. M'CLURE — In New York you were all together in a room while. the depositions were made before the Commissioner? — Yes.

And you were taken successively on to this chair? — The second day I was examined; the first day I had nothing to say at all; it was the second day, as far as I remember, that I was asked.

Were you not examined on the 26th of January? — I could not give the exact date.

Was it the day after your arrival? — No, I was not examined that day; it must have been the following day, as far as I can tell you.

Were you present when the girl Barrowman and the other girl Lambie made their statements in America? — Yes.

And they made their statements before you did? — Yes.

And, of course, both Lambie and Barrowman had indicated that Slater was very like the man before you went on to the witness stand to give your statement? — Yes.

And you knew precisely where the man in question was sitting when you went on to the chair? — Yes, I admit that.

So that when he was shown to you in America he was not placed among a lot of other men of the same appearance? — There was Slater, and then came Mr. Goodhart and Mr. Miller, but I knew who Mr. Miller was, because he asked me if my name was Adams, and if I was a Crown witness, and I said yes.

Sitting in a row there was Mr. Miller, that was Slater's counsel or agent in America? — I suppose they are both his agents.

And then Goodhart had something to do with the case also? — Yes, he had got to do with it, but Mr. Miller was pleading.

Mr. Miller was pleading, and Mr. Goodhart was telling him what to plead? — I suppose so.

And Slater was there? — I suppose that is the way of it.

And Slater had been pointed out twice already before you proceeded to give your evidence? — That is so.

And even after all you have heard you do not give an absolutely confident opinion that that was the man? — No, it is too serious a charge for me to say from a passing glance.

Do you say you had a passing glance? — Well, you know the time it takes for a man to come from a room.

You identified him as a clean-shaven man? — I meant from here (indicating the upper lip); but there was very little on it.

Did you not say clean shaven? — If he had a moustache he had not any more than I have got, and that is not much.

You are not clean shaven? — Well, very near it.

I see in America you were asked, "What did his face look like?" and you said, "Just an ordinary face, a sharp-featured man, nothing special about him, clean shaven"? — Yes.

That is what you mean still? — Yes.

Then the agent asked you, and you said he ha-d a hat on; you said, "I think it was a hat, I do not say he had, but I think so"? — Yes, I said it was not a cap; I wanted to explain to him that I could not be sure on that point.

Was it a bowler hat, or do you mean you do not know what it was? — I have said I am not sure on that point; I have said that all along.

You would not identify it as a Donegal hat? — No, I did not know what a Donegal hat was until I was told about it.

You have heard about that now? — Yes, plenty.

Do you know now what a Donegal hat is? — Yes.

Well, it was not that? — No; of course, I did not pay much attention to the hat.

Then I think you were asked, "Did you notice anything remarkable about his gait and walk?" and you said, "No, I thought he walked like a commercial traveller"? — No, I said I thought he had the appearance of a commercial traveller.

And then you were asked "An ordinary walk?" and you said "Just an ordinary walk"? — As far as I could tell.

At the time you went to this door, the door was opened by Lambie, who had the keys? — Yes.

Now, did you stand upon the mat outside? — No, I stood over the threshold of the door.

Where did Lambie go? — Lambie made straight for the kitchen.

Now, when the door was opened the first time was anybody in the hall? — No.

I think I heard you say that Lambie had got along as far as the clock on her way to the kitchen before a man appeared? — That is so.

Then, would it be incorrect for Lambie to say she was at the door when the man passed her? — Well, I think so, but I think the girl was excited.

That is not in accordance with her recollection? — No, I have nothing to do with her recollection.

At the time the man passed you where was Lambie? — She was in the hall.

By the clock, you mean? — No, the man passed, and she went into the kitchen and just came out and told me it was all right. I took that to mean that it was the pulleys in the kitchen.

Where was the man who had come out of the room when Lambie came back and said to you, "It's all right"? — He was down the stair.

Had Lambie gone into the kitchen by the time the man passed you? — No, I think the man had passed me before she went into the kitchen, as far as I remember.

And then, as I understand, if you stood at the door the man was walking towards the door from the right hand side of the hall? — Yes.

And Lambie was going towards the left hand corner to get into the kitchen? — Yes.

Past a clock halfway down? — Yes.

You said you had a passing glance at the man as he went past you? — Yes.

Did you see anything special about his nose? — No.

It did not attract your attention? — No.

His walk did not attract your attention? — No, but his dress did.

But not the hat? — No.

And not the boots; you did not see them? — No.

What kind of trousers had he? — they were dark.

And a light coat? — Yes.

You said that the coat was either fawn or grey; are you definite about its colour? — No, it was a light coat.

That is all you know? — That is all.

How far had the man got down the stair before you started going down after him? — I had just time to go into the room — I looked into the room, and the girl said, "Oh, you go down the stairs as quick as you can," and I went down the steps, and nearly fell down.

Can you give any idea as to how long you would be in the house after the man passed you at the door before you started after him? — Not more than half a minute.

Did you say that he went down like greased lightning? — Yes.

You mean that he went down as fast as he could? — Yes.

And you thought at that time that he was anxious to get away as fast as possible? — I knew he was a thief then.

When you went into the dining-room Miss Gilchrist was lying on her back? — Yes, but I did not uncover her at all the first time.

What had she over her? — She had a big rug over her.

She was lying on the top of the hearth rug, with her head rather towards the fire? — Yes, and with her feet towards the door.

In a diagonal position? — Yes.

There was a lot of blood about her, as you saw afterwards? — Yes.

The other rug that had been produced was laid on the top of her? — Yes.

Do you remember whether it had the hairy side up? — Yes, the hairy side was up.

And the other side was on the top of the lady? — Yes.

Did you notice that there was a great deal of blood on the hair also of that rug? — No, I did not observe that. It nearly made me sick.

You did not look at it too much? — No.

From where you were when the man came out do you think you were in a better position to observe the man than Helen Lambie? — Yes.

Why do you say so? — Because I practically faced him. He did not cross the hall, but walked quite coolly as if the house belonged to him.

Lambie in the meantime was on the other side of the hall, near the clock? — Yes.

You say decidedly that you had a better opportunity of seeing him? — Yes, I have no doubt about that at all.

At this time, I understand, it was your sister, Miss Laura Adams, who asked you to go upstairs? — Yes.

Was Mrs. Liddell also in the house at the time? — Yes.

How long had she been in? — She came in at five minutes to seven with my mother. The whole thing was done by ten minutes past seven.

Re-examined by the LORD ADVOCATE — Would a couple of steps or so take Helen Lambie in so far as you saw her? — She was further in than that.

How many steps was she in? — Eight or ten I would say — perhaps a little more — between the kitchen and the dining-room.

How many steps would she be in at the time when the man appeared? — She was just going to enter the kitchen.

Did she have an opportunity of seeing the man? — Yes, she saw the man, because she stood and stared and did not open her mouth.

When he passed her? — Yes, she had a good enough view of the man.

She turned round? — Yes, she stood and looked, and never said a word.

Was she plainly taken aback? — Yes, thoroughly. That is my impression.

And excited? — I think so.

You saw her turn round? — Yes, she turned round and stood.

Was the man in your view until he disappeared down the stair? — Yes, till he got past me.

Did you turn round a little, too? — Yes.

Is the prisoner the man you saw in New York and the Central Police Station? — I would not like to swear to it. I am a little near- sighted.

Go near to him and say whether he is the man you saw in New York and the Central Police Office? — Yes, that is the man.

He is the man that you think resembled the man that you saw? — Yes, closely.

By the COURT — What kind of light was there in the lobby? — It was well lit. There was an ordinary lamp with, I think, a blue glass, but I could not be positive. It is a nice hall lamp. The house is well furnished.

It was fully lit? — Yes.

Was there any light from the rooms, the doors of which were open, as well as from the lobby lamp? — The only light I could see was from the dining- room.

Did it throw any light into the lobby? — The lobby light there was the light above.

When you saw the man was his head up or down; was there anything noticeable about that? — It might be slightly down, but very little.

It did not attract your attention? — No, I was thoroughly off my guard.

Was he dark or fair? — Dark.

He had a hat on? — I am not certain of that.

Had he a covering on his head or not? — I am not certain.

Had he his coat collar turned up or down? — Just ordinary, I think, so far as I could tell. His dress put me thoroughly off — I thought he was a visitor.

Till he came up to you. you did not pay the special attention that you would have done if you had thought there was anything suspicious? — That is so.

Then when he passed you and ran, you looked at him also? — Yes. By that time you could only see his back? — Yes, that is all I saw. Is it your evidence that what Helen Lambie saw would be a side view, whereas you had a front view of the man? — I had a front view, and she got a good side view.

But you had a front view only at the time when your attention was not drawn specially to him from any idea of wrongdoing? — Yes.

LAURA EMMA ADAMS, examined by the LORD ADVOCATE — I live with my brother, the last witness, at 51 West Princes Street. Our dining-room is immediately below Miss Gilchrist's. I knew Miss Gilchrist as a neighbour.

By the COURT — I had never been in Miss Gilchrist's house.

Examination continued — I came into our own house about ten minutes to seven on the evening of 21st December last. I went to my own room and then into the dining-room, which was immediately below Miss Gilchrist's dining-room. I was reading the paper in the dining-room about seven o'clock. I heard a noise from above, then a very heavy fall, and then three sharp knocks. I looked up and said to my brother, "Miss Gilchrist evidently wants something." I connected the three sharp knocks with Miss Gilchrist's house because at one time we said that if she wanted anything she was to knock, and some of us would go up. My brother instantly went upstairs. He came back in two or three minutes and told me he had rung the bell two or three times, but he thought there was nothing wrong, because the house was lit up, and he heard the girl cracking sticks. I said to him, "That is not cracking sticks," and he said, "If it will please you, I will go up again." When my brother was upstairs I heard something going on, but not so distinct as the knocks. I could not say what the noise I heard resembled. It was very unusual. I advised my brother to go up again, and he went instantly.

Two or three minutes after he went up again what did you hear? — I heard nothing until I heard a rush down the stair. When I heard the rush I said to my sister, "Something is wrong," and we went to look out. One of us went to the window and the other flew to the door. I looked out of the window and I saw the maid wringing her hands. I could then see something was wrong, and I went to the door. I went upstairs immediately afterwards. There was not a soul in the house when I went up. I had to get the key from the maid and open the door.

Was the sound that of some one rushing down the stairs? — We could hear the feet. It must have been my brother and the maid, and probably some one else. It was a rush of feet down the stairs.

Mrs. ROWENA ADAMS or LIDDELL, examined by the LORD ADVOCATE — I am a sister of the last witness, and I reside at 63 Elmbank Street, Glasgow. On Monday, 21st December last, I went along with my mother to her house at 14 Queen's Terrace. I reached the house from the St. George's Road direction about five minutes to seven. My mother is an old lady. Before I reached the door of the house I saw a dark form leaning against the railing, just under my mother's dining-room window. I only saw a dark form, but, as I approached, I looked at the face of the man who was standing there. I gave a good stare — almost a rude stare— and I took in the face entirely, except that I did not see his eyes. He had a long nose, with a most peculiar dip from here (pointing to the bridge of the nose). You would not see that dip amongst thousands. He had a very clear complexion; not sallow nor a white pallor, but something of an ivory colour. He was very dark, clean shaven, and very broad in this part of the head (points to the cheek bone or temple). He had a low-down collar. His cap was an ordinary cap, I think, of a brownish tweed. He was very respectable. The man was just under the eastmost window, the window furthest away from the close, facing towards St. George's Road. He was on the same side of the street. He was leaning with his arm on the railing, nearer St. George's Road than the close entrance. After I passed him I looked over my shoulder, and he glided from the railing and disappeared, and I thought no more about him. West Princes Street is becoming a thoroughfare now a good deal.

But it is a quiet street as compared with Great Western Road, for example? — Yes, it is not a main thoroughfare. I did not look where the man went. The whole thing passed in a few seconds.

Would you recognise the man again? — I believe I have recognised him, I believe so, but, of course, I might be liable to error.

Look at the prisoner? — I cannot recognise him on this side. It was the other side I saw. (The accused turned round with his left side to the witness.) I do believe — I am afraid he was there — he was there at any rate; I believe he was the man that was standing at the railings.

Do you say that just from what you recollect of the appearance of the man's face? — Yes. It was hardly a passing glance; it was a stare. I heard the noise when I was in the house, all but the fall of the body. I joined in sending my brother up.

Cross-examined by Mr. M'CLURE — Have you forgotten to mention to us that the man was wearing a coat? — He had on a big coat.

A tweed coat? — I believe it to be a browNish tweed.

A heavy coat? — I believe so.

Not a waterproof? — I cannot say whether the material was waterproof or not, but it was not what you would call a gentleman's waterproof.

Not like the waterproof that has been produced? — Let me see the collar.

Have you not seen this before? — No; they have not bothered me before but once. Show me the hem.

Did you see the hem that night? — Yes. I am going by the hem considerably, because it was not a thin paper-like edge. It was a hemmed edge, whatever the coat was.

Do you mean a heavy seam inside the edge of it? — It was not like a thin waterproof.

It was not like the waterproof which has been produced? — It was not that material. It was a thick coat. I have stuck to that all along, and I will stick to it still.

You also said it was not a fawn coat? — Well, first of all, I said browny fawn, but Mr. Hart seemed to have a good deal of difficulty about browny fawn, and so I was quite agreeable that it should pass as a coat the predominant colour of which was brown.

You were ready to slightly change the colour to please Mr. Hart? — No. I have said all along that it was brown or fawn. Of course, there are so many shades, you see. 86

Evidence for Prosecution.

R. Liddell

I understand. It was a brown coat and a heavy coat. When did you first make a statement about this man? — On the Wednesday following the murder.

You had not thought of this man for two days? — He never came back to me for two days. The murder was so unusual and exciting that everything else was out of our heads.

Your brother was the first man on the spot? — Yes.

Did you not mention this man to him? — I mentioned it on the Wednesday, and they laughed at the matter.

Why? — They said, "What was the man doing at the railing? What had he to do with the murder?" That was very reasonable.

May I take it your family treated your alleged man at the railing as rather a jest? — They did, and they said, "There are quite enough mixed up in this miserable affair," and why should I have anything to do with it.

When you were taken to identify this man at the police office, did you not say that he resembled the man slightly? — I said in front of the prisoner, when Mr. Douglas asked me, "Yes, slightly." He was in his blue coat then.

Is that still your view? — I saw him again in another coat. I went back to look at him, and then I got the thicker coat as I had seen it. He was not standing upright; he was bending, and had the appearance of a delicate man even at that time. He was drawn together.

Was your first impression of him that he was a delicate man? — he had not the robustness of youth to look at.

The man you saw against the railings you thought was delicate? — He was not standing as a robust young man would. He was rather drawn together.

Were you rather surprised when you saw a man of Slater's build down at the police office? — Very much.

It was not like the man you had seen? — The face was there, but in that coat he was totally different from what he was in the first coat.

You would never have recognised him in the first coat? — No; but a tailor, you know

You had never seen him really till this day in the coat which you thought he was wearing that night? — I had never seen him since I looked at him that night.

On what date was it that you went to the police office for the purpose of identifying him? — I cannot remember, but I could easily find out. I went down with the crowd.

Did you see any other man like him? — No.

He was the only man who was the least like the person you recollected? — Yes; I scanned him closely as a matter of form. P would rather not even say that he resembles the man, but, still, I am on oath, and, being called as a witness, I must say

You must say as near the truth as you can speak? — Yes.

Then, do you go back from your original statement that he was slightly like? — No. I told Mr. Douglas that he strongly resembled him. and I said, "May I look at him again?" because if I could have only said that he was not a bit like I should have been pleased, but when I saw him

87

Oscar Slater.

R. Liddell again he came back so strongly on me. Then he had a cap on; it was pretty well down, and I got the face much better.

The delicacy you spoke of was totally absent? — No. He did not look the same figure in this waterproof — he did not look so nice as in the blue coat. He was a fine figure in the blue coat.

When did you see him in the blue coat? — In the row of people to be identified.

The waterproof did not show him so well off? — No.

Neither the waterproof nor the blue coat is the coat that you saw him in that night? — No.

Re-examined by the LORD ADVOCATE — Do I understand you to say that it was by his face you judged? — Yes. I was shown his photograph in the paper, and I could not tell that I identified him. When I went down to see him I thought that he was not certainly the man I had seen, and therefore going down I said to myself — of course I had heard, I confess, about the beautiful blue coat — I said to myself I shall only make for the features that are strong in my memory, and if they satisfied me then I could identify him again. The figure and the clothes came as secondary to me. I do not know whether I was right or not.

When you say the features had strongly impressed themselves on you, do you mean the side face that you saw? — Yes. I could not recognise any other.

You did not see the full face? — No, nor the other side. They are both quite different.

May I take it that your identification is entirely from your view of the side face that you stared at? — Yes. First I thought he was a loiterer, and I have a special animus against loiterers, and I was beginning to get bristly. Then I wondered and thought that perhaps he might be waiting for the maid upstairs. Then I thought he might be waiting for one of my sister's pupils, and therefore I stared at him.

And only at that one feature, the side face? — Yes. He was clean shaven.

Mrs. BARBARA MACDONALD or BARROWMAN, examined by the Lord Advocate — I am the wife of Robert Barrowman, a moulder, and I live at 9 Seamore Street, Glasgow. The witness Mary Barrowman is an adopted daughter of mine. She has lived with me and my husband since she was nine days old, when her mother died. She has always considered me and my husband to be her mother and father. She was born on 16th January, 1894. No. 55 of the productions is her birth certificate. She has been known as Mary

Barrowman all along. She was employed in December last with Mr. M'Callum, bootmaker, in Great Western Road, and her hours were from nine o'clock in the morning till eight at night. I remember on Monday, 21st December, Mary coming home late at night. She said that an old Indy had been murdered in West Princes Street, and she went down from her Band of Hope with some of the children to see where it was, as she had seen a gentleman coming out of the close, and she wondered what he was doing. She said that she did not know that the murder had happened then, but she said it was out of that very same close that the man came. She said she was sure she would know his face if she saw him again. I took no notice, because I thought it was just a story, and I said, "Now, Mary, hold your tongue, because you do not know anything about it." There was no more said that night. She said she was sure she would know the man if she saw him again. In the afternoon of Wednesday, 23rd December, when I was going upstairs to my house, I met Detective M'Gimpsey, who lives in the flat immediately below us. I asked him if he had not got word of that man yet, meaning the murderer of Miss Gilchrist, and he said that he had nothing to do with it, that he was in the Northern Department, and that it was the Western Department that had to do with it, and they had got no word of it. I said to him, "Then, if it will do any good our Mary saw a man coming running out, and she would know him if she saw him. She says he has a turned nose, and he came out just at that time." Mr. M'Gimpsey said, "Well, I will tell that, and you may expect the detectives up." I said, "I don't want anything to do with it, because I do not know anything more about it." Following on this conversation a detective came up about an hour afterwards, but Mary was not in. He said he would call back again. Then two came up after that. Mary had gone to a Rechabite meeting, and they said that they would wait for her, which they did, and then she gave her statement to them. That was on the night of 23rd December.

MARY BARROWMAN, examined by the LORD ADVOCATE — I am now fifteen years of age. I am employed with a Mr. Malcolm M'Callum, bootmaker, Great Western Road, Glasgow, and I live at No. 9 Seamore Street, Glasgow. I remember that on the night of 21st December last I left my employer's shop in the Great Western Road with a parcel to be delivered at Cleveland Street, off St. Vincent Street. I left my employer's place about seven o'clock, and I went from Great Western Road up Barrington Drive into West Princes Street, and I walked along West Princes Street in the direction of St. George's Road. I walked eastwards on the south side of West Princes Street. West Princes Street is a quiet street. When I came opposite the close a man came running out of it and knocked up against me. He wore a fawn overcoat, a dark suit of clothes, and a Donegal hat; he had dark brown boots. He ran towards West Cumberland Street, and I could see he turned down there. I was just at the lamp-post near the close when this happened. I saw him coming out of the close. I saw him coming down the steps. He was coming very fast. When he came down to the foot of the steps he turned towards me. He was running. I did not see anything in his hands. I was at the lamp-post when he ran up against me. I was walking towards St. George's Road. It was quite bright near the lamp-post where I was when the man knocked up against me. I had a look at him coming towards me when he got out of the closemouth.

Did you see whether the man saw you? — He knocked up against me. He did not say anything, but just ran on. When he passed me I turned to look after him. I walked after him a bit, but I did not keep up with him. I kept looking in the direction in which he was going. I did not walk fast; he was getting away from me all the time. When ho turned round into West Cumberland Street I stopped and went back in the direction from which he had come. I got a good look at him both when he was coming up to me and when he knocked against me. He was tall and broad-shouldered, and he had a slight twist in his nose. He was clean shaved, and had dark hair. He had a Donegal hat on, and was wearing it down on his face. I got a look at his face. I would know him again if I saw him. When I went back to the closemouth I did not see anybody there, and I went on with my message. When I went home that night I told my mother what I had seen. I told her that I thought there had been an old lady murdered there. I had gone with my message and then back to my employer's shop, and then to a Band of Hope meeting, where I heard about the murder, and then I went back to West Princes Street. I went there because of hearing about the murder. I saw a number of people there. I told my mother that I thought I would know the man if I saw him again. Two nights afterwards, on 23rd December, two detectives came to our house to see me. I told them what I had seen, and I described the man to them just as I have described him to-day. On 12th January I started for America with the girl Lambie, and Mr. Adams, Mr. Warnock, and Detective Pyper. The day I arrived at New York Mr. Pyper took me and the girl Lambie to the Law Courts, where we were to be examined. I remember standing in a corridor or passage along with Mr. Pyper and Helen Lambie, before going into the room. There were three men coming along the corridor, and in between the two men I saw this man, the man I had seen on the night of the murder. I told Mr. Pyper that this was him coming. I had no difficulty in telling that he was the man. Mr. Pyper had not asked me any questions about him in the corridor. Nobody had told me when I was in the corridor that I would see the man pass. I just picked him out that way without anybody speaking to me. I remember Helen Lambie doing the same. I saw him going into the Court-room. Afterwards I went into the Court-room along with Mr. Pyper and Helen Lambie. There were a great number of men in the Court-room when I went in. They were nearly all standing when I went in. I was examined there to see if I could recognise the man. I was seated when I was being examined. There were a number of other men seated in the room at the time I was seated. I was asked to point out the man, and I did so. He was sitting about 10 feet away from me. Mr. Goodhart was standing in front of him when I was asked to point him out.

How did you see him and point him out? — I looked round the Court, and I could not see him, and then I saw a man at the back of Mr. Goodhart, and I looked at that man, and it was him, and I pointed him out. I had no difficulty in pointing him out.

Did you think anybody else in the room was the man except this man? — No.

How did you recognise him; was he dressed the same or not? — No, he was not dressed the same. I recognised him by the face. When I saw him in New York he had a black coat on, with a navy blue collar and a hat. The hat was one of those hard hats, a bowler hat. That was the only dress I saw him in at New York. I came home after I was examined in New York. After I came home I remember going down to the Central Police Office. That was shortly after I came home. When I went down to the Central Police Office I went into a room where there were a number of men. There were ten or a dozen men in the room. I was asked to point out the man I had seen in New York. I pointed him out. It was the same man. That was the man I had seen the night that I was going my message. I had no difficulty in recognising him. I did not think that any of the other men who were there was the man. When I first went into the -room at the Central Police Office he was dressed in the same clothes as he had on at New York. A little while afterwards I remembered that he had other clothes on. He had on a fawn overcoat and a Donegal hat. (Shown production No. 43.) That is the coat that I saw. That is like the coat he had on that night when he knocked against me. (Shown production No. 44.)

Is that the hat? — He had it bashed down in the crown.

Is that the hat? — Yes, it is very like it. That is very like the hat he was wearing the night he knocked against me. I remember asking if he would pull the hat down a little more. I asked that because it was not far enough down, the way I saw him that night. When he pulled it down I then recognised it as I had seen it that night. I said so to the police. It was pulled pretty well down that night. I had no difficulty about recognising him.

Look at the prisoner; is that the man? — Yes, that is the man who knocked against me that night.

Cross-examined by Mr. M'CLURE — Did it strike you when he came out of the close as if he was running away from something? — No, I thought he was running for a car, or that something had happened.

He was running fast? — Yes.

As hard as he could go? — Yes.

Did he come running down the steps fast? — Yes, he took about two at a time.

He came down two at a time, and then did he bolt along as fast as he could in the direction of West Cumberland Street? — Yes.

Then when he passed you he was running at his top speed? — Yes.

And with his hat over his eyes? — Yes.

Tell me how far it was pulled down? — A good bit down his brow.

Was it further down the face than it is generally worn by a man? — Yes.

Was it down as far as his eyes? — Yes, just about as far as his eyes.

And with the brim hanging over? — No.

Can you tell me what kind of hat it was; wasn't it a cloth cap? — Yes.

Could you tell me whether it was a light cloth or not? — Dark.

And was it a round hat with a brim all round it? — Yes.

Did you see that quite distinctly? — Yes.

You said the man was clean shaven? — Yes.

Did you have a good look at him as he was passing under the lamp? — Yes.

Are you quite distinct about that? — Yes.

You have no doubt about that whatever? — No.

No hair on his face? — No.

Had you time to see whether his coat was a waterproof or a cloth coat? — Yes.

Was it a cloth coat? — No, it was a waterproof.

Tell me how you could distinguish that? — Because I saw it when he was running out of the close.

You have just told us that the man was running past you as hard as he could go? — Yes.

Do you say that just in the flash in which he went past you were able to take in all these details? — Yes.

By the COURT — Was it fully buttoned? — No, it was not buttoned at all.

Cross-examination resumed — Was he holding it up as he ran? — Yes.

How? — With his hands in his pockets like that (illustrating) and holding it up.

And running hard along? — Yes.

As I understand, you distinguished the man by the twist in his nose? — Yes.

That was really what you made him out by? — It was by the whole face.

His clothes had nothing to do with it, because in America you picked him out at once in different clothes? — Yes.

And when he came back to this country you saw him in two different sets of clothes, and you identified him from his face at once? — Yes.

When you saw him in the police office and identified him there you noticed he had a moustache on? — Yes.

Well, that was different from the man you saw coming out of the close? — Yes.

And the man whom you saw in America had a moustache on? — Yes.

And the man in the photographs you saw in America had a moustache on? — Yes.

And all these were different from the man you saw coming out of the close in that particular? — Yes.

You have made no mistake about that at all? — No.

Now, a hat was shown you just now, and, while you say that that hat was like the hat, you do not profess to say more than that? — It is very like the hat.

The hat was like and the coat was like? — Yes.

Did you and Helen Lambie occupy the same cabin when you were going across to America? — Yes.

And did you have a talk about this on the way over? — No.

You mentioned it sometimes? — No.

Do you mean to say that you and Helen Lambie, going across to America to try and identify the man who had done this thing, never once spoke to one another on the subject? — Not that I can remember.

Did you ever ask Helen Lambie what she thought he was like? — No.

Or did she ask you what you thought he was like? — No.

Had anybody told you not to mention it, or was it just yourself? — Just myself.

Did you wonder what the man in America would be like when you went over? — Yes.

Did Helen Lambie wonder? — I do not know.

Did Helen Lambie never say at any time to you what she thought would bring the man back to her? — No.

And you never said to Helen Lambie that if the man had a twisted nose in his face you would know him? — No.

You never spoke about it? — No.

Was it not an interesting subject to you both? — Yes.

Tell us why you never mentioned it to one another when you were occupying the same cabin for about twelve days? — She had her own ideas and I had my own ideas, and I did not want to tell her what I knew.

How do you know she had her own idea of the man? — She saw him that night.

Did she tell you she had seen him? — She saw him coming out of the house.

Did she tell you? — No.

Who told you that she had seen him? — I knew she saw him coming out of the house.

Who told you? — It was in the papers.

Had you seen it in the papers stated anywhere how Helen Lambie would likely identify the man? — No.

Was anything said to you at all about the man having a peculiar walk? — In the Court-room she said something about what a funny walk he had.

Did she say that at any time to you before she was in the witness chair in, the Court-room? — No.

Did you and she never speak about this at all until you were in the Court- room? — No.

You did not converse about it outside before going in? — No.

You were shown a photograph at Mr. Fox's office before you went to the Court? — Yes.

How many photographs? — Three.

And were any of them like the man at all? — Yes.

Now, as soon as you saw the photographs, did you recognise the man? — Yes.

And was Mr. Pyper, the detective, there then? — Yes.

I want you to be particular about this; he said you did not recognise any of them; is that the fact? — No.

You recognised the photographs at once? — One of them.

Then when you went down to the Court were you looking for a man who was like the photograph? — Yes.

And when you went into the Court there was nobody there the least like the photographs, except the man you saw and pointed out; is that so? — Yes.

Helen Lambie had given evidence in the Court: before you did? — Yes.

And you were sitting there present? — Yes.

Did you see Helen Lambie point out the man? — Yes.

And when it came to your turn you pointed out the same man? — Yes.

What was it that was funny about the man's nose? — It had a peculiar twist in it.

Could you see that from in front as he was coming to you? — Yes.

Is it twisted to one side? — To one side.

Which side is it twisted to? — To the right.

Are you quite sure it is to the right? — Yes.

Is it much twisted to the right? — Not very much.

How last do you think the man was going past you that night when he ran; was he going very quick? — Yes.

Were you looking more at his face or at his boots as he came along? Did you manage to see he had brown boots on? — Yes.

Do you know whether they were brown boots of the yellow type or of a darker type? — A dark type.

Do you know whether they were laced boots or buttoned boots? — I did not look.

Did I understand you to say that you went after the man? — Yes.

You said you thought the man might perhaps be running for a car? — Yes.

Why did you go after him? — I looked to see where he was going to.

Do you mean you just turned and looked over your shoulder? — No, I turned right round.

Did you go after him? — Just about the next lamp-post or so.

Did you run? — No.

You walked for about 50 yards along the street? — I do not know how many yards it was.

What were you going to see that you went after a man who was running fast; you said you thought perhaps he was going to the car? — Yes.

What did you go after a man who was going to the car for? — I thought he was running to catch a car, or there had been something wrong as he was running.

Did you want to see him climb on to the car? — (No answer.)

Did you think he was running from a place where something had happened, or running to a place in order to get something? — To a place.

When you were in America and saw the man for the first time, I think you said first that he was something like the man you had seen? — Very like him.

But you said "something like" first, did you not? — Yes.

And then you said afterwards, "I said, 'something like him' the first time, and then 'very like him' after I said 'something like'"; is that just your frame of mind — that is what you meant? — Yes.

I suppose you would not see his face for more than a couple of seconds altogether? — No.

When he came down the steps did he just come down as you said, two at a time, and instantly turn and run past you? — He looked towards St. George's Road and then ran to West Cumberland Street.

As fast as he could lay his feet on the ground? — Yes.

Were you carrying anything at the time? — I was carrying a parcel.

The first time you saw this man in America was he coming walking down the corridor between a great big man and another man with a medal on his breast? — Yes.

And as they came down they just walked him into this room? — Yes.

I suppose you saw quite well that he was in charge of these two people? — No.

What did you think he was doing between them? — (No answer.)

By the COURT — Were there other people coming down the corridor at the same time, or were these the only people? — No, there were other people.

Cross-examination resumed — What length of view had you of these men coming walking down the corridor? — About over to that wall there (pointing to the wall behind the jury).

And there was no person between him and you at that time? — No.

And he was marched down between the big man and the man with the badge on? — Yes.

Where was the door into which he turned; was that close by where you were? — Yes.

And I understood you saw nothing peculiar about his walk in any way, but just noticed his nose? — Yes.

Re-examined by the LORD ADVOCATE — When you saw him coming down the corridor first was he just about as far off from you as when you saw him coming out of the close? — Not so far.

When you were first asked if you could identify him in New York did you say he was like the man? — Yes.

Have you any doubt now that that is the man? — No.

After you took a good look at him did you think it was very like him? — Yes.

You have seen him now two or three times? — Yes.

Do you recollect whether before you started for America you were told not to converse with Helen Lambie about the case; just try and recollect whether anybody told you not to speak about it on the way out? — (No answer.)

By the COURT — Do you remember anything about that? — No.

Re-examination resumed — Did you know that the man you were to see out in America was accused of being the murderer? — No.

Did you know that he might be accused? — Yes.

And did you know it was a very serious matter that you were going out about? — Yes.

WILLIAM WARNOCK, examined by Mr. MORISON — I am a Sheriff criminal officer in Glasgow. I accompanied Mr. Pyper and the three witnesses to New York in connection with the prisoner's extradition proceedings. I got possession of Slater's luggage. It was in New York before I arrived there. There were seven pieces of luggage sealed with the United States Customs seal, and they were handed over to me and Mr. Pyper. I had it transferred to the "Columbia," by which I returned to Glasgow. The baggage was delivered scaled to the Central Police Office, and on Sunday, 21st of February, it was opened in Slater's presence. (Shown productions Nos. 43, 47, and 44.) No. 43 is a waterproof coat, No. 47 is a hammer, and No. 44 is a hat. These were all found in Slater's luggage. The hammer was found in a black leather travelling case, which is produced. The hat was in a hat box, which is here, too. The waterproof coat was got in this same travelling case. It was part of my duty also to search Slater. I found in his possession a pocket-book which contained a pawn-ticket, which is production No. 52. I examined some papers also in a leather case which was found in one of his trunks, and from it I took the production No. 58. No. 58 is a business card with the name and designation, "Oscar Slater, dealer in diamonds and precious stones, 33 Soho Square, Oxford Street, West." That is printed on the card. I also obtained an account form (label No. 59), showing a purchase transaction by the prisoner from one D. R. Jacobs, diamond merchant, New York, of a brilliant of extra fine quality, dated 29th February, 1908. I found also an extract entry of his marriage (label No. 60). (Shown production No. 46.) These caps were found in the hat case. There were only two caps. There were no other caps in his luggage. There was no other hat of the pattern of production No. 44 in his luggage, I took certain articles to Professor Littlejohn — these were the hammer, the waterproof coat, and the auger. There were no dentist's instruments or materials in his luggage. There were no brown boots found in his luggage. The waterproof coat was the only light- coloured coat that he had. I have seen the prisoner walk. He walks with his toes slightly pointing inwards, and when he raises his left foot his knees point slightly outwards. His left knee projects outwards slightly when walking.

By the COURT — More than his other knee does? — Yes, I observed it more.

Examination resumed — I heard the witnesses examined before the Commissioner in New York. I heard the girl Lambie referring to the peculiarity in Slater's walk.

Was her description of it very much what you had observed? — Well, I did not see her description of it, but she did imitate the walk before Mr. Miller, the counsel; I was rather to the side, and I did not see it; there were a number of people between. All I know is that she was asked to give this demonstration of his walk. I did not see what she did, but she was asked several times, and did it more than once. I heard the witnesses Mary Barrowman, Mr. Adams, and Miss Lambie being examined by the solicitors or counsel in New York and by the Commissioner.

Cross-examined by Mr. M'CLURE — I am sorry to put a personal question; is it the fact that the girl Barrowman, in describing the nose of the man that she had seen in the street, said it was very like yours? — Yes, she was led into saying that.

Do you remember this being said; the agent asks a question of the girl, "How was the nose bent, was it bent anything like Mr. Fox's nose towards the end?" and the answer is "No"; then, "Was it bent down the middle like the Lord High Marshal of Glasgow's nose?" — that is the name the American gives you — and Barrowman said, "Yes. It was bent down the middle? — Yes. Kind of hollowed out, so to speak? — Yes.

Very much of the order of the gentleman from Glasgow, who is the High Sheriff of the King's forces of the city? — Yes. Who testified just now, Mr. Warnock? — Yes. Is it not of that order, and bent that way?" and Barrowman said "Yes." You heard all that said? — Yes.

She, in point of fact, said that the man whom she had seen had a nose, not like Mr. Fox's in America, but like yours? — Yes, she was led into saying that.

As regards the walk of this man, would you say that was a very noticeable feature? — Oh, yes, it is very noticeable.

Mr, Pyper, who was out with you in America, says that it is not a thing that would make any impression upon him; do you agree with that or not? — I differ from him in this respect, I made it a point to observe his mode of walking, and I did observe his movement.

Is it a peculiarity that a person would pick up just in a casual glance? — Well, it depends; the person who saw the movement of the feet might not take any notice of it.

Would you require to look closely at the feet before you would notice this peculiarity 'I — Yes.

By the COURT — You said at a casual glance you would not notice it? — Well, if you were taking notice of the movement of his feet you would notice it.

But Mr. M'CLURE put it as a casual glance passing along the street? — Well, I would not like to give an opinion on that.

Cross-examination continued — When the girl Lambie professed to recognise the man in America she referred to his walk, but did she refer either to his having a turned-in toe or to any movement of the knee? — She referred to the movement of the knee — a bend of the leg.

Did she not refer to a kind of shaking of the shoulders? — She did.

Well, that has not got to do with either the knee or the foot? — No.

ANNIE ARMOUR, examined by the LORD ADVOCATE — I am a booking clerk with the Glasgow District Subway Company, and I am at the Kelvinbridge station. I was there on the 21st of December last in the evening. I was standing there giving out tickets at the turnstile. I am inside a box, and there is a small window to which the people come to buy their tickets. It is the ordinary size of a kitchen pane window. It is about that size. (Indicates.)

By the COURT — It is about 2 feet by 2? — I could not say.

Examination continued — Just what you have shown us with your hands? — Yes. It is clear glass. You can lift it up and give the ticket out and take the money. The turnstile is at the side of the window. I look right out on the turnstile. When I was there that evening, 21st December, I remember something happening. I was leaning against the counter, and a man came rushing in, flung down a penny, and did not wait for the ticket. He was so excited looking, and he gave me such a fright that I shouted, "Oh!" He ran down the stairs, and I shouted "Here," but he never paid any heed. He ran on, and did not wait; he never looked back. I heard him clattering down; he ran right downstairs. I noticed that he sort of stumbled and caught hold of the railing, he was in such haste. He was of medium height, dark, clean shaven, and wore a light overcoat, but I could not say whether it was a hat or cap that he had on, but I know it was something dark he had on his head. I saw his face. I could see after him from where I was; you can see right down the stairs and to the first step of the turn. There are eight steps, so that I would see him when he was going down these eight steps until he turned. I looked out at him and shouted "Here," but he paid no attention.

I suppose it is very unusual for a man to pass you at that breakneck speed? — Yes, it is very seldom that one goes away without their ticket. Trains go every four minutes on the Subway. I went down to the Central Police Office on 21st February last. I was shown into a room where there were a number of men — about a dozen men. There were some with hats and others with caps. I was asked to point out the man who had run past me without his ticket that evening. I pointed him out. I had no difficulty in pointing him out.

Will you look at the prisoner; is that the man? — That is like him. That is the man whom I saw in the Central Police Office. There was no other man there that I thought was like him. I had no difficulty in picking him out. I have no difficulty now in knowing that that was the man I saw in the Central Police Office or who passed me that night.

Did you take the time when the man passed? — Well, I looked at the clock either before he passed or just at the time, and it was between the hour of half-past seven and eight, but I could not say to the exact time. It was some time between these two hours I have mentioned. Sometimes my inspector comes at eight, and at other times at nine. It was before the inspector came. (Shown production No. 43.)

Is that like the coat the man wore who rushed past you that night? — Yes, that is like it — no, I think it was a shade darker than that. I think his coat was buttoned; the one side of the collar was turned up. (Shown production No. 44.) I could not exactly say whether it was a hat or a cap he had on, but it was something dark. It was by his face that I recognised the man; I thought he was so excited looking, and he gave me such a fright when he passed me that I had a good look at his face.

Cross-examined by Mr. M'CLURE — I take it that you cannot say what boots he had on? — No.

You cannot say what colour of trousers he had on? — I think they were dark; they were darker than the coat was.

But the coat was not a light coat like that, but a pretty dark one — a darker coat than the one that was shown you just now? — Well, not much darker.

Was it much darker? — A shade darker.

Then you mean it was not the same coat as that? — Well, it was the same style of coat, but a shade darker.

Then you mean that it was not the same coat? — Perhaps it was in the light that I thought it was darker.

Then may the colour of all his clothes have looked differently to you from what they look now? — And it was raining that night.

I want to know, are you able to identify now any of the articles here as articles which were worn that night by the man? — Yes, that is the kind of coat the man had on.

But you cannot say it was the same? — Only a shade darker; of course the rain could make the coat darker.

You are not sure of the trousers? — No.

And not sure of the boots? — No.

And not sure of the hat? — No.

And it may have been a bowler hat? — No, it was not a bowler hat, it was of cloth.

You said it was a hat or cap? — Yes, but it was not a bowler hat.

It was either a dark hat or a dark cap of cloth? — Yes.

Can you say whether it was a black one? — I only know it was dark; I cannot say the exact colour.

Did you have to press your foot upon the turnstile to let him through? — Yes.

How long did it take passing your window? — It does not take long to pass the window.

Did he fly through? — Yes.

As fast as he could? — Yes.

But you had time to observe he had no moustache of any kind? — No moustache of any kind.

Was there a train due about the time? — I do not know.

Did you ever see people rush in a hurry for the trains at this place? — Yes, but not in such a great hurry, and going in without their tickets.

I think you said they sometimes go in without their tickets, too? — I said it was not very often; it is very seldom.

But still you know they do on occasion go without their tickets? — Well, an odd one.

Could you see the man's face quite well through the window? — Yes.

Had he any peculiarity about his nose? — I never noticed the man's nose.

It had not a twist? — I never noticed his nose.

Which part of his face did you concentrate your attention on? — I had a view of the side of his face.

You are quite certain he had no moustache at all? — Quite certain.

Had the man you saw at the police office on 21st February a moustache? — Yes.

Before you went down to the Central Police Office to identify the man, I think you had seen his photograph and his description? — Yes.

And when you went down there, there was nobody the least like him except this person? — No, not that I saw.

The other people were quite different in appearance? — Well, there were some of a sallow complexion — dark.

None the least like this man? — No; none the least like him.

As regards the hour when this happened, you said you looked at the clock? — Yes.

What was the hour? — Well, I cannot say the exact hour, but it was between the hour of half-past seven and eight.

If you looked at the clock you can surely tell us? — No; I cannot remember. It might have been half-past seven or it might have been eight. It was not exactly eight; it might have been half-past seven or twenty-five to eight, but I am not sure of the exact time.

But you looked the clock? — Yes.

Can you tell us what the clock indicated? — No.

Might it have been a quarter to eight? — It might have been.

Might it have been ten minutes to eight? — No; it could not have been any later

Why? — Because I was expecting the inspector to come, and it was not ten minutes till the time he came.

And he comes at eight? — Sometimes at eight, and other times at nine.

So that it may have been ten minutes to nine? — No.

If you were judging the time by the fact that you were looking for the inspector, and he comes sometimes at eight and sometimes at nine, do you know what hour you are referring to — Yes, I know it was about half -past seven or eight, and that is all I know; it was between these hours.

May I take it that you cannot tell us to within half an hour? — It was between half-past seven and eight.

By the COURT — Do you know where Miss Gilchrist's house is? — No; I do not exactly know where the house is, but I know where the street is.

How far is it from your place? — I could not exactly say; I have never gone that way; I have been in St. George's Road, and seen the street from St. George's Road, that is all.

You cannot tell me how long it would take one to walk? — No.

JAMES DORNAN, examined by Mr. MORISON — I am a detective sergeant in the Western District of the Glasgow police force. I pointed out to the witness George Bell, photographer, the points marked Nos. 1 to 6 on the photograph of West Princes Street. No. 1 signifies 15 Queen's Terrace; No. 2 is the close, 46 West Princes Street; No. 3 is 58 West Princes Street; No. 4 is the corner of Queen's Crescent and West Princes Street; No. 5 is 16 West Princes Street; and No. 6 is a point in West Princes Street quite near St. George's Road. I know the locality round about Miss Gilchrist's house. West Princes Street is a very quiet street at night. There are a variety of ways by which you can reach the Woodlands Road Subway station from West Princes Street; a variety of routes can be taken.

How long would it take you to walk between Miss Gilchrist's house and that Subway station? — By West Cumberland Street, Grant Street, Arlington Street, Woodlands Road, and South Woodside Road, nine and a half minutes or thereby; going direct by West Princes Street to South Woodside Road and then to the Subway, seven and a half minutes or thereby.

By the COURT — That is walking at an ordinary pace.

Cross-examined by Mr. M'CLURE — I want to ask one question, because I know Glasgow pretty well. Woodlands Road is a main car line? — There are cars perpetually running on the Woodlands Road.

Isn't it the fact that the Woodlands Road is the main artery for all pedestrians who are walking from the Hillhead district into Glasgow and out again? — I would not say that. For the West End of Glasgow, from Hillhead, I would say Great Western Road was by far the most busy thoroughfare, which is the route to the Subway.

I am referring to pedestrians? — There may be some of them frequent that road, but it is not so frequented as the Great Western Road.

Isn't it the fact that Woodlands Road is very much frequented, and that a person passing any time between seven and eight would be likely to pass dozens, or even hundreds, of people? — No; not hundreds of people.

How many would you put it at — a much frequented road? — No; it would not be to the extent of hundreds of people.

Dozens of people? — There might be a dozen of people, but it is not a busy road at all.

JOHN ORD, examined by the LORD ADVOCATE — I am the superintendent of the Criminal Investigation Department of the Glasgow police. On the evening of the 21st December last I received a telephone message which had been transmitted from the Western District of the city. I at once proceeded to the Central Police Office and 'phoned to the Western for information. I then sent a telephone message to all the detective offices that all the officers should remain at their posts at the various offices. I then went to the scene of the murder along with Detective Gordon. I reached Miss Gilchrist's house about half-past eight at night. Superintendent Douglas and Detective Pyper were there at that time, and a constable. I went into the dining-room. I was informed that the body was lying just in the same position as they had found it. There were spots of blood on the fire-irons and fender, and also on the coal scuttle, and I found some on the hearth rug too. I went into the larger of the two bedrooms and I saw there a small box lying on the floor, with a number of papers scattered about. On the evening of 23rd December I got information by telephone of a girl, Barrowman, being able to give information, and I instructed her evidence to be taken. It was taken that night; it was the next morning before I got the evidence in full, on the 24:th. On the 25th I issued to the Glasgow newspapers a notice containing a description of the man as given by the girl Barrowman. I did that after approaching the chief constable and asking whether it would be judicious. Accordingly, a notice appeared giving the description of the man in the *Evening Times*, the *Evening News*, and the*Evening Citizen*. It would be published about two o'clock on the 25th. About 6.10 on the same evening, on the 25th of December, the witness Allan M'Lean called at the Central Police Office. He gave me information where a man of that description was to be found. He said that, in consequence of the description having appeared in the papers, he had called to give me information about the man. I found he was known at a club which is known as the Sloper Club, and that his name was Oscar Slater. On the night of the murder we knew that a valuable diamond brooch was amissing from the house. I heard that the man Slater had been trying to dispose of a pawn ticket for a brooch in the club. I subsequently discovered that that was not the brooch. In consequence of the information received from M'Lean I sent Detective Powell along with M'Lean to the place where Slater was said to live. M'Lean said he could not give the address, but he thought he could point out those close. It was reported to me that night that he was believed to be living at 69 St. George's Road under the name of Anderson. About midnight I instructed Detectives Lyon and Millican to go with Detective Powell to Anderson's house for the purpose of apprehending the man. About three o'clock in the morning it was reported to me by telephone that the man had gone. There was handed to me a piece of wrapper paper which was said to have been found by our detectives in the house. No. 28 of the productions is that torn paper wrapper. It is registered and addressed to Oscar Slater, c/o A. Anderson, Esq., 69 St. George's Road, Glasgow, and the word "Dent" is underlined. Dent is the name of a jeweller in London. I immediately gave instructions that all south-going trains should be carefully watched. In consequence of inquiries made at the railway stations it was reported to me that two single tickets for London had been issued for the 9.5 train from the Central Station. I wired to the London police. On 29th December I received information from Liverpool that Oscar Slater and a woman had arrived there early on the 26th. We had several telegrams with regard to men believed to be Oscar Slater. The information we received from Liverpool was that Oscar Slater and this woman had sailed by the "Lusitania" for New York, under the name of Mr. and Mrs. Otto Sando. A cablegram was sent to New York. I made the arrangements necessary for the identification of the man when he returned. I arranged to have quite a number of people in the room where he was to be seen by the witnesses. I did not go myself. I set apart two officers, Trench and Cameron, to look after the identification. I arranged to have a number of people there, some policemen in plain clothes, some railway servants, and others. There were about twelve altogether. Some people were coming in making inquiries, and we asked them to step into the room also.

Cross-examined by Mr. M'CLURE — You were not there when the identification was going on? — No, I did not go into the room.

We have been told that there were just two railway officials, and that the rest of the men were policemen along with Slater, is that correct? — I am confident that there were more civilians than that. I sent several people into the room.

We have been told there was no other person put in the least like Slater? — One of the railway servants is very like him. I refer to Inspector Lang, of the railway.

Is he here? — I do not know that he is here. He has dark hair, and his nose is slightly of the same description.

Detective Trench has given us a contrary impression? — I do not know about that, but the others will bear me out that this railway man's nose is slightly like that of Slater's. It is not so pronounced a Jewish one.

Did you understand the twisted nose that was referred to by the girl Barrowman to be just a Jewish nose? — No, not at first, not particularly Jewish.

You expected something different, in fact, from what Slater's nose turned out to be? — I did not expect anything.

But when you put in "twisted nose" you were not describing an ordinary Jewish nose? — The description was "thinks slightly twisted to the right."

Quite noticeable? — Those are exactly the words. I cannot tell what the person meant by it.

Why did you say that you discovered that upon the Friday night there were two single tickets taken for London? — That was reported to me, I said. I had officers making inquiries at all the railway stations, and it was reported to me that two single tickets had been taken for London.

And you naturally thought that Slater and his travelling companion had taken tickets for London, and then changed to Liverpool to put the police off the scent? — Yes, I believed that at the time.

Have you discovered since that the Caledonian Railway time books of that night show that two single third-class tickets were taken from Glasgow to Liverpool, and that Slater and his travelling companion travelled in a through carriage to Liverpool? — I have not discovered anything, because I have not seen a railway book belonging to any of the railway officials, nor have I interviewed any of them.

Look at production No. 69. You see the 9.5 train from the Central. Did Slater travel by the 9.5 train from the Central? — I cannot tell you definitely, because I was not there. It was reported to me that he was supposed to be travelling.

In point of fact, the reports you received were to the effect that Slater and his travelling companion left the Central Station at 9.5 p.m.? — Yes, it was reported that a man and woman, believed to be Slater, had left.

Do you find that two single tickets for Liverpool were issued for that train? — I see Liverpool, Birmingham, and London mentioned here.

Do you see that two tickets were issued for Liverpool for the 9.5 train? — Yes

And these are the only tickets for Liverpool that night? — That is all that is there.

Do you know whether the man's luggage was labelled "Glasgow Central to Liverpool"? — I cannot tell you anything about that.

Are you satisfied now that the man did not start with the London tickets? — No, certainly not.

Have you heard of any other people who travelled that night to Liverpool? — No, it would need a great deal more than an entry in a book to satisfy me that Slater did not travel with London tickets.

Do you not know that the railway official has to keep a record of the tickets issued with these trains? — Yes.

And there are entered two single tickets for Liverpool by the 9.5 train? — Yes.

Have you by any investigation got upon the track of any persons who were travelling to Liverpool from the Central that night? — I cannot say that I have.

And you are not satisfied that Slater went by that train to Liverpool? — I am satisfied of that.

But not with Liverpool tickets? — I cannot say that. I have other information to the effect that he did not, but that is not evidence.

Did you see the labels on his luggage? — No.

Have you not examined that? — No.

"Liverpool, Lime Street," is on his luggage? — Yes.

Is it probable now that he travelled with London tickets? — Yes, very.

Why do you say so? — Because I know he covered up his tracks as far as he could.

Have you made any investigation to try and find out any other passenger except Slater and the woman who went from the Central Station to Liverpool that night? — Yes.

And you found no persons who travelled except these two? — That is so. It was several days after that before we got information that he had gone to Liverpool.

Have you got any information that Slater took out two London tickets at the station? — Yes.

From any person who still remains of that opinion? — Yes. There is an official of the Central Station I believe who could have spoken to that if his name had been on the Crown list.

It is not on the Crown list? — No.

So the only person who could have proved that Slater and this woman took tickets for London and then changed to Liverpool is not present? — So far as I know. Of course, the whole of that is hearsay. I was not at the station.

But everything is reported to you? — Yes.

That naturally would have been a very suspicious circumstance if a person had taken a London ticket and changed to Liverpool? — Yes.

Do you still persist in saying that that is what Slater did? — I do not say that I persist, because I do not know definitely.

Do you not give him even the benefit of the doubt? — In this case I do not.

As regards the pawn ticket, was it reported to you by M'Lean that this pawn ticket for a crescent brooch with diamond stones was being offered for sale by Slater? — It was a man Cameron that had been offering it for sale on behalf of Slater.

And naturally you thought this might be a clue? — We associated it with the case.

You knew that the old lady had lost a crescent brooch? — Yes.

Did you find out that the crescent brooch which Slater was endeavouring to sell through Cameron was one which had been in pawn originally in the month of November? — Yes.

And that two sums of £10 and £20 had been advanced on it, and then on 21st December (the day of this murder) an additional £30 had been advanced on it? — Yes, that was reported to me.

Was it the coincidence in the date, 21st December, of the last advance upon this brooch that made you think it might be Miss Gilchrist's brooch? — Most assuredly that had some bearing on the case.

Did you discover immediately that this was not the brooch at all? — We knew that that morning.

Did you make inquiry at Cook's office? — I made no personal inquiries at all.

Did you direct inquiries to be made? — Yes.

Did you find that some days before the 25th Slater had been at Cook's office to find out about the sailings for America? — Yes, I heard that, too.

And that he had been at the Cunard office? — I did not hear that until about the 29th or 30th.

In point of fact, have you not information which goes to show that from the 21st Slater was going about billiard rooms and other places quite publicly in Glasgow, from the 21st until the 25th? — No, the information is just the other way. The information was that he had not been seen at the club that he used to frequent regularly. He was not back at it after the night of the murder.

Did you find he was going to billiard rooms in the city? — I did not find that.

Do you know that that was found by your agents? — I do not know that. I have not heard that part of the case. That was one of the things that the man M'Lean put some stress upon, the fact that Slater had not been seen at the club after the night of the murder.

Has he been to Johnston's billiard room since? — I do not know.

Or Gall's public-house? — I do not know.

And the Cunard offices and Cook's office on two dates? — I do not know that he was at Cook's office.

And Messrs. Cook afterwards telegraphed to Liverpool to see about the sailings of the Cunard steamers, and it was for Oscar Slater that their inquiries were made? — I cannot personally answer that question because I did not make inquiries, neither were they done by my department. A good many of these inquiries were done from the Fiscal's office.

But is that not your information? — I heard something about them, but I do not know the particulars.

Do you know that a telegram was sent to Dent in London for the return of a watch by Slater, and it was sent to him in his name? — The account was handed to me. It was found in his house. I wrote to find out what relations he had with Dent, and I got the telegrams referred to there.

Did you find it was about a watch that Slater wanted to get back because he was going abroad? — Yes.

Did you find also that in a letter, dated 20th December, and despatched at five o'clock on 21st December, Slater wrote to the Post Office Savings Bank in London before the murder asking that his deposit should be forwarded to Glasgow as he was going abroad? — This is the first time I have heard about that letter.

I refer to Nos. 4 and 5 of the defence productions. Did you know of these letters? — I never heard of them.

You have assumed all through that this man was going abroad as the result of a published description in the evening papers of 26th December, 1908? — Not necessarily.

But was not that the evidence you were suggesting just now? — I had no doubt in my mind that that was partly the result — that is to say, the hurried leaving of Glasgow at the time I supplied the first information to the Crown — I was satisfied he was leaving hurriedly on account of his description having appeared in the newspapers on the 25th. That was the inference.

Did you find that he informed the barber Nichols, who is on the Crown list, in the forenoon of 25th December, that he was going to sail from Liverpool by the "Lusitania" the next day, and was leaving that night from the Central Station? — I never interviewed the barber. His evidence was supplied by another officer. I heard that, but I never interviewed him. I found from the letter from Jacobs that he was going. I inferred he had meant to go then, because Jacobs says that he could not be out of his money for three months. That letter was written on 28th December, 1908.

Do you admit that all that information which has come to you since puts a different complexion on the matter? — No doubt it modifies it to a certain extent.

Re-examined by the LORD ADVOCATE — You said to Mr. M'Clure that you were informed that there was an official or servant at the Central Station who knew about the issue of the tickets, and you added that his name was not on the list? — That is so, because we were too late in getting him. The explanation is that the man's name and address were obtained after the prisoner had been served with a copy of his indictment, and he could not be added to the list.

Do you know whether the two tickets for Liverpool were issued to separate people? — I could not answer that.

Was that the reason why you said to Mr. M'Clure that the entries in a book alone would not satisfy you? — My reason for giving the answer was that I was satisfied that really the tickets issued to him were tickets to London.

In the course of your inquiries did you ascertain that on 9th December Oscar Slater communicated with Dent in London regarding his watch? — I could not repeat the date from memory.

Look at the print of productions, page 18. Did you ascertain in the course of your inquiries that on 9th December Oscar Slater, whoever he may be, communicated with Dent regarding his watch, and bid him not return same till the 30th of December, the address being 69 St. George's Road? — Yes.

Did you ascertain that Oscar Slater on 21st December asked Dent, if possible, to send the watch at once? — Yes.

He asked that by a wire? — Yes.

Did you ascertain that two days later, viz., on 23rd December, Oscar Slater, care of A. Anderson, telegraphed to Dent, "Must have watch. Leaving to- morrow night for the Continent"? — Yes.

Did you ascertain when the telegram of 21st December was sent off? — No, I do not know the hour.

Did you ever hear of Slater going to the Continent? — No. I did not hear of him having gone to the Continent.

When you saw the telegram you saw that apparently it was his intention on the 24th to go to the Continent? — That is the inference to be drawn from it. He says that he is going to the Continent.

Did you ascertain that the house he occupied at 69 St. George's Road was taken in an assumed name? — Yes, in the name of Anderson till May, 1910.

Did you ascertain also that there was no dentistry carried on there and no dentistry implements? — That is so.

By the COURT — Did all the advertisements or police notices in the papers contain a description with reference to the peculiarity of the nose? — Yes. After we got the girl's statement in any public notice that we issued we always referred to the nose, although I may explain that we kept the matter open and suggested that there might be two men, and we kept the first description alongside the second one.

The first description containing no reference to the nose? — No.

Did either of the descriptions contain any reference to the peculiar walk? — I could not answer that. There is nothing apparently about the walk in any of the intimations.

You referred to Slater having had another name, the Scotch name of Anderson. Is there anything peculiar in that in the case of foreigners, especially Jews, working in this country? — If they cannot speak the English language very well, and if other people cannot pronounce their names, then they often adopt a Scotch name, but an educated man usually keeps his own name.

Have you not met many cases of men like Slater taking a Scotch name? — No, not a man of his intelligence. In the mining class they nearly all adopt Scotch names.

Did you attach importance to the fact that he had taken another name? — I did not attach much importance to that.

But did you attach any importance? — Yes.

He took this other name before the murder? — Yes. He was known to some persons as Anderson and to others as Slater.

Did you attach any importance to it in connection with the murder? — After we got the third name, O.Sando, then the coincidence struck me as singular. That was three names.

WILLIAM NEIL, examined by the LORD ADVOCATE — I am a constable in the Western District, Glasgow. About a quarter past seven on 21st December last I was on duty in West Princes Street. The witness Adams came to me and informed me that Miss Gilchrist had been murdered in her house. I went straight to the house. I had passed the house six or seven minutes before that on the north side. When I went up to the room I found the old lady was lying murdered in her dining-room with a mat right over her. I was the first officer there. Her body was kept in the same position in which I found it till after the doctors came. I found a a set of false teeth and a half-sovereign lying on the table close beside her. I went to the police office on Monday, 22nd February, and I saw a man there whom I recognised. I did not know his name previous to that. The prisoner is the man whom I saw in the police office. I have seen him in St. George's Road several times in November and December. I saw him there about the latter end of November and twice in December.

You had known him before in Glasgow? — Yes, about five or six years ago. I had seen him then in Grant Street, which is the next street to West Princes Street. There was a club there that he used to frequent. I saw him occasionally then for about a minute, I would say. I did not know his name, but I recognised him as the same man as I had known before.

Cross-examined by Mr. M'CLURE — 'Was that about the time of the Glasgow Exhibition of 1901 or later? — I think it would be about that time.

ANNIE GILLIES, examined by Mr. MORISON — I am twenty-three years of age, and saleswoman with Messrs. Hepburn & Marshall, hardware merchants. Charing Cross, Glasgow. I recognise the prisoner. He first came to our premises on 7th November, and he made a purchase. He gave us the name of Anderson, 69 St. George's Road. He came back afterwards on 10th November and bought a set of tools. Production No. 31 is the duplicate sale note for these tools and a few other things. (Shown labels Nos. 47 and 48, consisting of a hammer, screw driver, pliers, &c.) These are the articles that we sold on the card of household tools. I was shown that hammer in the prisoner's presence in the police office. I identified it as the one I had sold him.

Did you notice anything about the handle at the time you saw it in the police office? — I thought it was not the same as when I had sold it on the card. I thought it had the appearance of having been washed. I do not think that the lower part had been washed, but the part towards the head had been washed. The wood there was different from the lower part. Looking at it now I think it shows the same appearance of having been washed as I noticed in the police office. I think it still shows that the portion of it towards the head had been washed.

Cross-examined by Mr. M'CLURE — You do not say that with any confidence, do you? You can see that the lower part of the hammer has been dirty, but can you say that the top has been washed? — It has not the appearance of a new piece of wood.

I quite agree. It has been in use for a good while? — Yes, six weeks.

You do not suggest seriously that your evidence is that that bit has been washed at the top, and the lower bit has been unwashed? You are not very confident about it, I think? — It has not the appearance of new wood.

By the COURT — Is it the lighter colour as compared with the darker colour below that makes you say that? — As compared with a new one.

Cross-examination resumed — Did you not sell us this card with tools since? — Yes.

On 10th November, when you sold the card with the pincers and hammer and other implements to A. Anderson, 69 St. George's Road, it was just a card like that which you sold for 2s. 6d.? — Yes.

Except that the hammer is dirty, do you see any difference? — Just a slight difference in the wood.

You do not profess to say whether it has been washed or what has been done? — No.

You see some coal dust under the head there? — It is difficult for me to tell what is on the handle now. It is not in the same condition as it was when I sold it.

Hall, 15 Queen's Terrace (looking east)
Showing inner side of outer door (left); dining-room (centre); door leading to kitchen (right)

Professor JOHN GLAISTER, examined by the LORD ADVOCATE — I am Professor of Forensic Medicine in Glasgow University. On the instructions of the Procurator-Fiscal, I visited and inspected on 22nd December the house at 15 Queen's Terrace occupied by the late Miss Gilchrist. In conjunction with Dr. Galt, I prepared the report No. 2 of the productions. That report is correct.

University of Glasgow,
22nd December, 1908.

At the request of James Neil Hart, Esq., Procurator-Fiscal of the county of Lanark, we, the undersigned, on this date visited and inspected the house at 15 Queen's Terrace, or 49 West Princes Street, in which on the previous evening a murder was alleged to have been committed on the person of Miss Marion Gilchrist. The police were in possession of the premises on our arrival.

The body was identified as that of Miss Marion Gilchrist in our presence by the following persons, viz.:—

1. Nellie Lambie, domestic servant to the said Miss Gilchrist, residing at 15 Queen's Terrace;

2. Arthur M. Adams, residing at 14 Queen's Terrace; and

3. William Neil, police constable, 178 B, Western Division of Police.

We first examined the apartment in which the body of the said Miss Gilchrist had been found, viz., the dining-room. The body had been left undisturbed in the position in which it had been found, and with the exception of a chair and a hair rug which had been displaced from their original position when first found, and of a coal scuttle the position of which had been slightly altered, all the other contents of the room were in their respective positions as when the body was first found.

The dining-room is a fairly large apartment. Its windows (two in number) look into West Princes Street. Along the east wall of the room is the fireplace of the apartment. On a carpet rug in front of this fireplace the body was lying. The head was pointing diagonally to the fireplace, and the feet towards the dining-room door. The right arm was extended at right angles from the body, and the left arm was lying alongside of and parallel to the body. The left leg was crossed over the right below the knees.

Without disturbing the body, it was observed that the head and face had been very much smashed. There were wounds on the right cheek extending from the mouth, wounds of the right forehead, and of the right side of head. There was a deep hole on the left side of the face between the eye socket and the left ear.

The left eyeball was entirely amissing, having either been driven into the cavity of the brain or having been gouged out. The right eye was partially torn out of its socket by the deep fracture of the right side of the brow. There was much blood on and among the hair of the head. On the carpet rug beneath the head on both sides was a considerable amount of clotted blood, and fluid blood had soaked into the substance of the rug. Between the head and the fender of the fireplace a piece of brain tissue weighing about three- quarters of an ounce, as well as smaller pieces, and several pieces of bone covered with blood were found. Two of these pieces were retained.

The fire-irons were in their places. They were bespattered with blood, as was also the grate and the fire-bars. The legs of some of the chairs in the neighbourhood and the coal scuttle were also bespattered with blood. All these signs indicated that the injuries had been inflicted in the neighbourhood of where the body was found lying, and that the injuries had been produced by very forcible application of some instrument.

There was also found between the head and the fender a complete plate (gold) of artificial upper teeth.

Both hands were remarkably pallid. There was no blood on the right hand or fingers, but there was dried blood between the fingers of the left hand. The skin rug already referred to was found when the body was first discovered to be more or less covering the body. On examination of it blood was found among the hair about the middle of the rug.

The spectacles of the deceased were found on the table in front of an open magazine. The chair, referred to as having been removed, originally stood, when the body was found, in front of this magazine, standing on its four legs.

The body was, in accordance with our instructions, approved by the said Mr. Hart, removed to the mortuary of the Glasgow Royal Infirmary for further examination and dissection.

We examined the room for any likely weapons. From our examination it did not appear that any of the fire-irons had been used for the purpose of inflicting the injuries; nor had any of the mantelpiece ornaments. We were shown a piece of a large auger or screw-bit, which we were informed had been found in the back green in a line with the kitchen window of the house. On examination we found that adhering to the metal of the instrument were several grey hairs, and, in addition, what seemed to be blood. We appended our signatures to the label attached to the instrument.

JOHN GLAISTER, M.D., &c.
HUGH GALT, B.Sc, M.B., &c.

Subsequently, on 23rd December, I received a warrant from the fiscal for the purpose of making, along with Dr. Galt, a post-mortem examination of the body, and I did so. No. 3 of the productions is the report by me and Dr. Galt. It is correct.

University of Glasgow,
23rd December, 1908.

By virtue of a warrant of the Sheriff of Lanarkshire and at the instance of James Neil Hart, Esq., Procurator-fiscal of the said county, we, the undersigned, on this date and within the mortuary of the Glasgow Royal Infirmary, made a post-mortem examination of the body of Miss Marion Gilchrist, which was removed thither for the purposes of examination from 15 Queen's Terrace, and which was identified in our presence by the following persons, viz.:—

1. Nellie Lambie, domestic servant to the said Miss Gilchrist, residing at 15 Queen's Terrace;

2. Arthur M. Adams, residing at 14 Queen's Terrace; and

3. William Neil, police constable, 178 B, Western Division of Police.

EXTERNAL EXAMINATION.

The body was that of a well-nourished elderly woman. Death- stiffening had disappeared from the body. The skin was markedly pallid in appearance.

The following marks of violence were seen externally: — Generally speaking, the face and head were both badly smashed. In particular, the following injuries were found: —

(1) Extending from the right angle of the mouth backwards on the right cheek for 2¼ inches was a gaping, ragged wound, divided into two parts by a bridge of skin 1½ inches broad, the mouth cavity and the wound being one continuous cavity. At the base of this wound several fractures of the lower jaw, upper jaw, and cheek bones were found, the bones being driven into the mouth.
(2) On the inner side of the right orbit was a lacerated wound, irregular in shape, 1¾ inches long and ¾ inch broad, which extended deeply into the base of the nose. On deeper examination it was found that the bones of the orbit, the nose, and the forehead were completely smashed in and broken into many pieces.
(3) From the upper part of the former wound (2), a wound extends upwards on the brow and head for a distance of 3 inches and towards the right temple for a distance of 2 inches, in which the right frontal bone of the skull had been smashed asunder from the rest of the bones of the skull and exposing the brain and brain substance, from which a considerable portion of the brain matter has escaped.
(4) The lobe of the right ear was completely torn away from the cheek connections.
(5) In front of right ear (¾ inch) was a spindle-shaped wound measuring ¾ inch long and ¼ inch broad, which extended deeply into tissues down to the bone.
(6) Behind the right ear was a series of wounds — (a) at a distance of ½ inch from ear was a spindle-shaped wound of like dimensions to the last; (b) a wound of similar shape 1 inch long by ¼ inch broad; and (c) a like wound ½ inch long by 1⁄8 inch broad.
(7) At a distance of ½ inch behind the series just described was an irregular-shaped, lacerated wound which measured 3½ inches long by 1 inch at greatest breadth, and which was divided in the middle by a bridge of

tissue, at the bottom of which several fractures of the bones forming the right temple and back of the head were found, some of the broken pieces of which were driven in upon the brain.

(8) On the top of the head behind the line of hair at top of the right brow was a lacerated wound 1½ inches long by 1 inch broad, which led down to a fracture of the bone beneath, which communicated with the skull cavity.

(9) Half an inch to the right side of wound last described was a lacerated wound 2 inches long by 3⁄8 inch broad, at bottom of which was a large fracture of the skull, from which brain matter was protruding.

(10) On left side of face there were the following injuries: — (a) A lacerated, irregular-shaped wound at left side of nose and left lower eyelid, which measured 2 inches by ¾ inch. In this wound the entire eyeball and parts of both eyelids were found to have been driven into the brain cavity, the eyeball itself being burst and collapsed. Dissection of this further showed that the floor of the left orbit had been completely broken away from surrounding bones. It was also found that the fracture of the right frontal bone extended across the brow into the left frontal bone; (b) on the left cheek, 1 inch from outer angle of the left eye, and on the same level, was a lacerated wound 2¾ inches long by 1¼ inches broad, the backmost part of which extended into the middle and upper portions of the cartilage of the left ear. At bottom of this wound fractures of the upper jaw and upper part of lower jaw were found which were quite loose; (c) 1 inch above the upper level of the last wound was a spindle-shaped wound passing down into the deeper tissues, which measured ½ inch by ¼ inch, and at the lower edge of this another wound of like shape and dimensions, but not so deep; (d) on the upper left temple, 2 inches back from the outer side of the left eye, was a semicircular-shaped wound with comparatively clean-cut edges, which measured 2¼ inches round its outer edge. In the base of this wound was an area of exposed skull bone measuring ¼ inch in breadth, in which was a linear fracture of vault of skull.

The entire hair of the scalp, which was greyish at the roots, was, with the scalp itself, saturated and covered with blood.

INTERNAL EXAMINATION.

Head Cavity. — The deep tissues of the scalp, more or less over the whole head, were considerably bruised and discoloured with effused blood, but more especially over the vertex and right side of the head.

The coverings of the brain were torn through in different places where were the fractures. The brain itself was greatly torn and disorganised. Several pieces were amissing, especially from the front portion of the right side of the brain. Several pieces of bone of different sizes were found driven into the brain substance at different points.

On removal of the brain it was found that the skull was fractured through its base, extending from the front right to the back. The skull bones were thicker than usual in the average woman.

Chest Cavity. — On dissecting this cavity it was found that the breast bone had been fractured completely through its entire thickness, about its middle, the area of fracture being surrounded with bruised blood. On the right side of the chest in front, fractures of the third, fourth, fifth, and sixth ribs were found, the third rib being broken in three different places, the fourth and fifth in two places, and the sixth in one place only. On the left side of front of chest the fourth rib was found to be broken close to the junction of bone and cartilage.

The right breast was slightly discoloured on the surface from bruising. Both lungs were healthy. The heart was very healthy for an old woman. Any slight departure from normal was due to the degenerative change from age.

Abdominal Cavity. — All the organs of this cavity were examined separately and in detail. The stomach contained some partially digested food. Both kidneys were granular from chronic kidney affection. There were small tumours of the womb and appendages. The rest of the organs were normal.

Opinion. — From the foregoing examination we are of opinion that the cause of death of the said Marion Gilchrist was extensive wounds and fractures of bones of face and skull, already described, and fractures of breast bone and ribs, together with shock and bleeding therefrom, that the said injuries were produced by forcible contact with a blunt weapon, and that the violence was applied with considerable force. These are testified on soul and conscience.

JOHN GLAISTER, M.D., &c.
HUGH GALT, B.Sc, M.D., &c.

I did not find in the dining-room any implement which looked as if it had been used for the purpose of murdering Miss Gilchrist. The fire-irons were undisturbed in their places, and all the ornaments were undisturbed. I saw marks of blood on the fire-irons. The fire-irons, the tongs, the poker, and the fender, the fire-bars and sides of the grate and the coal scuttle all bore marks of blood, as well as the legs of an easy-chair and a portion of the tablecloth which stood opposite the fireplace. That was not owing to any contact with the blood; they were bespattered with blood. I was clear that the injuries had been produced practically at the point where the body was found. I inferred that from the spattering of blood in the neighbourhood, and also from the fact that round the head there was a considerable quantity of blood. From my experience, my view is that the assailant knelt on the woman's chest, and, kneeling upon the chest, he struck violently at the head with the implement that he employed. The weight of his body, plus the force exercised in violently attacking the head, accounted for the rib fractures and other fractures of the chest bone. The bones in a person over eighty years of age are much more brittle than in younger persons. I formed an opinion as to the character of the weapon with which the injuries to the face and head had been inflicted. From the nature of the wounds I arrived at the conclusion that the weapon was not uniformly the same at the striking part, for this reason: we found several wounds of different sizes and of different shapes; and also for the reason that we found the left eyeball, in a burst condition, driven into the brain. That indicated that the weapon must have been of a pointed character to have enabled the eyeball to have been driven into the brain, because a large weapon that would have been likely to have caused the larger wounds could not have entered the orbit, because the orbit is bounded by bone. The spindle-shaped wounds were either produced by a relatively sharp surface of a blunt instrument, such as the head of a hammer, or the claw end of a hammer, or any such similar instrument. (Shown hammer, label No. 47.) I have examined this hammer before for another purpose. This hammer could, in my opinion, in the hands of a strong man and forcibly wielded, have produced the injuries found on that body.

Plus the kneeling on the chest? — Yes. Of course, the purchase which the assailant could have when kneeling on the victim's chest would be all the greater than if he was standing on his feet and using the same violence to a body prostrate on the ground.

If the assailant had five or six minutes at his disposal, and used the time well, could he with that hammer have inflicted the wounds you saw on the old lady's head and face? — Yes, I have very little doubt from experience of similar injuries and relatively similar weapons that these injuries could have been produced in that way. I carefully examined the claws of the hammer; I made measurements of the hammer. The total length of the metal head is 3½ inches, the breadth of each individual claw is ¼ of an inch, and the gap between measures 5-16ths of an inch, so practically the whole distance from the point of one claw to the point of the other claw is about ¾ of an inch, corresponding very closely to certain of the spindle- shaped wounds found in the skull. The diameter of the head is ¾ of an inch one way and 5/8 of an inch the other way, also closely corresponding with certain of those spindle-shaped wounds I have mentioned in my report. That is to say, the length of the hammer from my finger there (pointing) is ¾ of an inch, and the cutting margin would be ¾ of an inch.

That instrument, used in the different ways you have described by a strong man, could have inflicted all the wounds you have found? — I can only say that this instrument accounts most easily for the different classes of wounds, and particularly the eye mischief. I cannot see any other instrument that could do it unless an instrument of the same type, the head of a crowbar of varying sizes.

Is it the case that, in the case of a very old lady like this, the bones being brittle, the injuries could be more easily inflicted than on a young person? — Once a fracture of the skull was produced, then it would be much easier later to extend the fractures by repeated blows.

I was asked, along with Professor Harvey Little John, to examine certain articles that were submitted to us, and to make a chemical examination of certain stains found upon them. We made chemical and microscopical and other examinations of certain stains. On 11th March Professor Harvey Littlejohn and I issued a report upon the examination we had made on the articles handed to us. No. 4 of the productions is our report, and it is correct.

University of Edinburgh,
11th March, 1909.

We hereby certify on soul and conscience that on the 24th day of February and following days we examined certain articles which were handed to one of us, Harvey Littlejohn, on 23rd February, within the Forensic Medicine Laboratory of this University, by William Warnock, Sheriff criminal officer, Glasgow.

I. A coat labelled "Waterproof coat. Police Office, Central Division, Glasgow, 21st February, 1909. Found in trunk belonging to Oscar Slater, and referred to in the case of himself by John Pyper, William Warnock, Harvey Littlejohn, A. Cameron."

II. A hat labelled similarly.

III. A claw-hammer labelled "Claw-hammer. Police Office, Central District, Glasgow, 21st February, 1909. Found in trunk belonging to Oscar Slater, and referred to in the case of himself by John Pyper, William Warnock, Annie Gillies, Harvey Littlejohn, A. Cameron."

IV. An auger labelled "Police Office, B District, Glasgow, 22nd December, 1909. Found in back court at 15 Queen's Terrace, and referred to in the case of Marion Gilchrist (murdered), by Alexander Rankin, William Warnock, Harvey Littlejohn, John Glaister, Hugh Galt."

Coat. — This article appeared to be a new waterproof coat.

On inspection small stains were visible on different parts of the garment, externally and internally. These numbered twenty-five in all. They varied in size from 5⁄8 inch long by ¼ inch broad down to pinhead size, and varied also in shape, many of them having the appearance of spatters.

To the naked eye most of them presented a brownish-red colour, the remainder being blackish in colour. The latter on examination with a hand lens proved to be frayed rubber.

After treatment of the brownish-red stains, and on microscopic examination, corpuscular bodies resembling in general appearances mammalian red blood corpuscles were found in certain of the stains.

We are unable, however, to affirm positively that these were red blood corpuscles, because by reason of the small amount of material at disposal confirmatory tests for blood could not be employed.

Hat. — No stains were found upon this article.

Hammer. — From the head of this instrument to about half-way down the shaft the shaft had the appearance of having been scrubbed, the surface of the wood being roughened and bleached.

Yellowish stains were found on both sides of the head of the hammer and on both flanges.

Portions of these stains, as well as some adherent matter found between the claws, were scraped off and examined microscopically.

In addition to particles of rust and of a tissue which in our opinion was vegetable in character, corpuscular bodies were found. These resembled red blood corpuscles of the mammalian type.

For the reason already adduced, however, we are unable to state positively that these were red blood corpuscles.

Auger. — This instrument, which measured 13 inches in length, was thickly coated with rust. To it there was attached by means of string a small quantity of loose human hairs.

Examination of scrapings of material from various portions of the instrument gave no indications of the presence of blood.

The hairs above mentioned were found to be greyish in colour, to measure in length from 18 inches downwards, and to have well-defined diameters. Some of these hairs possessed roots which on microscopic examination proved to be healthy roots.

These hairs were compared with a quantity of hair cut by one of us — John Glaister — from the head of the deceased Marion Gilchrist at the post-mortem examination of the body, and which bore the following label: —

"Hair of scalp of the late Miss Marion Gilchrist, 15 Queen's Terrace, West Princes Street, which was removed at post-mortem examination by Professors Glaister and Galt, on 23rd December, 1908. John Glaister, Hugh Galt."

These hairs when compared with, hairs attached to auger were found to correspond generally in length, colour, and diameter.

HARVEY LITTLEJOHN, M.B.
JOHN GLAISTER, M.D., &c.

The hammer referred to in our report is the one which I have beside me now (label No. 47.) I see upon it now what we described in our report, the shaft having the appearance of having been scrubbed. Between the flanges by which the head is joined to the wooden shaft, and particularly at the sides and half-way down, the shaft looks as if it had been washed, scrubbed, or sand- papered. The iron has the same appearance, but that I have seen also in a comparatively cheap hammer where the polishing has not been very carefully done. I do not attach importance to the auger. The auger, when I first saw it, was wet. It was an old auger covered with rust. In my first report I said that the auger seemed to have what might be blood, but it proved on examination not to be blood. If there had been blood stains upon the coat, they could have been much more readily detected by analysis if the coat had been obtained by me sooner. To my mind, these stains had been subjected to the influence of water. When a waterproof coat gets wet with rain, the water keeps on the surface of the cloth. I do not know whether it was rain that got on the stains or whether they had been subjected to washing, but they were not stains as I should have expected them to be after immediate effusion on the cloth. They were paler in colour. We could not tell from the appearance of the cloth whether the coat had been actually scrubbed or whether there had simply been rain upon it.

I suppose there was no doubt that the injuries could have been inflicted by only one instrument that you saw, viz., the hammer? — That is the most likely of all the instruments I saw in the place or have seen since to have produced the injuries. I was quite satisfied, after my examination, that none of the fire-irons had been used.

Cross-examined by Mr. M'CLURE — I understand that you cannot say even that the hammer was used? — I cannot say positively that the hammer was used.

There is no trace of blood on it whatever? — We found certain corpuscular bodies that looked like blood corpuscles, but I am not able to say positively that they were blood.

You cannot say that there was any blood on the hammer? — I cannot say it positively.

You cannot say positively that the hammer was washed? — No, I said it bore the appearance of having been probably washed and scrubbed or sand- papered, but I cannot say positively.

Do you observe that it has coal dust at the top where the handle meets the head? — I am not so clear as you are about that. I think it is ordinary dirt, a miscellaneous collection of material which accumulates on any instrument that is exposed to the air in a dirty room.

If any washing of the hammer had taken place that dirt would have been washed up into the head? — It depends how it was washed. If it was washed by a scrubbing brush that is where they would try to get the dirt out.

We are now in the region of hypothesis? — Speculation.

So much for the hammer. I understand that you cannot say that there is any blood on the coat? — For the reasons I have given you, that the corpuscular bodies, which I personally believe to be blood corpuscles, I cannot in a case like this be positive about, because I cannot get the necessary corroboration from what was at my disposal.

And yet you would say it is blood? — Not in the absence of corroborative tests in a case of this kind.

Do you say that the coat bears any trace whatever of having been washed? — I said an application of water. I cannot say here that the appearance of the stains was due to their being washed, but I am clear that it was due to the influence of water.

Rain? — It might be rain.

That is -what a waterproof is generally made to do, to keep the rain off the body? — I think I am aware of that.

As regards the coat, you cannot say that there is blood on it, and you cannot say that it had been washed? — For the reasons I have stated.

A great many of the stains were other things altogether? — Some of them, of course, were. In examining a garment we look at everything. Some of these were little frayed pieces of rubber due to the manufacture. We examined twenty stains in all, and it was only in some of them we got these corpuscular bodies that I have named.

Suppose the murderer had knelt upon the body of his victim and used an instrument like a hammer or a crowbar, or anything which would cause these wounds, looking to the extensive spattering of blood that there was about this room and on the articles of furniture, would you not expect that the murderer himself would get badly bespattered with blood? — I would expect the man who applied the violence in the way I think he did would have his clothing more or less bespattered with blood.

To a large extent? — That, of course, would depend. Judging from the amount of injury in this case, I would say to a fairly large extent.

His hands could not escape, I suppose? — I should hardly think not, nor the hammer, nor any other instrument he employed.

He would likely have blood upon his sleeves and hands? — He might have gloves on — I cannot say.

Or on his gloves? — Anything that came in contact with the body would have blood on it.

This was a head that was so smashed that bits of the brain tissue were found on the hearth rug? — Yes, it was one of the most brutally smashed heads I have ever seen in my experience. A good deal of blood came from the old lady after death.

As regards the direction the blood went, I understand that not only were the fire-irons and grate bespattered with blood, but also the coal scuttle to a considerable extent? — A fairly large extent.

And also the tablecloth that was on the table? — The drooping portion at the side next where the head was was bespattered, but not so freely as some of the other parts.

The body was covered with the rug with the red hair? — I was told so. I did not see it.

Can you tell me which side of the rug was resting on the old lady's body? — No. I can only say that the hairy side was said to be downwards.

From the description you got it had been drawn over the body by the murderer? — That I could not say. It was a matter of very little consequence to me. I was not concerned with the rug. I was concerned with the body.

Suppose the hairy side was on the top of the body, and on the upper side there was found to be a considerable stain of blood, where might that come from? — That might easily come from some of the blood bespattered on the old lady's clothes.

If this was found on the top of the rug, after it was laid on the body, is it not probable that it came from the instrument which had been used to murder the old lady or some part of the murderer's person? — That is again a speculation. I can give no view except this, that that is not a large stain; it could not have been a stain produced from contact with the weapon. It looks like a small soaking or staining from the place where the blood was.

Did you examine the coat that was found, internally as well as externally?—Yes, we examined certain stains from the interior of the coat as well as from the exterior.

Provided the person who did this deed murdered the old lady with his coat on there probably would be a good deal of external blood stains? — Yes, that is where you would expect it to be, unless the coat was open and reflected back during the actual assault.

And if the deed was committed with the coat off, then, I suppose, if he put on his coat again the inside would be extensively stained? — It would be more or less stained. The stain might not be so defined, but there would be smears on the inside of the coat.

And the sleeves, of course, would show internally? — Yes.

They would show stains of blood? — Naturally anywhere where there were stains on the inner coat those would be reflected on the waterproof coat, if that were put on after the assault had been committed.

And if the person put a bloody hammer into his pocket then the pocket would be stained with blood? — Yes, unless the hammer was wiped or washed beforehand.

Were there any stains in the pockets? — No, we examined the pockets.

So what you have given us to-day is the result of a thorough and exhaustive examination of all the clothing? — Yes. I think I may claim that for the examination.

I suppose if the murderer took up and put on his hat he would probably leave blood stains on his hat? — That depends on whether his hands were clean or not, or whether he wore gloves or not. It is too speculative to answer.

This whole thing is speculative? — I would not like to say that, but I think the question is too speculative to enable me to give an intelligent answer.

Do you not think that any of these wounds were caused by the auger? — Some of them could have been produced by the auger.

Which ones? — Some of those slighter ones.

The spindle-shaped ones? — One or two of the smaller of these might have been, but they would be very limited as regards the wounds we found.

I notice in your report you say that there was a deep hole on the left side of the face between the eye socket and the left ear. Might that have been the result of a blow with the auger? — No. An auger could not have gone through the bone there.

The auger had attached to it some grey hair. What is your theory as to how the grey hair became attached to the auger if the auger had not been used at all in connection with this offence? — I have not any theory at all. I was shown the auger with a certain number of grey hairs attached to it, which auger, I was informed, had been found in the back court immediately below the kitchen window.

Do you think that the attachment of the grey hairs is a mere coincidence, and has nothing to do with this crime? — That I cannot say. The finder of the instrument will be probably better able to tell you than I.

I see in your earlier report, dated 22nd December, you state, "On examination we found that adhering to the metal of the instrument were several grey hairs, and in addition what seemed to be blood." Did you think it was blood at that time? — Yes. It is one of the commonest possible mistakes people make to think that when they have got a very rusty instrument, particularly an auger, which has a spiral screw on it, when that implement is wet, the colour is due to blood. I protected myself by using the words, "What seemed to be blood."

Of course, naturally your report was the first report drawn up immediately after the occurrence for the police? — I understand it was simply to visit the locus of the crime in order to find out if there was anything there to throw any light on the mode of causation of the crime.

Further examination led you to say, "Examination of scrapings of material from various portions of the instrument gave no indications of the presence of blood"? — I have said so — it was not blood on the auger that we discovered, and we looked very carefully for its presence.

The result of your examination comes to this, that no blood has been found anywhere except on the rug in the house, upon the old lady's body itself, upon the various surroundings, the fire-irons, coal scuttle, upon the tablecloth in the room, and upon the mat that was covering the old lady? — Your view is quite right, subject to the explanation I have already given with regard to these corpuscular bodies.

And you cannot say it is blood? — By reason of the absence of corroborative tests I am not able to say here that it is blood, but I have no doubt in my own mind that these were blood corpuscles.

Is not that a funny thing to say — a thing you will not swear to? Is there anything except those articles in the room which I have mentioned which you can say are blood stains? — No. Putting it as you want me to put it, I am inclined to say that I cannot positively prove that any instrument found in the possession of the accused contained blood.

Or any article of raiment? — Or any article found in the possession of the accused.

By the COURT — Looking to the length of the hammer, if the hammer had been put into any of the pockets of that coat would it have disappeared, or would a portion stick out? — My recollection is that a portion of the handle, if it had been put head downwards, would have stuck out from the top of the pocket by perhaps 4 inches.

How far had any of the blood gone in distance from where the body was lying? — Well, I can answer that by explaining the precise surroundings. The body was lying on the rug in front of the fireplace, the head being about 15 to 18 inches from the edge of the fender. The feet were towards the doorway of the dining-room. On the left side of the head of the body came the fender, the fire-irons, the grate, and the fire-bars — the back of the grate. On the right of the body came the table at which the deceased had been sitting, within not more than 2 feet at the very furthest, perhaps less than that; then the chair upon which the deceased had been sitting, and next to that the droop of the table-cloth from the table. Beyond the head of the deceased was a soft bottomed easy-chair, some of the fronts of the legs of which were also bespattered with blood, towards the head of the deceased; that would be probably 2½ and 3 feet. Then towards the feet of the body, but on the left side of the body, came the coal scuttle, which stood beside the fireplace; and then there was a smaller chair which stood at the head.

Was it marked? — The coal scuttle, but not the easy-chair; my impression is that the deed occurred within an area bound by a radius of 3 feet from the head.

When the injuries were inflicted would there be a spurt of blood from any artery, or simply the scattering of the material? — It depends entirely upon where the first stroke was; it is quite obvious that there must have been spurting of the blood where the wounds were caused over the temporal arteries; there were large wounds there; and then there would be spurting of blood where certain arteries on the front of the brows were opened up, but I cannot say in point of time when that had happened.

Suppose the old lady was on the ground and blows were the inflicted by a person bending over her, if there was a spurt then that would probably come in contact with this person? — It might. It would depend altogether on the incidence of the angle and the force.

What is your view, from what you saw of the position and the nature of the wounds, as to the course of the assault; take it that she was sitting at the table reading, the door opens, and the murderer enters; what is your view as to what happened? — My view is that the old lady was not sitting when she received the blows". The chair, I am told, was standing on its four legs beside the place at which it was left when the servant girl went out. My view is that the woman when she saw a stranger entering her room stood to her feet, that she received a blow with something, and was knocked down.

Front or back? — I think the front; she was knocked down on the floor; the assailant instantly pounced on her, and knelt on her, fracturing her ribs and breast bone during the act of the repeated blows, and that the instrument, whatever it was, produced those frightful injuries upon her head and face.

Have you any idea how many blows might probably have been inflicted? — No, but there must have been several — a very large number I should say; to give a rough guess, judging from the wounds and the size of them, anything between twenty and forty blows.

Of course, looking to the time available, with great rapidity? — Oh, it must have been with almost lightning rapidity. It must have been a furious assault, a continuous assault, before the assailant rose to do anything further he wanted.

And then, if it be the fact that the rug, which had been in front of the sideboard, was found on the old lady, he had then taken the rug and put it over her? — That is so.

You say in your report that you cannot affirm positively as to the red blood corpuscles, "because by reason of the small amount of material at disposal, confirmatory tests for blood could not be employed." Suppose you had had such an amount as would have enabled you to apply confirmatory tests, is it your view that they might either have confirmed your first view or they might have failed to confirm, or they might have disproved it? — That is so; one of these three conclusions might have been arrived at. The presumption, of course, is when we find corpuscular bodies in a red-coloured stain we then proceed to the corroboratory tests, both spectroscopic and chemical. Now, if we do not find corroboratory tests, both spectroscopic and chemical, then we must give up the idea of their being blood. We do not feel justified, I do not feel justified personally, in the case of a serious charge like this, to say, merely on the presence of corpuscles, that there was blood, without corroboratory tests.

It is quite reasonably possible, even in the case of what you ascertained, viz., "on microscopic examination, corpuscular bodies resembling in general appearances mammalian red blood corpuscles" — it is quite reasonably possible that confirmatory tests might have disproved there being mammalian blood corpuscles? — We must assume that; I am quite willing to assume that.

Apart from disproving, it might have altogether failed to prove it? — If we had had sufficient material we should either have been able to prove it or to disprove it; there should be no difficulty about either one or other of these conclusions.

You said, "In a case of this kind." Suppose it were not a case of this kind, but some commercial question, how would you act? Having found what you thought resembled mammalian blood corpuscles, but not having sufficient to apply confirmatory tests, would you or would you not proceed on the footing that they were blood corpuscles? — If it were not a case of the kind it is, judging from my very long experience of examination of these stains, I would, without hesitation, say that, in my view, to the best of my knowledge and belief, these were red blood corpuscles.

What is the difference; why do you put mammalian red blood corpuscles? — Because the red corpuscles of different classes of animals differ in appearance. The mammalian corpuscle is a circular disc with no nucleus in it, no little kernel in it inside. In birds, and fishes, and reptiles they are oval shaped, with a nucleus or kernel.

But in mammalian animals, whether lower animals or man, there is no characteristic distinction, is there, between the blood corpuscles? — Do you mean in the mammalian class?

Yes? — No, except with regard to one class, the camel tribe.

As between man and certain of the lower animals, there is no distinction? — You mean as differentiating by the corpuscle the nature of the animal?

Yes? — No; I should not like to say, from what is here, that there is anything to differentiate between the human and the general class of mammalian.

Dr. HUGH GALT, examined by the LORD ADVOCATE — I have been in practice as a physician and surgeon for about seventeen and a half years. I hold the degrees of Bachelor of Medicine, Master of Surgery, Bachelor of Science, Fellow of the Faculty, and Diplomate in Public Health of Cambridge. Along with Professor Glaister, the last witness, I made an examination of the surroundings of the murder at 15 Queen's Terrace, Glasgow. (Shown production No. 2.) That is our report. It is correct. On the following day I, in conjunction with Professor Glaister, made a post-mortem examination of the body of the late Miss Gilchrist at the Royal Infirmary. (Shown production No. 3.) That is the report.

It is a true report. From what I saw at the house on the 22nd December, it is my opinion that none of the fire-irons had been used, and nothing else in the room had been used as the implement with which the wounds were inflicted. I found that the fire-irons were in their places. They had simply spatters of blood on the top surface.

Was the area within which you found blood spots comparatively limited round the old lady's head? — In one direction it was limited; it was limited in the direction of the chair and table, but it extended pretty far over the fire-irons and grate. That is to say, in the direction of her feet there was little, but in the direction away from her feet, on one side of her head, there was a good deal. That was just what I would have expected from the character of the wounds. There were a great many wounds on the head and face, and, of course, a number had coalesced to form one large, ragged wound. The number of blows that had been struck must have been very great, certainly not under fifty or sixty, I should fancy; probably a good many more. They must have been delivered by a strong hand or a powerful weapon. I formed an opinion as to the way in which the ribs and the breast bone had got fractured. They were broken by the assailant either kneeling or jumping on the old woman's chest. I think she was standing first and facing, and was knocked down, and then battered. From the character of the injuries, I conjecture that her assailant was kneeling upon her body, probably while she lay on the rug. I saw this morning the hammer produced in this case. (Shown production No. 47.) If that hammer was wielded by a strong man kneeling on the old lady's body, and a succession of severe blows were struck, it could produce the injuries I saw.

Is that the kind of implement that you think must have been used to inflict the wounds? I do not say that that was the exact implement, but an implement of that kind? — Something of this nature. All the wounds that I saw could have been inflicted by using that hammer in one or another of several different ways; sideways, or with the claw, or with the head.

Cross-examined by Mr. M'CLURE — Isn't it more likely to have been a heavier hammer that did this extensive damage? — Well, if I had been asked in the abstract, I would have said, "Yes, the weapon was likely a heavier weapon."

I mean the smashing in this case is very extensive? — Most extensive.

And, in fact, the different blows had been administered over areas of the skull repeatedly so as to make one large wound? — In a number of the cases.

I suppose it is really impossible to say now what instrument exactly was employed? — It is impossible to say exactly; it just means that it was a weapon with some weight, and with sharp edges to it; something of the nature of this undoubtedly.

But unlikely to have been this, you would have thought? — A 'priori, yes.

Re-examined by the LORD ADVOCATE — Why do you say a priori? — If I had heard the story and was asked what kind of weapon was employed, I would have said probably something heavier, of the nature of a butcher's cleaver.

A heavier weapon? — A heavier weapon.

But if that weapon were wielded by a powerful hand, it would be quite capable of inflicting all the wounds? — That comes to the same thing, greater force with a lesser weapon.

By the COURT — Were there any holes where the eye was driven into the brain that must have been produced by a weapon with no greater diameter than a hammer, as compared, I mean, with a coal hammer? — Yes, a smaller head than an ordinary coal hammer.

Were there, or were there not, certain wounds which could not have been produced by a heavy coal hammer or anything of that kind? — That was one, the one you have mentioned; that was really the only one.

But if that existed, there must have been for that one a small weapon such as that hammer? — Yes, with a weapon of that nature, with a head of no greater diameter, or very little, at all events.

Professor HARVEY LITTLEJOHN, examined by the LORD ADVOCATE — I am Professor of Medical Jurisprudence in Edinburgh University. In conjunction with Professor Glaister I examined certain articles that were handed; to me by the police authorities at Glasgow, and in conjunction with him I made a report. (Shown production No. 4.) That is my report. It is a correct report. I examined carefully the auger that is mentioned in the report. I have read the two reports made by Professor Glaister and Dr. Galt. I think it is impossible that the auger could have inflicted the wounds that I see described in Professor Glaister' s and Dr. Galt's report, because the injuries are very serious; the auger is comparatively short, only 13 inches long, and it is comparatively light.

Cross-examined by Mr. M'CLURE — Have you any theory as to the attachment of the grey hair to the auger? — No, I cannot say that I have thought about it.

JAMES BARR, examined by the LORD ADVOCATE — I am a fishmonger in Glasgow. I am a member of a club called the Sloper Club at 24 India Street. I am also a member of the Motor Club next door, at Nos. 26 and 28 India Street. I know the prisoner. I knew him by the name of Oscar Slater. I knew him by sight about ten years ago in Glasgow. He lived there ten years ago. I do not know the address; I understood he lived in Kelvinhaugh. I could not say how long he was in Kelvinhaugh when I knew him. It would be a short period. After losing sight of him for five or six years I saw him in November last year. I first saw him in Kelvinhaugh Street, Glasgow. I saw him in a public-house there. I could not fix the date. It was in November. About ten days afterwards I met him in the Sloper Club. He was with a person named Hugh Cameron, whom I knew. He was not introduced to me at that time by Cameron. He went out, and Cameron asked me to propose him as a member of the Sloper Club. I demurred to doing so.

Why? — Well, his reputation was not good, and I objected to him. I agreed to do it afterwards. I do not think he was introduced to me before I did it. I put him up under the name of Oscar Slater. The address was an address in Renfrew Street; I do not remember the number. That was in November.

Was it towards the end of November or near the middle of it? — I could not be sure what date it was. There was no designation given that I remember. The name remained on the notice board of the club for fourteen days, I think. He was then elected a member.

Was he elected a member by the beginning of December? — I could not be sure about the date.

Was it about that time? — It would be near December if it was not. After he became a member I saw him in the Sloper Club at nights very frequently.

Can you say whether or not he came every week-night? — Not every night; I saw him very often while I was there. I do not think I was in the club on the night of Miss Gilchrist's murder, the 21st of December; I could not be certain. I remember hearing about the murder.

Can you try and recollect whether you were in the club that day or not? — No, it was the next day I heard about it. I do not think I was in the club on the night of the murder. I could not be certain whether I was in the Motor Club that night. I think the last time I saw Oscar Slater was about the week-end previous to the murder. I had no official connection with the club; I was not on the committee at that time.

When you saw him in the club did you notice what he was dressed in? — He was in a grey worsted suit at one time; he was always well dressed.

Did you see him in different dresses? — Well, he had a different suit on one or two occasions. I never saw him on any occasion wearing a drab or fawn-coloured waterproof.

Did he intimate his intention to resign the membership of the club, or intimate that he was going away? — I heard a remark passed one night that he intended going to America. That was some time previous to the murder.

By the COURT — I could not say whether that remark was passed by him or by another member.

Cross-examined by Mr. M'CLURE — How long was it before Miss Gilchrist's murder that you heard he was going off to America? — I think it would be some days before that.

Would you put it at the week preceding? — Quite possible.

Might I ask you a question; why cannot you remember whether you were in the Motor Club upon the Monday night or the Sloper Club? — I cannot remember whether I was in either of the clubs that night.

Why not? — Well, I do not keep a diary.

I suppose, looking back at this distance of time, you find it rather difficult to say what nights you were in the club and what nights you were not? — That is so.

About the address in Renfrew Street, I meant to ask you this, do you know whether the man was living at Renfrew Street at that time? — I could not tell you.

Who entered his address in the club book; would it be Cameron? — That would be the secretary's work.

Who would provide the secretary with the address in Renfrew Street; it would be either the proposer or the seconder? — I do not think so; a form was filled up and I was asked to propose him.

Re-examined by the LORD ADVOCATE — Was the address on the form? — Yes.

By the COURT — Did you know him under any other name than Oscar Slater? — No.

Did you know what his occupation was? — I certainly had formed opinions previously, but I did not express them.

Did you know whether he had any regular occupation or did you not? — I do not think so.

You mean that you do not think he had any? — I do not think so; of course, that is only my opinion.

Did he appear to be a man of education? — Yes, he was very cultured.

Did he speak English well? — Pretty well.

With a foreign accent? — You would know he was a foreigner.

Do you know what other languages he spoke? — No, I do not.

Have you ever had a letter from him? — No, I had no personal connection with him.

GORDON HENDERSON, examined by the LORD ADVOCATE — I am club-master of the Motor Club at 26 India Street, Glasgow. I reside in the club-house. The Motor Club was registered in November last. We have a membership of about 150 now. There was a member of the club called Hugh Cameron. He was a frequent visitor. I could not tell the date in November when the Motor Club was registered, but it was about the 4th of November when we opened. About three weeks after the club was opened I remember a stranger calling at the club and asking for Mr. Cameron, and my son went next door to the Sloper Club and inquired for Mr. Cameron and brought him out. The gentleman remained at the door in the hall until Mr. Cameron came out, and then Mr. Cameron took him upstairs. I saw the man that Cameron brought upstairs. I could not tell at that time what his name was; he went under the name of Oscar Slater. (Shown prisoner.) That is the gentleman. As far as I can remember Mr. Slater was in the club about three times. The second time would be about a fortnight afterwards, as near as I can remember. It was Mr. Cameron who brought him that time. His name was not entered in the visitors' book. As far as I can see, it was not entered as Oscar Slater. The third time that Oscar Slater came to the club, to my memory, was on the 21st of December, a Monday night. He came somewhere about a quarter to ten, as near as I could remember. He rang the bell. I answered it. When I opened the door when the bell was rung I found Mr. Slater there. Mr. Slater stepped into the hall, and he said to me, "Have you any money in the club, Mr. Henderson?" and I said, No." He said, "Give me what you have and I will give you a cheque for it." I said, "My committee do not allow me to lend money, and all I have got is just a few shillings and coppers for change," but I said, "If you go next door you will find Mr. Cameron there likely, he might assist you." He made the remark that Mr. Cameron was no use, and he turned to go out, and I opened the door and he went downstairs. By "next door" I meant the Sloper Club. I saw the man was excited a little. He seemed to be very anxious to get money. He was dressed that night with a fawn-coloured overcoat and a round felt hat which we call a Donegal hat. I did not observe his boots at all. It is not a usual thing for members of the club or their friends to come late at night asking money from me. On Monday night, 22nd of February, I went to the Central Police Office in Glasgow. I went into a room where there were a number of men. I was asked to point out the man that had come to me at the club for money. I pointed out Mr. Slater, the man in the dock. I had no difficulty whatever in pointing him out.

Cross-examined by Mr. M'CLURE — You knew him personally, and had known him a good long time? — No, I only spoke to the gentleman, I think, twice.

And you knew him then as Oscar Slater? — I did not.

When did you get to know his name as Oscar Slater? — When the two detectives came in four or five days after the murder.

At any rate, it was the same man who had been at the club before, and you recognised him at once? — Yes.

Was Slater at any time a member of the club? — No.

Had he ever a member's card? — Not that I am aware of; he might have had one.

I want to ask you this, what did you mean just now when you said he had a Donegal hat on his head? — I mean one of these round hats with a rim right round — a soft hat.

Anything about its colour-? — I think it was a greyish colour — a dark greyish colour.

How long did he stop there on the night he came in? — About four or five minutes altogether that night he came in to borrow the money.

And he was inside the hall? — He was inside the doorway.

Was he wearing a moustache that night? — Well, he was wearing a moustache, but it was like a stubble.

A short moustache? — Yes, a short moustache.

And when he came in he had a waterproof coat on? — Yes.

(Shown production No. 43.) A thing like that? — Something after that style.

Did you notice any discomposure about his dress at all? — No, I did not.

Do you know whether you had ever seen him with that waterproof on before? — No, I could not say I had.

Had you taken any particular note of the dress that he wore on previous occasions when you had seen him? — No, I had no occasion to take particular note of the gentleman at all; all I know is that when he came into the place he was a gentleman; he conducted himself like, a gentleman, and I had no reason to come into contact with him other than passing him along with a member.

Do you know what kind of clothes he was wearing at the previous time he was in the club — about the second time he was in the club? — I think he had a bowler hat on, and a Melton overcoat, or something of that style. I could not give you a description of the gentleman's clothing at all, but I only refer to the Monday night, I know what he had that night.

You said you thought he was excited; what did you mean by that? — Well, I may tell you that when Mr. Slater asked me for money I thought it very strange that he should ask me for money, and I just thought to myself that Mr. Slater had been playing cards somewhere and had lost some money, and he wanted something to go on playing with to get it back. At that time, or even the day after, I knew of no event that would make me take any particular notice of Mr. Slater.

He did not go into the club next door? — No, I happened to look down the stairs while Mr. Slater was going; he turned to the right, to Elmbank Crescent.

Is your club up a stair? — Ours is up about six steps; the Sloper Club enters off the pavement direct to the left of mine.

(Shown production No. 44.) By the COURT — Would you look at that dark hat that is there; was the hat that Slater had that night at the club like that or unlike it in colour and in shape? — Well, my idea of the hat that he had on that night was of a different make from that — a Donegal.

You do not call that a Donegal? — Well, no — not me.

Is your idea of the Donegal hat one that goes down in the centre with a cock or is worn without being touched? — No, my idea of the Donegal hat is a complete round hat; you can put it into any shape you like.

Is it like a bowler hat but soft? — Soft.

So that you may have a depression if you choose? — Yes.

What is the difference between a Donegal hat and that one? — Well, I could not tell you the name of this one.

In what respect does that hat differ from a Donegal hat? — Allow me to shift this; the Donegal hat is more like that (illustrating), with the rim coming that way, coming up; the rim sits up right round, and you can put the Donegal hat any way you like. My idea of this hat is that it is too dark.

It is not the shape, and it is not the colour? — Not to my idea.

PETER CRAWFORD M'LAREN, examined by the LORD ADVOCATE — I am manager to Alexander Liddell, a pawnbroker, at 8 Sauchiehall Street, Glasgow. I recollect of a man coming to my premises on the 18th of November last. He signed his name as "A. Anderson." He pledged a diamond brooch, and he got £20 on it. (Shown production No. 51.) That is the brooch. I handed him over the £20 in notes. The address he gave was 136 Renfrew Street. He signed his name and address in that way in our private loan book. (Shown production No. 52.) He got a copy of the contract with him like this. I had seen the man before, on the 14th — four days before. He was at our premises then, and he pledged a diamond scarf pin for some £5. On that occasion he gave the same name and address, "Anderson, 136 Renfrew Street." The same man returned to my place of business on the 9th of December last. He then wanted mother £10 on the brooch, which he got. On that occasion he signed his name as before, "A. Anderson, 136 Renfrew Street." The next time that he came was on the 21st December. He got £30 more. I think it would be about half-past twelve mid-day when he came on the 21st December. He redeemed a pledge, which cost him £6 4s. That pledge was a gold purse, a fountain pen, three pearl studs, and a ring. I think he would get about £23 5s. of money. I think the money was partly in notes and partly gold, as far as I remember. These articles that he redeemed were pledged by him on Tuesday, 17th November, for £6. I was not present when he pledged them. I am only speaking from having seen the signature in the book. I had no hesitation in giving him back the articles; he presented the ticket for them. (Shown prisoner.) That is the man. I was asked to go down to Duke Street Prison on the 10th of March, and I identified him there. I had no difficulty in identifying the man as the man who had called at my premises.

Cross-examined by Mr. M'CLURE — As I understand, this diamond crescent brooch was pledged on the 18th November; is that right? — Yes.

And £20 advanced on it? — Yes.

On 9th December there was a further advance of £10, making £30 in all? — Yes.

And on 21st December he got a further advance of £30 on it, making £60 upon this diamond crescent brooch? — Yes.

He had had some dealings with you in between for some smaller articles? — The 14th November was the first time I saw him.

The 14th November was one time; was that the time he pledged the other articles? — Personally with me — the second was on 17th November.

On the 21st of December, what he did, I understand, was to raise £30 more upon this diamond brooch, and lift the other things he had pledged with you? — Yes, to the extent of £6.

From that date, 21st December, you held only the one article, and there was £60 advanced on it? — Yes.

Is this kind of transaction one which is common enough in your business? — It is quite common in our office, anyway.

For people to deposit things with you and to get advances from time to time? — Yes.

Is it a fact that Oscar Slater had done business with your employer, Mr, Liddell before? — Yes, about January, 1900, his name appears in our books.

Is that the only time it is in your books? — Well, a few months after that it continues, until 1902, periodically.

Did your master, Mr. Liddell, know him as Oscar Slater? — Yes.

Did you know him as Oscar Slater? — Well, Mr. Liddell told me on the 17th; he had seen the scarf pin on the 14th, and on the 17th he said, "Do you know who pledged the scarf pin?" and I said, "No," and ha ¦ said, "That is Oscar Slater."

There is another thing I want to ask you: are pawn tickets, to your knowledge, ever sold? — Quite commonly, I believe.

And, of course, the person who presents the pawn ticket, as I understand, is the person with whom you settle? — He is the owner of the goods, as far as we are concerned.

So that if a person sold a pawn ticket in order to raise money you would recognise the buyer as the owner of the goods, and all he would have to do to get the goods back would be to pay your advances on it? — That is so.

So that any person to whom Slater sold the pawn ticket for the crescent brooch would be entitled on payment of the £60 to receive the brooch back? — Yes.

You say that kind of transaction is a common enough one amongst people who lodge deposits? — Quite common.

ALEXANDER RANKIN, examined by Mr. MORISON — I am an inspector in the Western District of the Glasgow Police. In consequence of instructions which I received from Detective-Inspector Pyper I went, on 22nd December last, to the house at 15 Queen's Terrace. That was to search the back green there, to ascertain if anything could be discovered that had some connection with the murder that had taken place the night before. 1 reached the back green about 10 a.m. on that day. I searched the back green. I found a piece of iron, or an auger. I found it lying in the grass opposite Miss Gilchrist's kitchen window. It was on the grass. There was grass below it — only grass. I lifted up the auger. I saw something else below it when I lifted it up. Some lady's hair came up along with it. I did not form any opinion as to how the hair had come there. It was like combings. The hair was sticking to the auger. It was raining at the time, and the hair and the auger were both wet. I did not see any mark on the ground that could have been made by the auger having been thrown from a height. I cannot say from my examination of the ground whether the auger had been thrown out or not. I examined to see whether there was any mark on the ground round about it, but there was none. The grass upon which the auger rested was not in any way pressed down. It seemed to have been there for a short time only. If it had been lying there for a long time the grass would have been stained with the rust. I took the auger and the hair to the police Court and labelled them. (Shown label 35.) That is the auger. I looked to see what had caused the hair to stick to the auger, but I could not say whether it was rust or blood. It was some wet substance. The hair was sticking on the smooth part of the auger up to the point.

Cross-examined by Mr. M'CLURE — Was it your idea that this had been used in any way in connection with the murder? — That was my opinion at the time because of the hair.

GEORGE FINDLAY, examined by Mr. MORISON — I am a timber merchant in the firm of James Dowie & Co., 50 Wellington Street, Glasgow. Before that I carried on business for a number of years under the name of J. & D. Findlay, wrights and contractors, Grant Street, Glasgow, where we had premises consisting of an engine house, sheds, and so on. We stopped work there about the end of 1907. Although the gates were closed access could easily be got to the premises. Part of our premises were just behind Miss Gilchrist's house. We had augers in our premises. The auger under label No. 25 is like the type of auger that we had in our premises just behind Miss Gilchrist's house. That type of auger is used for a steam boring machine.

Are you aware that after your works were stopped boys used to frequent your premises? — I am not aware of that, but it is possible that they would do so. It frequently happened that some of the augers disappeared. Inspector Rankin showed me the place where that auger was found. I noticed that our "workshop windows were broken just opposite the garden. There were similar augers in the machine shop at that point. Although I cannot particularly swear to the auger that has been produced, still it is like those that we had.

Cross-examined by Mr. M'CLURE — It might belong to anybody so far as you know? — Yes, it might.

And you do not know how it came there? — No.

You had been away from these premises over a year before? — Yes. quite a year before.

And that is all you know about it? — Yes.

The Court adjourned at half-past six o'clock.

Dining room, 15 Queen's Terrace (looking west) showing door (right)

THIRD DAY — WEDNESDAY, 5TH MAY, 1909.

The Court met at ten o'clock.

JOHN BAIN, examined by the LORD ADVOCATE — I am a clerk in the employment of Thomas Cook & Son, tourist and shipping agents, Buchanan Street, Glasgow. I remember that on Wednesday, 23rd December last, a man called at the office when I was in, between four and five o'clock in the afternoon. He gave me as his name and address "Oscar Slater, c/o Anderson, 69 St. George's Road, Glasgow." He wanted a two-berth cabin in the Cunard Line steamer "Lusitania," second-class, for himself and his wife. The "Lusitania" was to sail on the Saturday, 26th December. I told him that the fare was £12 each, and I said that that was the minimum rate, that the price would rise according to the accommodation. I told him that it was too late to wire the company at Liverpool that night, but I promised to write and ask the company by wire in the morning. (Shown production No. 37/1.) I wrote that letter.

83 Buchanan Street,
Glasgow, 23 Decr., 1908.

Messrs. Cunard Line, Liverpool.

"Lusitania," 26 Decr., 1908.

Dear Sirs, — Kindly wire us to-morrow if you can offer married couple a second-class room at £24 (£12 each), per the above to New York, and oblige. — Yours

THOS. COOK & SON,
per J.B.

I asked the man before he left to call next morning at 11.30, but he did not call then. He called in the afternoon about the same time, between four and five. By the time he had arrived we had received the telegram No. 37/2.

TO COUPON, GLASGOW. SECONDS, "LUSITANIA." SATURDAY. OFFER COUPLE ROOM E76, TWELVE POUNDS RATE. — CUNARD.

I told him what the contents of the telegram were; I believe he would see the telegram. I showed him the ship's plan and the room offered, but he was not satisfied. He said he thought he could do better in Liverpool, that he preferred an outside cabin. I told him that if he booked the cabin that was offered he could adjust matters at Liverpool. He said he would look back next day (Friday, Christmas Day). He did not come on Christmas Day. That is all that passed between him and me. In consequence of his call we wrote the letter to the Cunard Line, No. 37/3 of productions.

83 Buchanan Street,
Glasgow, 24th December, 1908.

Messrs. Cunard Line, Liverpool.

"Lusitania," 26th December.

Dear Sirs, — We beg to thank you for your wire of date, offering room E76 at the £12 rate in favour of Mr. and Mrs. Oscar Slater. This gentleman has called to-day, and is very much disappointed at not having an outside room. We, however, explained to him that the rate of £12 provided only for inside accommodation. He, however, replies that he could do better with you in Liverpool. We asked him if he would take out ticket for room E76 and endeavour to adjust with you in Liverpool on Saturday. He has promised to give us his decision to-morrow, on receipt of which we will advise you. — Yours truly,<7P>

THOS. COOK & SON,
per W. Dalziel.

That correctly represents what passed. When he failed to call as he had promised on Christmas Day we wrote the letter of that date to the Cunard Company, No. 37/4.

83 Buchanan Street,
Glasgow, 25 Deer., 1908.

Messrs. Cunard Line, Liverpool.

"Lusitania," 26.12.08 to New York.

With further reference to your wire of yesterday offering Cabin E76 per the above in favour of Mr. and Mrs. Slater, please note they have not called here to-day as promised, so we shall be glad if you will kindly release cabin.

We shall be glad to know if they book with you to-morrow. — Yours truly,

THOS. COOK & SON,
per W. D.

We got a letter from the Cunard Company saying that no one of his name had sailed with the steamer. I identified the prisoner as the man who called at the office. I went down to the Central Police Office on 21st February last, and I identified him amongst a number of other men.

Cross-examined by Mr. M'CLURE — When he called did he seem to be quite cool and collected? — Yes.

He just made inquiry for a berth in the usual way? — Yes.

When you showed him that he was to get room E76, and that was an inside berth, did he express disappointment? — Yes. He said that one reason was that his wife was a bad sailor. That was all.

An outside berth is fresher? — Yes.

He called back on the Thursday, but not so early as you expected? — That is so.

When did he call? — To the best of my knowledge it was between four and five on Thursday afternoon.

Your letter of 24:th December expresses accurately what Slater expressed to you? — Yes.

He suggested that he might arrange with them in Liverpool? — Yes.

You expected him back on the Friday to say whether he would take it or not? — Yes.

And he did not turn up? — That is so.

By the COURT — How was he dressed? — I cannot remember.

You cannot remember his coat or hat or anything? — No.

Did you think he was a foreigner? — Yes, that was my impression.

When you saw him and identified him was there anything except his general appearance that enabled you to identify him? — No, I knew him. I had seen him twice on the Wednesday and on the Thursday.

But had you noticed anything peculiar about his appearance on which your identification went, or was it merely his general appearance? — I noticed this much, that he looked much older then than when I had seen him before.

But did you identify him by any peculiarity distinguishing him from other people or by his general appearance? — I knew him by his face.

Did you notice any peculiarity in his face or general appearance? — No.

There was nothing about either his nose that struck you, nor his walk, nor anything else? — No.

JOHN FORSYTH, examined by the LORD ADVOCATE — I am manager of the second-class department in the offices of the Cunard Steamship Company in Liverpool. About 12.30 on 26th December a man came to the office. I saw him personally. He asked for accommodation in the "Lusitania" sailing that day. I told him that we could give him accommodation, and I asked whether the accommodation was required for himself or for a gentleman and wife. He replied that it was for gentleman and wife. I offered him a certain room. Strange to say, I offered him the identical room that had been offered to Messrs. Cook. He said he would not take that as it had been offered through an agent in Glasgow, and he kind of turned to withdraw the statement, but he made no remark.

How do you mean? — I offered him E76, and he said, "No, I do not like that, it is inside; it was offered by your agents in Glasgow." He kind of wanted to withdraw the remark. He made no further remark. I offered him another room, which, being inside, was again refused. I asked what he required, and he said he wanted an outside room. I offered him another room, an outside room, but the price was somewhat excessive. I stuck to my figure, however, and eventually he accepted the room. He paid me £28 for two tickets — at least he paid £30 in notes, and I gave him £2 in change. He produced a £1 Scotch note, for which I gave him a sovereign. The money he paid me was in the form of Scotch notes, to the best of my knowledge £5 notes. I asked him his name, and he said "Otto Sando."

Did he ask you whether you wanted his full name? — I cannot recollect the circumstances exactly. He told me how to spell his name. He repeated it, "S-a-n-d-o," and he remarked, "It is not Sandow, the strong man." I then handed him the application form No. 37/5 of the productions in accordance with the United States law, which makes it necessary that the form should be filled in by all passengers. He filled in the form himself in my presence.

APPLICATION FORM to Cunard Co., for Contract Tickets.

CUNARD LINE.

(1) Steamer, "Lusitania," sailing from Liverpool on the 26.12.08;
(2) Name in full, Otto Sando and Anna Sando;
(3) Age 38 years;
(4) Sex,;
(5) Married or single. Married;
(6) Calling or Occupation, Dentist;
(7) Able to read and write, Yes;
(8) Nationality (country owning political allegiance or of which citizen or subject), Germany, U.S. citizen, American address, Chicago, 30 Staate Street.

I recognise the prisoner as the man that came to me on the day I have spoken to. He is clearly the man, and he can recognise me, too.

Cross-examined by Mr. M'CLURE — Was this matter carried through by the man apparently just in the ordinary course? — Just in the ordinary course — just an ordinary business arrangement.

And he indicated to you that he had come from Glasgow? — Yes,

But because he signed on board as Otto Sando, you did not identify him with the Oscar Slater you had been reading about? — Not at the time.

When he said, "Your agents in Glasgow," did that indicate to your mind that he was about to refer to the previous correspondence? — Well, I had previously no knowledge of anything having gone wrong, and furthermore, I have so many people coming in and making various inquiries that unless there is something actually drawn to my mind at the time I take no notice, and when Mr. Sando or Mr. Slater came in and made the reference, "I had this offered from another agent," and when he filled in the contract, I thought nothing more about it.

And you would not identify him as the man you had the correspondence about? — Not at the time.

Are there any regulations about the entry of people into the United States; I mean have they strict rules about allowing people to land? — Yes.

And is the object of this thing which was filled up practically to satisfy these rules? — To satisfy the authorities as to the intentions of the parties entering the States; to show they have visible means of support or to show what they intend to do there.

Is there anything which asks about their financial condition? — Yes.

In this, is there? — Yes, questions No. 30, 27 to 30 — not on the contract, but on another pink form. They must have not less than fifty dollars.

Then do you take the man's word as to his possession of fifty dollars? — You must do that; you cannot put your hand in the man's pocket and satisfy yourself.

Then as to the occupation given as the occupation of dentist, you do not know anything about that either? — No.

So far as you recollect, was the man quite cool and collected when he was transacting this business? — I rather fancied he was somewhat nervous; I do not know; it happened that while he was talking to me he looked at the door as if he expected some one to come in. I thought he was expecting his wife or some one else.

There was nothing at the time to draw special attention? — Nothing out of the ordinary.

I suppose you have seen many passengers more nervous? — Yes.

By the COURT — When he spelt the name "Sando," and added that he was not "Sandow," did he say the strong man? — "Not the strong man."

Did he make that remark in an easy, jocular way, or was it simply to guide you in the spelling, seriously said? — A jocular way.

Did he laugh at it? — Just a smile, merely "Otto Sando, not Sandow, the strong man," with a smile.

Did you notice what kind of clothes he had on? — Well, it is rather a hard question to answer; I have so many people coming in, but, to the best of my knowledge, he had a soft hat on and a blue overcoat, either a blue serge or vicuna overcoat; I could not just specify myself.

Was the soft hat dark or light? — To the best of my knowledge it was a dark one; of course, I had quite a number of passengers, ladies and gentlemen, afterwards.

That day, Saturday, the 26th, interviewing you or you interviewing them, could you give an idea how many you would have — 100 in the course of the day? — Oh, yes! more than that. With that particular steamer I had somewhere about 200 people.

But you identify him now quite easily? — Quite easily and distinctly.

Is that from his general appearance, or did you notice any peculiarity about him that struck you? — No, nothing peculiar; I have a very good memory for faces.

When he referred to agents, just tell me to the best of your recollection what he said. — When he came and asked for the accommodation I offered him E76 or E77, whichever room it would be, and he said, "No, I will not take that; it was offered me in Glasgow."

He said in Glasgow? — In Glasgow.

And did he also refer to agents? — "Your agents in Glasgow," and kind of withdrew it.

And when you say he apparently wanted to withdraw that, do you mean he did not want to pursue that or seemed to regret having said that? — Well, it seemed to me that he was rather sorry he had made the remark.

ALLAN M'LEAN, examined by the LORD ADVOCATE — I am a cycle dealer in Glasgow. I am a member of a club called the Sloper Club. The club-house is at 24 India Street, Glasgow,

Was there a man named Oscar Slater a member of the club in December last? — Well, I cannot say whether he was a member or not, but I have seen him in the club often.

Could you describe the man to us? — Yes. He is about 5 feet 8 or 5 feet 9, of sallow complexion, pointed jaws, and I think he was clean shaved the last time I saw him, or he had a very small growth on his moustache. He wore a dark suit and a fawn overcoat — a rainproof coat, I think it was — and a dark cap. I noticed a peculiarity about his nose; he had a twisted nose — a twisted or broken nose. (Shown prisoner.) That is the man. I recollect the night of Miss Gilchrist's murder. I never saw Oscar Slater in the Sloper Club after that night. He had been there pretty regularly before it.

Could you give us an idea how often he would be in the club during the preceding fortnight; I mean in the fortnight before you heard of the murder? — Well, he may have been every second or third night. On the 25th of December — Christmas Day — I went to the Central Police Office and gave certain information to the authorities.

What led you to do that? — Well, a friend of mine had been offered a pawn ticket of a diamond brooch, and when I saw in the papers about the murder I thought that the brooch corresponded with the one for which the ticket had been offered for sale, and it had been offered by Oscar Slater to a friend of mine. I read the description in the paper. When I saw the description in the paper I thought he was the man, and that is the reason I went and informed about him. I undertook to show the detectives where Oscar Slater lived. I accompanied Detective Inspector Powell to the house.

How did you know where he lived? — I had seen him — I cannot remember whether it was the morning before the murder or two mornings before the murder — but we came up from the club and he walked in front of us, and I saw him go up that close, and I thought he stayed there when he went up that close. When I say in the morning, it would be between one and three o'clock in the morning. I never spoke to the man. I never knew him under any other name than Oscar Slater.

Cross-examined by Mr. M'CLURE — I suppose this murder attracted a great deal of interest and notice in the club? — Yes.

Can you tell me when it was that you heard that a man whom you thought corresponded with Oscar Slater, according to the description, was offering a diamond brooch? — It was on the Monday of the murder.

On the Monday of the murder a diamond brooch was offered to a friend of yours called Anderson by Slater? — Yes.

And did you later in the week notice that a diamond brooch of the same kind of description was missing from Miss Gilchrist's house? — Yes.

And you put two and two together and thought that very probably that might be the brooch? — Yes.

Then, I suppose, taken along with that, was the fact that the man was described as having a sallow complexion — was it a sallow complexion? — Yes.

And that he had not been in the club since you had seen him the previous Sunday; was that what brought suspicion into your mind and led you to go to the police? — Yes.

You found out afterwards that the brooch that had been pawned had really nothing to do with Miss Gilchrist? — Yes.

You knew Slater quite well by sight? — Yes, I knew him by sight.

How often had you been in his company in the club? — Well, I had never been in his company in the club, but I had seen him there often.

What do they do to amuse themselves in your club? — Well, sometimes we play at cards and have concerts.

Was the purpose of your going to the club so late as that generally to play cards? — Yes.

And you have seen Slater playing cards? — Yes.

You do not know whether he was a member of the club or not? — I do not know.

Did you not ever yourself walk home with Slater and Anderson? — No,

I think you have walked home in the company of Slater before now? — No—well, he has been walking in front of Anderson and me; that is the only time, but he never walked alongside me.

And you and he and Anderson have gone home together, walking along the street together? — Well, he has walked in front of me.

Were the three of you together, you and Slater and Anderson? — There was Slater and some other party that morning walking in front of Anderson and me, perhaps about 10 yards in front of us.

Had you all left the club together? — Yes.

Had you all been playing cards together? — I do not know whether we had been playing cards that night or not.

Try and remember; would you not be playing cards? — Well, we did play probably every night.

Tell me this — this is no idle curiosity — what was the game of cards you did play? — A game called "muckie."

It is not played by partners, but each man for himself? — It is played by partners.

Is it a game for four, or what is it? — Any number can play.

By the COURT — Was he one of the partners? — No, he was playing at "poker" that night.

Cross-examination resumed — Did he lose money that night? — Well, I really cannot say.

Can you not remember; I am wanting you to remember? — Well, you know, the poker room is off the other rooms; there are different rooms laid off in the club, so that I was in another room altogether.

And you do not know whether he lost money or not? — I do not know; I have seen him lose money.

You went down about 11th March, or was it in February you went, to identify him when he came from America? — I think it must have been March; I cannot really say.

You had no trouble whatever in recognising him as Oscar Slater, whom you had known at the club? — None whatever.

By the COURT — You know the murder was on Monday, 21st of December? — Yes.

How long before that had you seen Slater in the Sloper Club, to the best of your recollection? — Well, I think it would be three or four weeks before that that I had known him.

What was the last time before that that you had seen him? — I saw him either on the Sunday morning or the Monday morning previous to the murder.

Do you mean the same morning as the murder and the Sunday, the day before the murder? — Yes.

What hour is it open on Sundays and other days; when does it open in the morning? — I could not really say.

The club is open on Sundays? — Yes.

A member can get in at any time? — You can get in at any time.

Did you know what Slater did — what his business was? — No.

Did you know whether he had any business? — No.

MARGARET FOWLIS — Examined by the LORD ADVOCATE — I live at 69 St. George's Road, Glasgow, on the top flat. I recollect in November last of a house on the flat immediately below us being taken. I observed a name-plate being put on the door of the house with the name Anderson. I saw a servant maid at night going out and in, and various men went out and in at all times. I saw one lady besides the servant maid. I never spoke to her. I once passed the man Anderson on the stair. I would recognise him. (Shown prisoner.) That is the man I passed on the stair. I do not know whether he carried on any business or not; I did not know anything about him. I recollect on Friday, 25th December last, two men called for luggage. My sister opened the door to them. We said we had no luggage to go. They handed a paper with Anderson on it, and we said that the house was downstairs. We stood looking over the stair when the porters went away, and we saw boxes being taken downstairs. Mr. Anderson was throwing them out of the house and getting the men to carry them downstairs. That was the man that I had passed on the stair, but he had no moustache then. The time was between half-past eight and twenty minutes to nine at night. He had black trousers and vest, and was in his shirt sleeves. He had a blue overcoat, and a hat, and patent boots, or what looked like patent boots. He had a long blue overcoat with a velvet collar. He did not leave the house in a cab; he walked, and he was followed by two ladies, one of whom was the servant. That was the last I saw of them. I was taken to the Central Police Office on 22nd February last, and I there identified Anderson amongst a number of other men. The prisoner is the man that I identified.

Cross-examined by Mr. M'CLURE — Was it about the beginning of December that you saw him first? — No; it would be about the middle of December.

You met him on the stair at that time? — Yes; I passed him.

Had he a moustache? — I think so.

Now, then, the next time you saw him was the time he was going away on Christmas Day? — Yes.

I wish to ask you now, and to seriously consider this question. Had he a moustache then? — No.

Had you an opportunity of observing? — Yes, because he came out, and he looked up. My sister and I and a man were standing talking, and he came and looked up.

I am putting this question with a definite intention, and I hope you will give it a deliberate answer, as we have had some evidence about this. Is it the case that at that time he had a three weeks' growth of black hair or a noticeable moustache to any one who looked at that time, on 25th December? — I said he had no moustache.

By the COURT — Was his upper lip clean shaven? — Yes.

Cross-examination continued — And you had a good opportunity of seeing that? — Yes.

How far would they be in your sight? — Just a few minutes, till he went round Charing Cross.

Where is the nearest cab stand to your house? — In North Street, in the direction they were going.

Did the porters take the luggage down in a barrow? — Yes.

Do you know whether the servant was in the house the same night and handed over possession of the house to two women who came next morning? — I do not know. Two women took possession, but I did not see them.

And they lived on there for some time? — Yes.

I suppose at that time the house would be under the constant supervision of the police? — It was.

ISABELLA FOWLIS, examined by the LORD ADVOCATE — I live at 69 St. George's Road, Glasgow. I am a sister of the last witness.

(This witness corroborated the evidence of the previous witness.)

RUBY RUSSELL, examined by Mr. MORISON — I am twenty-two years of age. I am a domestic servant with Mrs. Bernstein at 69 St. George's Road, Glasgow. I remember the house on the flat immediately above our one, which had been empty for some time, being tenanted in the month of November last. After the tenants came there was a plate put on the door with the name Anderson. Prior to Christmas Day I had on two occasions seen the man who lived there. When I saw him before Christmas he had a moustache on. I identify the prisoner as the gentleman. He was always dressed in dark clothes, but I could not say whether it was the same suit that he had on. I remember a detective calling at our house and making inquiries about seven o'clock or 7.30 on Christmas Day. My attention was attracted by something on the stair shortly after that, two men taking luggage downstairs from Anderson's house. Anderson was dressed in dark clothes that night. There was a woman standing on the other side of the street. I was standing at the window, and I saw the prisoner going across to the lady, and then they walked away together. They walked a few yards and then separated, and he went away himself.

Cross-examined by Mr. M'CLURE — What do you suggest was their object in separating? — I think they saw me, and did not want to go away together.

Did you know Slater personally? — No.

Did Mrs. Bernstein have any dealings with Slater? — No.

Was there any communication at any time between Mrs. Bernstein and her household and Slater and his household? — No.

Do you happen to know that a detective called on Mrs. Bernstein? — Yes.

How long was that before Slater left? — About half an hour.

Do you suggest that Slater left because the detective had called at Mrs. Bernstein's — I thought it was very funny.

His visit to Mrs. Bernstein had never been communicated at any time to Slater or his household? — Not that I know of.

How many boxes and bags went away upon the barrow? — I saw one large trunk.

Were there not nine packages taken away by the porter? — I never saw nine packages.

Do you suggest that Slater did all his packing in the half-hour which intervened between the visit of the detective to Mrs. Bernstein and his leaving the house? — I do not say that.

Would you kindly explain if you can what it is that connects in your mind the departure of Slater from this house with the visit of a detective to Mrs. Bernstein which had not been communicated to Slater by Mrs. Bernstein? Did you just think it funny? — I thought it very funny, going away so quickly.

JOHN CAMERON, examined by the LORD ADVOCATE — I am a city porter in Glasgow, stationed at the Central Station. On the evening of Christmas last, 25th December, I was at the Central Station, in Gordon Street, Glasgow, with my barrow. Between six and seven o'clock a man called and asked me to go on a job. He wanted me to go to 69 St. George's Road and lift some luggage and take it to the Central Station. He told me that the name was Anderson. I had never seen the man before. He told me to be at the house at the back of eight o'clock. I went there and found the house three stairs up. By mistake I went to the top flat, and then I came down when I found my mistake. I found at the house the man that had engaged me, and I think there were two women in the house. The man gave me the luggage and told me to carry it downstairs. There was another porter, Mackay, with me to give me a hand. There were ten pieces altogether, composed of trunks, portmanteaus, and a parcel. Mackay and I took them to the Central Station. The man let me out of the close, and said that he would go in the car and meet me at the station. I did not see how he went down. He was waiting on me when I got down to the station. I could not say whether the women were with him; I would not swear to that. I saw one at a fruiterer's store at St. George's Road, but I do not think I saw her after that. I am not quite sure whether I saw her at the station. I am not sure whether the man that ordered me to do this work was clean shaved. I would know him again if I saw him. I recognise the prisoner as the man that engaged me to remove his luggage. I did not wait to see him enter the train. As soon as he paid me I came right away.

Cross-examined by Mr. M'CLURE — Did you hear him telling the porter to label his luggage? — I heard him giving the porters instructions, but I am not sure where he told them to label the luggage to.

Have you not got an idea? — I think it was Liverpool, but I would not swear to it.

Before leaving, did you not see the two women at the station? — I saw one, but I would not swear to two. I saw them up at the train along with the prisoner.

Did you put the luggage into the train? — I backed the barrow up, and the porter took the luggage off and gave me a hand.

What van did you put it into? — I think it was a back van.

Do you remember if it was a van in a composite carriage which was through for Liverpool? — I am not sure.

Would you recognise any of the baggage if I showed it to you — Yes, I think so.

Is that box that I show you one of the baggage? — I think so.

Do you see the label there, "Lime Street, Liverpool, from Glasgow Central"? — Yes; but I never paid any particular notice.

When was it that you got your orders from the man to be up at his house in order to take away the baggage? — Between six and seven o'clock, at the Central Station, as far as I can remember.

Were you informed at the time what train you were to take the luggage to? — Yes; the 9.5 train.

When you got orders to remove the luggage, did the gentleman help you in any way to put the luggage on to your barrow? — No.

Did he hand the luggage out to you? — Yes, from the house. He told us to carry the luggage down the stair, and we did so, and put it on the barrow.

Did you go into the house and get it yourself and carry it down? — Yes, as he instructed me to do.

Did the gentleman seem in any way excited? — No.

He did not seem to be in any special hurry? — No, not to my knowledge.

Do you remember whether he said anything about your being late for the train? — I remember him saying, "You will have to hurry up, or you may be late."

Did you see anything in this man's demeanour or behaviour that night to suggest to you that he was more in a hurry than any other person to catch a train? — No; not at all.

JOHN BROWN, examined by the LORD ADVOCATE — I am booking clerk at the Central Railway Station, Glasgow. I was on duty there on the evening of 25th December last. There is a train leaves the Central Station at 9.5 p.m. for London, Liverpool, Birmingham, and Preston. There is not usually a through carriage for Liverpool on that train. I understand there was a through carriage for Liverpool on the 25th of December last. Usually passengers change carriages at Preston or Wigan. A single ticket from Glasgow to London is available to go via Liverpool. You stop at Liverpool and then prosecute your journey afterwards. I recollect what tickets were taken out for that train, the 9.5, on the evening of 25th December; I have them before me here. There were comparatively few people travelling by that train that night, being Christmas night. I have in my hand a scroll balance book. I keep it myself — the booking-office clerk. It is taken after each issue for the train. I made it up immediately after the train departed. Amongst the tickets which I issued for that train were two singles Liverpool, third-class, and two third singles to London. I recollect it was a man who bought the two single thirds to London. I saw him at the window of the booking office. I recollect selling him the two tickets.

Do you think you would know the man again if you saw him? — Well, I might give my recollection. (Shown prisoner.) That is very like the man, but on oath I could not swear to it. I did not observe any one with him. My recollection is that the two thirds for Liverpool were issued to separate parties — issued separately.

One man bought one ticket? — Either a man or lady; I cannot remember. I was not very busy that night, nothing extra.

Had you time to observe the man who bought the two London tickets? — Well, just a passing glance, as it were. I have no recollection of what money he offered. With a single third for London you can travel by Liverpool and break your journey there. If you did so you could retain the ticket.

Cross-examined by Mr. M'CLURE — So far as the book goes, the entries just show Liverpool two third-class, £1 10s? — That is so.

London two third-class, £3 6s? — That is so.

Do you remember to whom you issued the Liverpool tickets? — No.

May you have issued the Liverpool tickets to a man? — I may have.

Is there any way of finding out whether London tickets are collected at Liverpool? — They might be; of course, they do not collect them if they are going on to London.

Suppose a person with a London ticket was going to change his journey and going to Liverpool, he would give up the London tickets at Liverpool? — Not necessarily.

What would happen with them? — He could break his journey at Liverpool and proceed on with them within ten days.

Would they be shipped at Liverpool? — Quite likely they would be.

Suppose a person has got tickets for London, and he changes his journey at Liverpool upon the London ticket, what happens as regards the ticket when he arrives at Liverpool? — I really cannot tell you that; the tickets would be checked at the collecting station for Liverpool, and the passenger would be allowed to retain them.

And if the person went to America without ever going on to London, would it not be quite possible to find out from the numbers at the Clearing-house that these two tickets had disappeared? — I cannot say as to that.

If the tickets with the numbers on them did not turn up at the Clearing- house, it would be known there that two tickets of a certain number had been issued and they had never come back? — I should think it would.

Has any inquiry been made, as far as you know, to find out whether the two tickets issued for London have disappeared altogether or not? — Not that I know of.

Do you know whether the two tickets for Liverpool issued that night were collected in due course at Liverpool? — I do not know.

When was it that you were asked, to begin with, about the issue of tickets on the 25th? — On the night after.

At your place are tickets issued for anything except the English train? — Just the English train.

And I understand your evidence, then, to be this, that you have a recollection that a man — had he a moustache? — Slight.

With a slight moustache took the two tickets for London; is that so? — That is so.

And you think on your recollection that he was like this man here? — Very like the man.

Who took the tickets for Liverpool, whether a man or a woman, whether a person with a moustache or not, you cannot possibly tell? — No.

Can you tell me this: in ordinary course, I suppose the tickets would be checked before the train started, when the people had taken their seats? — They usually are.

And if a man was sitting in a through carriage for Liverpool with a London ticket, I suppose the ticket collector would speak to him about it? — Perhaps not; he might.

Do you think a man would be allowed to sit in a Liverpool carriage with a London ticket and not be given a hint to change? — He might be.

Suppose a person were wanting to go to Liverpool, this, of course, would be the only train he could go in that night? — There is one at ten minutes to six.

I mean there is no later train? — Not after that.

And there is not another one till ten o'clock next morning? — That is so — 10.10.

Would the 10.10 train in the morning take a person in time for the sailing of the "Lusitania" at four in the afternoon? — Yes.

Re-examined by the LORD ADVOCATE — I suppose, if a man broke his journey at Liverpool and retained his ticket he could hand it over or sell it to somebody else? — That is so.

And so it would be used? — That is so.

You know that is sometimes done? — I understand so.

But is it a perfectly regular practice to travel from Glasgow to London with a London ticket and break your journey at Liverpool? — Yes.

JOHN MILLICAN, examined by the LORD ADVOCATE — I am a detective constable in the Central District of Glasgow. By instructions of Superintendent Ord, I, on the 25th December last, accompanied by Detective Sergeant Lyon and Detective Inspector Powell, went to the house at 69 St. George's Road about twelve o'clock at night. We went there to see who was the resident there — for a Mr. Oscar. I heard the name Anderson given; I saw the name Anderson on the door. We rang. The door was opened by a maid — a German. We asked for Mr. Oscar. She said, "No man here." We asked who lived there, and she said, "No one but Madame." We asked where Madame was, and she said that Madame was away for a short holiday. We then asked to go inside the house, and she allowed us to go into the house. We went into the house and looked all round, and there were a lot of papers lying in the front bedroom, and amongst the papers I picked up a piece of paper. We did not search the house minutely; we just looked round the house. We went into all the rooms. We found nothing in the way of baggage.

Could you tell from the appearance of the house that baggage had been taken away? — By the appearance of papers lying about, as if things had been packed. We did not find any dentist's instruments in the house or see any. I did not see any appearance of a dentist's business having been carried on there. The servant said that no man lived there. (Shown production No. 28.) That is the piece of paper I picked up. The following is on it: — "Registered fragile, with care — fee paid — Oscar Slater, Esq., c/o A. Anderson, Esq., 69 St. George's Road, Glasgow. Dent — R., London, W.C, 1, No. 1292." I examined the other papers on the floor and found nothing of any importance amongst any of them. On finding that paper with the address on it, I pointed it out to the servant girl who was there, and asked her what about the man. She said. "That is a friend of Madame's; he is away with Madame for a short holiday." I asked her if she knew where he had gone. She did not know. I looked through the other four rooms and kitchen, and found nothing in any of them. From the people below I learned that a man Anderson had disappeared that night shortly after eight o'clock, and that a woman had gone with him; he was joined by a woman on the opposite side of the street.

Cross-examined by Mr. M'CLURE — Who gave you that information? — The servant of White, two stairs up.

What is the name of this servant of the Whites? — I do not know.

She is not here as a witness? — Not that I am aware of.

When you went into the place to begin with, did you explain to the servant, who was alone in the house, that you were detectives? — We did.

And that was twelve o'clock at night? — It was.

Did you explain any special mission? — We did not; we only wanted to see Mr. Oscar.

Did you not know his name was Slater? — I did not.

"Who gave you the information that his name was Oscar? — I got the information from Detective Inspector Powell.

And he did not call him Oscar Slater, but Mr. Oscar? — Just Mr. Oscar.

Then you went into the place and looked through the room? — Yes.

Did you notice that the paper from Dent's address to Oscar Slater, c/o Anderson, 69 St. George's Road, was dated 23rd December, 1908? — Yes, I read the date.

And it showed that it came from Dent's, in London? — Yes.

Does the servant speak English well? — Well, broken English.

DAVID LYON, examined by the LORD ADVOCATE — I am a detective officer in the Central District, Glasgow.

(This witness corroborated the evidence of the previous witness.)

REGINALD GEORGE TUCKETT, examined by the LORD ADVOCATE — I am chief assistant to Messrs. Dent, watchmakers, 34 Cockspur Street, London. I know a man named Oscar Slater, and we had some dealings with him. Our first transaction with him was on 24th November, 1905, in connection with the repair of a watch. He was then in London. Our second transaction was on 25th August, 1908. So far as I remember, he handed me the watch at that time; I will not be positive about that. He gave the address of ¥o. 36 Albemarle Street, Piccadilly. He paid me for the repairs of the watch on 21st October, 1908. I do not recollect of him calling at our shop on 10th December last; I do not think he called in person. As far as I remember, the watch was sent on that date. I received the letter, dated 9th December, addressed 69 St. George's Road, c/o Anderson — "Enclosed you will find my watch you delivered at 36 Albemarle Street. The watch is 15 minutes or 20 minutes fast. Kindly put the watch in order and return same to this address till 30th December." On 21st December I received the telegram No. 36/2, "Dent, watchmaker, Trafalgar Square, London. If possible please send watch at once, Oscar Slater." The watch was still in our keeping. I received that telegram on the same day on which it was despatched. At that time we closed at seven o'clock in the evening. On 23rd December I received a subsequent telegram, addressed 34 Cockspur Street, London. "Must have watch, leaving to-morrow night for the Continent. Oscar Slater, c/o A. Anderson, 69 St. George's Road." The previous telegram was signed "Oscar Slater." I sent the watch, I think on the 23rd, but I will not be positive about that. It was sent to the address given. That was the last transaction that I had with Slater, and I have not heard of him since. (Shown production No. 28.) That is the label upon the watch which I returned. It is addressed in my handwriting. To the best of my belief Oscar Slater is the prisoner; I think I have waited on him.

Cross-examined by Mr. M'CLURE — Did he stop in London at the time of the previous transaction with you while he was there? — Yes.

On 9th December, as is shown by the letter signed Oscar Slater, No. 69 St. George's Road, Glasgow, did he send you a watch for repair? — No, it was sent to us while he was in London. We received the watch from Albemarle Street.

I show you No. 36. Are you not wrong in saying what you have said? — I may be wrong; my impression was that it was left by hand. In any case I received it, and my statement was to the effect that the watch had received a blow or fall.

Did you receive the letter dated 9th December, which says, "Enclosed you will find my watch you have delivered to 36 Albemarle Street, London"? — Yes.

Is that dated from 69 St. George's Road, Glasgow? — Yes.

And one would think that the watch was enclosed along with it? — Yes. My impression was that it was left by hand, but about that I will not be sure.

Was the same watch twice with you? — Yes.

May it not have been that the first time it arrived it was handed in by hand, and the second time that it came in a package along with that letter? — That may be.

Was there enclosed also a card? — That may have been enclosed.

Was that not enclosed with the letter? — It may have been.

"Address till 30th December, 69 St. George's Road, c/o A. Anderson, Glasgow "? — No.

Does that card in front of you have on the face of it "Oscar Slater, dentist, 36 Albemarle Street, W., Telephone 1624 Mayfair"? — Yes.

And on the back is there written "Address till 30th December, 68 St. George's Road, c/o A. Anderson, Glasgow"? — Yes.

Do you remember receiving that? — It was with the letter of 9th December.

And that was an intimation to you that the address, 69 St. George's Road, was good till 30th December? — Yes.

You apparently have had this watch in your possession for repairs from 9th December right up to the 21st? — Yes.

There is a telegram there to "Dent, watchmaker. If possible send watch at once"? — Yes.

Did you see from the telegram that it was handed in in Glasgow at 6.12 at the Central Station? — Yes.

Apparently the watch had not arrived by the 23rd. Did you, on the 23rd, receive another telegram, "Dent, 34 Cockspur Street, London. Must have watch, leaving to-morrow night for Continent. Oscar Slater"? — Yes.

All your communications were with him under the name of Oscar Slater 7— Yes.

And he put "c/o Anderson" when he went to Glasgow? — Yes.

Do you see the last telegram of 23rd December, handed in at Charing Cross, Glasgow, one minute past twelve? — Yes.

And it was sent off at 12.7 and it arrived in London at 12.44? — Yes.

It was in answer to that telegram that you sent off the parcel which was in the wrapper No. 28? — Yes.

And it contained the watch? — Yes.

I suppose when you got notice by the second telegram that they were leaving to-morrow night for the Continent that hurried you up? — Yes, it hurried us up considerably.

You had thought that they were to be there for a week longer? — Yes, our intention was to send it off after Christmas.

MARIAN CARSON, examined by Mr. MORISON — I am twenty-four years of age. I am a telegraphist in the employment of the Caledonian Railway at the Central Station Telegraph Office, Glasgow. I was on duty on 21st December till 6.37. (Shown production No. 36, addressed "Dent, watchmakers.") I can tell from the marking of the code time on the telegram when I received that. I took it in. It was handed in at 6.12, and it would be sent into the tube and sent to the Post Office at once. I cannot tell whether it was handed in by a man or a woman; I do not remember anything about it.

Cross-examined by Mr. M'CLURE — Is it signed "Oscar Slater"? — Yes.

(Shown prisoner.) Is that the man? — I do not remember him.

MARY ANDERSON M'MURDO, examined by Mr. MORISON — I am a sorting clerk and telegraphist at Charing Cross Branch Post Office. (Shown production No. 36, addressed "Dent, 34 Cockspur Street, London," and signed "Oscar Slater, 69 St. George's Road, c/o Anderson.") That telegram was handed in at my branch on 23rd December. It says, "Must have watch, leaving to-morrow night for the Continent. Oscar Slater." That was handed in at my branch post office at one minute past twelve on 23rd December. The message was despatched at 12.7. That was two days before Christmas, and we must have been specially busy that day. I cannot recollect whether it was a man or woman who handed in that telegram to me; I have no recollection who handed it in.

Cross-examined by Mr, M'CLURE — Look at the prisoner — was that the man? — I could not say.

FREDERICA CAROLINA LANG, examined by Mr. MORISON—I am a sorting clerk and telegraphist in the General Post Office, Glasgow. Prior to November last I was acting in the same capacity in the Hope Street Branch Post Office, and after leaving it I was temporarily employed on 23rd, 24th, and 25th December. While in the Hope Street Post Office it was part of my duty to keep the book called the Counter Register Letter Book. I have examined the letter book of 24th December, and on that date I find a registered letter or packet. No. 421, sent off to an address in Germany — the address being, Adolf Leschzinger, 5 Klukowitzer Strasse, Bentham O/Sohl*, Germany. I cannot recollect whether I saw the person who handed it in.

[*Sic*. Should evidently be "Beuthen, O/Schl," where "O/Schl" stands for Oberschlesien (Upper Silesia). Former name of the then German and now Polish town called Bytom.]

Have you seen the prisoner before as far as you know? — I think I have seen him before.

Where at? — I could not say.

But can you say whether it was in your branch post office on the 24th or not? — I could not say.

Can you say whether he was there on 22nd or 23rd? — I could not say.

Do you just remember the face? — Yes.

Cross-examined by Mr. M'CLURE — You saw the prisoner in Duke Street? — Yes.

Is it from that recollection that you think that you have seen him? — No, I think I have seen him before.

But you cannot recollect whether he sent the package to Germany? — No.

Was it a registered letter? — It was either a letter or a packet. Each one has the same entry.

WILLIAM GORDON, examined by Mr. MORISON — I am a detective lieutenant in the Central District of the Glasgow police. I called at the house 69 George's Road on 26th December, 1908, in order to make inquiry at the accused's house. I saw a person who said that she was the maid there, and she told me that they were away to London. I asked for Anderson, because the name was on the plate on the door. I called again on Monday, 28th, and Tuesday, 29th December, to see if any letters had come for Anderson. There were no letters. I learned on the 7th of January that the two women who occupied the house were going to London. I did not see the maid then; she was away. She went to London on the night I called, on the 26th.

By the COURT — How do you know that? — She told me that she was going to London.

Did she say whether she was to join them? — No; she said that she was going to 72 Charlotte Street, London, that night, care of a Mr. Sancroft.

Examination continued — The maid told me that Madame and Anderson had left the night before for London. I made inquiries as to the movements of Anderson on the Monday night, and she told me that he was in at seven o'clock at dinner, but that she did not know anything further about his movements after that.

I called afterwards on 7th January. (Shown production No. 27.) I was handed that letter on 7th January. The envelope is addressed, "Oscar Slater, c/o Mr. Anderson, 69 St. George's Road, Glasgow, Scotland, Eng." There is also an intimation, "If not delivered, return to D. R. Jacobs, 326 Third Avenue, New York, U.S." The letter bears the American postmark, and appears to have been posted at Madison Square, at New York, on 29th December. The letter itself is dated 28th December.

Do you know when the two women actually left the house? — It was reported to me that they left on the 8th of January. They told me on the night of the 7th that they were leaving on the 8th.

When did these two women arrive in Glasgow? — They told me that they would arrive here about the 24th of December. I did not see them until the 26th, a Saturday.

Did you see them in the flat that had been occupied by Slater when you called on the 26th? — I did.

Did you find that the keys of the flat had been handed over by Slater's servant to them? — She told me so..

And did she inform you that these people were taking up the occupancy of the house? — No. The maid did not tell me, but they themselves told me so.

Can you tell me when these two women came to Glasgow? — They told me that they had come two days previously.

Do you know where they had been between times? — In the Alexandra Hotel, in Bath Street.

Did you make inquiry? — No, I did not.

Where did you get the letter dated 7th January? — I got it from Mrs. Freedman.

Did she say that she had come from London? — Yes.

And was to continue the occupancy of the flat after the letter had gone? — She said that it was arranged between Slater and her that she should do so.

Was it not between Slater and Mr. Freedman, in London? — No; it was between Slater and her. The words she said were that they were away to Monte Carlo.

Who were away? — Madame and Mr. Anderson. She called the lady Madame. She said that they were away to Monte Carlo, and that he had asked if they had any money and wanted a loan of £25.

Who wanted it? — Mr. Anderson. He asked it from Mrs. Freedman.

Do you understand that the story was that they had gone off to London and then to Monte Carlo? — It was the maid's story that they had gone to London, and Mrs. Freedman's story was that they had gone to Monte Carlo.

Cross-examined by Mr. M'CLURE — I show you the envelope No. 27; you were asked about something that appears on the envelope at the foot of page 17 — "If not delivered, return to D. R. Jacobs, 326 Third Avenue, New York, U.S.," and it is headed "Scotland, Eng."? — Yes.

The words, "If not delivered, return to D. R. Jacobs, 326 Third Avenue, New York, U.S.," are not in any printed form, but written in ink? — Yes.

Apparently by the person who wrote the letter? — It looks very much like it.

Would not that suggest to you as a detective that the person who sent off the letter had in his mind that perhaps the addressee would be away from the address at the time the letter had arrived? — There was no indication on the letter to that effect.

For what purpose would he write on the envelope, in his own handwriting, "If not delivered, return to D. R. Jacobs," unless he thought that there was a probability of the man being away at the time the letter arrived there? — There might have been a change of address.

He might be away from there? — Yes, supposing he was still in Glasgow.

There is another thing I call your attention to. From the terms of the letter itself, is it quite plain that Mr. Jacobs, who wrote the letter to the accused, was expecting to be shortly over in America, as he says, "Buy all you can when you come over"? — Yes, there is something there about that.

Putting these two together, does that seem a fair inference that he wrote the letter to a man whom he expected was going over to America, and who might not be at the address at the time the letter went there? — There is a possibility that he might do it, but the other probability is just the same that he might change his address from that house.

But the words "come over" mean that he was going over to America, do they not? — Yes.

Re-examined by Mr. MORISON — When was it that Mrs. Freedman told you this about Slater having gone to Monte Carlo? — On Saturday, 26th December.

Did she say when she had come to the address 69 St. George's Road? — She had arrived that morning.

You said something about £25 which I did not quite catch. Did she tell you that she had given Slater the loan of £25, or that he had asked the loan? — Mrs. Freedman told me that she had called the previous evening at the flat and found Mr. Anderson, the accused, busy packing up his luggage, and Madame, as she called her, was crying, and she had asked what was up, or what was the matter, and then Anderson said that he had received

Mr. M'CLURE — If Mrs. Freedman is not coming, this is not relevant.

LORD GUTHRIE — If you object, we cannot take anything.

By Mr. MORISON — What about £25? Did Mrs. Freedman tell you that she had given the prisoner the £25, or merely that the prisoner had asked it? — Mrs. Freedman told me distinctly that she gave him £25.

[The LORD ADVOCATE here proposed to recall the witness Lambie.

Mr. M'CLURE — My lord, my friend is proposing to recall the girl Helen Lambie, with whom we parted some two days ago. I do not know the purpose of her being recalled at the present time, but I think it is quite enough for me to say that she has been in Court since she was examined, and has heard certain of the evidence, how much I do not know. I should suggest that this is an absolute disqualification, although I am absolutely ignorant of the points she is to be examined on.

The LORD ADVOCATE — If my friend says she was in Court I cannot contradict him.

LORD GUTHRIE — She was in Court.

The LORD ADVOCATE — My friend may be perfectly correct. I do not propose to ask her a question about anything that has been said in the evidence. I will put to my friend the few questions that I proposed to ask. If he adheres to his objection, then I do not insist.

Mr. M'CLURE — I would rather not know anything about it, because it would seem to be departing from the strict line I am entitled to take up, and I do not wish to have anything like negotiation in a case of this kind.

LORD GUTHRIE — If something had come out in cross-examination, it is conceivable that occasion might have arisen for a witness to be recalled. It would be a very unfortunate thing if the occasion did arise, but it might arise.

The LORD ADVOCATE — Yes, it did arise out of one or two questions put by my friend in cross-examination.

LORD GUTHRIE — You do not insist on recalling the witness?

The LORD ADVOCATE — No.

Mr. M'CLURE — I am objecting in absolute ignorance of what the questions were to be.]

WILLIAM SANCROFT, examined by the LORD ADVOCATE — I am employed by the Glasgow Corporation in the Tramways Department. On 23rd December last I was conductor on a car on the passage northwards at Union Street, about five minutes past six on that evening. I remember one man in particular joining the car at the end of Union Street next Argyle Street. He went upstairs in a hurry and seated himself at the far end of the car. There was a boy reading the *Citizen* on the opposite side of the standard, on the left hand side. Near West George Street I went upstairs to collect the fares from the passengers. I asked the man where he was going, and he mumbled something. He had a penny in his left hand. I took it for granted that he wanted a penny ticket, and I punched it. When standing at the standard, half-way covering his seat, I asked the boy if there was any clue to the murderer, and he said, " No, there is not any clue yet, and I don't think there is any likelihood of getting one." All of a sudden this man who was sitting on the seat got up in a hurry and passed by, pushing me to the side. He went downstairs in a hurry. I went after him and tried to tap him on the shoulder, as I usually do to draw the attention of passengers in case they have made a mistake. I was three steps down when I saw the man running full speed across to Garscadden Street. That was long before he had got his pennyworth or even a half-pennyworth. I spoke to the motorman about what had happened, and I delayed the car about a minute or so. I would most assuredly know the man again. I recognise the prisoner as the man.

Cross-examined by Mr. M'CLURE — Did you think that night he was the murderer? — No, I did not.

That night, I suppose, you only thought this, that there was a dark- complexioned man on the car who came on for a little while and left in a hurry, before he got his penny's worth? — A dark-complexioned man resembling very much the description given in the papers, I think, the night after the murder.

You did not think that this was the murderer that night? — Not at the time he was on the car.

He seemed to be in a hurry to join the car, and, later on, in a hurry to leave the car? — Yes.

Is that the only thing you have got against him? — Another thing was taking 1d. ticket and going off before the ½d. station.

I understand that you said that you did not know whether the man had heard your remark to the boy? — I do not remember if I said so. I think I said that when the remark was passed as to there being any clue of the murderer, this man, according to my opinion, must have heard us.

You said the car was not very well lighted where the man was sitting? — It is not very well lighted in a December night.

Who is the boy that was reading the paper? — I tried to trace that, but I have not been able to get hold of him. I have been told that he has been in some employment in the city, about St. Vincent Street, as a clerk, and has been dismissed. He was a regular traveller at that time of the night. I have not been able to get a hold of him. I have tried my best.

The Clerk of Court then read the following declaration which had been emitted by the prisoner:?

At Glasgow, the twenty-fourth day of February, one thousand nine hundred and nine, in presence of Arthur Thomson Glegg, Esquire, Advocate, Sheriff-Substitute of Lanarkshire.—

Compeared a prisoner, who had had a private interview with a law agent prior to this examination, and the charge against him having been read over and explained to him, and he having been judicially admonished and examined, declares: My name is Oscar Slater. I am a native of Germany, married, thirty-eight years of age, a dentist, and have no residence at present.

I know nothing about the charge of having assaulted Marion Gilchrist and murdering her. I am innocent. All which I declare to be truth.

OSCAR SLATER.
A. T. GLEGG.

James N. Hart,
Duncan Lee,
Wm. Warnock,
Witnesses.

The LORD ADVOCATE then intimated that this closed the case for the Crown.

———————

EVIDENCE FOR DEFENCE

JAMES DOW, examined by Mr. M'CLURE — I am in the accountant's office in the Post Office, Edinburgh. I have been cited as a witness to speak to a letter which was addressed to the Comptroller of the Post Office Savings Bank, West Kensington, London. The letter is dated 20/11/08, Glasgow. The letter is addressed from 69 St. George's Road, Glasgow, to the Comptroller of the Post Office Savings Bank in

London. It is dated the 20th of the eleventh month of 1908, which apparently would be 20th November, but it arrived at its destination in an envelope which has got the Glasgow postmark of 21st December, 1908, 5 p.m.

That is 5 p.m. on the 21st December, about two hours before the murder? — I do not know when the murder was. The letter is in these terms:—

Glasgow, 20th/l 1/1908,

69 St. George's Road. Dear Sir, — Enclosed you will find my Savings Bank book. Be kind enough to send me the money at once as I have an urgent call to America because my wife is ill. If possible wire the money on and I will pay all expenses here. — Yours truly,

Adolph Anderson.

In answer to that letter there was one addressed from the Post Office Savings Bank, West Kensington, London, to Mr. A. Anderson. That was dated 22nd December, 1908. The letter was in these terms—

Post-Office Savings Bank,
West Kensington, London, W.,
22nd December, 1908.

Sir, — I am directed by the Post-Master General to acknowledge receipt of your Deposit Book, Investment Certificate, application, and letter of the 20th inst., and to inform you that steps are being taken to sell £59 2s. 7d. 2½ per cent. Consolidated Stock on your behalf, but the transaction cannot be completed until to morrow. A warrant for the sum due in your Savings Bank account is, however, enclosed, and instructions have been sent to the Postmaster of Glasgow to pay the amount without production of the Deposit Book. — I am, Sir,

Your obedient Servant,
H. DAVIES, Controller

Dining-room, 15 Queen's Terrace (looking east).

Do you find that, following upon that, the 2½ per cent. stock which stood in the name of Slater was sold on his instructions, and the proceeds given to him at the Glasgow Post Office on 24th December, 1908? — In the name of A. Anderson, yes, that is so. He received £49 7s. 2d. I find also that the balance remaining due in his Post Office Savings Bank account, namely, £39 18s. 3d., was paid to him on 23rd December.

Take it from me that the murder of this lady was accomplished at seven o'clock upon the 21st December, 1908. Were instructions given for the delivery of the Savings Bank deposits and stock of Slater by the letter posted at 5 p.m. on the 21st December, and therefore before the murder? — I should say so.

You take, I suppose, the post office stamp as conclusive of the date? — Well, I am not conversant absolutely with the stamp, but I should say it was.

Cross-examined by the LORD ADVOCATE — Who is Adolf Anderson? — I could not say — a depositor in the Post Office Savings Bank.

Did you ever see him? — No, never to my knowledge.

Do you know anything about him? — No, not at all.

You mentioned the name Oscar Slater? — No, not I.

I heard it mentioned in connection with the consolidated stock? — "A. Anderson," I think I corrected; A. Anderson was the name the stock was in.

Did you ever hear the name Oscar Slater in connection with this person Adolf Anderson? — No, not to my knowledge.

Do you know when the bank account was opened? — Yes. On the 12th of November, 1908.

In London? — In Glasgow.

And what is the designation of the person? — Dentist.

And the address? — 69 St. George's Road, Glasgow.

When was the last transaction — the last deposit of money? — On the 17th December, 1908.

How much was deposited that day? — £5.

Then, when was the last money drawn out? — The last sum was drawn out on the 24th December, 1908.

Do you know whether the depositor, Adolf Anderson, attended at the bank to get the money? — Well, I could not say. It was paid at the Glasgow head office.

When was the consolidated stock that you have mentioned bought? — On the 13th November, 1908.

Is it bought from Glasgow? — It is bought through the Savings Bank in London, by request of the depositor in Glasgow.

Was there any interest paid upon it when it was paid up? — Not yet; there has been no interest yet.

How long does Government stock require to be deposited before any interest is paid on it? — I think there is interest payable for any length of time.

Was any interest paid on the £69 2s. 7d. worth? — No.

Was there any claim made for any interest? — Not that I am aware of.

If it had been left for a further period would interest have been paid upon it? — Upon the stock, yes; as a matter of fact, there is interest due; it has been added to it, I believe, for the time it was in.

That has not been claimed, as I understand? — No,

Re-examined by Mr. M'CLURE — Adolf Anderson opened an account on the 12th November, 1908? — That is so.

In the Post Office Savings Bank? — Yes.

And he requested payment of that on the 23rd of December, and was paid £39 18s. 3d.? — He requested payment with a letter that reached London on the 22nd.

And he got paid? — He got paid at Glasgow, by London's request.

On the 13th November, in London, 2½ per cent, consolidated stock was bought for a certain amount for Adolf Anderson? — For Adolf Anderson, 69 St. George's Road, Glasgow.

And he requested that that should be sold by the letters which have been referred to? — That is so.

And it was sold and he was paid £49 7s. 2d., the proceeds, upon 24th December? — That is so.

The point I wish to make clear is this, the instructions as regards the uplifting of the amount in his savings bank book were given on the 21st December, at 5 p.m.? — That is the date on the envelope.

HUGH CAMERON, jun., examined by Mr. M'CLURE — I reside in Cambridge Street, Glasgow. I am a bookmaker's clerk. I have been at odd times a dealer in jewellery. I go about clubs in Glasgow where gambling takes place. In particular I know the Sloper Club, 24 India Street, and the Motor Club, 26 India Street. I also went to the Mascot Club, Renfield Street. That club is now out of existence. With regard to what the people do in the club at night, some utilise the reading rooms, some play billiards, and others play games at cards. I play cards a good deal at these various clubs. I have known Oscar Slater since 1901, the year of the Glasgow Exhibition. I met him first in the Crown Hall billiard rooms, Sauchiehall Street. I met him a good deal at that time. He did not play cards at that time; he backed horses. He was not a member of a club in Grant Street at that time. It was later on that he became a member. I should say that he was in Glasgow about nine months in 1901. I saw him about three or four years afterwards, in 1905 or thereabout. After another interval of something like three years I saw him again in November, 1908. I met him in Sauchiehall Street. He had been in town some little time.

He was staying at the Central Station Hotel under the name of A. Anderson. After that he went to lodgings in 13G Renfrew Street, and later on he removed to a flat in St. George's Road, which he took in the name of Anderson. From the time he came in November, 1908, to stop in Glasgow at the Central Station Hotel, in lodgings in Renfrew Street, and in St. George's Road, he was known as Anderson. I saw a considerable deal of him from the time he arrived in November until he left on 25th December. I would not say that we met very nearly daily, but we met pretty frequently. We employed ourselves probably by filling in the time, such as going to the skating rink, and then to a music hall in the evening, and from there to the Sloper Club, where he subsequently became a member. When meeting in the clubs in the evening card playing was indulged in until well into the morning. That was the ordinary kind of way that I and others had of passing the time. There is not much horse racing in December; it is practically the close season. So far as I know, Slater was never a dentist. I heard later on from him, after he had been in Glasgow for some time, of his purpose to go to America, and I got his address. It would be fully a fortnight before 21st December that I heard from Slater of his intention to go abroad. He spoke quite freely about his intention among his friends. I got the address from him in his handwriting, and I have it here. This matter was brought to my notice specially by a letter I saw from San Francisco. That letter was shown to me about a fortnight before he went away. I cannot say whom the letter was from. I do not remember anything about the terms of the letter further than that things were going very well and asking him to go out. That was the gist of the letter. Either at that time or shortly afterwards Slater gave me his address in San Francisco. It was Oscar Slater, c/o Caesar Cafe, 644 Broadway, San Francisco.

Do you swear you got that a week or ten days before 21st December? — I cannot swear to that. I cannot swear that I got it at a given time, but I know I got this given in his own handwriting, I got it from himself, but as regards the time I got it I cannot swear.

May I take it that you got it before there was any question about this murder? — Yes. I am not definite as to when I had seen Slater before the day of the murder, 21st December, but it must have been somewhere about the week-end; either the Friday or the Saturday of the previous week. I saw him on the Tuesday or the Wednesday after the murder had taken place, but I am not quite certain about that. When I met him I received from him a pawn ticket to dispose of, for a brooch which had been in pawn for £60. He gave me the ticket, and said that I knew a great many more people about the city than he did, and that I was perhaps in a better position to dispose of the ticket, and I might dispose of it for him. I took the ticket from him, and I approached two people, Mr. Donaldson, who has a billiard room in Crown Street, and Mr. Allan, the poulterer in Sauchiehall Street. I was not successful in disposing of the ticket, however, and I gave it back to Oscar. It was a ticket for a diamond crescent gold brooch, upon which £60 had been already advanced. There had been an advance of £20 in November, and in December another advance of £10, and a further advance of £30 had been made on it on 21st December, the day of the murder, making £60 in all. The sale of the pawn ticket would involve this, that the brooch would be delivered up to the person who had purchased the pawn ticket upon payment of the £60, with interest, to the pawnbroker. That is a sort of transaction with which I am familiar enough. The brooch was in the pawnshop of Mr. Liddell, Sauchiehall Street. I do not know Mr. P. C. M'Laren in that shop. When I failed to dispose of the ticket, either to Mr. Donaldson or Mr. Allan, I returned it to Oscar Slater. I do not think he made any remarks about making further efforts. I remember meeting him after the time I have mentioned, the Tuesday or Wednesday. I had made an arrangement to meet him in the Crown Hall billiard room at 5 p.m. on Thursday, 24th December, but I did not meet him then. I met him passing the comer of Gordon Street and Renfield Street. I was along with my wife, and I saw him passing there. I mentioned to my wife that I had a prior engagement with him at five o'clock in the Crown Hall billiard rooms, and I said it was no use going there when I could see him now. I told her that I would be home about six o'clock, and left her, and followed him. I met him either at four o'clock or shortly after four on 24th December. I asked where he was going, and he said ho was looking for the Cunard Line shipping office in Jamaica Street. I went down to Jamaica Street with him, and he went into the Cunard offices. Immediately he came out he asked me if I would mind going upstairs to get an English £5 note for five Scotch £1 notes. I went upstairs, but I was not successful in getting the £5 note. He told me that he wanted the note to send to his people in Germany, which he had done, as he stated, almost every Christmas. I did not get the £5 note at the Cunard Offices. We went next to the Central Station and tried the booking-office there, but were unsuccessful. We then went to the Central Station Hotel, where he had originally been, but he was not successful there. Then we went to Forsyth's, and then to the Grosvenor Restaurant, where he got the note. On getting the £5 note he enclosed it along with a letter in an addressed envelope. I went with him to the Hope Street Post Office. He got the letter registered there, and the money was sent off. I saw the letter handed over and the registration fee paid at Hope Street. After that we went to Miss Cranston's tea-rooms in Sauchiehall Street, and then to Brechin, the butcher's shop. We parted after that in Sauchiehall Street. I arranged to see him after he had taken his dinner. He dined, as a rule, at seven o'clock. I had tea at six o'clock. I called at his house a few minutes before eight. I was told by the servant girl he had gone out half an hour ago, that a gentleman had called for him. The last I saw of Slater was a few minutes before six o'clock on 24th December. As early as two o'clock on the Saturday morning, 26th December, some detectives came to my house and asked me if I knew Oscar Slater. I said that I did. I never saw Oscar Slater dressed in checked trousers or light-coloured spats at any time during November and December. As a rule, his clothes were dark, with the exception of the waterproof coat, of course. I am not very clear as to the shape of a Donegal hat. I have seen him wear a cloth hat with a circular rim right round, and with a split in the centre — I mean the kind of hat like the production No. 44. I never saw him with a cloth hat with a rim round it, and without the split. He generally wore a black bowler hat. I have seen him with the cloth cap, No. 46 of productions.

Do you remember being in Johnston's billiard rooms with him on the Wednesday night before he left, the 23rd? — I cannot say that I do. At the time I saw him last on Thursday, 24th December, he had a very stubbly moustache which was quite noticeable. I am aware that Slater, before he left, had lost money at the Sloper Club. I knew that because I had seen him lose money at the Club. I did not, in point of fact, know that Slater was going off on Friday, the 25th. I understood that he was going to America soon, but I did not know the precise date. I did not know that he was making inquiry at shipping offices during the week of his departure. I understood that he went to the Cunard office to make inquiry as regards the sailings of the Cunard Line to America. That was upon Thursday, the 24th. He did not communicate to me any definite plan at that time as to when he was leaving, further than he said, when he came out of the Cunard office, that perhaps the "Campania," sailing on Saturday week, might suit him.

You saw Slater two or three times between the day of the murder, 21st December, and 25th December; did it occur to you that there was anything in his demeanour, his manner, or his habits different from usual? — No, there was nothing.

Did he show any anxiety at all to secrete himself or to hide himself? — Not that I know of. In fact, it was the opposite.

You were round about in public places with him during the afternoon, as you have mentioned? — Yes, on the Thursday afternoon.

And you saw nothing that would lead you to suppose that he was a fugitive from justice? — No.

Cross-examined by the LORD ADVOCATE — Under what different names did you know the prisoner? — Anderson and Oscar Slater.

Adolf Anderson? — I never heard of the Adolf; any indication was "A. Anderson" on a card that I always saw.

When you first knew him in 1901 what was the name he went by? — Oscar Slater.

What was he? — I am not aware when I met him what he was.

After you became acquainted with him did you become aware what he was? — He was a gambler.

Anything more? — Yes, I had it that the man, like a great number of those who came to Glasgow, lived on the proceeds of women.

Did you not know from the first that his mode of living was on the proceeds of women's prostitution? — I cannot say that I knew from the first; I had no knowledge of the people.

When did you come to know that? — When we came to have sufficient knowledge to know the people that came about the locality the story went round.

When was that? — Some time after they arrived in Glasgow.

Can you fix the year? — The year of the Glasgow Exhibition, 1901.

Where did he live? — I do not know.

Had he any place of abode in Glasgow that you knew of? — I did not know of his address in Glasgow at that time.

For how long did you know him in 1901 without knowing whether he had any address or not? — I knew him all the time he was there till he left without knowing his address.

Did you ever ask him where he lived? — I did not.

What part of the city did you and he frequent, or did he frequent? — We did not at that time frequent any part of the city together.

Where did you meet him? — In the Crown Hall billiard rooms in Sauchiehall Street.

Is that the only place you met him then? — At that time, yes.

Later on did you meet him in a club in Grant Street? — Yes.

How far is Grant Street from Queen's Terrace? — It is a street further along; I should say about 70 yards to the west.

Did you meet him there often? — Yes.

Was that a gambling club? — Yes.

In what year was it that you met him often in the Grant Street gambling club? — As near as I can remember, the latter part of the year of the Glasgow Exhibition.

How long did he remain in Glasgow at that time? — I cannot be definite as regards that.

A year? — I have stated about nine months, I think, but I am not very sanguine about it.

Where did he go to then? — I do not know.

Did he never tell you? — No.

Did he just disappear, as far as you were concerned? — As far as I was concerned, yes.

Did you know of him being a dealer in diamonds and precious stones? — I cannot say that I have known him to be a dealer in diamonds and precious stones.

Is that news to you now? — No, it is not exactly news, because I know that he, along with many others, all did in that way, buying and selling, but whether it embraced the words "diamond merchant" I would not say; they all more or less deal in jewellery.

When he disappeared, had you no communication with him? — None whatever.

Did you never hear of him being in Soho Square, London, dealing in diamonds and precious stones? — No.

When did he reappear? — I am not definite as regards that either.

Was it years or months afterwards? — Oh, it was some years, I think.

Where? — In Glasgow.

What part of Glasgow? — In Sauchiehall Street.

What part of Sauchiehall Street? — Hope Street.

Was it a house? — No.

You mean, you met him casually on the street there? — I cannot say where I met him.

Why did you mention Hope Street; what happened in Hope Street? — That is the street adjacent to the Crown Hall billiard rooms, which we, as a rule, frequent.

Was it again in the Crown Hall billiard rooms that you saw him when he reappeared in Glasgow? — I cannot say that.

Can you recollect any place that you met him after he reappeared in Glasgow? — No, I cannot say that I can.

Did you see him at all at the time that he reappeared? — Yes.

You could not fix the date of his second appearance? — No.

Can you not recollect any place you met him in Glasgow the second time he reappeared? — No, I cannot say that I can.

You just remember that he was in Glasgow? — Yes; I remember that he was in Glasgow.

And you saw him? — Yes.

Under what name was he going then? — Oscar Slater, as far as I can remember.

How long was he in Glasgow at that time? — I cannot say.

And you tell us that you cannot remember a single place you met him in Glasgow during his second visit; do you really say that? — Well, I may have met him in the Crown Halls, but that is not definite, so that I cannot definitely state any particular place that I met him on his second visit to Glasgow.

Did you meet him in any of the gambling clubs on his second visit to Glasgow? — I do not know that any of the clubs were in existence at that time during his second visit to Glasgow.

Had the Grant Street Club been suppressed or not? — Yes; it only lasted the one year or part of a year.

And was there not another club where you met him the first time in 1901? — The West End Club.

Was it suppressed also? — Yes, it was suppressed also.

Then, after his second visit, when you do not remember where you met him, did he disappear again? — Yes.

Did he tell you when he was going away, or did he just vanish? — I do not remember him having stated anything about when he was going or where.

How long did he disappear for the second time? — Till November, 1908.

And then did you meet him casually on the street? — Yes.

Do you know under what name he was going then? — Yes.

What was it? — A. Anderson.

Did he tell you that himself? — He gave me his card.

Did he tell you why he had taken the name A. Anderson at this time? — He did not.

Did you ask him? — I did not.

Did you not think it curious that he should have changed his name the third time he came to Glasgow? — Yes.

And when you thought so, did you not ask him what reason he had for taking a different name? — No.

Does it not seem curious to you now that you did not inquire of him? — I meet many men in that kind of way. I never was sufficiently curious to ask the man why he had changed his name.

But amongst yourselves, in the clubs, is he still known by the name of Oscar Slater? — Yes.

Did you know his German name; did you ever hear it? — I did not.

Did you know that he had another name? — I was always under the impression that Oscar Slater was his name.

Now, did you meet him very often at nights during the second half of November and the first three weeks of December in the Sloper Club? — Yes.

In the Motor Club also? — Yes.

Were these both clubs very much of the same kind as the Grant Street Club and the West End Club? — Very much.

And had they been started comparatively recently? — Both clubs — well, the one is a transfer from another.

Did he still continue to gamble at both the clubs? — Not so much in the Motor as in the Sloper Club.

Was he practically at the Sloper Club every night gambling during the latter end of November and the beginning of December? — No, not every night.

But almost every night? — I should not say that; not every night.

Give us an idea how many nights a week? — Three or four.

And sometimes more, I suppose? — Three or four.

Do you know where he went on the other nights? — I do not know, I am sure.

Do you know what he did during the day? — As far as I understand, he was not much out until mid-day.

And from mid-day onwards do you know what he did? — Sometimes he was along with me.

Where? — At the skating rink in Victoria Road, Glasgow.

In the afternoons? — Yes.

And at other times? — Walking round the town.

So far as you know, had he any occupation? — Not that I know.

Did you know that he was in the way of pawning jewels? — I was conversant with the fact of anything having been pawned, such as the brooch and the pin, and some other things, on account of him being short of money.

Did you know in the middle of November that he was short of money and went with a diamond ring to a man called Jackson, South Portland Street? — No; I was not conversant with that fact.

How did you come to know that he was short of money? — I was in a position to lend him some.

Did you? — I did.

When? — I cannot state the date.

Was it November or December? — I could not be certain.

How much? — £4.

Did he repay it? — He did.

When was that? — In December, I think.

You said that he lost money at gambling; do you know how much he had lost just before he went away? — I could not say.

Did he tell you what money he had — what he possessed? — No, he did not.

Did you know that he had money at his credit in the Savings Bank? — I did not.

Did you know that he had pawned jewels with Liddell? — Yes.

Did he tell you that? — Yes.

Did you know where he got the jewels? — I did not.

Do you know what he got for them at the pawnshop? — Yes.

Did you know that he had obtained £30 upon a brooch? — Yes.

And did you know that on the 21st December he raised other £30 upon it? — I got to know that afterwards.

From whom? — From himself.

Now, why was it that he wanted to sell the pawn ticket to you, or you to get a purchaser for the pawn ticket? — Because it would very likely realise money.

What did he want money for at that time? — As far as I understand, he did not wish to redeem the pledge when he took the extra £30 on it, and he wanted to take any little value out of the ticket that remained then.

Did he tell you why he was eager to get the balance of value out? — No.

Was he so anxious for the money that he trusted you with the pawn ticket to try and find a purchaser? — Well, I do not know. I trusted him before.

Did he trust you this time? — Yes, with the pawn ticket.

And was he very anxious that you would find a purchaser? — Yes.

And did you do your best for him? — I applied at two different places.

And failed? — And failed.

By the COURT — How much was he willing to take; did he give you a limit? — I think he mentioned £10.

Cross-examination continued — Did he tell you at that time what he wanted the money for? — He did not.

Did he tell you at that time that he could get command of about £80 from the bank? — No.

Now, you said that he told you about a fortnight before the murder that he was going to America? — Yes.

Did he tell you why? — On account of a letter that he had got from a friend.

Did he show you the letter? — Yes.

Who was the friend? — I do not know; I did not read the signature.

Where did the letter come from? — I understand from San Francisco.

Who was the friend in San Francisco? — I cannot tell you.

What did he want him to come over to San Francisco for? — Business was pretty fair; very good, it stated, I think in the letter.

By the COURT — What language was it in? — In the English language.

Cross-examination continued — I thought you told us that the man had no business; I thought you said that the man had no calling? — Not as far as I knew.

Then what did you understand by a letter from San Francisco bidding him to go there because business was good? — Well, I understand that Slater and this man had had a club in conjunction before, and he wanted him to come out and join him again.

To run a club? — Yes.

Can you recollect anything more about the letter about which you have just told us? — No, I cannot.

Why did he not go? — I do not know.

Did he tell you why he did not go? — No, he did not, but his intentions were sincere; he intended to go as soon as possible.

Did he ever tell you of a friend Jacobs in New York? — No.

Do you know anything about his dealings in emeralds? — No.

Did you never hear of that? — No.

Did you ever hear of him going to Chicago? — No.

Did you know when he left on the 25th of December that his destination was Chicago? — I did not.

Were you surprised to hear that? — Yes.

Did he ever tell you that he meant to go to Queensland? — No.

Did you never hear of that? — No.

Did he ever mention to you that he intended to go to Monte Carlo? — Yes.

When? — I think it was prior to this letter arriving.

That would be early in December? — Yes, I believe it would.

By the COURT — Had he been there before? — Yes, he had been at Monte Carlo before.

Cross-examination continued — Did he tell you? — On account of some friend in the club stating he was going to Monte Carlo; that was before he produced the letter from San Francisco.

Do you know why he did not go to Monte Carlo? — I do not.

Did he ever tell you that he had changed his mind? — I think I heard him mention to these people who spoke of going that he would not manage to get to Monte Carlo.

Why? — He did not mention or state reasons.

Did you know by the middle of December that he had abandoned his intention of going there? — Yes, I believe so.

Did you ever hear it said that he intended to go to London? — No.

Or to the Continent generally, just across to the Continent; you never heard him say that? — Of course, Monte Carlo is the Continent.

Did he ever say that he was just going to the Continent, without mentioning any particular place? — No, Monte Carlo was what I heard said.

Did he seem to think the day when you saw him going to the Cunard Line that the "Campania" that sailed a week later would do him well enough? — Yes.

And did he tell you that he was at the Cunard office to inquire about the sailings? — Yes, about the sailings, and he got a pamphlet.

Did you know when he was speaking to you about going off to America or Chicago and the rest that he had taken his house for eighteen months from the 28th November? — I did not.

Did you know that he had bought a considerable quantity of furniture and furnished the house? — On the hire-purchase system, yes.

He told you that? — Yes. I knew that.

And did you know that he had set up as a dentist? — So the card read.

By the COURT — You saw the card? — Yes.

Cross-examination continued — I suppose you knew otherwise; did you not know otherwise? — Well, I thought I did.

You have been up in his house at 69 St. George's Road? — I have.

Did you ever see any dentist's instruments there? — No.

Or any sign of any business being earned on? — No.

You knew him well; how do you account for him taking his house for eighteen months and going away without mentioning the fact to the landlord? —I cannot say.

Does it strike you as curious? — With a man such as he is, I should look upon nothing with surprise.

Was the last time you saw him 24th December? — Yes.

And did you make an appointment with him, which he did not keep, immediately after that? — On the 24th I had to see him in his own house, and I was told he had gone out.

Did you call at a certain time to see him, and when you went were you not told that he was out? — Yes.

And you never saw him afterwards? — I did not.

And you had no idea that he was going off the following night? — None whatever.

He did not tell you that? — No.

Had he not a large quantity of clothes? — Yes.

He had eight or nine different packages full of clothes? — He had eight or nine different suits of clothes and so many coats; I do not know about packages.

Did you know that he shaved his moustache off in the middle of December? — Yes.

Did you remark it at the time? — Oh, yes.

Did he tell you why? — He mentioned to me that it was getting a bit scraggy.

Did you notice there was a few days' growth the last time you saw him? — Yes.

Did he write you a letter from New York? — Yes.

Were you his most intimate friend in Glasgow? — I question that very much.

Do you know anybody that was more intimate with him than you were? — Well, there were some of his own countrymen; I don't know who they were.

(Shown No. 53 of Productions.) — Was that the letter which he sent? — That is the letter.

Re-examined by Mr. M'CLURE — My friend says he had "a few days' growth" of the moustache the last time you saw him; do you know when he was shaved? — I do not exactly know the date.

Well, the barber has told us that he shaved it a fortnight before the 21st; was the moustache perfectly observable the last time you saw him? — Yes.

I mean, a feature in his face? — Yes.

Would it be incorrect to describe it as a few days' growth? — Rather more than a few days' growth I should say.

And he has a very black moustache? — Very dark.

You never would have taken him for a clean-shaven man when you saw him last? — No.

As regards dentist, have you any notion of the purpose for which Slater, and I suppose other people, take a designation of that kind? — To have a vocation of some kind, if they are required to state what their business is.

He has not pretended to be a dentist at any time to you? — No.

And you never knew him touching anybody's teeth? — No.

So far as you knew him, was he a man who lived like the rest of the people in these clubs, mainly by backing horses in the season or gambling at clubs? — Or gambling at clubs.

And that was the ordinary life of a lot of them who were there? — Yes, I may say that.

Now, did you hear him complain over and over again of -what he called business being bad in Glasgow? — Yes, I have heard him state that.

And you are quite familiar with the idea that he was on the move, so to speak, and was going away? — He spoke of going to America certainly, but I did not expect that he would go as soon as he did.

You thought it was to be the "Campania," instead of which it was the "Lusitania," a week earlier? — Yes.

Did you ever hear him saying that he would go when he got some one to take over his flat? — I know that he was negotiating for his flat being taken over, because I came in contact with a man who came up for a negotiation of that kind and saw him in Slater's apartments.

Tell me who that was? — A man called Aumann, as far as I understand.

Was Aumann up seeing Slater's flat? — Yes.

With a view to taking it over? — Yes.

Can you tell me how long that was before Slater left? — Some considerable time; I cannot tell you just exactly how long.

Do you know anything at all about Mrs. Freedman, who ultimately came into the flat after Slater left? — No.

In order to have lifted the brooch which had been deposited, he would have had to pay £60 down? — Considerably more — £61 odds he would have required to pay for the brooch.

And having raised as much money as he could by advances on the brooch he was then willing to sell any odd value it might have to a purchaser? — He was; the ticket was a valuable asset — a brooch pawned for £60.

You said he intended to go abroad, you thought to San Francisco? — Yes.

That was your understanding? — Yes.

And it is only a question whether it was sooner or later? — Exactly so.

By the COURT — Do you know whether Slater had any training as a dentist? — I do not know whether he may have had before he came to this country or not, but not since I knew him here.

And you think he merely took that name just to give an appearance of having an occupation? — Yes.

Do you know that in his declaration he calls himself a dentist? — I did not know.

At the time, on 21st December, was he well off or hard up? — Well, you see, there were £30 got at mid-day on the 21st, so that you would not say that a man in possession of £30 was hard up.

You told us he had no occupation, that he lost money at gambling, and that he was anxious to sell the pawn ticket; how did he live, if he had no occupation and had lost money; what was he living on? — On the gambling.

But he had lost in gambling, you told us? — Well, not all; he was still in possession of jewellery which he had pawned, and up till then he got £30 more, and what he still holds, and I believe he had other things that he could have realised money on, had he not gone away, so that he was not absolutely penniless.

You have told us that he called himself a dentist so as to have an occupation; he had an occupation as a dealer in diamonds and precious stones; you have seen his card with that on it? — Yes.

Having an occupation as a dealer in diamonds and precious stones, why did he require to call himself a dentist, or can you tell? — I have no explanation for that.

Where was he on Monday, 21st December? — That I have no conception of.

Where was he on Sunday, the 20th of December? — I could not say.

Was it on the 19th, the Saturday, that you saw him? — I am not certain about that — either the Friday or the Saturday; it was the week- end prior to the 21st, some time about the week-end I saw him.

He was not with you on Monday, 21st December, at all? — No.

He refers in his letter to you to his friends; in his letter to you he winds up by saying, "My best regards to you and all my friends "? — Yes.

Will you name them? — I take it that it was members of the club that had been in the habit of playing with him, a matter of seven or eight of us altogether; we played at poker, and I think that his reference to "friends" there meant those boys that played at cards, at poker, in the club, because outside of that I know of no others.

He says in his letter to you, "I will prove with five people where I have been when the murder was committed"; did you understand these were among his friends? — No, I did not — not the friends that I refer to, the club friends.

And you do not know who these people are? — No.

I did not catch the name of the person to whose care the San Francisco address was to be sent, 544 Broadway, San Francisco; what was the name? — Caesar Cafe.

Have you heard him speak in any other language besides English in the club or elsewhere? — No.

Had he associates who were not Scotch or English? — Yes.

Germans? — Yes.

How much have you known him lose at the Sloper or the Motor or the Mascot Clubs on any one occasion? — From £15 to £20; the bulk of his money was lost at clubs before he was a member of the Sloper Club — a club that I did not frequent at all, a club in Glasgow.

You said in reference to Monte Carlo that there were people in the club who were going there? — Yes.

Who were these? — Mr. Dewar and Mr. Dillon and a Mr. Maclean.

Are they still in Glasgow? — Yes.

And were those friends of his; did he go about with them? — At the club.

And outside? — I will not say outside.

Who besides you did he go about with outside? — German friends of his own.

Can you name any of them? — I did not come into contact with these people at all — his German friends, but still I know that he had them.

Can you name any of them? — Rattman, Aumann, and Max Brooks.

Do you recollect any others? — That is all I know of.

MAX RATTMAN, examined by Mr. M'CLURE — I was cited here for the Crown, but I was not called. I know Oscar Slater, and have known him for the last six years. He and I are fellow-countrymen. I was in Glasgow when he came to it. I arrived one train later than he did about 29th October, 1908. I met him frequently between that date and the 25th of December, when he left; I met him nearly every day. I met him generally in Gall's public-house in the Cowcaddens, and I met him at various clubs in the evening, sometimes in the Mascot Club, in Virginia Street, and sometimes in the Motor Club, in India Street, and I met him in Johnston's billiard saloon, opposite the Pavilion, in Renfield Street. I heard of Slater's intention to leave this country. As soon as he arrived in Glasgow he expected a letter from San Francisco or New York from a friend, and as soon as he received an answer he was willing to leave. About ten days before he left I saw a letter that came to him from San Francisco. It was sent to him by a friend of his, I believe, but I do not know the name, but it was signed by some one.

Would you recognise the name — was it anything like Devoto? — I am not positive about that. I read the letter. He said something about the reason for his stopping in this country, as he expected some one from London to take the house, and he could not leave till that party arrived. He was intending to go out in response to that letter as soon as he could arrange for the house being taken over. He told me that at the time he showed me the letter. On 21st December I was with Slater at half-past four in Gall's public- house. Slater came in, and he asked me to come over with him to the bar, and he spoke to me about a pawn ticket which he would sell me for £4. He said that he had a brooch which was pawned for £60 in Sauchiehall Street, corner of Buchanan Street, in Mr. Liddell's pawnbroking office. I had seen the brooch before; I have seen his wife wearing it. It was a half-moon with a row of diamonds. I refused to buy it myself, and I asked Mr. Aumann, with whom I had dealings at the time, whether he was willing to buy it. I said that it was pawned at the corner of Sauchiehall Street. Mr. Aumann said that it was no use, as the pawnbrokers had already advanced too much on it, and he would not have any profit, because he would have to repay £60. It was I who spoke to Mr. Aumann on Slater's behalf in Gall's public-house. Slater then left, and soon after Mr. Aumann and another person, whom I did not know, left, and had a game of billiards in Johnston's billiard room. We stopped playing a little later than half-past six. I saw Slater that evening before I left the billiard room. He came into the billiard room about twenty minutes past six, and I asked him whether he had sold the ticket or not, and he said no.

I find a telegram was sent by Slater from the Central Station at twelve minutes past six that night; would it take him about six or seven minutes to go from the Central Station up to the billiard room? — Not much more.

Does that support your view that it was about twenty minutes past six when he came to the billiard room? — I think it was twenty minutes past, because soon after he left we finished off playing, and he was only there for about ten minutes. I am speaking generally, because I was not looking at my watch at the time. Slater left Johnston's billiard room on the night of the 21st about half-past six. I am sure about that. He said that he was going home for dinner, and he asked me where I was going. I said, "Very likely to a music hall," and he said that he would see me there, if possible. I think I said that I was going to the Palace, and he said, "Very likely I will come and see you." I knew that he dined about seven o'clock every night. I did not go to the Palace Music Hall. I saw some one off to Germany by the 9.30 train from St. Enoch Station. I got home about twelve o'clock. That was on the Monday, and I believe it was the Wednesday night when I next saw Slater after ten o'clock in Johnston's billiard room. It was after ten or eleven, because I had been at a music hall, and I would get to Johnston's billiard room about a quarter to eleven. He was sitting there with Mr. Cameron, the last witness. I think that would be about eleven o'clock at night. He was sitting on a bench near the door; I was playing with Mr. Aumann, and he was watching us. Aumann and I had a game at a table opposite him. We had only 100 up, and we left about twenty minutes past eleven o'clock. Slater, Cameron, and I left together. Cameron left us at the corner of Cambridge Street and Sauchiehall Street, and I went on with Slater as far as his place in St. George's Road. I never saw Slater wearing light, checked trousers of any kind. I have seen him wearing brown boots sometimes, but very seldom — once or twice. I never saw him with a Donegal cap on, but I have seen him with a cap with the sides up. I never saw him with light-coloured gaiters. His ordinary clothes were generally dark or brown. I was aware of his desire to get some one to take over his flat before leaving. I received a letter from him from Liverpool. It was a letter in German, and is on page 16 of the print. I translated it. (Shown production No. 26.) That is the letter I received from him. He says there "that Freedman's girl took over my flat." I see that the translation says, "Dear Max, surprisingly leaving Glasgow."

Does that mean unexpectedly? — I did not translate it like that. I would translate it, "Having left Glasgow suddenly, I am very sorry I was not able to say good-bye." I was aware that he was negotiating with Freedman. He expected a letter every day, but the letter never came, and when Mrs. Freedman came she was sitting in the flat waiting for him. I know that he was expecting Mrs. Freedman to come down. That letter was the last that I heard of him before this affair. I am perfectly certain that I can speak to the fact that the accused was in my company till at least 6.30 on the night of the 21st. So far as my recollection goes, we left off playing at 6.35, and Slater left before we stopped playing billiards. I knew that he was in the billiard room for a very short time — about eight or ten minutes. I believe it would take some seven or eight minutes to come from the Central Station, where the telegram was sent off at 6.12, up to the billiard room where we were. On the 21st of December last Slater had a moustache about ¼ an inch long. It was quite noticeable, it being dark. I would never have taken him for a clean-shaven man that day. I am not quite positive how he was dressed when I saw him last, but I know that he had a dark suit of clothes and a bowler hat.

Cross-examined by the LORD ADVOCATE — What are you? — I am a commercial traveller representing a firm in Germany.

Where are you situated? — In Edinburgh now.

Where is your place of business? — I have not got a place of business. I am a traveller.

Is your real name George Schmidt? — No; my real name is Max Rattman.

Do not you often go by the name of George Schmidt? — No.

Never? — I once did.

When did you come to know the prisoner? — About five or six years ago.

Where? — In several places in London.

Where? — In the Traveller's Retreat, for instance.

Where else? — Denmark Street.

What are these places? — Gambling places or clubs.

What was his means of livelihood? — As far as I could see he was gambling; he was a sportsman and making a book.

How long did you know him at that time in London as a gambler? — I did not know him long in fact, I did not know him personally at all in London. I got to know him better personally in Glasgow.

What were you doing in London at that time? — I had a restaurant.

And he came about that? — No; he did not.

When did you meet him again in Glasgow? — About 29th October.

What name was he going under? — I only knew him under the name of Slater. Having been at his place, I saw that he went under the name of Anderson.

Why did he go under the name of Anderson? — I could not tell you.

Do you know that he called himself a dentist? — I do not know anything about that.

Did you not know that he called himself a dentist? — No.

You never heard of that? — No; I never heard anything about his being a dentist.

Did you ever see him in possession of jewels? — Yes, I did.

Where? — One day he offered me a ring for sale, but not for myself.

When? — About four weeks before the murder.

Did you know that he called himself a dealer in diamonds and precious stones? — I did.

Was that correct? — He was known to me as a dealer in diamonds.

When? — Lately.

What do you mean by lately? — Since I knew him again in Glasgow.

"Who told you, when you knew him in Glasgow, that he was a dealer in diamonds? — He often had some diamonds about him.

Where did he get them? — I do not know.

You just knew that he was a dealer in diamonds and precious stones because he had them? — Yes.

And he tried to sell one to you? — One ring.

Do you know any other people besides yourself to whom he tried to sell them? — He tried to sell to Mr. Aumann.

Any one else? — No.

Do you know that he tried to sell to another of your countrymen, Jackson? — No.

Did you know about him pawning a brooch at the time ho did it? — I knew about it.

Where did it come from? — I do not know; I could not tell.

Are you sure he had no place of business then? — Not so far as I know.

Can you fix the date when you saw the letter from San Francisco? — No. It was some time before the murder.

But how long you do not know? — No. It was eight or ten days, or something like that.

Who was the man who wanted him? — His friend, with whom he had a club in New York.

Was it a man Jacobs? — Jacobs was mentioned in the letter, but I do not know whose was the signature.

Was it not a man Jacobs who dealt in precious stones? — I do not know.

Try and recollect. — I could not tell you.

Did he say he would join his friend in San Francisco? — Yes.

Did you know that when he went his destination was Chicago? — No; he said America.

Did you ever hear of that till to-day? — No.

From your knowledge of his manner and ways, can you account for him going to Chicago? — No.

You cannot explain that? — No.

Under how many different names did you know him going? — Only Slater and this name Anderson.

Did you ever hear of a name Otto Sando? — No.

Did you know that when he went away he took that name? — I read it in the paper; that was all.

Can you explain that? — No.

You don't know why he took that name? — No; I could not tell you.

He had no reason to conceal his going away from you? — No; he did not conceal it from me.

Why did he go away so quickly? — Because the person was waiting in the flat for him, and he packed up his things.

Did you not know that the person was not waiting in the flat for him but in the Alexandra Hotel? — I do not know.

You thought the lady was waiting? — In the flat.

And he left suddenly because she was to take possession of it? You just judged that from the letter? — Yes.

From what passage in the letter is it that you judge that the lady was in the flat, and he had to get out of it? — "As soon as I arrived home I found Mrs. Freedman waiting." That is what he says in my letter here.

Is it? — No; I find it says, "Freedman's girl has taken my flat over."

Did you think he had suddenly departed because Freedman's girl had appeared on the scene? — I believed so.

Who was Freedman's girl? — I do not know.

Did you never hear of her before? — No.

Did he say in his letter that he was sorry he had forgotten to say good- bye to you? — Yes.

Did he say good-bye to you? — No; simply in the letter.

Did he say he forgot to say good-bye to you because Freedman's girl had appeared? — No; it was because I did not go up. He asked me to go up on the Friday, and I did not go up. That is the reason I did not see him any more.

Did you know he was sailing on the Saturday? — I did not know — yes, he said in the letter that he was in Liverpool, and was leaving for San Francisco, and his wife was going to Paris.

Did you know he was sailing on Saturday before you got the letter? — No; I did not know until I got the letter.

Was the last time you saw him the Thursday? — Yes; I think so.

And he said nothing to you on the Thursday? — He said I was to come up on Friday and see him, being Christmas Day.

He said nothing to you on the Thursday about starting for Chicago on the Saturday? — He said San Francisco.

Did he say anything to you on Thursday about starting by ship? — He said nothing on Thursday. He simply said I was to come up on Friday, and nothing else.

By the COURT — There is nothing about that in the letter? — He says in the letter he was leaving for San Francisco.

Where is that? I do not see that? — (No answer.)

Cross-examination resumed — Would you be so kind as to translate for us the two sentences, the one about the French girl and the other about San Francisco? — It says here, "The French girl is going to Paris from Liverpool, and I go on to San Francisco, and I shall write you a letter how things are."

By the COURT — Where does he say he is going on Saturday? — He says it in the letter.

Read the portion in the letter where he says he is going to San Francisco on the Saturday? — He says the girl is going to Paris, Saturday morning.

Does he say Saturday morning? — No.

Why did you say that if the letter does not have Saturday morning? — The letter was Saturday morning. "And I shall let you know how things are in San Francisco." That is all. "Give my best respects" to So-and-So. There is nothing else mentioned except that he will let me know from San Francisco.

It does not say when he is leaving Liverpool? — Not in the letter.

Cross-examination resumed — Did you know to-day for the first time that he was not on his way to San Francisco, but was on his way to Chicago? — I do not know anything about Chicago.

Who was the French girl referred to in the sentence immediately before? — That was the person who was living with him at the time.

Where? — 69 St. George's Road.

Does he say that she is going to Paris from Liverpool? — Yes.

You knew that she went with him to America? — I did not know. I only read that after he was arrested that the girl was in his company.

You found that out afterwards, that that was not true about going to Paris? — Yes.

Tell us what is the word that you have translated here by "surprisingly"? — It says "absolutely suddenly," literally translated.

"Absolutely suddenly"? — "Having left Glasgow, I forgot to say good-bye to you because Freedman's missus has taken my flat over."

Does he really say that he forgot to say good-bye to you because Freedman's girl had taken over his flat? — Yes, absolutely.

We may take it as "absolutely suddenly leaving." Did he give any explanation in his letter to you for his absolutely suddenly leaving Glasgow? — Because Mrs. Freedman had taken the flat over.

That is the explanation? — That is the explanation in the letter.

Who is the marker in the billiard room in Renfield Street? — A very old man; I do not know his name.

Was he in the billiard room on the 21st of December? — I could not tell you. I did not take any notice.

How do you recollect it was 21st December? — Because, as soon as I arrived home, I heard about the murder. I was not living far from it.

Was there anybody else in the billiard room at the time? — I believe there were two or three other persons, but I could not tell you.

What were their names? — We were playing three — Aumann, myself, and another man that I do not know — we were playing a three hundred game when Slater came up.

Are you just given us your idea of the time? — Yes.

As I understand, you did not look at the clock? — No, but I was home about ten minutes to seven, because I was wanting to see some one off at the station.

You are giving us your guess at the time? — Yes.

You say you reached your home at ten minutes to seven? — Yes.

Where is your home? — At that time it was at 23 Cromwell Street, New City Road.

Did you finish your game after Slater left? — Yes, there was only a minute of difference when we finished the game and when Slater left.

That is to the best of your recollection? — Yes.

You neither took the time when he came in nor did you take the time when he went out? — No.

All you know is that you reached your own home at 23 Cromwell Street at ten minutes to seven? — Yes.

And you were in the billiard room after Slater left — Yes.

For some time, which you have guessed at? — Yes.

May I take it that you do not recollect what clothes he was wearing that night? — No, but I am certain that he had a dark suit and patent boots.

Had he a great number of suits? — Yes.

And hats? — Mostly a bowler hat or this one cap that I have mentioned.

Did he tell you why it was that he was so anxious to get money on the pawn ticket on the 20th or 21st? — He said he had no chance at present to get it out, as he was going away.

Was he very anxious to get the money? — No. He simply offered it for £4 or £5 — he said he would let me have it for that price, but he would not let others get it for that. He said he was to offer it to Miller in a public-house in Cambridge Street.

Re-examined by Mr. M'CLURE — Suppose Slater was at the Central Station telegraph office at twelve minutes past six, can you give us any idea how long it would take him to walk up Renfield Street and along Sauchiehall Street to where he lived, the corner of St. George's Road? — About twenty minutes.

So that even if he went quite straight from the Central Station to St. George's Road it would take him that time? — I think so.

How long do you think he stopped in the billiard room? — About ten minutes.

So in that way he could not have arrived until after twenty minutes to seven? — No, because he only left at 6.30.

Suppose he left Johnston's billiard room at 6.30, how long would it take him to walk at an ordinary pace? — About twenty minutes.

Johnston's billiard room down to the Central Station, down Renfield Street, is a considerable distance? — I think I could do it in about eight minutes. Of course, Slater was a very fast walker.

You have no manner of doubt at all that it was on 21st December that you saw him there up till 6.30? — I am positive about that.

By the COURT — What country was it that you and Slater came from? — From England.

You said you were a fellow-countryman of his? — Yes, German by birth.

Is Slater a German by birth? — I am not positive. I do not know where he comes from or where he was born.

You said you were a fellow-countryman of his? — He told me he was a German.

Do you know what he was trained as? — No.

Do you know whether he was ever trained to any occupation? — No.

I notice in the letter that was written to you there is a reference to Karl Kunstler, Soldata, and Willy. Who are they? — People living in Glasgow.

Are they all Germans? — Yes.

Who is Willy? — A little wrestler.

What is his name? — Hoyne.

Is Slater an English name? — As far as I know it is an English name.

Do you know what the prisoner's German name was? — No.

You have no doubt that he has one? — I could not say.

Do you know any person in Germany, of German birth, called Slater? — I do not know.

PETER JOHNSTON, examined by Mr. M'CLURE. I am a billiard room proprietor in Renfield Street, Glasgow. I know the prisoner Slater. He frequented my billiard rooms. He came to Glasgow about November. Pie w-as in the habit of coming to my billiard rooms pretty frequently between that and the time he left Glasgow. I do not know the names of those who came with Slater to the billiard room. Sometimes he came himself and mixed up with the company. I know a man called Cameron. He was in with Slater two or three times. I know Rattman and Aumann. These are all people who were frequently about my rooms. The table at which these people usually played was No. 6, in the far-away corner. I could not say whether

Slater was playing in my rooms on 21st December or not. I find that table No. 6 was continuously engaged from 5.8 to 6.40. I do not remember who were playing at that table. I was away for my tea at the time. I remember Slater coming in on Wednesday, 23rd December, about 10.25 at night, along with Cameron. I would ask him when he came in if he wanted a game.

He said that they did not care about playing that night. They stayed on for some time in the place.

Cross-examined by the LORD ADVOCATE — Is it not the fact that you saw Slater in your billiard room only twice? — I have seen him two or three times. I have seen him more than twice.

When was the first time? — I could not say — he was coming about it for a month.

Was not the first time you saw him in your rooms about 14th or 15th December? — I do not remember the dates.

Did he play the first time? — I could not really say.

Did you see him, do you think, more than three times altogether? — Yes, I would see him maybe six or eight times.

From what time till what time? — He generally came in in the evening.

But can you tell us what was the earliest date, or about the earliest date, that you saw him? — He might come in about five or six o'clock. It was generally about eight or nine.

That was in November or December? — November, I suppose.

You do not know? — No.

On the last occasion, on 23rd December, he came in about eleven o'clock at night? — About 10.25.

And waited till midnight? — He waited till his two friends played their game.

Did you see him on 21st December at all? — I do not remember.

Was he clean shaven? — I would not like to say. I rather think he was a little dark, but he might not have very much to show. I do not know that he was exactly clean shaven.

If he had anything on his upper lip it was very little? — Yes.

By the COURT — Except on the 23rd, had he always played any time you saw him in the rooms before? — He played very regularly when he did come in.

ADAM GIBB, examined by Mr. M'CLURE — I was a billiard marker in Johnston's employment on 21st December last. I have seen Slater at various times in the billiard rooms, two or three times a week at least. I could not tell the names of the friends that he played with, but I could recognise them. Being foreign to me, I did not know their names. They were German. (Shown witness Max Rattman.) I recognise that man as being one of his friends. (Shown witness Josef Aumann.) I also recognise that man. I remember seeing Slater in the billiard rooms on 23rd December about eleven o'clock at night. He was by himself. He was not joined by somebody that I saw. I did not see Cameron that night. I remember distinctly that he had a moustache on that night. It was quite noticeable to me, and I was at a billiard table at the opposite end, 16 feet away. No person who had a look at him could have taken him for a clean- shaven man that night. He appeared to me to be a man that had neglected to shave his upper lip for about a fortnight.

Cross-examined by the LORD ADVOCATE — When did you first see him coming about your saloon? — I could not specify any date. He came back and forward for about three months.

Do you remember any time when he had a full moustache? — No, never at any time. It was always short and stubbly.

Did you know or did you not know that his moustache was shaved off in the middle of December? — I did not know.

Did you see at any time during the period he was frequenting your rooms that he had shaved his moustache off? — No; I cannot say that he did shave it off.

Did you notice at any time during the three or four months any difference in his appearance? — There have been times that he came about the rooms and has been playing when I probably have not looked much at him. In a public billiard room I do not take exact stock of every one. It was always a short moustache that he wore.

You saw him going about the room in November and December, and you never saw any change in his appearance so far as his moustache was concerned? — I never saw much change in him.

You did not observe it? — No.

Do you say that the last time you saw him he had a stubbly moustache? — Yes.

Were you in the billiard room on 21st December? — Yes.

The day of the murder? — Yes.

Did you see him there that day? — No.

Re-examined by Mr. M'CLURE — Was the table engaged upon the Monday, as you find from your books, from 5.8 till 6.40? — Yes.

Is that the table, No. 6, which was usually played on by Slater and his friends? — Yes; that was the table they generally played on.

As I understand, you do not remember who was playing that afternoon? — I cannot remember.

JOSEF AUMANN, examined by Mr. M'CLURE — I live at 282 Buchanan Street, Glasgow. I have known Slater from October last year. I met him first in Gall's public-house in Cowcaddens, and I saw him sometimes after that. I remember Slater speaking to me about going to America. He spoke to me three weeks before about going to America. He told me that as soon as he could sell his house he was going to America. He also told me about a letter that he had from America, but I did not see that letter. I did not see him showing it to anybody. Mr. Rattman told me that he had seen the letter. I did not see it myself, but Slater told me he had received the letter. After that he came to me and asked me to take his flat off his hands. He said that he would sell his house, and asked me to take it. He offered to show it to me, and I said that if I liked the house I would take it over. I went to the house to see it. I went one evening about seven or eight o'clock, and I looked over the house and looked at the furniture. I did not take it because my wife did not wish me to buy a house. She would not have the house. He did not say anything to me as to what he was going to do with it when I did not take it. He told me that he would look out for somebody else. I remember that on 21st December I was in Gall's public-house in Cowcaddens, about three o'clock or half-past three, and I stayed on for some time. I played billiards that afternoon in Johnston's billiard room, and, while I was playing, Slater came in from five o'clock to half-past; I am not exactly sure. I played at billiards that night till about a quarter to seven o'clock, and then I went home. Rattman did not come with me. I had been playing with Rattman, and, while we were playing. Slater was looking on. I think I went home by myself about a quarter to seven. I do not know whether Slater left the billiard room to go home before I had finished playing my game. I do not remember Slater or Rattman going out. When I left I do not remember whether Slater was still there or whether he had left us.

I must ask you again, in case there is any mistake. Can you tell me whether Slater was for some time in the billiard room that afternoon when you were playing billiards? — I do not think he stayed long.

Can you tell me when he went out? — Yes, in the afternoon he was there. I was with Rattman, and Slater came up and asked Rattman about this ticket. Slater went out by himself, and by that time the game was finished. That was some minutes before the game was finished. I think I left the billiard room about a quarter to seven. I left a short time before I got my supper, and I went directly from the billiard room for my supper at home. I think Slater was away from the billiard room a short time before me. I do not think the game was quite finished when he left. I think the game was finished a short time after Slater went away. After Slater went away the game was finished in two or three minutes. My house where I stay is about three minutes' walk from Johnston's billiard room. I lived in Hope Street at that time, at the Theatre Royal, and I walked home for my supper. The flat which Slater wished me to take over from him is a good bit further out west; it was in St. George's Road. That is a good way out beyond Hope Street; about ten minutes' walk further than Hope Street. I remember on the Wednesday, after that, which was the 23rd, being in Johnston's billiard room again, and I saw Slater again. I think that was after closing time.

Was that after the public-houses were closed? — Yes, Mr. Cameron was with him. (Shown the witness, Hugh Cameron.) That is the gentleman I mean. Slater sat down with his friend Cameron, and he stopped a longer time for a drink along with his friends. I saw Slater about two times or three times in the billiard room. I did not see him more than two or three times altogether when he was in Glasgow. I have been with him only two or three times, but I have seen him at other times. I saw him in black clothes. I never saw him with light, checked trousers or with light-coloured spats. He was only in dark clothes. He wore black boots, I think.

Was it patent leather ones? — He had sometimes clean boots.

Do you mean bright, shiny boots? — Yes.

Cross-examined by the LORD ADVOCATE — Did you say that Slater came into the billiard room between five and half-past five o'clock on the afternoon of the 21st? — Yes, I did.

When he came in between five and half-past five, were you playing a game of billiards with Rattman? — Yes.

Did you commence the game before Slater came in? — Yes; I was playing a game as he came in.

Did Slater stop a very short time in the billiard room? — Yes.

And then did he go away? — About some minutes before I finished the game.

But your game had begun before he came in? — Yes.

And he came between five and half-past five? — Yes.

Do you remember for what purpose Slater came to the billiard room? — He came and asked Mr. Rattman about this pawn ticket for the brooch.

Was his purpose in coming to the billiard room to get Rattman to give him money for a pawn ticket? — Yes.

And did Rattman refuse? — He said that he would not buy it.

When Rattman said that he would not buy it, did Slater then go away? — Yes.

You understood that he was going to try and get money somewhere else? — Yes; he only spoke to me and Rattman.

Just about the pawn ticket? — Yes.

Did you look at the clock when Slater came in? — No, I do not think so.

Nor when he went out? — No, I do not think so.

When did you look at the clock that night? — I never looked at the clock.

Do you recollect whether it was a wet evening; was it raining? — I do not know.

Had Slater a waterproof on? — I think he had a waterproof on in the afternoon. I do not know whether he had a waterproof on in the billiard room.

Had he a waterproof on when he was in Gall's public-house? — Yes. I think he had a waterproof; I cannot remember exactly.

Look at No. 43 of the productions. Did you sign that card? — Yes.

Is that the waterproof you have seen Slater wearing? — Yes. It is a waterproof like his, but I do not say that is it. He had a waterproof of the same colour.

And you signed that label? — Yes.

Was it a waterproof like that that he was wearing that afternoon? — Yes.

Do you recollect what sort of hat he was wearing? — He had sometimes a cap.

Was it a black hat that you could pull down? — No.

What kind of hat was it Was it like any one of these hats? — He had a hat sometimes like a bowler hat.

Can you say what hat he had that night? — No.

Did you know of him doing anything except selling jewels? — No; I did not see Slater much.

Did you know of him doing any business except selling jewels? — No.

Do you remember meeting him in Gall's public-house in Cowcaddens one day in December, 1908? — Yes, with Rattman.

Do you remember him offering for sale a diamond ring, with twenty-five diamonds in it? — Yes. He showed it, and he asked me what I would give for it. I offered him £.30 or £35, and he said he would not sell it.

Did you think that Slater was the owner of the house that he wanted you to take over — did you understand he was able to sell you the house that he asked you to buy? — I do not understand very well.

Did you understand from him that if he could find a buyer for the house he would go off to America? — Yes.

Did you understand that he was only waiting on in Glasgow till he could get the house taken off his hands? — I do not understand.

Re-examined by Mr. M'CLURE — What o'clock do you have supper? — Seven o'clock, and sometimes after eight.

Is seven o'clock the hour of supper in your house? — Yes.

When you left the billiard room on Monday, 21st December, was that shortly before seven or shortly before eight? — Shortly before seven.

How long, do you think, after Slater left the billiard room? — He went away about half-past six.

JAMES TRACEY, examined by Mr. M'CLURE — I am a porter in the employment of the Caledonian Railway Company at the Central Station, Glasgow. I was on night duty on Christmas Day, 1908. I remember being down about the weighs before the 9.5 train started for London and Liverpool. I remember a badge porter coming with a lot of luggage on his barrow. He told me that he was waiting for the arrival of the party to whom it belonged. I saw a cab arrive after that, about 8.45. There were a gentleman and two ladies in it. The gentleman came out and claimed the luggage which the badge porter had. I am quite certain they all arrived together — the three of them. I opened the cab door, and they got out. The gentleman told me the destination of his luggage. He told me to have it labelled for Liverpool, and that he was going by the 9.5 train. I got luggage labels, and I labelled all the pieces of luggage. There were nine altogether. I took the luggage up to the train; it was taken up to the train on the badge porter's barrow. I put it on board the train. I put it in the rear brake van of the 9.5 train.

Was the rear brake van a through van for Liverpool? — Well, when I took up the luggage I asked the guard where he would have it, and he told me to put it into the rear van. I had told him by this time that it was destined for Liverpool, and he told me where to put it. I do not know what tickets the gentleman had. He asked me to send a parcel to Paris. It was a small paper parcel, about 1 foot square. He asked me if he could have it forwarded through to Paris, and I went to the excess clerk, and I told him that the gentleman wanted to have it forwarded through to Paris, and the excess clerk informed me that the parcel office was shut, but that he could have it forwarded by post, and I told the gentleman he could have it forwarded straight from Liverpool when he arrived there. One lady travelled with the gentleman. The gentleman had a dark coat and a dark cap. I saw him in the train, and the tickets being checked; he was in a compartment a few compartments from where the luggage was placed. The other porter had let him in for some excess. He was grumbling a bit at that.

Except for the grumbling about the excess luggage he had to pay for, did you see anything remarkable about the passenger? — No, nothing. He seemed to be quite cool and collected, but he was annoyed at having to pay the excess; that was the only thing.

He did not seem to be hiding from anybody? — No; he told me he had travelled all over the world, and he had never been asked to pay excess before.

But he did not seem to be wanting to escape observation? — No, he was just the same as any other passenger. (Shown prisoner.) That is the gentleman. The night he travelled to Liverpool he had a moustache. It was quite noticeable.

Cross-examined by the Lord Advocate — Did you just see him at the station when you were putting in his baggage; had you ever seen him before? — No, I never saw the gentleman before.

And you just saw him when you were putting his baggage into the luggage van? — Yes.

And have you any difficulty at all in recognising him? — No, that is the man there.

You recognise him at once? — Yes.

Did you notice whether he had a slight moustache or a moustache like he has now? — He had a moustache something similar to the one he has now.

Was there as much as he has now? — Yes, something similar to the moustache Tie is wearing now.

Did you know what tickets he had? — No.

Did you see them examined? — No.

By the COURT — Have you seen either of the ladies here? — No.

About what age was the one that went with him? — She would be a woman about forty or thereabouts.

The one that went with him? — Yes, thirty-five or forty.

(Shown Andrée Junio Antoine.) Is that the one that went with him? — I could not say.

You do not identify her? — I could not say.

(Shown Catherine Schmalz.) Do you know that one? — No.

HUGH MURPHY, examined by Mr. MAIR — I stay at City View, Larkhall. I am a railway official at the Central Station, Glasgow. I am in charge of the train running department books. I have examined the books for the night of 25th December, 1908. There were two carriages for Liverpool on the 9.5 train that night —

a brake composite and brake third. One of these carriages went direct to Liverpool and one did not; the brake third went direct to Liverpool. That carriage would leave the London train at Wigan to go to Liverpool.

Suppose passengers were in a London carriage of that train would they have to change at Wigan? — That is the last point for changing. They would have to change somewhere. Their luggage would have to be changed unless it was loaded in the Liverpool carriage van. There was luggage accommodation in the Liverpool carriage.

Cross-examined by Mr. MORISON — It would not be necessary with a London ticket to travel by a London carriage? — No, not necessarily.

A passenger with a London ticket might desire to go to Liverpool first, and he could do so with his London ticket without extra charge? — He could.

WILLIAM KEMPTON, examined by Mr. M'CLURE — I am manager to James L. Bryce, pawnbroker, in Oswald Street, Glasgow. I saw Slater on 3rd November. I had known him before, about the Glasgow Exhibition year, but on this occasion I saw him about 3rd November. I did not see him frequently between 3rd November and the time he left; I only saw him once, when he redeemed a pledge. On the 3rd November he pledged with me two gold rings, three pearl studs, a gold pencil-case, a gold purse, and a fountain pen, and he got £5 for these articles. He redeemed them on 13th November. He dealt with me as Oscar Slater. The last time I saw him was on 22nd December. He called in the afternoon about four o'clock, and he redeemed a pair of prism binocular glasses. He had pledged them on 7th December for £2 10s. When he came in he was dressed in a dark overcoat and a hard hat. He did not seem in any way excited in his manner. Upon Tuesday, 22nd December, he told me he was going to America.

Did he say he was making any inquiries about steamers? — He wondered whether he would go by the Anchor Line; he thought he might go by the Anchor Line, and he asked me about that; of course we could give him no information. I am quite certain that was on the 22nd December, because that was the day the prism binoculars were redeemed. At that time, on the 22nd December, he had a slight stubbly moustache. It was quite noticeable.

Cross-examined by the LORD ADVOCATE — Did you know him in 1901? — Yes.

How long was he in Glasgow then? — Well, I could not exactly say, but most of the Exhibition time.

Did you do business with him then? — Yes.

What sort of business? — Pledging jewellery; he always redeemed it.

Did you know that he was a dealer in precious stones, diamonds, and jewels? — Well, I had an idea that he was buying and selling.

Where he got them you did not know? — No.

Did that business dealing between you and him continue during the time he was in Glasgow in 1901? — Yes.

Then did he disappear for some years? — Yes.

And then did he reappear on the 3rd November, 1908? — That was the first time.

What address did he give on the 3rd November? — Central Hotel, Glasgow.

Did you ever know he had any other address in Glasgow during November and December at that time? — No.

Did you think that it was the Central Hotel all the time? — Yes.

Did you notice whether on the 3rd November he had a moustache? — No, I really could not say then.

Can you say whether he had one when he was in Glasgow in 1901; did he wear a moustache? — Well, I would say he had always a slight moustache.

Did you notice it was stubbly on the 22nd December? — Yes, just growing.

How was it he came to speak, on the 22nd December, about taking a ship for America? — Well, I really could not say, except that it might be in regard to saying something about these glasses he was redeeming.

He wanted the binoculars for the voyage? — Well, I thought perhaps he might want them.

What did he say to you about going to America? — Oh, well, he did not say what he was going to do when he got there.

Did he say anything about the time he was going to start? — No, he did not say.

Or the line he was going by? — Well, that was all he asked about — the Anchor Line; of course I could give him no information.

Did he say. anything about where he was going to in America? — No, he did not say definitely.

Or why he was going? — No.

You say that he was redeeming the binoculars on the 22nd? — Yes.

Do you recollect when he pledged them on the 7th December what address he gave? — No, his address was not asked; it was taken for granted.

You just kept it on the books as it was? — Yes.

Re-examined by Mr. M'CLURE — I suppose you do not care what the man's address is? — Well, we ask the address, but knowing Slater so well we thought it was good enough at the Central Hotel.

After all, he would not get his pledge back without paying you your advances and interest? — Certainly not.

And if he changes his address in the meantime it makes no difference to you? — None to us.

My learned friend always asked, "Did he disappear?" — it is an awkward way of putting it; when my friend put the words, "Did Slater then disappear" into your mouth, do you not just mean that he left Glasgow? — I do not know where he went to.

And when he came back he reappeared, I suppose? — Yes.

Were all your transactions with the man *bona fide* loans upon property deposited? — Yes.

And do you say he always redeemed by and by the goods he left with you? — Yes.

ANDRÉE JUNIO ANTOINE, examined by Mr. M'CLURE — I was born in Paris, and I am now twenty-three years of age. It is about five years since I first met Slater. I met him in the Empire Theatre in London. He was a married man. He did not take up living with me at that time. When I met him first he was living alone, and not with his wife. He called himself a dentist. I never knew of him doing anything in the dentist line at all. He never worked as a dentist so far as I am aware. He used to manage clubs. I cannot tell whether he had any connection with clubs where cards were played in London, but I knew that he used to go to clubs. About three years ago I went with him to America. I was living with Slater in Brussels at that time, and we left from Boulogne for America. Slater went to America because of his wife, as she was always bothering him and came after him. He went to New York. In New York he managed a club. We travelled to New York under the name of Mr. and Mrs. A. George. We took that wrong name so that his wife might not find him. There is produced a house agreement between Peter de Sylvestri, Oscar Slater, and John Devoto, taking premises 114 West Twenty-Sixth Street, in the burgh of Manhattan. That is the first place where Slater carried on business. Devoto was his partner and de Sylvestri was his landlord. The rent was sixty dollars a month. On the first occasion we were in America for one year, and then we returned to Paris for my health.

And to visit your people? — The principal thing was my health. We were away from America for about two months, and then we returned under the name of A. George. While Slater was over in America he carried on the business of the club as Oscar Slater. We came back again to France in June, 1908. We came to England in August, and to Glasgow in October. When we came to Glasgow first we stayed in Renfrew Street. We were only a few days there before we got a fiat at St. George's Road. We went to Glasgow because Slater thought that there was good business to be done there. After we were there for some time he found that there was no good business to be had, and he made up his mind to return to America. He made up his mind to do so a month after we arrived in Glasgow, somewhere about the beginning of December. When in Glasgow Slater went about the clubs gambling. He had one or two friends who came to the house, namely, Cameron and Reid. I never saw Rattman. Slater received a letter from San Francisco, from John Devoto, the person who was his partner in New York, telling him to come, that there was good business over there.

Was there anything that prevented him going off at once? — Yes, because we had the flat. I knew that he intended to leave if he got the flat disposed of. I remember of Aumann coming up to look over the flat, but he did not take it. Mr. Freedman, a German gentleman in London, wrote saying that if Slater could find a place where Mrs. Freedman could live, she would come down. Slater offered him the flat. We left Glasgow for America on 25th December. Before we left Mrs. Freeman had arrived. She arrived on the Friday morning, 20th December. I got a postcard from the Alexandra Hotel, in Bath Street, saying that she had arrived. I sent my servant over to tell her to come to the flat.

[At this stage the witness, feeling faint, had to leave the Court, and the examination was adjourned.]

CATHERINE SCHMALZ, examined by Mr. M'CLURE — I came to Glasgow from London along with Madame Junio on 4th November. Madame Junio is the last witness, Andrée Junio Antoine, but she was known in London as Madame Junio. We took up house at 136 Renfrew Street. We were about a week there before changing to the house at St. George's Road. Oscar Slater left Glasgow on 25th December. From the time we arrived in November until that time I acted as the servant in the house. Slater usually got up about nine o'clock or 9.. 30 in the morning, and he sometimes went out. He was always in for lunch. He took dinner at home at seven o'clock.

Did he take dinner always at seven, or was it sometimes a little later? — It all depended on whether I was ready with the dinner, but it was generally at seven o'clock. I do not remember of him being away at dinner time so long as I was there. I heard it proposed that Slater should go back to America. That was three weeks or a month before 25th December. I remember a gentleman coming up to look over the flat. He was a German, and I think his name was Aumann. He came into the kitchen as well as going over the rest of the house. His purpose in looking over the house was that he proposed taking it. If he had taken the flat then Slater was going to America. I heard that spoken of in the house three or four weeks before Slater left. Aumann did not take the flat. After that fell through I heard conversation about some one named Freedman coming from London. Slater was writing to Freedman to take over the flat. I was not sure that he would take it, but I heard them talking about it. I remember the Sunday before Slater left, that being Sunday, 20th December. Slater was never out of the house on a Sunday and on that particular Sunday he was in the house, in his dressing gown. He was at dinner in the house that night. Reid and his little boy and Madame were also at dinner that night. I am quite positive on that point. I know now that Monday, 21st December, was the date of the murder that was committed.

As regards Monday, was there any difference in Slater's ordinary habit of coming home to dinner? — No; I never noticed anything.

During that week was there any departure from his ordinary habit of coming home for dinner about seven o'clock? — No.

On Monday, the 21st, did he come home for dinner? — Yes. I remember two letters arriving by the morning post on Monday, 21st December. In the afternoon, after lunch. Slater said that I could go away to London to find another situation on the Saturday. One of the two letters came from London and the other came from San Francisco. I do not know anything more about them than that. Mrs. Freedman came on the Friday of that week. Mr. Slater sent me in the morning to the Alexandra Hotel, as they had received a postcard in the morning saying that Mrs. Freedman was at that hotel. I went over, but I did not bring her back, because the porter told me that she was not up yet. I went back about half an hour later, and she said that she would come directly. She came at 12. .30. Upon that Friday preparations were being made by Mr. Slater for going away; he was packing. Later on, about 8.20, men came or the luggage, and it was then taken off in a barrow. We went down to the station in a cab, which we got in Sauchiehall Street.

Did anything like this happen, that you and Slater and Madame went down to the station by separate ways? — No; we all went together. When I got down to the station, I remember the door of the cab being opened by a porter. After getting out of the cab I went with Madame, and Mr. Slater went for the tickets. By and by the train left. They went to Liverpool. I got instructions from Mr. Slater before leaving to hand over the keys to Mrs. Freedman. Mrs. Freedman came at 10.30 on Saturday morning and got the keys of the house. I stayed on in Glasgow till ten o'clock at night, when I took the train for London. Before Mr. Slater left

Glasgow he gave me instructions that I was to say to any one asking where they were that they were off to Monte Carlo. He did not explain to me why he wanted that. At twelve o'clock at night the police came.

Did you say then that they were off to Monte Carlo? — I said I did not know then.

Did you explain to another policeman that they were off to Monte Carlo? — Yes, on the Saturday morning.

Do you know of any reason why they should have fled from Glasgow? — Mr. Slater's wife bothered him.

But do you know anything which would associate Slater with the murder of Miss Gilchrist? — No.

Did you see any change during that week from the ordinary habits of the household? — No.

Did you see any attempts to burn clothes or to wash clothes which had been stained in any way? — No. The house went on just as usual. I am perfectly certain that upon the Sunday night Mr. Slater dined in and was never over the door, and upon the Monday he was home about his usual horn-. I have seen the hammer (label No. 47). I used that to break coals with. I remember the hammer coming into the house when we moved into the flat. It was bought upon a card with some other tools on it, exactly like the new card that is now shown to me. The hammer was kept in a drawer in the hat-stand in the hall. So far as I know, the hammer was never out of the house. I never saw that hammer being washed or scraped, or having anything done to it. About three weeks before Mr. Slater left Glasgow he got his moustache taken off. I do not know why he had it taken off. At the time he left Glasgow his moustache was growing again; it was quite noticeable, and one would not have taken him for a clean-shaven man at that time.

Cross-examined by the LORD ADVOCATE — Who engaged you? — Madame Junio.

Was she living then at 45 Newman Street, London? — Yes.

She received gentlemen there? — Yes.

And among the gentlemen was Oscar Slater one? — Yes.

Did he come oftener than the other gentlemen did? — Yes.

Did he sometimes live there? — He stayed sometimes there.

For a night? — Yes.

Stayed there as the husband of Madame Junio? — Yes.

Did you ever hear her called by the name of Kiebrow? — No.

Did you know what Slater was doing in London? — I do not know.

Do you know when he went to Glasgow? — In the end of October.

Why did he go there? — I think to start some business.

What sort of business? — As a dentist.

Was he a dentist? — I do not know.

Why did you say just now that he went to Glasgow to start business as a dentist? — I do not understand properly what you mean.

Why did you say that he went to Glasgow to start business as a dentist? — I think I heard it in conversation.

Between him and who? — Madame.

Did you hear him saying that to Madame? — Yes.

Did you know at that time that he was a dentist? — No.

After he went to Glasgow did he write asking you and Madame to come? — Yes.

Did Madame ask you if you would go to Glasgow? — Mr. Slater asked me before he went away if I would like to go to Glasgow, and I said "Yes."

When you went to the house at 6U St. George's Road, did you see that he had a brass plate on the door with the name Anderson? — Yes.

Did you ever know him in London as Anderson? — No.

Did you think it strange to see that on the door? — I thought he took the name because his wife might not find him.

Where was his wife? — I do not know.

Did you eyer see her? — No.

Or know anything about her? — No.

Is she alive or dead? — I think she is alive, but I do not know.

By the COURT — Who told you about her? — I heard her name from other people.

From whom? — From strange people.

In Glasgow? — No, Inspector Fowler asked me if I knew where his wife was living in London.

Cross-examination continued — Was Slater quite safe from his wife in London by the name of Slater — was he bothered in London by his wife at 45 Newman Street living under the name Slater? — Mrs. Slater was not living there.

Why did he take the name Anderson when he went to Glasgow, when he was safe in London with the name Slater? — Mrs. Slater did not find out where he went to when he went to Glasgow.

When you went to Glasgow, to 69 St. George's Road, did you find that he was not a dentist there? — Yes.

Did anybody come to have their teeth extracted in the house? — No.

Did anybody come to the house at all except Madame and Slater himself? — Yes, friends of Madame came.

Gentlemen in the evening? — Yes.

And did Madame go to the Empire and Palace Music Halls? — Yes.

Where did Slater go? — I do not know.

Did Madame go out immediately after dinner? — No, she went out about ten o'clock to the music halls — not always.

Usually did she? — (No answer.)

What did Slater do during the day? — He went out sometimes in the morning and in the afternoon — I do not know what he did.

So far as you know, he did no business? — Not so far as I know.

Did he usually come home to dinner? — Yes, always.

Was the dinner sometimes later and sometimes earlier? — Seven o'clock was the usual hour.

Was it sometimes nearly eight when he had dinner? — It was my fault; Mr. Slater was in.

But owing to your fault was it about eight o'clock before the dinner was served? — No. Mr. Slater was in after seven and was waiting for his dinner.

How late have you seen the dinner? — Between half-past seven and eight o'clock.

Do you recollect of any particular date last December — can you remember the 19th, for example? — (No answer.)

Did you read about the murder in the newspapers? — No.

Did you ever hear about the murder? — No.

As I understand, you did not know that a murder had been committed? — No.

Did you know the day of the month during December? — When the murder was committed?

No, did you know the day of the month, any day? — Yes.

How did you know that; did you read the newspapers? — No.

How did you know what the day of the month was? — On the calendar.

Did you look up the calendar every day? — No, I knew the day of the month.

Did you have a calendar beside you? — Yes.

Do you remember what day of the week the 21st was? — On a Monday.

How do you recollect that particular Monday? — Because I got notice on the Monday.

How long had you been engaged for? — I was only for a week — a weekly engagement.

What wages were you engaged at? — Eight shillings.

Were you surprised to get notice to go away? — No, because I heard Mr. Slater say that he was going to leave because he did not like Glasgow.

Did he say why he did not like Glasgow? — The climate did not suit Madame.

Was that the reason why he was going to leave? — I think it was, as far as I know.

Did he say on the 21st where he was going to get a better climate for Madame? — No, but I heard the conversation that he was going away.

Was it a conversation between Madame and Slater? — Yes.

Where did they say that they were going to? — San Francisco.

Did you ever hear them mention Chicago? — No.

Or Monte Carlo? — No.

Or Queensland? — No.

Do you know what he was going to do in San Francisco? — I do not know.

Did he tell you what day he was going away? — No, it was at the end of the week, because I had to leave on the Saturday.

You got a week's notice? — Yes.

And you were to wait till the end of the week? — Yes.

Did he ask you whether you would be afraid to go back? — He asked me if I could find my way back to London.

Did you ever see Madame Freedman till she came to Glasgow? — No.

Do you know whether she had been sent for — did Slater send for her or did she offer to come? — I do not know.

Did she send a letter or a message when she arrived at the Alexandra Hotel, Glasgow? — Yes, on the morning of the 25th — a postcard.

Did she and another lady come in the afternoon? — Yes.-

By that time had Slater begun to pack up his baggage? — Yes.

Do you remember when Madame Freedman came that Madame was crying—weeping? — Yes.

Do you remember Madame Freedman asking what was the matter and Slater saying to her, "We must go to Monte Carlo at once"? — I do not know that.

Do you remember anything like that? — No.

Do you remember Madame Freedman asking why it was that Madame was weeping? — I do not know.

Do you know why she was weeping? — Because Mr. Slater would not take her with him.

Did you hear him saying to Madame Freedman, "I do not want to take her with me; I want to go by myself. She is to go home to Belgium"? — No, I did not hear the conversation between Mr. Slater and Madame Freedman.

Was it before Madame Freedman came that you knew Madame was weeping because Slater said he would not take her with him? — Mr. Slater told me that I should speak to Madame — that the time was no good for her to go.

Did you think it curious that he should be going to San Francisco for Madame's health and then trying to get Madame not to go with him? — I do not know.

Did you understand why it was that he wanted Madame to stay at home if he was going to San Francisco for her health — do you understand? — Yes, because the time was so bad that she might be ill on the way.

Then you told me that he was going to San Francisco because the climate in Glasgow did not suit Madame's health? — Yes.

On this day, 25th December, when Madame was weeping, was it because he was not going to take her with him? — Yes; he arranged that Madame should come later on.

Did he say why he was going ahead of Madame? — I do not know.

Did Madame say that she wanted to go with him? — Yes, that she would like to go.

Did he give any reason to you when he said that if any one came inquiring for him you were to say that he had gone to Monte Carlo for a holiday? — Yes.

What reason did he give you? — I do not know. I did not ask for reasons.

By the COURT — He gave none? — No.

Cross-examination continued — Did he tell you where to forward letters? — Yes; to San Francisco.

General Post Office, San Francisco? — Yes.

Did he appear to be in a hurry to get away from Glasgow? — He was going away because Mrs. Freedman took the flat.

When they left at night, did a cab drive up to the door and take you and Madame and Slater to the station? — No; we took the cab in Sauchiehall Street.

Did you leave the house with Madame? — Yes, and Mr. Slater.

Did you walk? — Yes; up to Sauchiehall Street.

To the cab stand there? — Yes.

Did you walk all together or did he walk in front? — We all three walked together.

When you went back that night, do you remember detectives coming about midnight? — Yes; twelve o'clock.

Do you remember them asking if Mr. Oscar Slater lived there? — Yes.

Do you remember saying that no man lived there? — He asked if a young man, a lodger, Oscar Slater, lived there, and I said, no; he was not a lodger.

Did you know him as Oscar Slater? — Yes.

Never as Anderson? — No.

Did any one come to the house asking for him under the name of Anderson? — No.

Do you remember the detectives finding an address on the floor? — Yes.

And did they ask you, "What about this man"? — Yes.

"What did you tell them then? — I do not know.

Did you not tell them that he had gone off for a holiday with Madame? — Yes.

Did you say to Monte Carlo? — Not that night.

What did you say? — I do not know — that they had gone off for a holiday.

Did you know that Slater did not want you to tell anybody that he had gone to San Francisco, only that his wife should not find where he went to? — (No answer.)

By the COURT — Did he give that as a reason why you were to say that he had gone to Monte Carlo — that his wife might not find out? — No; I thought so.

But he did not say so? — No.

For some reason or another, did you know that he did not want to tell anybody that he had gone to San Francisco? — I do not know the reason.

Did he not tell you? — No.

Did he not tell you that you were to say that he had gone to Monte Carlo? — Yes.

Did he give you any reason? — No.

Do you know that on the evening of 25th December he went o\it about six o'clock? — Yes.

Do you remember him telling you that if Cameron came that he (Slater) had gone out? — That he was not in.

Do you remember Cameron calling at eight o'clock? — Yes.

Were you taking in the dinner at that time? — They had had dinner.

When Cameron called at eight o'clock, did you tell him that Slater was not in? — Yes.

Was Slater in? — Yes.

Did he give you any reason why he did not want to see Cameron that night? — No.

You say that he had shaved off his moustache — how long before he went away? — A fortnight.

Do you know whether he had shaved it a second time? — No, I do not think so.

Was it just stubbly? — Yes.

At the time that he went away? — Yes.

Re-examined by Mr. M'CLURE — No person could fail to see it? — I do not know.

The moustache that he had was one that you could not help seeing? — You could see it easily.

You say that Madame broke down and was crying because she was not to be taken to San Francisco? — Yes.

Did you hear that matter discussed between Slater and Madame — speaking about it at all? — If Mr. Slater was going, I should tell Madame not to go, because the time was too rough, and she might come later on.

ANDRÉE JUNIO ANTOINE — Examination resumed — A postcard had arrived in the morning, and the result was that I sent over for Mrs. Freedman. She did not come the first time, and I sent the maid back again, and then she came.

Would you tell me how it was that Mrs. Freedman came down to Glasgow from London? — I think she wanted to stay for a time in Scotland. There was an arrangement made that if she came down she would get the flat.

Was Slater anxious to get the flat off his own hands at that time? — Not so very anxious.

But was he wishing to go away from Glasgow? — Yes; to San Francisco. This had been spoken of for some time before the 20th. I remember Sunday, the 20tli, which was the last Sunday that we were in Scotland. Mr. Slater was not out that day. The time he was in Scotland he never went out any Sunday. Mr. Reid and his little boy came to see Mr. Slater about six o'clock on that Sunday, and they remained till 10.45. The ordinary dinner hour was seven o'clock; it was always ordered for that, but it was sometimes as late as ten minutes. Mr. Slater always dined at home; he never missed his dinner.

On Monday, the 21st, or on any other day during the last week that you were in Glasgow, did he depart from his ordinary practice of dining at seven o'clock? — No, he always dined at seven o'clock. There was no day that he missed having his dinner at home. I did not notice any difference in his manner on any day during that week. I do not know of any clothes belonging to Mr. Slater having been washed that week. I do not know of any clothes having been burned or anything of that kind at all.

Did you see anything at all that would lead you to believe that he had any hand in this affair that happened on the 21st? — Oh, no! I did not see any change in his ordinary habits. After dining at seven o'clock he usually went out. I do not know where he went, but I have heard from him where he had been at times. He did not tell me where he was going as a rule. Two letters were received on the Monday morning, one being from San Francisco and the oth6r from London. The letter from London was from a friend of Mr. Slater, Mr. Rogers, saying that Mr. Slater's wife was still bothering him for money. Mr. Rogers had paid her money on frequent occasions for Mr. Slater. The letter from San Francisco was from John Devoto, saying that there was very good business there, and to go there. There had been a previous letter from Devoto. After receiving these letters Mr. Slater gave Catherine Schmalz notice on the Monday. When he received the letters he said that he was going to America, and in the afternoon he gave notice to Schmalz. On that day he wrote for money from the Post Office Savings Bank. I do not remember whether he got that money later on in the week. I knew about his raising some money upon a diamond brooch. That brooch was mine. It was given to me by Mr. Slater about two years ago. I began to pack up myself on the Friday afternoon at four o'clock, and Mr. Slater packed some time in the morning, after Mrs. Freedman went away. Mr. Slater said I was to go home to my people in Paris, but I did not wish to do that; I wished to go with him. The girl Schmalz also spoke to me, and said that I should go to my people. In the end I said that I would go with Mr. Slater, and he said that I could go with him. One reason he gave for not wanting to take me was the bad weather in America at the time; it was not good for my health to travel in the winter season. He said that I could go to him in the summer time; but I wished to go with him. A man came up to our house to take away our luggage to the station, and he took it away in a barrow. Mr. Slater, Schmalz, and I walked to Charing Cross, Sauchiehall Street, and took a four-wheeler there and drove to the station. It is not the case that we all went away separately. I remember when we arrived at the station a porter came and opened the door of the cab, and we came out. I went to buy some newspapers for the journey. Mr. Slater and I left for Liverpool, while Schmalz went back to the flat. She had instructions to hand over the keys of the flat to Mrs. Freedman.

Were you present when Slater gave Schmalz instructions to tell any person who asked that you were off to Monte Carlo? — I cannot remember that. I think he said that if any one called for him to say he was in Monte Carlo.

Have you any notion why he did not want it to be known where he was going? — In the first place, because of his wife; and, secondly, in case of the landlord of the house and the furniture company bothering Mrs. Freedman about the flat. I have seen the hammer (label 47). The maid used that hammer for breaking the coals. It was not used for anything else. I remember that it was bought when we took the house in St. George's Road. It was bought on a card with a number of other articles. It was not washed or scraped in any way to my knowledge. I never saw Mr. Slater washing his waterproof. I never saw him doing anything which might be supposed to be concealing stains upon his clothes. His conduct during that last week in Glasgow was in no way different from his ordinary conduct. I knew that during that last week he was making inquiry at shipping offices. I never knew of him having any checked trousers or light- coloured spats. He had a moustache when he left for America; it was quite a noticeable moustache. I do not think that any person seeing him could have mistaken him for a clean-shaven man at that time.

The LORD ADVOCATE — I have no questions to ask.

The Court adjourned at a quarter to seven o'clock.

———————

FOURTH DAY — THURSDAY, 6TH MAY, 1909

The Court met at ten o'clock.

SAMUEL REID, examined by Mr. M'CLURE — I am acquainted with the prisoner Slater. I was in Glasgow when Slater came to the city, about the beginning of November last year. I met him in Hope Street. When I met him he had not taken the flat at 69 St. George's Road; he was staying in Renfrew Street. He told me he was taking a flat at St. George's Road. I was up in that house before the furniture was put in, and I saw the house. At the time the furniture was put into the house I put in two sacks of coal. After they were living in the house I was there on the Sundays. I remember the Sunday before Christmas. I left for Belfast on the Monday before Christmas, that being Monday, the 21st December. I went to the house on Sunday, the 20th, at six o'clock, and I stayed there till about 10.30. I dined with Slater. I had my little boy with me. I have got a little girl as well. There was a Sunday before that when I was in the house and dined with Slater, and had both my children there. The latest I would leave on the 20th would be 10.30, but any other Sunday I stopped a bit later. During the time I was in the house on the 20th Slater was there. My little boy is getting on for five years old. After the murder the Glasgow police followed me to Belfast. They saw me there, and I made a statement, and told them that I had been in Slater's house on the Sunday. On the day when I was dining with Slater his moustache was growing. It was very noticeable. His hair, of course, is very black, and I do not think that any person could have mistaken him for a clean-shaven man.

Cross-examined by the LORD ADVOCATE — What are you? — I am an agent.

For what? — A commission agent.

For what? — For anything — horse racing.

Were you a bookmaker in Glasgow? — I was.

When did you first come to know Slater? — I have known Slater these last twelve or fourteen years.

When did you first come to know him? — In London some time ago.

How many years ago? — Twelve or fourteen years ago.

What was he then? — Supposed to be a dentist.

Was he? — I could not say whether he was, but I was told he was.

Who told you? — Different people.

Were you ever at his place? — Not in London.

Where did he live? — I could not say.

Where did you meet him? — In a restaurant.

Where? — Broad Street, Golden Square.

Where after that? — In different clubs.

Do you mean gambling clubs? — Yes.

How did he make his living? — I think by gambling.

How else? — That is all I know.

Do you know he had another way of making his living? — I could not say.

Tell the truth? — I am speaking the truth.

Do you not know quite well that he had another way of making his living? — No.

Gambling was the only way you knew? — That is what I understood.

Did he deal in jewels? — I could not say.

Did you ever see him with jewels? — I have seen some of his things, but I have never seen him dealing with them.

Do you know that he pawned jewels? — I could not say.

Have you not seen pawn tickets in his possession? — No.

How long did you know him in London? — I could not say exactly, but I have known him for some years.

Did you then come tO' Glasgow? — Yes.

Where did you live in Glasgow? — In Renfrew Street at first, and then, after I was married, I stayed off the New City Road.

Were you a bookmaker in Glasgow? — Yes.

When did Slater come to Glasgow? — This last time?

Yes? — I could not say exactly. I think it was in November.

Where did you meet him? — On the Friday, in a public-house in Hope Street.

Just casually on the street? — In a public-house.

What public-house? — Galloway's.

During the day? — Yes.

Were you surprised to see him in Glasgow? — I was.

Did he tell you why he had come? — I could not say what he had come for.

Did he tell you where he was living? — Not at the time.

Where did you meet afterwards? — In the clubs.

What clubs? — In the Vaudeville.

Where? — At the back of the General Post Office.

Is that a gambling club? — Yes.

Where else? — Main Street, Gorbals.

What was there? — A club.

A gambling club? — Yes.

Did you see him frequently at these two clubs in November and December? — Yes.

Was he gambling there? — Yes.

When did you come to know where he lived? — I could not say the date.

Did he tell you where he lived when you first met him at the public- house? — No.

How did you come to know where he lived? — We went home together, and he told me to meet him.

Where? — In his private house.

Where? — Lodgings in Renfrew Street.

Did you meet him there? — Yes.

When? — On the Saturday morning.

In the beginning of November? — I could not say whether it was the beginning or the end; I could not say the date.

When did he leave from there? — He shifted, I believe, on the Saturday.

Did he tell you where he was going? — Yes.

Did he tell you under what name he was going? — Anderson, I believe.

Did he tell you why? — No.

Did you ask? — No.

Did he tell you he was going as a dentist? — No, I could not say; he never said anything to me.

In November or December did you hear anything about his cari7ing on business as a dentist? — I could not say.

Did he invite you to come and see him at his house? — Yes, on the Sundays.

Every Sunday? — Yes, every Sunday.

Did you go every Sunday? — Yes, four Sundays.

On his invitation? — Yes.

Did he just give you a standing invitation at the beginning to go on the Sundays? — Yes.

Did you ever meet anybody else at his house? — I do not remember meeting anybody.

Have you any special recollection of Sunday, 20th December? — No.

You did not note the date at the time? — No.

And you have no special recollection? — No.

What hour did you usually go? — Six o'clock.

And sometimes later? — No.

Did he dine at six? — No, we dined at seven.

How did you spend your time? — Playing with the children.

Did you see anybody else there besides yourself and your children? — I do not think so; I could not say.

Was there any woman there? — Yes, there was a lady there.

Do you know her? — Yes.

Do you recollect of him telling you on any Sunday that he was going to America? — No, I could not say that.

Had you ever any talk at any of your Sunday meetings about his leaving Glasgow? — No, he did not say that, but he said he liked America better, that there was more business there.

"What sort of business? — I could not say.

Did you ask him? — No.

What did you think at the time? — I did not think anything.

Did you know how he was getting his living? — By gambling.

In Glasgow? — Yes.

Did you know whether he was making money or losing money? — I could not really tell you.

Did he never tell yon? — No.

Were you surprised to find that he had left Glasgow without saying good- bye to you? — I said good-bye to him.

Where? — In his house.

When? — On the last Sunday I was up. I went away to Belfast.

Were you surprised to hear that he had left Glasgow? — I was surprised for the time.

He had never indicated to you that he was going away? — No.

Hall, 15 Queen's Terrace (looking west),
showing door leading to bedrooms (left), drawing-room (right).

DR. WILLIAM GEORGE AITCHISON ROBERTSON, examined by Mr. M'CLURE— I am a Doctor of Medicine, a Doctor of Science of the University of Edinburgh, and a Fellow of the Royal College of Physicians and of the Royal Society of Edinburgh. I have specialised in medical jurisprudence, and have lectured on it for the last twelve years, and I am the author of a work upon medical jurisprudence. I examine in that subject for the Royal College of Physicians. I have had submitted to me certain productions in this case, a skin rug, a carpet rug, a claw hammer, and a waterproof coat. I have read the medical reports of Dr. Glaister and Dr. Galt. I read also the medical report of Dr. Glaister and Dr. Littlejohn as regards the tests for blood. Looking to the extent of the injuries inflicted upon this woman, Miss Gilchrist, I think the sort of instrument used was some blunt weapon. The hammer produced does not strike me in the least as being a likely one, because the multiplicity of wounds and their extent is out of all proportion to the size of the hammer. The hammer is a very light one. Of course, theoretically, if a light hammer is wielded with terrific force, it may cause injuries which a heavier weapon would with less force, but from the very extensive smashing of the skull, I would consider that this small hammer is a very unlikely weapon. I examined that hammer for blood stains, and there are no blood stains upon it. I see under the head of it some material which looks like coal dust.

Do you see anything which suggests to you that the top of the hammer, the upper part of the handle, has been washed or scraped? — No appearance whatever of either having been washed or scraped, but the lower part somewhat dirtied by being held in a dirty hand. That is all I can discover about the handle.

Have you made as careful an examination as you could for the purpose of detecting the presence of blood corpuscles upon it? — I have not, but I see that there are no clots of blood upon it, absolutely no appearance of blood whatever, even in the crevices, where it might have lodged, where it would be impossible almost to remove it by washing or scraping. There is absolutely no sign of scraping. The hammer has absolutely no signs of blood about it.

Would the murderer who carried through this murder be likely to have blood upon his clothes? — I should think he would be bespattered thoroughly with blood. I say so because of the injuries, which would splash up blood on the surrounding objects for a very considerable distance. I am informed that the fire-irons had blood over them, that there was a considerable quantity upon the coal scuttle, that the hearth rug had a great deal of blood upon it, and that the tablecloth, which was hanging down the table on the other side of the body, had a considerable amount of blood upon it.

Do you think it would be possible for a person who knelt upon the body and smashed at the face with the implement to escape considerable blood marking? — I should think he would be more or less covered with blood. I have looked at the waterproof coat (production No. 43). I have found no signs of blood whatever upon it. Supposing the murderer had done the deed with that coat on, I certainly agree that the outside of the coat should be much marked with blood. I would expect that.

Would you expect that his clothes, and about his wrists and the ends of his sleeves where his hands were, would probably show signs of blood, almost certainly? — Certainly.

Suppose he had concealed the instrument with which this was done in his pockets, would you expect to find blood in the pockets? — There are no signs whatever of blood in the pockets. If he had done this with his ordinary clothes on and then put on the coat, I would expect to find the inside of the coat showing blood deeply. I have made an examination, and I find no trace of blood whatever. There are some small spots on the coat; larger ones have been cut out, and therefore I have not seen them. They are not produced here at all.

From the spots that are on the coat, is there any one of them indicative of blood? — Not in the least resembling blood stains. The coat showed no signs whatever, so far as I can make out, of having been washed.

Were those stains which were upon it stains that looked as if something had dropped on the coat and there remained? — They might have been drips from an umbrella, or mud stains.

But you do not think in any way characteristic of blood? — Not in any way characteristic of blood. There is no spreading of the stains which I can see as if water had been applied. They are quite clean where they occur, and are quite distinct. I also examined the auger (production No. 26). The result of my examination of it is, that the upper part — at least the part nearest the hands, not the curling bit, but the plain bit, and the upper circles here (indicating) — are much more corroded with rust than is the lower part; and an examination of a part of this deep corrosion yields the presence of one test for blood. I cannot say definitely whether there is blood on that or not. I have no theory as to how the grey hair became attached to it.

Do you think that it is a likely weapon to cause the wounds which you have described? — Of the two it is more likely to have caused the wounds than the hammer, but I do not think it is the instrument. I should expect to find an instrument of heavier weight than that. There was a skin rug laid over the top of the head of Miss Gilchrist, with long hairs; there was a considerable amount of blood upon the hairy side of that rug, which I was led to understand was next the body.

Did you find blood upon the other side of it, on the top? — There are a few stains, one large one, about 1½ inches square, with from it a trail of three or four drops, as if it had dropped from perhaps the coat of the assailant.

If only one side of the rug was in contact with the body, what would you expect to have caused the stains on the other side? — It could only be droppings from something. That is only a surmise.

Cross-examined by the LORD ADVOCATE — I understand that your evidence is given entirely upon the facts disclosed in Professor Glaister's report? — That is so.

I suppose you would agree that the two medical gentlemen who actually saw the body, and saw the wounds, would be in a much better position to judge than you who only read their report? — Yes.

You offer the opinion that because of the multiplicity and the extent of the wounds you do not think the hammer could do it? — I do.

What do you judge to be the number of blows inflicted? — That would be impossible to say.

What would you judge to be the number of wounds inflicted? — I think they are narrated in the report given.

Do you infer from the report that the old lady's face and head were simply battered in? — Yes.

Did you notice that a number of wounds were spindle-shaped? — I did.

Did you observe that one of the blows, at all events, had just driven in the left eyeball? — Yes.

Leaving a round hole? — Yes.

Must that, therefore, have been done by a probably rounded instrument of comparatively small diameter, driven straight in? — I see the wound to which you refer is 2 inches by ¾ of an inch; that, of course, is much larger than the head of the hammer we have here.

Do you say that if the hammer was wielded by a powerful hand and a rapid succession of blows struck with it by a powerful hand on the head of a lady over eighty-three years of age, these wounds could not have been inflicted? — It is possible, but not probable.

What instrument do you think would be more likely? — I should think a heavy poker.

Do you mean a long instrument? — It might be long or short; it might be a crowbar.

Beating with it? — Beating and thrusting with it.

By a crowbar you mean a bar about 2 or 3 feet long? — It may be any length.

Well, the usual crowbar is 2 or 3 feet long? — Yes.

You think that might be it? — Yes.

With the head of the hammer, and with the hammer turned sideways, and by the use of the claws of the hammer, could not all the wounds that you have seen described in the report have been inflicted? — No, I cannot see how these spindle-shaped wounds could ever have been inflicted by the hammer.

Do you not see how with the claws of the hammer it could be done? — Then there would be a portion of skin between; each claw would make its own injury.

Have you measured carefully the claws of the hammer? — Yes.

And the distance between the claws? — Yes.

What are your measurements? — I have not got them here, but I have compared them with the wounds that are described, and the wounds do not in the least degree appear to me to correspond to the injuries which might be inflicted by the claw end of the hammer.

But you would not expect, would you, that they would leave the exact marks of the claws of the hammer on the face or head? — I should think that we should have at least had some that would show the direct impression of the claw end.

Do you mean with a rain of thirty or forty blows? — I do.

When did you examine the hammer? — On Friday and Saturday of last week, on 30th April and 1st of May.

Do you say that about halfway down the shaft, the shaft of the hammer has no appearance of having been scrubbed, or the surface of the wood of the hammer having been roughened and bleached? — Yes, I say that.

Is there no difference to your eye between the half near the head and the half near the handle? — Do you mean in colour?

Yes? — Certainly there is the dirty end of it.

And do you see no evidence of scraping or scrubbing? — None.

Or of the wood having been roughened or bleached? — It is natural. If you look at any ordinary hammer you will see that in the wood.

Did you make any test for the purpose of ascertaining whether there was any blood? — I did not.

Are blood stains easily removed by water? — If they are immediately removed they are, but not when the blood clots or coagulates.

But if they are treated afterwards with water, are not blood stains very easily removed? — By no means; they are exceedingly difficult to remove, and in the soft wood of this hammer they would be very difficult to remove indeed.

If you take the waterproof coat or the head of the hammer, what would be the best means of removing blood stains? — A little cold water, or cold water in which a little salt has been dissolved.

And will that effectually remove them? — It would not effectually remove them; it would remove a few of the corpuscles.

Would you be able by analysis to find traces of the blood if, shortly after, the blood on the hammer or on the coat had been treated as you have described? — I think so.

How? — Do you mean me to describe the tests for blood?

No; I mean, suppose it is treated effectually as you have described with water or with water and salt, would you still find traces of the blood? — Yes, in a hammer such as this, which is full of crevices, it would be impossible to wash the blood clots out from those crevices.

Suppose that the man took means with water and salt to remove the blood from the crevices, do you say that could not be done? — I should think it almost impossible to be done, and if the hammer head were removed one would then find underneath the flanges evidence of the blood.

Then is it your evidence that once you get the blood on the hammer you cannot effectively remove it with water, even with water mixed with salt? — Unless it is immediately removed. If the hammer was put immediately under a water tap then it might be washed off with the water.

That would do it? — I do not say it would; I say that it might do it.

Re-examined by Mr. M'CLURE — Your conclusions really agree with the conclusion of Professor Glaister and Professor Littlejohn? — Perhaps you will state what they are.

You have seen their report where they say that they cannot state positively that there are blood corpuscles? — That is so.

You find no trace thereof whatsoever? — That is so.

Look at that card with a hammer and other implements upon it, and take it from me that this was bought at the same shop as the other hammer, and that similar implements were upon another card containing the hammer produced in the present case, do you see a general similarity between the shafts of the two hammers? — A very great similarity.

Can you really say anything more than this, that the older hammer is dirtier? — It has been used.

It is dirtier at the lower end than at the upper end? — Yes.

In fact, where the hand would be it is dirtier than higher up? — That is so.

Is not that the whole matter? — That is so.

Dr. ALEXANDER VEITCH, examined by Mr. M'CLURE — I am a Bachelor of Medicine and Master of Surgery of Edinburgh University. I have been in practice for almost nineteen years. I have had very many cases of injuries to the human body to investigate. I do not hold any appointments, but several firms of lawyers employ me to investigate accidents and alleged accidents. I have examined the productions in this case, especially the hammer, for blood. I found absolutely no appearance of blood whatsoever, I read the medical reports as to the injuries inflicted upon the body of Miss Gilchrist. I consider the hammer that has been produced to be an unlikely instrument to inflict the extensive injuries which are narrated in the report. My opinion is that it is quite impossible to determine either the size, the shape, or the weight of the instrument that would produce such injuries. From the injuries I could not myself say what the instrument was that was used.

Professor Glaister suggested that not only that hammer but other hammers or crowbars might have inflicted the injuries. Do you agree with that opinion? — Yes. I would suggest that a piece of a crowbar or a larger hammer would be more likely to have produced the injuries, but what instrument was used I really cannot say.

Supposing that hammer were used, could it possibly have inflicted the injuries? — I should say conceivably, but there is absolutely no evidence in my mind to support it. In my opinion it is not a likely instrument. I examined the coat which has been produced, and which belongs to the prisoner. I inspected it for blood stains. Considering the amount of blood that was scattered in the neighbourhood of Miss Gilchrist's body, the assailant could not escape getting a good deal of blood on his own person, because he must have been kneeling, or standing, or resting with one knee upon the chest of the old lady. Being told that Professor Glaister's theory is that the assailant was kneeling upon the body of Miss Gilchrist, and inflicting blows upon her head while in that position — I think he would be certain to come in for a good deal of blood splashing. If he was wearing that coat at the time, or if he put it on afterwards, it was bound to have shown marks of blood. I have seen no semblance of a blood stain on the coat — there is no stain with the characteristic appearances of a blood stain. Such slight markings as are on the coat are not of the appearance of blood. I examined the inside of the coat, the pockets, and the sleeve, and nowhere did I find any trace of blood whatsoever. The coat, so far as I could see, showed no signs of having been washed. The stains which were on the coat showed no signs of having been tampered with water. If water had been applied to the stains I think there would have been some appearance indicative that washing had been attempted. I would have expected certain appearances which are not there. I should have expected that the outer ring of the stain would have been denser than the centre. If the washing had gone to any extent the outer ring of the stain would have been indefinite. Such stains as are on the coat are quite distinct, and I would say that they are untampered with. To the best of my belief they are not blood. I found no traces of blood about the hammer. I am of opinion that it has neither been washed nor scraped. Close up to the end of the shaft the handle has been gripped more frequently, and there is an appearance of coal dust near the hammer head which would give a difference to the staining along the shaft. It is dirtier and blacker towards the lower end where the person chipping the coals would be clutching it. I saw some rust on the hammer, but there is absolutely nothing to suggest to me that that rust is blood in any form at all. Supposing that this hammer had been wielded by the assailant, and Miss Gilchrist's head was smashed, as we know it was, by many blows, the hammer necessarily would have had a lot of blood about its head and probably all over. I see no signs of scraping or scrubbing on the lower portion of the handle. If the assailant was wielding this weapon his hands would probably be bloody, and I should expect to see some sign of that on the lower part of the handle. There is no sign of scraping or scrubbing whatsoever. I am certainly dealing with probabilities here.

Bedroom, 15 Queen's Terrace,
showing toilet table and gas bracket.

Cross-examined by the LORD ADVOCATE — From your examination of the report how many blows did you think were struck? — It is impossible to tell.

Would you judge that there had been a great many blows struck? — A good many.

Have you ever, in your experience, seen a case where there was such an amount of mauling? — Never.

In your judgment, must it have been effected by a succession of blows? — I should expect so.

The assailant probably kneeling on the body of the victim? — Probably.

Do you judge it was in that way that the fractures of the ribs and breast bone were caused? — That is my theory.

Are you in as good a position to judge of the appearance of the wounds as the men who made the examination? — Certainly not.

Did you, in trying to conjecture what sort of implement had been used, come to the conclusion that it was a large instrument or a small one? — I thought it more likely to be something of the nature of a crowbar — I mean a portion of a crowbar, or a piece of railing, or something of that sort — a blunt instrument.

And used in two different ways by beating and thrusting? — Yes.

That would have done it? — Yes.

And you say conceivably the hammer, wielded by a powerful hand, would do it? — Conceivably, but unlikely. I should have thought of a larger hammer.

The shape of the instrument would do, but you think not the size? — I could not go that length.

What length do you go? You said you thought a larger hammer would have been necessary. How much larger do you think? — I thought you dissociated shape from size.

I thought you said that you would have expected a larger hammer? — Of course the shape of the thing depends on the size.

Certainly, to some extent. Describe to us the kind of hammer that you think, judging from the report, would have been sufficient? — Nearly twice as large as that hammer.

Would not a smaller hammer, if wielded by a powerful hand upon a very old lady, have effected the same purpose? — No, I should have expected different wounds.

You mean different in shape? — I should have expected a class of fracture that is not present in this case.

What class of fracture would you have expected to have been produced by a lighter hammer? — A depressed fracture, penetrating, and of comparatively small size.

Would not that again depend on the number of blows struck? — I should expect that any one wielding a hammer for that purpose would strike to the best of his effort at every stroke.

I suppose you made no analysis of the stains found either on the coat or on the hammer? — No, I made none.

And do you agree that water used immediately afterwards would remove the blood stains very effectually? — Very effectually.

Re-examined by Mr. M'CLURE — You had no opportunity of seeing this body? — No.

Miss Gilchrist was buried a long time before you were brought into connection with this case? — Yes.

And you are giving your evidence on a criticism of the report that has been lodged from the experience which you have gained? — Yes.

The evidence for the defence was then closed.

THE LORD ADVOCATE'S ADDRESS TO THE JURY

The LORD ADVOCATE then addressed the jury as follows: — May it please your lordship — Gentlemen of the jury, on the evening of the 21st December last a lady, upwards of eighty-three years of age, who had, so far as we know, not a single enemy in the world, was found murdered in her own dining- room, under circumstances of such savage ferocity as to beggar all description. There are no rival or conflicting theories in this case as to the way in which this aged and defenceless lady met her tragic end. She was literally battered to death by her assailant, who knelt on the body of his victim whilst he was inflicting a rain of fatal blows. I say, gentlemen, that the hand which dealt these blows was the hand of the prisoner, and I hope to be able to satisfy you that he, and he alone, was the perpetrator of an act of savagery which happily finds few, if any, parallels in the annals of crime. Up to yesterday afternoon I should have thought that there was one serious difficulty which confronted you — the difficulty of conceiving that there was in existence a human being capable of doing such a dastardly deed. Gentlemen, that diffIculty, I think, was removed yesterday afternoon when we heard from the lips of one who seemingly knew the prisoner better than any one else, who had known him longer and known him better than any witness examined, that he had followed a life which descends to the very lowest depths of human degradation, for, by the universal judgment of mankind, the man who lives upon the proceeds of prostitution has sunk to the lowest depths, and all moral sense in him has been destroyed and has ceased to exist. That difficulty removed, I say without hesitation that the man in the dock is capable of having committed this dastardly outrage, and the question for you to consider is whether or not the evidence has brought it home to him.

Now, the motive for the crime is as plain as daylight. This old lady, living in a plain, simple, and unostentatious way, as you have had described, with only a single servant, living in a respectable house, though no doubt a comparatively small house, had an exceptionally and inordinately large number of jewels. This seems to have been her only extravagance. At the time of her death, according to the evidence given before you, she was actually possessed of and had in her house jewels to the value of upwards of £1380, jewels which, if bought in a shop in the ordinary way, would have cost no less than £3000. It was so remarkable that it had become as it were the tittle tattle of the neighbourhood that she was possessed of these valuable jewels; it was not money in the house, it was this exceptional possession held by this lady living in this simple and defenceless way. We shall see in the sequel how it was that the prisoner came to know that she was possessed of these jewels.

If you will turn with me and examine for a few minutes the bare outlines, the undisputed facts, of this case, I believe you will find that they yield six or seven priceless inferences to enable you to form a judgment on the case. Gentlemen, the old lady and her servant were the only inmates of the house, a house situated in a respectable and very quiet and not much frequented street in the West End of Glasgow. The house was one stair up, and it was the only occupied house on that stair, there being no inhabitants in the house above at this time. The habits of the two inmates were simple and regular, almost monotonous. The old lady had a few visitors, but practically no male visitors. Her servant was, as a rule, the only other occupant of the house, and former servants seem to have been almost her only visitors to the house. The practice of the servant was to go out in the evenings about seven o'clock to do the messages and to fetch the old lady her newspaper. On the night of 21st December last the servant left as usual to get the newspaper and to come back with it, and then to go out for the rest of the messages. There were three locks on the door of the stairhead, two of which were opened by the latch keys which the servant had with her as a rule. The door at the foot of the stair, out of the close, as the Glasgow people would say. was locked by one key. That door at the closemouth could be opened by means of a handle, you will remember, close by the dining-room door inside the house. The servant took her latch keys with her as usual, and left the outer door of the close on the check, closed, so that no one could enter without the key unless the occupant of the house admitted him. According to the evidence she was out and away from the house for the best part of ten minutes. She had only to go to St. George's Road to buy the newspaper and come back. She met some one on the road and that detained her. She had left her mistress sitting at the dining-room table, with her back to the fire, reading a magazine. When she came back she found the outer door of the closemouth open, and when she ascended the stair she found, standing at the door of her house, her neighbour, Mr. Adams. Mr. Adams told her that there was something wrong inside, that he had heard noises down below, and had come up; he had rung at the door, and the door was not opened. They were both, therefore, on the alert; they both knew to expect something unusual, something wrong. The servant maid thought the sounds were possibly those of the clothes- line pulleys. She opened the door and immediately stepped inside — Mr. Adams was just at the threshold — when there emerged from the bedroom door a man. The bedroom was lighted; it had been left in darkness when the servant went out. The man walked steadily, deliberately, from the bedroom door to the outer door, and passed the servant and Mr. Adams. Immediately he passed, he darted down the stair at full speed. "When he had reached the closemouth he glanced to the east along St. George's Road, turned to the west, and ran along West Princes Street, westwards. A few yards from the door he knocked against a little girl and pushed past her, and turned down West Cumberland Street. He must have doubled on his path probably more than once, because between 7.30 and 8 o'clock he appeared at the Kelvinbridge Subway Station, which could have been reached in some seven or ten minutes' walking, and with running could easily have been reached in some five minutes. Probably he cannot have gone directly. He dashed past the turnstile and downstairs to the Subway, and probably caught a passing train. The man who passed Mr. Adams, and the servant girl, and the girl on the street, and the girl at the Subway, had nothing in his hands. There were no marks upon him to distinguish him from other men. The only feature about him was this, that he held his hands in his pockets, close by his side; his waterproof coat was open, and he held his hands in his pockets, pressing them to his sides. It is certain that the murderer took the weapon with which he inflicted the blows into the house with him, it is certain he took it out of the house with him, it is certain it was of a size which would go into his pocket. "When the servant girl and Mr. Adams rushed to the dining-room they there found the old lady drawing her last breath upon the floor, with her head towards the fire and her feet towards the door, the fire-irons all round undisturbed, not a weapon or implement of any kind left in the room, the fire- irons bespattered with blood. They found that the lady had been done to death. The medical examination, made a short time afterwards, showed unmistakably that her assailant knocked her down, and had knelt with his knees upon her body, fractured her ribs and her breast bone, and there, whilst kneeling upon her prostrate body, absolutely and literally rained blows oh her face and head in rapid succession. The doctors who saw and examined the old lady say that the blows must have been inflicted by a powerful hand, wielding probably, as they judge from the appearance of the wounds, a hammer. From the appearance of certain wounds, some of them being spindle-shaped, one of them having simply driven in an eyeball, they judged that the deed must have been done, not by a big coal hammer, but a small hammer, and they say that the hammer found in the prisoner's possession afterwards was an implement with which, wielded by a powerful hand, all the blows and the injuries which they saw could have been inflicted. When Mr. Adams and the servant girl went to the bedroom, where the gas had been lit, they found that a box had been opened in which the old lady had kept merely her papers. These papers were scattered about the floor. They found that one brooch, which the servant proved had been left, was taken away: — a valuable brooch — and a ring which was not of much value had been left. The rest of the old lady's jewels, which she kept in her wardrobe amongst her clothes and otherwise, were left untouched. Obviously the assailant had been disturbed before his work was complete.

Now, these are the bald, plain, undisputed facts, and from these facts you can draw the following priceless inferences:—

(1) That the murder was coolly and deliberately planned and executed by no bungler, but by a daring, clever, cold-blooded, expert performer.

(2) The murder was accomplished by a man who was familiar with the neighbourhood and with the surrounding streets.

(3) It was accomplished by a man who had familiarised himself with the number and character of the inmates of the house, and with their habits and ways.

(4) It was accomplished by a man who had watched and knew the movements of the policemen on the beat.

(5) It was accomplished by a man who had taken his weapon with him, and taken his weapon away from the house.

(6) It was accomplished by a man who was on the hunt for jewels — not money — and who knew how to deal with jewels, how to make away with them when he got them. Jewels are difficult things for those who are not experts to handle if they do not come by them by honest means.

(Last) It was accomplished by a man who was not familiar with the place in which the jewels were kept, who had never been in the house, and therefore was not familiar with more than the fact that there were jewels there, and that he had to find them when his deed was done.

Are there any of the inferences, think you, that clash with the evidence which we have heard in this case relating to the prisoner? Are there any of these characteristic qualifications of the hypothetical murderer which the prisoner has not? There are none. He was a man who was well acquainted with this locality and the streets round about. He had frequented clubs in the immediate vicinity six or seven years ago. He had taken a house early in November within three minutes' walk of this old lady's house in West Princes Street. I will show by and by that he was a man well acquainted, not only with the habits of the inmates of the house and the movements of the police outside, but he was a man who knew about jewels, and was accustomed to handle jewels. In his pocket book was found a card which intimated at one time or another that he was a dealer in diamonds and precious stones. We know from the earliest date that we know anything at all about him — to wit, back in 1901 — that he was dealing in jewels and precious stones. We know in this case that that was the way in which he raised money during all the weeks he was staying in Glasgow. He went to Jackson, on the South Side, and raised money upon a ring. He goes to M'Laren and raises money three times on a brooch. He tries to sell the pawn ticket for the brooch, and he tries to raise money on it.

We hear of him in no other connection but in connection with diamonds and jewels. When he leaves the place there comes a letter from some gentleman named Jacobs, in New York, telling him that he will send him over emeralds when he can get the money for them, and he bids him when he comes over bring as many as he can. We hear a great deal in the case about his dealing with jewels from the selling point of view, but we hear nothing about his dealings with jewels from the purchasing point of view. You will observe that none of these gentlemen was able to give you any account of how he had come into possession of these jewels. No man was examined in the past three days who had ever sold jewels to him. You will draw your own inferences. He was a man who had no acquaintance with the inside of the house, and did not know where the jewels were kept. That answers to the prisoner. He was a man who was certainly in possession of a weapon with which admittedly the deed could be done. It is no use speculating upon the size or shape of the implement. It was an implement that could go and did go into the man's pocket, for he was seen by at least four people immediately after the murder was committed, and not one of them saw a weapon in his hand, and you know that no weapon was left in the house. He was in possession of an implement which, say the two doctors who examined the body, could quite well have inflicted the wounds, Every wound, including the spindle- shaped wounds, could have been produced by that hammer; the wound which drove in the poor lady's eyeball could have been produced by that hammer. That hammer, wielded by a powerful hand, is the only kind of implement, they say, which could have inflicted all the wounds which were found upon her face and her head. The man who was seen emerging from the bedroom was the murderer. The man who was seen at the foot of the close running westwards was the murderer. The man who rushed at a great pace past the turnstile at the Subway was the murderer. And that man, I say, was the prisoner.

We shall now look at the evidence with regard to two of my inferences— first, that he was acquainted with the habits of the inmates of the house, and, second, that he was acquainted with the movements of the police. It is perfectly well known that blackguards who commit crimes of this order upon innocent, feeble, and defenceless people are themselves cravens at heart. There is nothing they dread so much as the noose. The only human instinct that animates them is the instinct of self-preservation. They never, under any circumstances, commit crimes of this kind without taking the most careful and elaborate precautions to secure their own safety in the end; and, happily, it is by these very elaborate precautions that the hand of justice is often able to reach them and we are able to hunt down the miscreant. So it is in this case. This man appears on the scene early in the month of November. He takes a house within a quarter of a mile of the old lady's house. He takes it under a false name; he takes it under a false designation. He takes the house under the name of Adolf Anderson, and he calls himself a dentist. He takes the house for eighteen months. Is there any reason that suggests itself to your mind why he should have taken a false name and a false designation unless it be to cover up his tracks and to baffle the hand of justice after his deed was done? There is no reason suggested, none whatever. He had no customers there; he had no people who came to trade with him; he had no reason to deceive anybody at that time; he had no character to lose and none to gain. There can be and there was no other object except to remove all traces of him when his deed was done and he found it necessary to make his escape.

Then, gentlemen, he required as part of his elaborate precautions to familiarise himself with the inmates of the house, with their movements and their habits, and also with the movements of the police. There was one method, and one only, by which that object could be accomplished, and that was by careful, prolonged, and steady watching with a skilled eye. He is seen early in the month of December by a number of people, to whose evidence I am going to call your attention, carefully watching the house and the movements of its inmates, and also the movements of the policemen on the beat. There was, as you will remember, a Mrs. M'Haffie, who lived at 16 West Princes Street, very nearly opposite the house where the old lady lived, probably a little further to the east in the direction of St. George's Road. Gentlemen, Mrs. M'Haffie, looking out of her window on to this quiet, unfrequented street, saw, she says, the prisoner moving slowly backward and forward on at least half a dozen separate and distinct occasions, for thirty minutes at a time. There was nobody in the case who had anything approaching so good an opportunity of seeing and observing his movements. She seemed not to be particularly busy with her housework at the time, and she was struck to find in this quiet neighbourhood, where she had never seen the like before, this man moving backward and forward between the corner of St. George's Road and the old lady's dwelling. She sees him coming back time after time, and observes that it is the same man. She is shown the prisoner, and she has not the smallest doubt that he is the man. Why should she have any doubt? Who, having once seen him, could forget his face? Her daughter had the same opportunities for observation, and took advantage of them. She, too, saw the man walking slowly backward and forward, examining the windows of the house, and looking up. Once or twice, says the mother, when he caught sight of them observing him, he turned his face away and moved out of their sight. The daughter, too, was perfectly clear and unhesitating in her identification of the man. She was asked whether, in the month of March, when being precognosced by the agent for the accused, she would swear to the man when she came to Edinburgh, and she very properly said that she would not. It was a very improper question to put on the part of anybody precognoscing, and it was only by my consent that the question was allowed in Court. That was the girl's answer. You will judge whether, when she was in the witness-box, she appeared to have any more hesitation than her mother had in identifying this man. A niece of Mrs. M'Haffie paid a visit one evening in December, about a fortnight before the murder, and when she was going upstairs she met a man coming down who, she says, was very like this man. When she went up she found from her cousin that he had come to the door and asked if there was any one of the name of Anderson living there, a peculiar question to ask when there was the name "M'Haffie" on the door. This niece came back to the house a second time, four days later, and from the window there was pointed out to her by Mrs. M'Haffie this very man walking backward and forward and making his observations. When the niece came downstairs she found him moving off towards St. George's Road, and she followed him as he was walking down, no doubt to his own. house. She noticed that he had a sort of slouching gait and was going at a slow pace. The cousin who opened the door said that he was very like the man who had come up and asked for Anderson.

Now, gentlemen, it does not stop there. On 14th, 15th, 16th, and 17th December he was seen by a very intelligent girl who had a most excellent opportunity of observing him, namely, the girl Euphemia Cunningham, employed in the photographer's shop, whose habit it was to go home for dinner about one o'clock, passing through West Princes Street on her way. At the comer of West Princes Street and Queen's Crescent, in full view of Miss Gilchrist's house, she observed the man standing and staring up at Miss Gilchrist's window. She had a most excellent view of his side face. She observed this same man on the three succeeding days, and she was very much astonished, as she had never seen loiterers there before. There was nothing to loiter about there for. On the three days, 15th, 16th, and 17th December, she called the attention of her companion, William Campbell, to the fact. She, without hesitation, said there was no doubt that this was the man she saw, because she took a good look at him, as it struck her as curious at the time. William Campbell, who was with her on the 15th, 16th, and 17th, says that he was very like the man he saw, and he remembers when Euphemia Cunningham said to him, "There is the same man again." The man apparently heard, and rapidly turned away his face. On the night before the murder, about twenty minutes to seven, Mr. Bryson, a cabinetmaker, an intelligent and respectable man, was going home, passing eastwards along West Princes Street. As he passed the house of Mr. Gillies, almost straight opposite Miss Gilchrist's house, he was struck by a man standing on the flat stone at the top of the little flight of steps leading to the close door, standing with his back to the close door and looking over at Miss Gilchrist's windows, two of which were lighted. He was so struck with the appearance of this man, and his long, steady gaze, that he actually went up and stared at him, thinking that there was something wrong. When the man saw him staring he was taken aback; he moved on, and walked away towards Queen's Crescent. Mr, Bryson had a most excellent opportunity of seeing him; he went for the purpose of seeing him. He took a long, fixed stare at him, and he had not the slightest hesitation in saying that the prisoner in the dock is the man he saw there. An hour and a half later Mr. Nairn, a provision merchant, a very respectable man, was passing in the same direction eastwards. He was ahead of his wife and children, and he stood near the corner of Queen's Crescent to wait for them. While he was standing there he says that within a very few yards further to the east he saw a man with his back to him staring steadily at Miss Gilchrist's house. It appears that that was the position from which you had by far the best view of the house. Inspector Dornan went down there and had it pointed out by Mr. Nairn, and he says that that is the place where you have the best view of Miss Gilchrist's house. There the man stood, says Mr. Nairn, for the best part of five minutes. Mr. Nairn was very much impressed with the fact, and you will remember he said, "I did not have an opportunity of seeing the man's front face." But when the prisoner turned he had no hesitation in saying, "That is the man." Then, in addition, you have the evidence of Constable Walker, who saw him on three different occasions, the first time standing at that very comer, in full view of Miss Gilchrist's house, the second time, a few days later, walking westwards on the north side of West Princes Street, right opposite Miss Gilchrist's house, and the third time loitering near the corner of St. George's Road. Lastly, you have Constable Bryan, who saw him the week before the murder close by the corner of St. George's Road and West Princes Street.

Gentlemen, if that was the prisoner, how do you account for his presence there? What was a respectable dentist doing day after day, hour after hour, carefully observing this house? I say that there was no other object that he had than to observe closely what was going on, so far as he could, with his skilled eye, to learn from prolonged observation what were the movements of the people in that house, who were the inmates of the house, and what were their habits and customs; when the servant went out, and when the old lady was left alone at home; what were the movements of the policemen on the beat, how often they passed, at what intervals, and at what times. If any other explanation suggests itself to your minds, I should be astonished. I am at a loss to give any explanation other than that the man was there with a purpose, namely, to make all secure when the supreme moment came.

It is said that in cases of this kind you are not safe to proceed upon the evidence of those who have had no personal knowledge of a man, and who merely speak to their having recognised his face. A mere passing glance at a man, a stare at a man, a long look at a man is not sufficient if you have not known him, because you may be mistaken. Now, I agree that that is true. I myself consider — but his lordship will guide you here — that it would be dangerous to go upon mere personal impressions formed of a man's appearance, because you may be mistaken. Gentlemen, you can be under no misapprehension, and there can be no mistake, if the man's appearance is distinctive and peculiar. In the case of ordinary and commonplace faces, faces which you see every day in the street, it would be a dangerous thing to go on your mere passing recollection that you had seen this man or that. But where you have a man with a peculiar, well-marked face, a face that you would not see every day, or once in a year, if even ever, then you are in a very different region. I say that the prisoner's face is one which no man with any observation at all could forget, having once seen it. You are capital judges yourselves, there are none better than you. Judge for yourselves in this matter. I would remind you, however, of some very striking testimony in this case. Mr. Marr, the house factor, saw the man once, and he had no hesitation in recognising him again. There is no dispute about it that the prisoner was the very man with whom Marr had bargained. The printer who printed his cards saw him once, or perhaps twice, for the briefest possible time, and he at once recognised him. The clerk in the Cunard office saw him once — he sees hundreds of passengers — and he recognised him instantly after the one brief look that he had had at him when giving him his tickets. The porter who carried his baggage had never seen him before, and had never seen him since, and yet he recognised him without hesitation. The porter at the railway station saw him once, and recognised him instantly and without the slightest doubt.

He could not recognise the ladies who were with him, although he had just as good an opportunity of seeing them; but he had not the slightest hesitation in recognising the prisoner. Mr. Jackson, to whom he went once in November to sell a ring, had never seen him before, and has never seen him since, and yet he recognised him without a moment's hesitation. There is not a single human being in this case who, having once seen the prisoner, has failed to know him again at once, so striking, so peculiarly distinctive is his face.

Gentlemen, that is testimony which, I submit to you, is absolutely overwhelming. You are not dealing here with the case of a man who is like or who resembles thousands of other men, you are dealing here with a man who, once seen by a competent and intelligent observer, is never forgotten, and these are very striking instances which I have just given you. I purposely selected people who saw him once, but did not fail to recognise him instantly they saw him again, and you, it is admitted, have recognised the right man. I ask you whether you are really going to accept the perfectly sound, good evidence of Mr. Marr, the Cunard man, the railway porter, and the others who did inevitably and surely recognise this man, and to put aside the evidence of the eleven people who saw him on that street watching the house carefully, several of whom had much better opportunities of observing him than Mr. Marr and the others had. Is it possible that these ten or eleven people may have made any mistake? I submit that it is not possible.

In a case of mistaken identity where a respectable man is had up, charged with having committed some crime, there is always some way to satisfy the jury that he is the wrong man, that there has really been a great mistake committed, that he is a perfectly respectable man who was not near the place. There is no man so destitute of friends and acquaintances that he cannot establish his identity, and show who he is and what he is, and what his movements were, and where he was at the time when the crime was committed which is laid at his door. This man had a communication with his intimate friend Cameron after the charge was made against him, and when he knew quite well what the situation was. He writes to his friend Cameron a letter, dated 2nd February, in which, after railing very hard at Gordon Henderson, whose evidence I will come to in a moment, he says, "I can prove my innocence before having a trial, because I will prove with five people where I have been when the murder was committed." He professes that he could meet the charge by producing five people to the authorities, and satisfy them where he had been when the murder was committed. Where are the five? Who are the five? What steps have been taken to show that he is an honest dentist, practising at 69 St. George's Road, and that this was an entire misapprehension on the part of the police? Not one. You heard the evidence. It is said that on the night of the murder he was seen in a billiard room in Renfield Street. The billiard room keeper and the billiard room marker were examined. One or other of them must have been in the billiard room, but neither of them would say that the prisoner was there. His friend Rattman, to whom he wrote the letter to which I shall refer a little later, was produced, but all Rattman says — and it is the best he can say — is that he was there playing billiards that evening, that the prisoner came in but did not play billiards, that he stopped a short time and then went away. Kattman never looked at the clock, either when he came in or when he went away; he never looked at the clock that evening. Kattman says it w as his habit to be home a little before seven; he says he expected to reach his home, which was two or three minutes away from the billiard room, at ten minutes to seven. Kattman never looked at the clock at any time, and he is only giving you a hazard guess or conjecture, with no foundation whatever. The other man who was present in the billiard room was a man named Aumann. He, like Rattman, never looked at the clock at all. He says that the prisoner came in any time between 5 and 6.30, that his object was to get his friend Kattman to buy the pawn ticket for the brooch, and when Kattman declined to buy it, the prisoner left. Remember this is 21st December. It is vain to say that Aumann subsequently added that it was 6.30 when the prisoner left. Aumann never looked. If Aumann's evidence is correct, then the prisoner came into that billiard room between 5 and 5.30 and tried to get Rattman to buy his pawn ticket, and, when he failed, off he went. That is all you know. There is no evidence on the part of these two men that the prisoner was in the billiard room at or near the time when the murder was committed. Keep in view that the billiard room is less than a mile from the scene of the murder, and the prisoner is said to be a remarkably rapid walker. Aumann and Kattman said he was a remarkably rapid walker when he pleased. Well, then, out of the five people "who will prove where I have been," that is the best that can be done. You are quite safe to assume that there is no case of mistaken identity here. The prisoner is hopelessly unable to produce a single witness who saw that he was anywhere else than at the scene of the murder that night.

Having seen the elaborate precautions that were taken to ensure safety, to ensure that he would not be confronted by some man who could say that he entered the house, I now turn to the evidence of those who saw the man who committed the murder; for, of course, the man who committed the murder was the man who came out of the bedroom, was the man who emerged from the close, was the man who dashed past the turnstile. Was that man the prisoner? That is the question which you have to decide. Well, gentlemen, the first witness who speaks to the prisoner's presence at the scene of the murder, and within minutes of the murder, is Mrs. Liddell, the married sister of Mr. Adams, who was coming home with her old mother to 14 We.st Princes Street, next door to Miss Gilchrist's house. As she approached Miss Gilchrist's house she saw a strange man standing against the railings, with his left side to her. She was much struck by his appearance, and she stared at him; not a mere passing glance, but she stared at the man she saw standing in this position against the railings. She describes his face with minute accuracy. She said that his was one face in a thousand. She said that she could not be mistaken as to it. She would pledge herself to nothing but what she herself had actually seen, and what had impressed itself on her memory. She said she was rather struck with the appearance of this man at this unexpected time and place. Gentlemen, she may have been theatrical in her way of giving evidence, but I am sure you will not deny she was a conscientious, careful, and unbiassed witness. She refused to give any evidence on the identification until she had seen the man placed in the exact position in which she had seen him that night; and then she said, "Yes, I believe, I must believe, that that man was there." She hesitated, no doubt, because she knew and realised the serious issue depending on her testimony in a case like this, but she says, "I know the face at once, now that I see it as I saw it that night." Then she describes his nose, his cheek, his complexion, in perfectly graphic language, and she cannot doubt it was the prisoner she saw that night a few minutes before seven. The next witness is the witness Adams. Now, he is a little short-sighted — that must be said — but when he stood at the door he expected that something was wrong. He had heard gruesome sounds down below a few minutes before, he had been sent up by his sister to see what was wrong, he had rung the bell three times and had got no answer, and while he was waiting there he again heard the gruesome sound of this old lady being done to death by her murderer. He went downstairs and told his sisters what had happened, and they bade him go up again as something surely must be wrong. He went up again, and standing beside the maid-servant when she opened the door, he was certainly on the alert. The man came out and passed him close by. He saw him, he saw his face. As he passed him he dashed off, and he turned round. and followed him with his eye till he disappeared down the stair. Now, Mr. Adams had just as much time as I have described — I do not say he had a long time — to make his observation. But I say that under these awful circumstances, and knowing as he did that something was wrong, he was on the alert. And he says that the prisoner was the man. "When he was taken to New York he identified him. He was taken to a room where there were upwards of forty men, and he had no difficulty whatever in picking this man out as being very like the man he had seen that night. That is to say, he did not hesitate between this man and the thirty or forty other people who were in the room. Never for a moment did he flinch. He picked out that man as the only man that was like, or, as he said, very like, the man he had seen that night.

Now, do not misunderstand a witness who says, "That is very like the man I saw; he has a very close resemblance to the man I saw." What more can a man say, what more ought a man to say who was not familiar with the man, and had only an opportunity of seeing him once? It is really a matter of phrase. "Yes," some one says, "That is the man," and he means no more than "That is very like the man," unless he adds, as you have sometimes heard, "But there is something about this man that is not like the one I saw," or "There is something about the man I saw which is not like this man; he is very like him, but there are some features different." Now, you must have observed that not a single witness in the box who said, "That is very like the man," added, "But there are some features present here that were not present in the man I saw," or the reverse. And, accordingly, do not be misled by phrases or words. No man, who has testified that he recognises the man in the dock now as the man he had seen on a former occasion, and only once, can ever say more than this, "That is very like him; that closely resembles him. I do not hesitate between that man and any other man I see before me." Mr. Adams came home and again saw him in the police office, and again identified him, and he gave the same story here in the witness-box. You cannot deny that Adams was a perfectly impartial and a perfectly respectable man. You cannot deny that he was under circumstances in which he could observe the prisoner. You cannot deny that he has never hesitated or flinched between this man and any other man; and he has not pointed out a single feature that the man he saw had and that this man has not. He recollects the kind of coat he wore and the kind of hat. It was the man's face that impressed him, as it impressed every other person.

I come now to the servant girl, Helen Lambie. There is a discrepancy between her evidence and the evidence of Mr. Adams, of which you must judge, a discrepancy as to the place where she was in the house when she observed the murderer coming out of the bedroom. She herself said in the witness-box that she did not get past the threshold of the door. Mr. Adams said she had taken several steps into the house, and that accordingly her observation of the man coming would be shorter than she says it was; but, on the other hand, her observation of the man as he was going away from her would be longer than she says it was, because Mr. Adams agrees in saying — and it is very important that you should remember this— that when the man passed her she turned round and watched him until he had disappeared down the stairs. She had therefore an opportunity, she says, not of seeing his face — his head was down when she saw him — but she saw his side face, his height, his general appearance, and his gait. Now, when she was taken out to America a very striking incident took place before the examination proper before the Commissioner. She and the girl Barrowman were standing with Inspector Pyper in the corridor of the Court. They had no reason to expect that the murderer would come that way. They were not told that the murderer was to be brought in. They were not asked any questions. They were standing there silent, whilst a number of different people were passing into the Commissioner's room, when there appeared in the corridor the prisoner at the bar and two other men. Simultaneously the two girls said to Inspector Pyper, "Oh! there is the man" — an involuntary exclamation. There was no question put to them, there was no information given beforehand to lead them to expect that they would see the man. They see him unexpectedly, and involuntarily and instantly they say, "Oh! there is the man."

Now, evidence of that kind is infinitely better, I should imagine, in your judgment than even evidence given upon oath in the witness-box. People get flurried and excited and agitated when they are placed in an unaccustomed position, and many witnesses do themselves very poor justice indeed in the witness-box. Here were the two girls standing there without expecting anything, without any questions being asked, and instantly they recognise the man. Now, when she was taken subsequently into the Commissioner's room I am bound to say that she was not treated very fairly. There were thirty or forty people in the room; the man Slater was seated in a position in which the girl Lambie could not see him from the place where she was standing. It appears from the evidence of Inspector Pyper that the agent or counsel representing Slater stood up in front of him and spread out his frock coat, and when the girl was asked if she recognised the man in the room she looked round thirty or forty men of all kinds that were gathered in the room, and, not seeing him, she leaned back in the way Inspector Pyper describes and caught sight of him behind Mr. Goodhart, and said, "That is the man there." Now, that is very striking evidence. We conduct our business in this Court with much greater propriety, much greater attention is given to fair play and justice. There the girl was put in a distinctly disadvantageous position, yet, without hesitation, she picked that man out of the thirty or forty men who were there. You must keep these two incidents in view, I think, in judging of Helen Lambie's evidence. There is no doubt she said in New York that she did not see his face, and that she was judging by his gait and general appearance. No doubt about that. She says now that although she did not see his full face, she saw his side face, as not only she says, but Mr. Adams says, that she looked over her shoulder when the man passed. It is for you to judge whether the girl who saw the side face was not labouring under excitement, agitation, and may be confusion, owing to the strange and unaccustomed surroundings in which she found herself after having been taken over to New York, in this room full of men, and subjected to such questioning and badgering as we do not tolerate here. That is the question pre-eminently for you to judge. Now, when she was here she unquestionably told you that there were three things from which she drew the inference of recognition — first, the side face; second, the size and general appearance; and third, the gait. It is also true that Inspector Pyper observed the man's gait, and said that it was not very distinctive. He says he could not rely on that. No doubt he has seen the slight in-toe and the slight turn-out of the knee, but he adds, with fairness and justice, that what impresses one man most may not impress another. It is the general appearance on which the girl relies. Furthermore, she remembers what he was wearing, and she says that this coat which has been exhibited was the coat that the man was wearing that night, and she remembers the dark hat, and nothing more. You are the best judges of all this. What I pray of you is, that when you are considering her evidence remember her natural agitation and excitement, first, when she saw her dead mistress lying on the floor on that awful night, and second, the unaccustomed surroundings in New York, when she was subjected to a good deal of badgering and questioning by the Commissioner and the agent. And I pray you not to forget the two incidents to which I have called your attention, the incident in the corridor and the incident in the Commissioner's room.

The third witness who saw the murderer that night was the girl Barrowman. She was going a message at the time, and she walked eastwards along West Princes Street. As she came within "12 or 13 yards of Miss Gilchrist's house she saw a man coming out at a break-neck pace. If you recollect, there is an incandescent lamp just a few yards to the west of the entrance to Miss Gilchrist's house, and that incandescent lamp throws an admirable light upon Miss Gilchrist's steps and the intervening pavement. This little girl had a full view of the man. She saw him glance towards St. George's Road, and then he ran westwards, and ran against her. She describes his coat; she describes his hat; she describes his appearance. When he dashed against her he still continued to pursue his flight westward, and she turned round and followed him a considerable number of paces, until she saw him turn round into West Cumberland Street, and then she lost sight of him. She went home and told her mother what she had seen. Her mother bade her be silent, because she might have been mistaken, though she said that she was not. By pure accident her testimony came to the knowledge of the police, and it was from her description that the man was traced. She never swerved — you saw her in the witness-box, and you will judge whether she was not a remarkably intelligent and clear observer — she never swerved from the description she had given. She said he was clean shaven. You will recollect about that. The prisoner was shaved about the middle of December, and there was only some growth. Is it not perfectly natural that the girl who had only a comparatively short opportunity, but a very good opportunity, of observing the man, should not see what is called this stubbly growth on the upper lip, a growth, the barber said, of about 3-16 of an inch? That is the one point on which it is said that her recognition of the features and the appearance of the man is defective. You will judge whether that is sufficient. She identifies him without hesitation from amongst the forty people in the Commissioner's room in New York, and she identifies him here. I ask you to remember the very striking incident which took place in the Central Police Office. She asked that he should be dressed as he was on the night in question. He puts on the coat No. 43 of the productions, he puts on the hat, and she makes him pull it down a little, and a little more, and then she says, "That is it; that is as I saw him on the night of the murder." Now, that is very striking testimony. I do not know that, under the circumstances, you could possibly have better testimony than that. I leave it with you to say whether it is likely, putting all things together, that that very intelligent and wholly unbiassed observer, that girl who had an excellent opportunity of seeing the murderer, could possibly have been mistaken.

The last witness who saw the murderer was the girl at the turnstile. Now, so far as I know, the only observation upon her evidence is with regard to the time. She said it was any time between 7.30 and eight o'clock when the passenger passed her at a break-neck speed. All she can say is that it was after 7.30, she says between 7.30 and twenty-five minutes to eight, but let it be later, if you please. I do not contend — no man would contend — that this man made a straight course from the scene of the murder to the underground station. If he had done so he could have covered the distance in about five or six minutes, and we know that the murder must have taken place, and the murderer must have escaped from the house by fifteen or twenty minutes past seven. Of course, there is a network of streets there, a network of streets that were perfectly familiar to Slater, up and down which he might have doubled, and no doubt did double, before he reached the Subway station. My point is that he knew perfectly where was the best place to get underground and to elude observation. He knew the whole locality, and he knew his best means of covering up his tracks was to get down below, to get to the Subway, and to be taken by a train to some remote part of the city and then come strolling back to his house. The girl had an excellent opportunity of observing. He comes up, pitches down his penny, passes the turnstile without picking up his ticket, and she looks out, and has an opportunity of seeing him while he goes down the flight of steps. She describes him exactly as Barrowman describes him. You would notice that both of them observed that he was holding his hands in his pockets, and that his coat was open. I suggest that the weapon was in his inner coat pocket, and he was holding it tight to prevent it falling out. Now this girl, having seen the man, having seen his face when he paid his money, has not the slightest doubt. She, like the others, picked him out from amongst the ten or twelve people she saw in the Central Police Office, and she never swerved between him and any one else. You have heard a body of evidence that cannot be lightly set aside, testimony which is in exact agreement with all the other evidence in the case, on the part of the four people who saw the murderer. The only question is, are you satisfied that their recollection of him and his appearance is so good that you can believe them when they say, without hesitation, that the prisoner at the bar is the man they saw?

Now, gentlemen, I come to a different class of evidence altogether. We know nothing of the man's movements until a quarter to ten at night, when he appears, excited, at the Motor Club in India Street. He interviews Gordon Henderson, the clubmaster, whom he has seen only two or three times before; he begs him to give him all the money he has in the club, and he will give him a cheque for it. Now, that is a strange request. Why does he now begin on this very day, 21st December, to collect together all the money that he can? Why was it he could not even wait till the next day to cash his cheque? I dare say you have your own ideas as to whether that cheque would have been honoured. Why does he go, gasping and panting, for money to this Motor Club, where he was but little known as compared with the club adjoining, the Sloper Club? How is it that Henderson had his suspicions aroused by the excited man coming at this late hour, not a member of the club, and begging him for all the money he can lay his hands on? Henderson is not able to give him anything, except a very little loose change, which is insufficient, and he suggests that he should go next door to the Sloper Club, where he would find his friend Cameron. I suppose he, knowing Cameron's financial resources better than you or I do, said that was no use, and then he left. Slater himself obviously felt that this was a very suspicious incident. Here is what he says about it in his letter, "I am very down-hearted, my dear Cameron, to know that my friends in Glasgow, like *Gordon Henderson*, can tell such lies about me to the Glasgow police. I have seen here his statements he made in Glasgow telling the police that a German came up to him and had told him Oscar Slater had committed the murder, and also that I have been on the night of the murder in his place asking him for mony, I was very excited and in hurry, I didn't think it was very clever from him, *because he like to make himself a good name by the police* to tell such lies. I don't deny I have been in his place asking him for mony, because I have been brocke in the Sloper Club. Only I will fix Mr. Gordon Henderson. I will prove with plenty of witnesses that I was playing there mucky, and I am entitled to ask a proprietor from a gambling house when I am broke for money. He would not mind to get me hangt, and I will try to prove that from a gambling point I am right to ask for some money. I hope nobody propper mindet will blame me for this." I wonder who are the gentlemen who were brought to prove that he was at the Sloper Club that night, that he was playing cards, that he had lost money and could not get money from his friends in the Sloper Club, and that he went to the adjoining club, where he was not a member, and asked the clubmaster at a late hour of night to give him money to pay his debts in the adjoining club, and offered him a cheque. He did not ask for any sum of money; he asked for all the money that the clubmaster had. I suggest to you that Slater at this time, having committed the murder, was now getting all the means he could collect in order to enable him to effect his escape, for you will recollect he was disturbed before he had possession himself of more than one of the old lady's jewels.

There is one other instance, and it is a very striking one. In the evening of 24th December — or it may have been the 23rd — there mounted the car at the foot of Union Street a man whom the conductor, who was a very good observer, identified as the prisoner. He went up on the top of the car and took his seat a little bit in front of the place where the electricity comes down to drive the car. On the opposite side there was sitting a boy reading about the murder in the *Evening Citizen*. As the car conductor comes up and asks the man where he is going there is a mumbled answer, and the conductor gives him a penny ticket. Then he turns to the boy, who has been reading about the Glasgow West-End murder, and asks him if the man has been got yet; and the boy answers, "No, and I do not think they are likely to get him." The conductor sees this man fidgetting and looking suspiciously at him, and within a few seconds after he has paid his fare he rises, darts down the stair, runs up a side street, and runs full speed up the street, without waiting for the car to stop. Well, it is suggested that it is not very economical for a man to pay a penny and leave before he has reached his destination, but that is not the observation I think that you are likely to make. He was very brave, he was perfectly cool, he was perfectly composed, amongst his cronies in the few days after the murder. He never went to any of his clubs or any of his other familiar haunts, and the only time we hear of him in the presence of the members of the general public we find that his guilty conscience is aroused, and he feels that the sooner he is out of the neighbourhood the better. At all events, there is that very striking incident. The conductor, having seen the man on the roof there, said of the prisoner, "That is the man "; and he has not the slightest hesitation about him any more than the other witnesses have.

I come now, finally, to his flight from justice. I say, deliberately, "his flight from justice," because I am going to demonstrate that there was one reason, and one reason only, for his leaving Glasgow at that time, and that was to escape the hands of justice. His departure from Glasgow was, to use his own expression in his letter to his friend Rattman, "absolutely suddenly." That is Rattman's translation, "absolutely suddenly," or, as we say in the letter as printed, "surprisingly." Gentlemen, he left Glasgow on the night of 25th December without saying farewell to a single one of his intimate friends and cronies, without a single one of his friends knowing that he was going away. It is said that a fortnight, or three weeks, or a month before he spoke of going to America. I dare say he did; I am certain he did. There is no doubt whatever he had made up his mind, as soon as the deed was accomplished, that he would not stay in this country one moment longer than was absolutely necessary. He had in view to go to America or somewhere else, and that he stated that to his cronies three weeks or a month before is, I think, not only highly probable, but absolutely certain. What I say is, that, having this intention of going abroad unquestionably fixed in his mind, he did go at the precise moment when he went suddenly, unexpectedly, and without giving a word of warning to a single one of his friends. I say that his flight was precipitated, and the moment fixed by the publication of his description in the newspapers at two o'clock on the afternoon of the 25th December. He had taken his house for eighteen months. Do you think that a respectable man, dentist or no dentist, having taken a house for eighteen months, and having made up his mind to leave his house, would not have given some notice? I am assuming at this moment that he is a respectable man, who has fallen into the hands of the authorities by a mistake. Do you really think that a respectable man who, having taken a house for eighteen months from respectable people, would have left without giving a word of warning? He gives no notice, and he leaves the house with the rent unpaid, of course. He has bought £178 worth of furniture, and he leaves that. Happily, that was purchased on the hire-purchase system, and the furniture people got back the furniture. No notice is given to them. You would expect that a respectable man would go to the furniture people and would say, " I am going away. Pray, take back the furniture." He leaves without giving any notice. On 9th December he sends his watch up to London to be repaired, and he tells the watchmaker that his address till 30th December will be 69 St. George's Road. At 6.12 p.m. on 21st December a telegram is sent off saying that he must have his watch at once, and on 23rd December he sends another telegram saying, "Must have watch now, leaving to-morrow night for the Continent." That was a falsehood, and he knew it, because on that very day, the 23rd December, he was at Cook's office in Glasgow finding out about sailings for America. He was minded to go on board the "Lusitania," which left Liverpool for New York on Saturday, the 26th. He was too late on the 23rd to effect arrangements for a berth, and he was asked by the clerk to come back the next day, that they were communicating with Liverpool, and would give him an answer then. On the afternoon of the 24th this man, who was instantly leaving for the Continent, comes back to Cook's office, and is offered an inside berth, which he thinks is unsuitable. He thinks he would like an outside berth, and he does not take the berth that is offered. The clerk asks him to come back next day, and he agrees to come back the next day, the 25th. He never appeared on the 25th. Now, mind you, at this time he had given his name to Cooks' people in Glasgow as Oscar Slater. On the 25th — the day he was to go back to Cooks' office — his name and his description, and all the rest of it, appear in the Glasgow papers, and he sees that the last thing in this world that he ought to do, if he studies his own safety, is to go back to Cooks' office as Oscar Slater. He accordingly straightway proceeds to pack up all his goods and effects on the 25th. So far as we know, he never leaves the house from the time he sees the paper until a little after six o'clock, when he goes down to the Central Station, and gets a porter to go up to his house. No arrangement was made beforehand. He walks down to the Central Station at six o'clock and gets a porter to come up for his baggage at 8.20, and he goes on with his packing. The porter comes, and then you will remember the curious departure. The cab does not drive up to the door. Down he goes with the lady and the servant. You will remember what the servant upstairs and the neighbours said. He looks suspiciously about, and the lady is behind him. No doubt they go on and find their way down to the Central Station and take their places in the train. The booking clerk at the Central Station says that a man very like Slater came and bought two London tickets, third class. He says that he cannot recollect who it was that bought the other tickets that are down in his book, the two third- class tickets to Liverpool. I do not attach very much importance to this, and I will tell you frankly it depends entirely on the evidence of the booking clerk, who simply says, "I recollect seeing that man, a man very like that man, buying two third-class single tickets for London "; and he says, what is perfectly true, that a man with a London ticket may travel to Liverpool and break his journey there, going in the Liverpool carriage. It seems to be the regular practice to take a ticket for London, and break the journey at Liverpool, and no question is asked. When he arrives at Liverpool he does not go to the Cunard office and say, " I am Oscar Slater, the man who was communicating with you through your agent Cook in Glasgow," but he lets slip, as some men do even when they seek to be most careful, what he thinks to be rather a suspicious expression. When he is offered a berth he says, "Oh, well, I was offered that by your Glasgow agents," and then, says the booking clerk, he seemed to have regretted having used the words "Glasgow agents." Whatever impression he may have produced upon the Cunard agent, he takes his passage on board the "Lusitania" under the name of Otto Sando, and the lady under the name of Amy Sando. Why? For two reasons. In the first place, because he knew that the police were on the track of Oscar Slater, and, in the second place, because he knew that upon a number of his packages were the initials "O.S.," and it would not do for him to travel under the name of Adolph Anderson, or George, or any other name but a name beginning with and S. And, accordingly, for some reason or another which has not been explained, which cannot be explained consistently with innocence, the man takes his passage for himself and the lady under false and assumed names. He does more. In the application form for tickets he puts in his name as Otto Sando, and his occupation as dentist. Where is his destination? His destination was Queensland to the barber, his destination was San Francisco to the watchmaker, his destination was Monte Carlo to the servant who was left behind. His destination was America generally. His destination is now changed, because the newspapers have reported his name and his description, and his destination now is, "American address, Chicago, 30 Staate Street." On the back of his ticket you find the name "Otto Sando and Mrs. Amy Sando." You find his occupation given as dentist, you find his final destination Chicago, and you find in pencil "Hotel Chicago." Now, I ask you, how can you account for this remarkable history of deception if this was an honest man, simply leaving this country for America in order to take up some business, in order to visit a friend for some entirely innocent purpose? Is there any sort of explanation consistent with innocence? I submit to you there is no explanation of it which is consistent with anything but the view that he, knowing that the police were on his track, took every step possible in order to baffle the ends of justice and to escape the hands of the authorities.

That was not the end of his deception. In the course of his preparations, when he was collecting his money, he had to lift some money from the Savings Bank and some money that was invested in the public funds; and he had to write a letter to London in order to get that money. He wrote that letter to London on the 21st, and he got his money from the Savings Bank, some ££39, on the 23rd, and his money from the public funds, some £49, on the 24th. In the letter which he wrote to the authorities asking for his money, he asks them to send it at once, "as I have an urgent call to America because my wife is ill." The postmark upon that letter is "Glasgow, 5 p.m., December 21st." There is no talk here about escape from an importunate wife. We were told that the whole object of the visit to America was either to benefit the health of one lady or to escape the pursuit of another, but here he is now going to America, not to escape, but on the urgent call of his wife, who is said to be ill.

What is the meaning of all this deception, what is the meaning of all these deliberate falsehoods, what is the meaning of this collection of all his available resources, what is the meaning of his call on the pawn-brokers on 21st December to get £30 more upon this brooch? What is the meaning of his attempt, his eager attempt, to sell even the reversion of the pawn ticket, having got into his hands upwards of, roughly, £135? Why was he collecting all this money? This man, who was hard up some weeks before, had begun to collect all his available resources in order that he might make his flight from justice absolutely certain and secure. My submission to you is that the circumstances connected with his flight bring home inevitable guilt to this man. These subterfuges and deliberate lies and falsehoods which he told, and the efforts which he made to conceal his tracks, are consistent with nothing but guilt on his part, and that synchronised in a remarkable degree with the publication of his description in the newspapers and the knowledge that was so brought home to him that the authorities were upon his track.

Gentlemen, I submit to you in summary that the evidence shows, clearly and beyond all dispute, that this man was a man who was capable of this atrocious crime; it shows that this man was a man who had the whole knowledge necessary to enable him to commit the crime with success; it shows that he was one of the few men who could commit a crime of this kind with any reasonable chance of escaping. As I said before, jewels are difficult things to deal with and to dispose of. This was a man who had been seen elaborately taking the precautions necessary to accomplish a crime which was carefully planned, which was deliberately carried out by cool and abandoned ruffianism. The evidence shows conclusively, not only had he taken elaborate precautions to cover up his tracks first, in anticipation of the accomplishment of his nefarious object, but he took the greatest pains when the supreme moment came to conceal his escape and to effect his flight with perfect safety.

Gentlemen, I have done. I cannot prove more in this case. I do not for a moment deny that you have to-day to discharge the most serious and the most responsible duty which you will probably have to discharge during the whole course of your natural lives. On your verdict undoubtedly depends a man's life; and I need say no more to bring home to you a sense of the responsibility which now lies upon you. If any reasonable doubt occurs to you, if you entertain any reasonable doubt as to the evidence bringing home guilt to this man, then you are bound to give him the benefit of that doubt. He may be, and probably is, the worst of men; but he is entitled to as fair a trial as if he was the best of men. He may be one of the most degraded of mortals, he may be a cheat, he may be a robber, a burglar, or the worst of characters, but that does not infer that he committed murder. He is entitled, therefore, to have all the benefit of as fair a trial as you can give to a citizen of most unimpeachable respectability. Gentlemen, he is entitled to justice, to no less than justice, but to no more than justice. My submission to you is that his guilt has been brought fairly home to him, that no shadow of doubt exists, that there is no reasonable doubt that he was the perpetrator of this foul murder. I adjure you to allow no feeling of sentiment — if, indeed, sentiment is admissible in a case like this at all — and no feeling of aversion to the consequences that may follow, to deter you from discharging the duty which you owe to your country, and the duty which is laid upon you by the oath which you took on Monday morning, to prevent you from finding and returning the verdict to which the evidence inevitably leads.

MR. M'CLURE'S ADDRESS TO THE JURY/a>

Mr. M'CLURE then addressed the jury as follows: — Gentlemen of the jury, I must confess to a feeling of very great responsibility in rising to address you now on behalf of the accused. Not only has he got, with slight resources and the assistance of a few friends, to fight his case single-handed against the forces of the Crown and the power of the Lord Advocate, but I think he has also to fight a most unfair fight against public prejudice, roused with a fury I do not remember to have seen in any other case. Certainly the newspaper campaign which has been conducted against this man Slater is without parallel for its absolutely irresponsible character, for the rumours it has set afloat, for the prejudice it has created. I am not saying this to you because I believe you have been moved by it, but I mention it because it is right that it should be mentioned and condemned. This man, in many quarters, has been convicted before he has been tried; but I ask you to bear in mind that you, gentlemen, and all of us here who have been present during these last three days listening to the evidence, are better judges than any outsider can possibly be of the rights and wrongs of this matter. If you ever had any preconception in your minds because of what you have seen in the newspapers before you were empanelled — even as late as Saturday last there was a disgraceful attack upon the prisoner in an evening newspaper — lay that aside, and remember that the accused has to be tried by you upon the evidence that has been laid before you upon oath. I am certain you will do nothing that is unfair, and I am certain you will act up to the high conception of duty which, I trust, you entertain. The case has many difficulties, and you will weigh them; but you will remember this, that if you come to an adverse verdict against this man there is not the lea-st doubt that it will be followed by sentence of death, and that will be followed by his certain doom. If he is convicted, I would have you remember that there is no possibility of a commutation of the capital penalty; and I say this to make you bear in mind the terrible power which you wield, and also to impress upon you your duty to weigh fairly the great issues which are before you.

There is no doubt whatever — it has been mentioned as the main thing against him — that the person you are trying is what is ordinarily described as a person of disreputable life. People who frequent the clubs to which he resorted, who have no means of livelihood except gambling, and have for their friends all kinds of outcasts, live a life of their own, and none of us here touches it. Therefore, when appeals are made to you by the LORD ADVOCATE, asking you to conceive what a respectable man would do under circumstances of this kind or of that, his appeal is beside the point. These people do not have influential friends, they have only friends of their own class; and surely this is certain, that if one of them is charged with murder, and may have to die for it, you cannot, in common fairness, disregard the evidence of the people he has been living among. You cannot say, "Because I cannot get people living under respectable social conditions to say something in his favour, he is therefore doomed." The LORD ADVOCATE says, "Where was he? If he cannot show to demonstration by respectable witnesses where he was, what do you think of him? Is he not guilty?" Gentlemen, that comes, in simple language, to this, that unless the man could demonstrate an alibi by the evidence of the respectable — that is, by persons he never mixed with and never met — then he is to pay the last penalty. That surely, gentlemen, is not the way in which this case can be dealt with. If you can find proof convincing to your mind that the prisoner did the deed, then I, no less than the Lord Advocate, would not ask you to hold your hand. But your judgment must be a careful and considerate judgment. When a man is being tried for his life he has a right to the benefit of all the doubts there may be. If you see any doubts in the evidence, then weigh them well. Remember that a fellow-creature is not to be sent to death unless his guilt is clear. Remember this also, that it is well to give a verdict in which there will be no after reproach for yourselves.

Gentlemen, there were some circumstances in connection with this case — occurring before the case itself was investigated — which started an almost overwhelming prejudice against the prisoner. Sympathy, of course, exists in the breasts of none of us for the crime which was committed; and if we had the perpetrator, there is no doubt what we would do with him. But the horror of this murder overhung the city of Glasgow, and, as you have heard in the evidence, all sorts of absurd rumours were in circulation. These rumours, some of which were put to the witnesses, were things that I had heard myself — that this old lady was the friend of thieves, the recipient of stolen property; her house full of jewels; one person said to be her illegitimate daughter, and Slater himself said to be her illegitimate son! There was not a word of truth in all that, but it shows how the public mind was taken possession of. It was something to strike horror into the heart of every household, that, in a common stair in Glasgow, at seven o'clock in the evening, when an old lady was left casually alone, a murderer could come across her threshold and kill her, and nobody know where the murderer was. It was the same excitement as there was in London when Jack the Ripper was feared — feared, indeed, not only in London, but all over the country. "When excitement of that kind takes possession of the public mind, the judgment becomes dangerously overbalanced; and I will make clear to you two matters creating totally unfounded prejudice against the prisoner which took possession of the public mind and influenced it wildly against him.

In the first place, when the pawning of a diamond crescent brooch was found to have taken place exactly upon the 21st of December, the very day of the murder, the whole place was agog. A diamond crescent brooch was missing from the old lady's house, and it was said, "There is the murderer already disposing of the stolen property!" How did this matter get to the police? It got to the police in this way, that Allan M'Lean was casually told at the club, by a friend of his called Anderson, that Slater, who had been a member of the club, and had been gambling there regularly for a period of weeks, had been disposing in Glasgow of a diamond crescent brooch in a pawn-shop. This, we now know, was not Miss Gilchrist's brooch at all, yet it is responsible for the blaze of suspicion against this man which immediately ensued. Two days after, a newspaper came out with a description of the supposed culprit. He was said to be a sallow-complexioned man, a dark man. And so was Slater ! And for some days Slater had not been seen about the club ! Then Allan M'Lean — I do not blame him for it; he was quite right — went to the police and said, "I know a man who answers that description, and I know he was pawning a diamond crescent brooch." So he took the police up to show them the place where this man Slater lived — and this fatal suspicion was afloat. Gentlemen, we all know now, as I have said, that the diamond brooch had nothing at all to do with this old lady. It was a diamond brooch which, so far back as the month of November, had been pawned by Slater in the pawnshop of Mr. Liddell. Twenty pounds had originally been advanced on it; on 9th December, a fortnight before the murder, £10 more had been advanced on it; and on the day of the murder the prisoner, who owned it, and was going abroad, went back and got as much more as he could get on it, viz., £30. That, of course, has nothing to do with this case, as we now know, but the coincidence set the public mind on fire.

Another circumstance — also, I shall show, of mere coincidence — strongly affected public opinion. When Allan M'Lean guided the police to Slater's residence, Slater had disappeared; he was gone ! What more natural than to suppose that this was, as my learned friend said, a "flight from justice"? It was a natural supposition, yet I will be able to show you, I think, quite conclusively that this was no flight from justice. I shall show you that Slater had long purposed going abroad, and you will judge whether the steps that were taken to that end long before, and the things which he did on the very day of the murder, are consistent with the action of a man who had still a murder to perpetrate — a man taking decisive steps to depart before he had murdered anybody — apparently, the suggestion must be, on the chance that he would commit a murder at some later time ! That is what it must come to, for the prisoner had, in fact, concluded a number of his arrangements to leave for America before this murder was perpetrated. I have told you about the pawning of the brooch being an entirely false scent. Everybody admits that now. What about this "flight from justice"? Let us see how this stands.

The key to the situation is to be got in the domestic establishment. What do Schmalz and Antoine say? Slater, according to their evidence — which, by the way, was not alluded to in the speech of the LORD ADVOCATE — had come down from London in November because, as he said, trade in his line of business was bad in London. No doubt that was the motive that brought him. He had not been very long in Glasgow before he was equally disgusted at the opportunities offered there, and he thought of moving. It is not as if this purpose was known only to himself and his immediate household — I mean Schmalz and Antoine. It was not so at all. It is absolutely proved, without any possibility of doubt, by a series of witnesses, that for at least three weeks before this murder occurred he had expressed to various people his intention to go abroad to America — to San Francisco. I want you to follow me here, because this does a great deal to clear up the situation. The intention of going to America, was expressed at least three weeks before to, first of all, Hugh Cameron. Hugh Cameron has sworn this explicitly; and, let me say this of him, that he cannot be called a witness who is specially favourable to the prisoner, because, whatever line of life was followed by the prisoner in Glasgow, to whatever depth he may have gone in his life, our information upon that depends entirely upon the evidence of Hugh Cameron. The LORD ADVOCATE, in connection with the prisoner's habit of gambling, asked, "Did you ever hear of him living in any other way?" and the answer of Cameron was, "Not at that time." Then the LORD ADVOCATE asked, "Did you subsequently?" and the witness said, "I heard it" — and you know what it was. There is no more evidence on that matter, unless what the girl Antoine said herself, that in the prisoner's absence she received gentlemen. That, however, is a subject we are not to go into. It should not have been referred to, and is not in the case; but you will remember the suggestion that was made upon it by the LORD ADVOCATE — that a man of a type so degraded was capable of anything. The prisoner does not look like it, but still, because of this vague and irrelevant accusation, he is supposed to be a man of such extraordinary brutal disposition that he will kill a woman. Well, Hugh Cameron, whose evidence raised this issue, cannot be accused of undue partiality. And what was his evidence? He stated that, three weeks before the murder was committed, this man was talking of leaving Glasgow, and the only thing that kept him from going was that he had a house on lease, and furniture on the hire-purchase system, and that he had to get some one first to take these over. When Cameron was asked, "Did he tell you that he was just on the eve of departure?" he said, "No, he did not tell me." But he added this — and you will bear it in mind — "I did not understand he was just going; I thought it might be by the 'Campania' the following week." The witness Rattman said the same thing. He said, "Not only did I know he was going, but I saw a letter from San Francisco; I do not remember the name of the writer of it." Antoine gave the name as that of a man called Devoto, and his letter was not only seen by Cameron and Rattman, but Cameron stated explicitly, "Although I did not know he was going that week, I knew that his departure was imminent."

Now, that being the state of mind in which the prisoner was, he did make an effort, which was spoken to yesterday, to dispose of his house and furniture. How did the witness Aumann impress you, gentlemen? He did not seem to be telling an untruth, and he stated that he was personally asked if he would take over the flat. He told you that he went over the flat with Slater, and saw the woman Antoine there; that he went home and asked his wife if he should take it, but that she dissuaded him. It therefore comes to this, that three weeks at least before the murder the prisoner's intention to leave was expressed to various friends, and, in point of fact, one of them had actually gone to look at the house with the view of taking it over from him. We have it in the evidence that some person in London called Freedman had also been approached with the same object.

Let us now come to the Monday morning, 21st December. Two letters arrived that morning for Slater, and these letters were followed by results which, I think, you will appreciate. There was a letter that morning from Devoto in San Francisco, and there was another that came from Mr. Rogers in London. It is said by Antoine that she and Slater had been living together for practically the last three or four years. Slater has a wife, and his wife, apparently, when he and Antoine were together in Brussels, managed to make it so hot for them that they left for Boulogne. They travelled across to America under the names of Mr. and Mrs. A. George, so as to give his wife no clue. On this morning of 21st December, when there came the letter from San Francisco, and the intimation from Mr. Rogers that Mrs. Slater was making further inquiries regarding her husband's whereabouts, Slater made up his mind that he would go to America, and expressed his intention in presence of Antoine and Schmalz. Now, it is not as if nothing followed upon that. You will ask me, "Where are the two letters you are talking about?" They are not here. But I ask you to note what followed. At two o'clock that day Schmalz was told that her services were dispensed with from the next Saturday, and that she could go back to London. Slater said to her, when he gave her her dismissal at lunch time that Monday, "You will be able to find your way back to London by yourself." Now, that was before the murder. The next thing is this, that, as we know, he posted a letter, the envelope of which bears five o'clock as the time of posting. That letter was sent from 69 St. George's Road, and was written before the murder. Here is the letter—

Dear Sir, — Enclosed you will find my savings bank book. Be kind enough to send me the money at once, as I have an urgent call to America because my wife is ill. If possible, wire the money on, and I will pay all charges here. — Yours truly, Adolf Anderson.

The LORD ADVOCATE, commenting on the terms of this letter, says that the prisoner's wife was not ill, and he asks, "What does he mean by saying that? He is a liar, and therefore he is the murderer." That hardly follows, nor is it to the point. The letter was all true except the words, "my wife is ill." Here, then, is a letter posted two hours before the murder, following upon the dismissal of the servant. It says that the writer is going to America, and, in order to hurry up the Savings Bank people and to get attention, that he is going immediately, as his wife is ill. I should think a stimulus of this kind is not unusual. Then we have this further circumstance, that he sent a wire to Dent, in London, who was doing something to his watch. In that wire he says, "Dent, watchmaker, Trafalgar Square, London. If possible, please send watch at once. — Oscar Slater." That was sent off from the Central Station, Glasgow, at twelve minutes past six on Monday, 21st December, and it is in Slater's handwriting. Now, the murder was not yet committed. It has been proved to you that he had got letters that morning which made him resolve to leave for America, and here are three facts which all go to show that he proceeded at once to make arrangements and realise what property he had. First, he dismisses the servant; second, he writes to the Savings Bank that he is going to America, and asks for his money; third, his watch being at Dent's in London, a wire is sent at 6.12, asking that it be returned at once. These are three things which show that he was on the move before the murder was committed. Another thing is this: he had now raised £60 upon this diamond crescent brooch which never belonged to the deceased lady at all. Having got the last advance of £30 — I suppose all the pawnbroker would give for it — he went immediately, as has been proved by Rattman and Aumann, to Gall's public-house, and he was there between four and five o'clock in the afternoon, with the pawn ticket, to see if he could raise some further money on it. That is to say, he wished to transfer his remaining interest in this diamond brooch, on which he had raised £60, and he asked Aumann if he would be prepared to buy the pawn ticket. Is it not obvious that the person who was doing all these things was carrying out his expressed intention to leave the country? He began by collecting whatever assets he had, and he was doing this up to the late afternoon of 21st December. There is no gainsaying that at 6.12 he was in the Central Station sending off a telegram. The telegram is in his handwriting, and 6.12 is the hour at which it was despatched. Accordingly, we have the prisoner, on the night when the servant girl says she left her mistress's house to buy an evening newspaper, at the Central Station sending off a telegram asking Dent to send on his watch. That is at 6.12 p.m. It seems to me an extremely unlikely preparation for a man who was going to murder some one at seven o'clock, to be entirely absent from the locality of the crime during the whole afternoon, to be walking about raising money on his possessions, to be writing for the money in his Savings Bank account, to be wiring for his watch to be sent on. Is the person so employed going to commit a crime at or about seven o'clock? But there is this further to be said. The telegram to Dent involved this, that he could not get the watch for a day or two. The Post Office Savings Bank letter involved this, that he could not get paid that money for some days to come. In point of fact, he was not paid it till the 23rd, and he did not get the proceeds from the sale of his 2| per cent, stock till the 24th. Can you conceive a man, who has been watching his chance to murder this old lady, spending the whole of the afternoon in walking round the pawn shops where his property happens to be, interviewing his friends and trying to sell them pawn tickets for the residue of his pawned property, writing letters for money, telegraphing for a watch, involving himself so as to hinder an early departure? Can you conceive that as being a probable or likely thing? Can you conceive it as the act of a person who has his victim in view, and means to commit murder?

"What was said about his movements afterwards? Rattman was absolutely clear on the subject. He said that after 6.12 — about twenty minutes past six — the prisoner came over to a billiard room where he (Rattman) v.-as playing a game with Aumann. They did not say that Slater stayed long with them; they both told you quite distinctly that Slater did not stay till the game was finished, that he left a few minutes earlier, and they put down the time as about 6.30. Slater had to go considerably further than Aumann; he had to go some 1400 yards in order to reach the vicinity of the deceased lady's house; he had just the same distance to go to reach his own home. I do not know how long he would take to do that distance, but, suppose he took between ten minutes and a quarter of an horn-, then it would be a quarter to seven by the time he could be at the spot. For a murderer who has got a victim in view, he is cutting it very fine, do you not think? What is the idea of the prosecution, I wonder? Is it that the prisoner secreted himself in some passage round about, and watched for his chance in the absence of the servant girl? That must, I should think, be the case for the Crown, but how can it be reconciled with the fact that the prisoner absented himself from the locality throughout the whole afternoon? Well, what about his subsequent proceedings? We cannot prove absolutely an alibi, but the evidence comes very near it. We have Antoine and the girl Schmalz, who both said that seven o'clock wag the prisoner's ordinary dinner hour; and, looking back, they can remember nothing exceptional that night. He was not absent from dinner. Dinner may have been earlier or later by a few minutes — that Schmalz admitted; but at any rate nothing happened to give these women an idea that they were living in the presence of the brutal murderer who had just despatched Miss Gilchrist. Things, they said, proceeded in the ordinary way; there was nothing to attract their attention. So far as I can see, we have proved that he could not have been near the scene till a quarter to seven; and his own people think that he was in about seven as usual, or a few minutes after. I would press upon you, gentlemen, the evidence given by Schmalz, the servant, and by the girl Antoine. You may call Antoine what you like, but did she look yesterday as if she was telling a pack of lies? Schmalz was cross-examined for about half an hour, and never lost a feather. She told a simple story, and she stuck to it, although she was tried and tested in every way. The girl Antoine — you saw how much moved she was ! What happened to her? Was it mercy, or was it because there was no success with Schmalz? The LORD ADVOCATE never asked her a single question in cross-examination. If a witness is dismissed without any questions being asked, is her story being accepted? The LORD ADVOCATE may say. "It was not worth my while"; but it remains the fact as regards this important evidence that he has not spoken about it to-day — he has not mentioned the name of Schmalz or Antoine. Did either woman strike you as being an untruthful witness? And if Antoine lives the life that is alleged, is she to be deprived of every human right? If she speaks a word for a man whom she believes to be innocent, is she to be told, "We know what you are, and we will not accept a word of what you say"! If the man who is being tried for his life says, "Here is a person who has something to say in my favour" — is your reply to be, "We cannot accept it: it may be the only thing you have to rest on, but still it is not to be accepted, because you lead a life that is deplorable"! In the concluding remarks of the LORD ADVOCATE he did tell you that you must have no reasonable doubt left in your mind before convicting the prisoner in this case. Do you see any reason whatever to doubt the evidence that was given by that loyal woman, be she what you like? The servant girl told us a plain story. Is she not to be believed either? Remember their evidence squares absolutely with the evidence given by Rattman and Aumann, and almost demonstrates the impossibility of the prisoner being guilty. The murderer must have been long about the place; how else could he see if there was anybody going in or out, or that the coast was clear? Yet Slater was elsewhere.

Now, gentlemen, the murder is committed, and there was the hue and cry. Everybody in Glasgow is up to see if they cannot hunt the murderer down. What is done by the alleged murderer? What about his "flight from justice"? On Tuesday he is at the pawn office redeeming his binocular glasses. When he was redeeming them he told the witness Kempton, "I am going to America," and he discussed the advantages of going by the Anchor Line. Now, that is on the day when all the papers are full of the murder. Is that like the action of a murderer — just doing the same thing as he had done the day before when he was collecting his things, and taking measures to get his money paid and his property realised? I ask you to consider this — he had succeeded (it is said) in perpetrating this crime, and next day he walks quietly down to the pawn-broker's, and does the same as he did the day before — only this time it is his binocular glasses ! That does not strike one as the proceeding of a man who was engaged in a "flight from justice." One other strange thing is this, which I omitted to mention, the prisoner was seen after the murder — upon the same night. His people say (as I have already said) that he went home in the usual course for dinner about seven o'clock on the 21st. Well, at 9.45 he presents himself at a club to see if he could raise the wind. The clubmaster refuses to give him any money on his cheque. What was his appearance when he presented himself there? The clubmaster says that he was absolutely composed; well, he said (I think) that he was excited a little, but so little that he thought he had been losing money. That is the man who was fleeing from justice; yet, at 9.45 he presents himself to the clubmaster Henderson, and Henderson sees nothing at all in his appearance to suggest that he had come from murder. He asks for money, and he is refused. He goes away making use of the expression that his friend Cameron, to whom he was referred, is "no use." If these are blood spots that are on that coat now, these blood spots were freshly on it then, and yet they were not seen ! If he was the murderer, what did he do with his coat? Where was he washing his coat so that nothing was seen, and there is not a speck of blood to be found on it? And, mind you, he has done the whole of that between 7.10 and 9.45. He has washed his clothes so thoroughly that the medical men cannot find a speck of blood now ! This is the coat that the murderer was wearing, if the Crown is right. Now, is there a man anywhere of such extraordinary callousness that he can remain in a billiard room to within a quarter of an hour of such a tragedy, and after coolly call upon this man at the club, wearing the very garments in which he committed the murder? The clubmaster says, "I saw no sign of his being put out in any way; I thought he had been losing money at cards, as he seemed annoyed." That is all. If this case is fairly considered, gentlemen, there is no answer to the case put forward for the defence.

But to proceed. Cameron says that on the 22nd or on the 23rd — I am not sure which he says — he got the pawn ticket himself. Slater had tried Rattman, and he had tried Aumann with the pawn ticket, but they would not purchase. Rattman gave the ticket back to Slater, and Slater, on the Tuesday or Wednesday, handed it to Cameron, who tells you that he tried Mr. Donaldson and Mr. Allan, but with no result. Now, that is Tuesday or Wednesday. Is this procrastination what you would expect from a man who had committed the crime? Again, either on the 22nd or 23rd, I do not remember which, Nichols, the barber, who has no association in any way with the prisoner, says that Slater came into his shop and talked about going to Queensland, and he adds that he also talked about going to San Francisco. We all know that the latter is quite probable; and it is worthy of remark that, according to Nichols, he had then a very noticeable moustache. I shall refer to that circumstance later. On the 23rd he wired Dent again from the Charing Cross Post Office, and, in order to hurry up Dent, I suppose, he wired, "Must have watch; leaving to-morrow night for the Continent"; he was going to America. By this time actually Rattman and Cameron had his address as "Caesar Cafe, 344 Broadway, San Francisco." Not only at twelve o'clock does he wire to hurry up Dent, but at four o'clock he is at Cooks' to see about tickets by the "Lusitania" for New York on the Saturday. He told Cooks' that he was going to America, and the only question was as to the price of the berth. A question was raised the following day as to whether it was to be an outside or an inside berth — but does not all this show that every action is directed towards getting his affairs put right and starting for San Francisco as the result of his resolve upon the Monday morning? We have the letter from Messrs. Cook to the Cunard Line, and the answer of the 24th that the applicants could have Room E76. The steamer plan was shown on the 24th to Slater, and he said, "That is an inside berth; I would much prefer an outside one." And then the letter of Messrs. Cook to the Cunard Line proceeds — "He, however, replied that he could do better with you in Liverpool. We asked him if he would take our ticket for Room E76 and endeavour to adjust with you in Liverpool on Saturday. He has promised to give us his decision to-morrow, on receipt of which we will advise you." Gentlemen, the murder had been committed three or four days ago by this time; the flight from justice has not yet begun! The prisoner, in the most leisurely manner, is going round the ordinary places that a man would go to when he is preparing a departure. The man in Cooks' office says that in manner he was perfectly cool and collected on the 23rd, and yet on the 23rd that extraordinary man Sancroft, the tramway car conductor, says that his mere asking of a boy if there was anything found out about the murderer led Slater to jump from a car and race for his life, apparently, up a side street. This is the man who is going about quite cool and collected! Sancroft made his evidence quite absurd when he said, "I cannot say whether the man heard the conversation between the boy and myself, but I thought it strange." Sancroft did not know at that time even what the suspected man was like — he said he had not yet got the published description of the man; yet, having seen a person leaving a tramway car in a hurry, and thinking back on it, Sancroft realises he is an amateur detective, and that he has got the man. As against that you have the evidence of those people among whom the prisoner went, cool and collected.

Slater did not go back to Messrs. Cook on the 25th, as was expected, and the reason is quite simple. These people, called Freedman, arrived in Glasgow on the morning of the 25th. It is suggested that this is all a story, that it is not true that the accused was trying to dispose of his flat before leaving for America; but you have got this fact, in the first place, that Aumann was up and looked over the flat, and you have this also definitely proved, that Mrs. Freedman, and another person arrived on the Friday morning from London. They were at the Alexandra Hotel. In reply to a post-card from them, Schmalz was sent over to the Alexandra Hotel twice on the Friday morning. She said that she did not see Mrs. Freedman the first time, but on the second occasion she brought her over to the flat. It was then arranged that Schmalz was to stop and hand over the keys to Mrs. Freedman on the Saturday, and then leave for London herself, and this she, in point of fact, did at 10 p.m. The Freedmans did arrive, and that put the arrangements a little out, and led to Slater failing in his appointment at the office of Messrs. Cook. Anyhow, we are now arrived at this point: on the 23rd the prisoner has lifted his £39, and on the 24:th he has got £49 as the proceeds of his 2½ per cent, stock. He saw Cameron the same evening. Further, Cameron, during the day of the 24th, went with him to the Cunard offices and tried to get a £5 note for five single notes. They were ultimately successful after trying two or three places; he got a £5 note at the Grosvenor Restaurant. They then went to the post office in Hope Street, where the accused got a letter registered and sent to Germany. Cameron says that he was told it was the prisoner's Christmas present to his people. The post office girl proved the despatch of that letter. Now we are at Friday, the 25th, the day they leave for America.

All these preparations, you will bear in mind, were carried through by the prisoner under the name of Oscar Slater. When it comes to the Friday he goes down to Nichols, the barber, and recovers the bottles, shaving materials, and things of that kind which he had deposited there. He tells Nichols, the barber, that he is leaving that night to join the "Lusitania" at Liverpool. He has gone as Oscar Slater all through' the week doing these things openly, and he tells the barber on the very night of his departure that he is going to travel by the "Lusitania" to New York. Is there a vestige of suspicion in all this of a person who is on a flight from justice? What plausibility is there in the suggestion that it was because of the evening papers on the Friday afternoon that he fled from justice? He has been doing all this through the week, and has not concealed his movements or his name in any way at all. On the Friday evening he goes down to the Central Station and engages a badge porter about six o'clock. The porter goes up to his house about 8.20. What possible suspicion is there about anything that happened that evening? Those two ladies, the Misses Fowlis, who lived in the flat above, took a very keen interest in the proceedings of the Slater household, and hung over the banisters to see what was happening; they said they were waiting for the postman. They saw the baggage being taken out of the house. Now, we know that was arranged for before. There was a servant from the Bernstein's house, which was on the same stair. She said she thought it was very strange, these people going away, because a detective had come to Bernstein's house half an hour before, and she thought that Slater was clearing out because the detective had been there. This, gentlemen, is a mere afterthought. You know that the prisoner had been preparing to go away for days before, and he knew nothing of the detective's visit. There was another strange suspicion. After the porters had carried away the baggage the Misses Fowlis looked out of the window, and they suggest that these people went away separately, as guilty people might — that Slater went by himself and the others went behind. Suppose you were going to the station with two ladies and wanted a cab. Would you not go in advance to get the cab? We know from the railway porter and from the badge porter that they all arrived at the station in a cab. "What ground is there for suspicion in this simple matter? Then it is said that the prisoner took tickets for London, and went off to Liverpool instead. This is a matter which has not been definitely cleared up; but is it not a curious thing that there were two third- class tickets taken for Liverpool by the 9.5 train that night, and no one can suggest whose tickets they were unless those of Slater and Antoine? Where is the flight from justice? It has not begun yet, and nothing suggesting subterfuge occurs until tickets were taken at Liverpool in the name of Otto Sando. Let me say a word upon that matter. I ask you to remember this, that the accused was a man living with a woman who was not his wife, and she was travelling with him to the States. On the previous occasion when they went abroad they took a false name, Mr. and Mrs. George. They are going abroad again, partly because of this bother with Mrs. Slater in London, which Mr. Rogers had written about, and also because Devoto had written for Slater to go to San Francisco. Remember the woman pleaded to be allowed to go when the prisoner thought it would be unwise for her to go in the winter, and it was her weeping that eventually led to her being taken. In the main facts there is nothing suspicious. Taking the name Otto Sando was very natural, because whatever name he took must coincide with the initials already on the luggage. They wanted to travel under some other name than that of Slater, and they wanted to arrive at America as man and wife, because there is trouble upon landing if a man comes with a woman who is not his wife. Now, that is plain enough. I have no idea why he put down " Chicago" as his destination. I do not know why he did a lot of things; but, on the broad facts and grounds of this case, it is surely very plain that this cannot be called a flight from justice. You see how slow the flight was; and it was only because, by a mere coincidence, the police visit inspired by M'Lean happened on the day already fixed for the prisoner's departure? the very day, too, upon which the description was published in the newspapers — that he was supposed to have fled at all. When this matter is examined there is nothing, I earnestly submit, to lead you to say that this man had anything to do with the perpetration of the crime.

I have disposed, I think, of those prejudicial matters which led everybody to regard Slater as being undeniably the murderer of this old lady. It "was because he had pawned a brooch which was supposed to have belonged to her, and because, when he was looked for, it was found that he had apparently fled from justice.

I now come to the direct evidence which had been led to support the allegation that he is the perpetrator of the crime. My learned friend began by saying that the first witness he had against the prisoner was Mrs. Liddell. Just about five minutes before seven, on the night of 21st December, when she was going home, she saw a man (so she said) leaning against the railings. She said she got "bristly," and she gazed at him. His face was not sallow; it was not white — but it was ivory white. She also explained the coat he was wearing, and she said it was this man Slater. She was a person who was anxious to give you the idea that she had very critically examined everything, and she asked the prisoner to turn round in the dock. This was unnecessary. She had seen him before at the police office. She was asked if the coat produced was the coat he was then wearing, and she said it was not, because she had examined the man's clothing very carefully, and there was a broad hem on his coat. She said his coat was not a waterproof coat, but was a heavy cloth coat. She just looked over her shoulder — and he glided away, and she knows no more about the man. That is not very convincing, and the coat she speaks to is not Slater's coat. Then how were you impressed with her evidence? The murder was perpetrated within a quarter of an hour, and she never thought of mentioning this mysterious man at all. She never mentioned him till Wednesday, the 23rd, and she said her statement was received as a jest in the family. Her brother said to her that there was no use in more of the family mixing themselves up in this affair, and the other members of the family received her story as a jest!

The next witness is Helen Lambie. I frankly confess that I do not know where I would have been in this case with the evidence of Helen Lambie, unless, by good fortune, I had got the shorthand notes of the inquiry in New York. It is deplorable to think that a man's life might depend on a chance circumstance of that kind. You got a story in the witness-box here months after the event, and I must say it had little correspondence with the first impressions of some of the witnesses. It is not that the people are consciously dishonest; but, having first thought the prisoner was only like the man, when they are taken back and are shown him another time they say, "Yes, that is the man we saw before." They identify him really as the man shown at the previous inspection, but from this gradually they become convinced that they were certain at first sight. The important thing, however, is, what did they say when they saw him the first time? Now, this is crucial, and I must refer you to the evidence that was given in America. Let me make a few preliminary observations. You remember that Helen Lambie travelled to America with the little girl Barrowman, and they occupied the same cabin. I do not know what you think would be likely to occur in the way of conversation between a girl of twenty-one and a girl of fifteen who were occupying the same bedroom for ten days, and who were both going to give evidence as regards this strange affair — they knew they were both to be witnesses. The Lord Advocate said to Mary Barrowman, "But, of course, Mary, you were advised by the people connected with the case not to speak about it," and she said, "Yes, I was not to speak about it." Do you believe they did not? What happened next was this. These two girls were in the corridor of the Court, and Slater came down between a man, who is 6 feet 3 inches, and another man who was wearing a medallion. Neither of these two was at all like the man who was wanted. With the two girls there was Detective Pyper. Detective Pyper tells you that he never saw the men approaching; the first he knew about it was both girls exclaiming, "Oh, there he is going into the Court!" He says that he was looking in the other direction, because he was expecting the arrival of a Mr. Fox, who was conducting the Crown case in America in the extradition proceedings. While he was looking for Mr. Fox the man had walked about 10 or 12 yards down the corridor. Helen Lambie's first remark was, "Oh, I could almost swear that is the man." The little girl Barrowman, you will remember, had been to Mr. Fox's office already in the forenoon, and had been prepared by photographs of Slater which had been submitted to her. Detective Pyper said that they were not very good, and that she failed then to recognise them as photographs of the man whom she had seen running down the street in Glasgow. But when the girl saw the man walking down the corridor, a man who was like (I suggest) the man in the photographs, she said that she identified him. What happened between Helen Lambie and the girl Barrowman while the man was walking towards them nobody knows, because no independent witness can speak to it; may the suspicion of one not have prompted the other? Well, at any rate, the evidence is distinct that all Helen Lambie said at first was, "I could almost swear that is the man." Now, let us see why she could almost swear it was the man. When she came into the American Court she was asked, "Now, do you see the man here you saw that night?" Here is her answer, which has been read to you before, "One is very suspicious, if anything." Gentlemen, is that an identification? She then proceeds, "The clothes he had on that night he has not got on to-day, but his face I could not tell." She was then asked, "What did you say about his face?" and she replied, "I could not tell about his face; I never saw his face." Gentlemen, she did not see his face— but perhaps it will be more satisfactory if I read her evidence in detail. It proceeds thus—

Tell us what kind of clothes he had on, if you can — a description? — It was a three-quarter, something like a waterproof coat, three-quarter length.

Had it any colour that you could recognise? — It was a kind of fawn colour.

What kind of a hat or cap or what did he have on? — It looks like one of those Donegal caps.

Now, can you give us anything further in connection with this man that you can tell us about? — No; I could not.

Did you notice anything about his walk? — Yes, sir, I did.

Tell us what about his walk that impressed you? — He didn't walk straight, but it was some

But his gait, his manner of walking, was there anything about that that you noticed? Did you notice anything about the style of walking? — Yes, sir.

What was there about that that impressed you? — He was sort of shaking himself a little I'll show you how he was walking. (Illustrating.)

Since you have been here have you seen anybody walking like that? — Yes, sir, I have, sir.

Is that man in this room? — Yes, he is, sir.

Point him out to us if you can? — I wouldn't like to say.

Now, point out the man; that is all we ask you to do.

MR. MILLER — I object unless you ask her whether she has seen more than one man walk like that.

THE COMMISSIONER — The question is, do you see in this room among all of us people here the man that you passed that night? — I think you ought to let the man walk, and I can pick him out.

You have seen him walk? — Let him get another chance; give the man a chance.

Cross-examination by Mr. MILLER — Didn't you state a moment ago that you did not see the man's face? — Neither I did. I saw the walk; it is not the face I went by, but the walk.

Now, gentlemen, that is the evidence that Helen Lambie gave in America.

LORD GUTHRIE — You might read the two or three intervening sentences.

Mr. M'CLURE — Very well. They are as follows:—

THE COMMISSIONER — Is the man in this room that passed you in that hallway?

THE WITNESS — Yes, sir.

THE COMMISSIONER — Where is he. Point him out? — He is sitting here. (Indicating the defendant.)

Is that all you have to identify this man as the man you saw in the hall? — Yes.

Now, that, of course, is not the story that was given by Helen Lambie here. It was the walk, and the walk only, in America. I know that yesterday, owing to the request of some of the jurymen. Slater was made to walk down one of the passages after the Court rose, and the gentlemen of the jury were present. I cannot tell what impression the parade made upon the minds of the jury — you will consider that for yourselves. I would submit that the way the man walked was in no way characteristic. There was nothing in his gait that would enable you — much less a person who saw a man walk across Miss Gilchrist's hall for two seconds before he got out of the door — to identify him as the person who had been in that hall. That is a matter for you to judge of; but you will also recollect that Detective Pyper was asked whether he saw anything characteristic in Slater's walk by which he could recognise him, and he said there was nothing in the walk of the man that impressed him. Mr. Warnock, who was in America, said that by looking very closely he thought he could see some sort of pitch of the knee. I only put it to you as fair men, is that evidence upon which you would ever think of taking a man's life? But Helen Lambie has gone back on her original story. She now says that she got a look at his face, and she says the man was clean shaven. Well, Slater was not, if you accept the evidence of Nichols, who shaved him on the 25th. He had then a very noticeable moustache.

The next witness is Mr. Adams. Mr. Adams says to you that he was standing in a better position than Helen Lambie to see the man who was in the house, and, while he thought the prisoner is very like him, he would not swear to him. Here is what he said in America — and I ask you to remember that he and the little girl Barrowman and Helen Lambie were all in the room together when this took place—

THE COMMISSIONER — Is there anybody in the room that you identify as the man?

THE WITNESS — I couldn't say positively. This man (indicating the defendant) is not at all unlike him. I only got a passing glance at him.

Mr. Adams I thought was very fair, and he said undoubtedly that there was a resemblance. Then I read this further from his evidence in America—

Did you notice his crooked nose? — No.

Did you notice anything remarkable about his gait and walk? — No, I thought he walked like a commercial traveller.

An ordinary walk? — Just an ordinary walk.

What, gentlemen, becomes of Helen Lambie's identification? —

You don't swear this is the man you saw? — No, sir.

You don't identify him with the man that passed you? — I say he resembles him in appearance. That is all I can say.

He had also seen a photograph before. Now, you are trying a man for his life, and there are two witnesses who (let us suppose) had equal opportunities of seeing the culprit, and the one said, "I will not swear to this man; he is like him, but I will not go further than that"; and the other said, "I could almost swear that is the man"; would you be prepared on that evidence to find it proved that he was the man and to take his life? Would you not, gentlemen, be taking a large responsibility? Mr. Adams, who failed to identify, says that he was in a better position to see than Helen Lambie; Helen Lambie says it was not his face at all that attracted her attention, but only his walk — which has no marked peculiarity — surely it is plain that the safe evidence was that given by Mr. Adams, and not by Helen Lambie ! The witnesses for the Crown have said that this man's walk is not peculiar in any respect at all.

Now, what about Barrowman? She is going along the road, when out of a close comes a man. You will remember it is seven o'clock on a December night. He ran down the steps very fast, we know — that is the evidence of Mr. Adams, who used the expression "like greased lightning." The person — whoever he was — hesitated for a moment, then turned and ran, as hard as he was able, past the little girl, and down West Cumberland Street to the left. Can you take it that the little girl's identification is worth your serious regard? It is said that the man had on a Donegal hat. A Donegal hat is a tweed hat with a rim all round it. It is also said that he had brown boots. Gentlemen, they have been through all his baggage — they have produced everything that would assist them — but there are no brown boots, and there is no Donegal hat! The only thing similar is the waterproof. Now, this man was running as fast as he could. I would ask you, would you undertake to identify a man who raced past you on the street — in the vicinity of a lamp, it is quite true? The description originally given in the paper was this — and this is from Barrowman — "The man wanted is about twenty- eight or thirty years of age, tall and thin, with his face shaved clear of all hair. A distinctive feature is that his nose is slightly turned to the right side." How could the little girl Barrowman possibly see all that when the man was flying past?" He wore one of the popular round tweed hats known as Donegal hats, and a fawn-coloured overcoat, which might have been a waterproof, and also dark trousers and brown boots." Who has come to say that the possessions of this man included brown boots or a Donegal hat? Can you yourselves now say that "a nose slightly twisted to one side" is rightly descriptive of the prisoner's nose? Would you say that all these things could be accurately observed by a young girl in a momentary glance like that? It is past belief.

The next witness is Annie Armour, who was employed at the Subway station. Her evidence is not of great importance. She heard about the murder some time after, and it recalled to her mind that one night between 7.30 and 8 — she cannot exactly tell when — a man hurried up to the booking office, laying down a penny, passed on without waiting for a ticket, and went down the stair to the station. She said that his coat was darker than the coat of the prisoner produced, and she had no doubt he was clean shaven. Now, the prisoner was not clean shaven. You know from Nichols, the barber, that he had a very noticeable moustache at the time, and I say no more upon this.

Accordingly you have these three leading witnesses for the Crown, Lambie, Adams, and Barrowman — Adams declining to say more than that the prisoner is like; Barrowman alleging that she, with an instantaneous glance at a man flying along the street, is able to give a detailed description, which, however, does not tally closely with the prisoner; and Lambie — if we take her American evidence, which was the first — only referring to his walk. As you saw, the walk has no peculiarity, and Detective Pyper said there was nothing in it to attract his attention. I do not see how, in a matter of this gravity, you can accept and act upon evidence so inconclusive and uncertain. And that is the only evidence of real moment in the case.

I make also this remark — do you not generally find that when a bloody murder has been perpetrated, the person who perpetrates the murder has blood upon him? The man who escaped that night certainly had blood about him. Where he is God knows, but we know where this man is! We have got this man's clothes, and they bear no trace of blood. Where did he wash his clothes between 7 and 9.45? How had he got rid of everything? Again, what about the weapon? The doctors are uncertain as to the hammer being a likely instrument to cause the injuries that resulted in death, but, even if it were, hammer and coat alike are absolutely free from blood. Do you see any plausibility in the suggestion that the hammer has been scraped and washed to remove traces of blood? Our doctors tell you that they would have great difficulty in removing traces of blood in that way; but, suppose it was tried, why did the murderer not wash and scrape the whole handle, and especially where his hand gripped the weapon? It must have been covered with blood if it was used, yet it has not been cleansed, and upon it there was no blood found. Why is the prisoner so different from all other murderers? There is no trace of blood on anything belonging to him, and how could he get rid of it all in two hours?

There is only one other point remaining, that is, as regards the very extraordinary identification of the prisoner as a man who was going about the neighbourhood, lurking, and secreting himself in closes. First of all, there was the family of M'Haffie. Mrs. M'Haffie identified the prisoner as the man who had walked backward and forward in this street. That, of course, would not prove that he was the man who committed the crime; it would only show that he was in the neighbourhood, and no more. The daughter, again, in the month of March, would not say that this was the man, although she now agrees with her mother. But there is another point — all the M'Haffies have described the man they saw as a man who was wearing checked trousers and light-coloured spats. The prisoner has never been seen anywhere with checked trousers or with light-coloured spats, and none of these has been found in his baggage. Was he so careful as to destroy not only the clothes that he wore on the night of the murder, but also all the clothes that he had worn at any other time I And you will recollect this: one of the Miss M'Haffies was asked by his lordship if, when the man asked at the door for Anderson, he had a foreign accent, and she said "No." Now, the prisoner's foreign accent is pronounced. That is the family of M'Haffies. Nearly every one of these witnesses contradicts the other.

Take now Miss Cunningham, who walked with the witness Campbell to dinner every day, and saw this strange man. She identified the prisoner, curiously, from a photograph. She says that "the man was absolutely clean shaven, and that she had a good opportunity of seeing him," while the photograph from which she recognised the prisoner was that of a man with a black moustache. That is not very convincing. When she saw the accused she said, "That is the man." Campbell, on the other hand, says that he was nearer the man than she was, and he declines to say that the prisoner was the man. He will only say that he resembles the man, and that is all. Then there are two other witnesses, Bryson and Nairn. These are both witnesses as to Sunday, 20th December. Bryson says that at twenty minutes to eight he was walking along the street and saw a dark- haired man with a sallow complexion, who had a long nose of a peculiar shape, prominent in the middle, broken, and had a slight moustache. He told you how this man was gazing, with an intentness that he had never seen equalled, at the house opposite. The man was at that time in a black morning coat or jacket, and with slightly grey trousers. Nairn saw, it is supposed, the same person at 9.15. Nairn is the witness who only saw his back, and he says that the man had dark hair. Now, there is an hour and a half between these two witnesses. When Bryson saw the man he had a black morning coat and slightly grey trousers; when Nairn saw him he had a light coat and a black cloth cap. Between 7.40 and 9.15 this man had presumably gone home and changed his coat before coming out for a second period of observation !

Against all that, I want to know what weight you are going to give to the evidence given by the witness Reid to-day and the evidence given yesterday by Schmalz and Antoine? Reid left for Belfast on 21st December, and his last Sunday in Glasgow, the 20th, was passed dining with Slater along with his little boy, aged five. He positively swore that on 20th December he dined with Slater, going there about six and not leaving till 10.30. If there is any truth in that — which is spoken to by three witnesses — what comes of the evidence of Bryson at 7.40 and of Nairn at 9.15? It cannot have been Slater. Then also I ask you to remember Bryson's statement that he made a remark to his wife upon the appearance of the man, and said that he was there for no good; but his wife does not remember of any man being there, or of her husband making any remark whatsoever. Would any one with a sense of responsibility accept such evidence?

Finally, there are two policemen. One of them said he saw a man feigning that he was drunk, and the other said that he saw the prisoner — and he identified him rather curiously. He had waved his hand to a man because he thought he knew him — mistaking him for his friend Paradise, to whom he thought he was waving his hand. If he could make a mistake like that, surely he might quite well mistake some one else for the prisoner. This kind of evidence is really no good at all; the possibility of error is manifest. Just take this contrast: the man wanted is alleged to have been clean shaven by Mrs. Liddell, Helen Lambie, Barrowman, Adams, and Armour. It is, on the contrary, proved that Slater had a moustache by Rattman, Aumann, Cameron, Reid, Nichols, the barber; Gibb, the billiard room man; Kempton, and Tracey. It is demonstrated by these people who knew him well that the prisoner had a noticeable moustache at the time the murder was committed. Now, I have really done with the evidence, and I believe I have demonstrated that, upon anything like a fair view of it, the prisoner cannot be identified as the murderer. No responsible jury, I think, would ever venture to convict.

I should like now, in concluding, to make a remark upon a case that happened. Do you remember the case of Adolph Beck? He was a man against whom allegations were made by a number of women in London. Beck, in mistake for a man called Smith, was sworn to by ten women and two policemen, and he got seven years' penal servitude. The women had all had full opportunities of knowing him; he had sat and talked with them all, at times, for half an hour or an hour; and all ten women swore that Beck was the man who had got jewellery from them on various representations. The charges were backed up by the evidence of two police constables who knew Smith; and so Beck got seven years' penal servitude. The unfortunate man served the whole of his time and then came out. Smith had not been convicted, and was by this time at his old game, with the same class of fraud on a new lot of people. Again some women who had been defrauded in this way came forward, and they accused Adolph Beck. He was once more tried, protesting his innocence as he had done during the earlier trial; but he was convicted again on positive evidence given by people who said they had passed a certain time with him, to whom he had talked, and whom he had defrauded. He was sentenced to five years' penal servitude. The judge who tried the case, on reflection, thought that there was something wrong about this conviction, and the result was a Parliamentary inquiry before Lord Justice Collins. After everything had been sifted out, both the convictions against Beck were quashed, and the taxpayers of this country paid him £2000 as a solatium for the injury that had been done to him.

Now, ten witnesses in Beck's case swore to the accused as a man whom they knew and had spoken to. In the subsequent inquiry witnesses came who said that, knowing both Smith and Beck, they did not think there was a great resemblance between them. Gentlemen, Beck was not tried on a capital charge. If he had been tried on a capital charge and convicted, what would have been the reparation? You cannot give £2000 to a dead man! In that case there was the sworn testimony of ten concurring witnesses who had ample opportunity of knowing him. Was that class of evidence not better than the stuff you have got here — self-contradictory, inconclusive, given by witnesses who had no personal acquaintance with the accused? What are you to do in this case? Are you going to say, with that warning in front of you, that you find this man guilty of the murder of this old lady? If you do so, then it is quite certain that it is final; no reparation can follow. I ask you to bear that in mind. I do not believe I am speaking at present to men who are in the least wanting in a sense of responsibility. I am speaking to men who have listened with great care, and are thoroughly prepared, I believe, to lay aside all prepossessions created by the newspapers, and to judge the case only by the evidence which has been led. Can you lay your hands on your hearts now and say that you are convinced that this is the man who committed that murder? If you are, then the responsibility is yours, and not mine. If you are not convinced up to that point, surely you will give this man — I will not say the benefit of the doubt — but the benefit of the evidence which has been led. I think it is proved that he was not out of his house on the 20th, and there is only a blank of about a quarter of an hour unaccounted for on the 21st, when this murder was committed. That might happen to any of us, and are you on that account to sacrifice a life? I do not believe it for a moment: the evidence warrants an acquittal. And, while nobody expects any of you sitting in the jury-box to do more than exercise a sound judgment, you will take care, I trust, that your judgment is sound. If, contrary to my expectation, it should lead to an irreparable wrong, then yours alone will be the responsibility.

LORD GUTHRIE'S CHARGE TO THE JURY

LORD GUTHRIE, in charging the jury, said — Gentlemen of the jury, there are cases in the criminal Courts, as well as in the civil Courts, where the judge, addressing the jury, draws their attention to the important nature of the issue they have to try. Obviously, in this case, any such observation would be an impertinence. You have shown by your close attention that you thoroughly realise the gravity of the charge against the prisoner, that this is a case where a human life is involved.

When a man, going on an unlawful errand, uses force which results in death, that is murder, whether he intends to kill or only means to overcome resistance, or to prevent an alarm. In this case, looking to the nature and number of the injuries, it is certain that the man who killed Miss Gilchrist meant, at all events in the later blows, not only to prevent her giving an alarm, but also to make certain that she should not ultimately recognise and identify him. In short, "dead men (and dead women) tell no tales." I do not agree with Mr. M'CLURE when he assumed, in the powerful, accurate, and judicious speech which he made for his client, that the man who entered Miss Gilchrist's house went with deliberate intention to murder her. He argued that the prisoner could not be the man who killed Miss Gilchrist, because his conduct immediately before was inconsistent with his having murder in his heart. Gentlemen, it may well be that the man who killed Miss Gilchrist went without any intention of murder. Why should he? She was at the time the only person in the common stair (the servant had gone out for an indefinite period), a feeble old lady of eighty-three years of age. He, no doubt, expected she would make no resistance, that she would give him the keys, and that he would get away, possibly masked so as to avoid her identification, without touching her at all. This expectation failed. She did resist, she cried out, she knocked on the floor (the meaning of which he would at once know), and then arose the necessity to silence her.

In this case there is no question of law for me to discuss and determine. There are questions of fact and of fact alone, and yours must be the responsibility, because it is your opinion on the facts that must determine the verdict. Therefore, it might be enough that I should now leave the case with that statement in your hands, but long experience in criminal matters and professional training may enable a judge to help a jury to make up their own minds, first by observations on the different classes of evidence led, and then by directing attention to the vital parts of the evidence.

As Mr. M'CLURE well said, it is only evidence that we have got to look at, not rumour, whether in the newspapers or outside the newspapers, and we have surely got enough evidence in this case to servo the turn, for the Crown examined sixty witnesses and the defence examined fourteen, making seventy-four in all.

The case appears to have given rise to the usual crop of rumours, mostly unfounded, or so entirely exaggerated as in no way to represent the truth. It would, again, be impertinent to suggest that you need to be warned not to take any of these into consideration.

First, let us consider the evidence as a whole. You have direct evidence, and you have circumstantial evidence. By direct evidence I mean evidence directly identifying the prisoner with the person who was undoubtedly the murderer. You will have no doubt that the man that Lambie and Adams saw leaving the house, and the man that Barrowman, the message girl, saw on the street coming out of the close was the same man, and was the murderer. You may probably also think the man who haunted the street in the vicinity of the house for days before the murder was identical with the person who was seen leaving the house by Lambie, Adams, and Barrowman. If you think he was the murderer, then, in regard to him also you have direct evidence. But, whether he was the prisoner or not, whether the man leaving the house was the prisoner or not, is for you to determine.

Then we have a good deal of circumstantial evidence in regard to the prisoner's conduct before, on, and after 21st December, which I shall refer to later. Much of that evidence is important, when taken along with its surroundings, although taken by itself it may be of little or no consequence. For instance, a man passing under an alias, a man giving a false address and a false profession, a man showing excitement, a man wanting to release his funds, a man wanting to go hurriedly to another country — these things by themselves are consistent with innocence, but, coupled with the direct evidence, if you accept it as applying to the prisoner, they may be suggestive or even conclusive of guilt. They may, to put it otherwise, afford important material in the way of corroboration.

You have heard a good deal about evidence of character and about evidence of financial circumstances. I think you will agree that both are double-edged. The prisoner may found upon these elements as being in his favour, and the Crown may found on them as being against him.

About his character, proved by his own witnesses, by Cameron, his companion and friend, and by Schmalz, his servant, there is no doubt at all. He has maintained himself by the ruin of men and on the ruin of women, living for years past in a way that many blackguards would scorn to live. That is an illustration of what I mean when I talked of evidence being double-edged. It is nothing remarkable to find a man of that kind taking a wrong name, telling a lie about his destination, going by different names, murder or no murder. He called himself Otto Sando after the murder, in view of going to America, the particular name being selected apparently to square with the O.S. (Oscar Slater) on his boxes, but then he had long before gone by the names of George and Anderson, and it is possible that a desire to avoid the pursuit of his wife

— rather a nebulous person, so far as the evidence is concerned — may have had something to do with this concealment. He called himself a dentist in Glasgow, although he did not possess a single dentist's tool; but he had assumed the same blind years before in London. He says to one person he is going to the Continent, to another that his destination is Monte Carlo, to another Chicago, to another San Francisco. If you or I had told false stories about where we were going, if we were to travel under an assumed name, there would be a strong inference that we had been doing something of a serious kind that we wanted to conceal. In the case of a man like Oscar Slater, whose life has been a living lie, that inference does not necessarily arise. These stories I have referred to are all lies. But, then, the man's life has been not only a lie for years, but is so to-day.

Gentlemen, I use the name "Oscar Slater." But that is not his name. I never knew a case like the present, either in my own experience or from reading. What is his name? He knows, and probably Antoine knows; but the Crown, with all its means of investigation, has failed to find out. We do not know who that man sitting in the dock really is. His fellow-countryman admitted that there was no such German name as Slater. We do not know where he was born, who his parents are, where he was brought up, what he was brought up to, whether he was trained to anything. We do not know whether he ever did an honest day's work in his life. The man remains a mystery as much as when this trial began.

The Lord Advocate founds on the prisoner's admittedly abandoned character as a point in support of the Crown. He is entitled to do so, because a man of that kind has not the presumption of innocence in his favour which is a form in the case of every man, but a reality in the case of the ordinary man. Not only is every man presumed to be innocent, but the ordinary man, in a case of brutal ferocity like the present, has a strong presumption in his favour. In addition, a man with the prisoner's sinister record may be capable of exhibiting a callous behaviour even immediately after committing a murder. You will remember that Mr. M'CLURE founded upon the prisoner's demeanour shortly after the time of the murder. The Lord Advocate replies that a man of such a character after the crime is over does not exhibit the symptoms that you would expect in the case of a man of ordinary respectability, who had been goaded into violence by drink or passion. You will consider that matter from both points of view, telling in favour of the prisoner and telling against him.

The financial circumstances also have been mentioned. The man is said to have been hard up; he urgently wanted to realise money. I do not think that these two circumstances, if they existed, would have much significance. They were not confined to that period. He was hard up and wanting to realise money for years before the murder was committed.

Gentlemen, all these circumstances are relevant to the case, but if you make up your minds to convict the prisoner, you ought to be able to say to yourselves, "We have disregarded his character, and we have disregarded his financial circumstances, we have convicted him irrespective of these." But, if you reach a conclusion against him, it may well strengthen that conclusion to reflect on the two elements that I have mentioned. In short, they should not be factors in reaching a conclusion, although they may very well support the conclusion after it had been reached.

Next we must consider the evidence of identification and its value. Not a word too much has been said on that matter by the Lord Advocate and Mr. M'Clure. It is extremely important. I express the point thus— it would not be safe to convict the prisoner merely on the evidence of personal impression of his identity with the man seen flying from the house, on the part of strangers to him, without reference to any marked personality or personal peculiarities, and without corroboration derived from other kinds of evidence. My proposition involves a distinction between the identification, by personal impression, of a strange person, and the identification, by personal impression, of a familiar person. Suppose a father told you that his son, who was resident in his house, had been seen by him in Princes Street yesterday. That would be admirable evidence. But if a person who had only seen the son once in his life told you that he had seen him in Princes Street yesterday that would be evidence of slender value, unless the son had a marked personality, or unless he had some peculiarity about him, such as a very peculiar walk, or unless there were corroboration, such as that the man, when spoken to, answered to the name of the particular individual. The distinction may be vitally important in this case. Some of us may have doubles. "We have been told that we have been in such and such a place by a competent and honest witness, who is quite sure about it, and yet we had never been there at all. The most august case is that of His Majesty the King. The illustrated papers are fond of publishing a double of His Majesty, a person who has superficially a startling resemblance to the King, but who would never be mistaken for the King by any one about the Court. Then, again, people differ as to the extent of a resemblance, or even whether there is any. You may have seen a strong resemblance, but one of your friends says that he can see no resemblance at all, and, when the two people are brought together, you see that there is nothing but a very general similarity. That applies to the personal impression of a stranger in reference to a stranger. Now, obviously, if the persons are not strangers, then the position is entirely different, and it will be for you to say in this case whether some of the evidence of identification — such as that of the M'Haffies, who say that they saw the person watching the house for days — is to be taken as the evidence of strangers, or as the evidence of persons who had an opportunity of familiarising themselves, and who did familiarise themselves, with the individual. Then you will say whether in this case there were the marked personality and also the personal peculiarities which may very well enable a man to be identified with certainty even by persons who are strangers to him. And you will say, thirdly, apart from all that, whether the points of corroboration detailed to you by the Lord Advocate are or are not sufficient to show that, if the identification is not by itself sufficient, at all events it is sufficient when taken along with the corroboration on which he founded.

The case of Adolf Beck was most properly dwelt upon by Mr. M'CLURE— a very startling narrative. In that case women — not of respectable character, but acting admittedly *bona fide*, and competent to form a reliable opinion, with no motive to make a wrong statement — swore, without doubt or hesitation, that the man in the dock, Adolf Beck, was the man who had defrauded them. And it turned out that they were wrong. They had mistaken Beck for another man. Smith, the real criminal. There was no corroboration, and in point of fact Adolf Beck had a resemblance to the man Smith. Sad to say. Beck was convicted. Now, in this case, there is one thing quite clear — the prisoner is like the murderer. But, then, he is not charged with being like the murderer; he is charged with being the murderer. Yet I do not think you can doubt, after the body of evidence led before you, that he has at least a marked resemblance to the man who haunted the street outside Miss Gilchrist's house, and to the man who was seen coming from the house. You have to say whether the Crown has proved that he is the man. Keep this also in view — the witnesses brought before you as to identification were all Scotch, while the prisoner is a foreigner. A Scotch person has a much more delicate sense of identification in regard to one of his own people than he has in regard to a foreigner. Suppose you are dealing with a negro. White people say that they cannot see any difference between negroes. That is because we are not accustomed to see them. In the same way with a foreigner. A Scotchman is apt to say, "Oh, he is a foreign -looking man," and he does not know the subtle differences that, of course, exist among foreigners as they do among our own people. Therefore the mere fact that a witness thought that the prisoner was the same as the man seen leaving the house, because both of them had a foreign appearance, goes for very little, if it goes for anything at all.

These are the observations I think it proper to make in regard generally to the different classes of evidence, and that brings me to the question of what the direct evidence is. It has been gone into very fully and very fairly and moderately by the Lord Advocate and by Mr. M'Clure, and I do not intend to go through it, but I may tell you that I have a note of the pages where each witness expresses the exact state of his or her impression, and I shall detail them, if you express a desire that I should do so. Some say, "I think he was like"; some say, "I think he was very like "; some say, "That is the man "; some say, "I will swear that is the man." Gentlemen, I do not think you will attach cardinal importance to the mere form of expression. That depends largely upon the idiosyncrasy of the witness. I take a single illustration. The girl Lambie was shown the coat No. 43, and when she was asked if that was like the coat, she said, "No, it is the coat." That is evidently inaccurate. Why, dozens of coats like that could be produced out of the shops, and, in the absence of accidental marks, nobody could be certain of the particular coat. If they professed to be certain, it would simply show that they did not know the meaning of language. They could only say, "It resembles the coat in every way." That is an illustration of how one witness — in this instance, a superficial and unreflective girl of small mental capacity — fails to see the difference between two things that are quite different, being able to say, "That is like the thing" and being able to say, "It is the thing." If you agree with the remark I have made about Lambie's evidence in regard to the coat, as involving a want of power of discrimination on her part, you may come to the same conclusion in regard to her identification of the man leaving the house. When she says that the prisoner is the man, you may think she only means that he is like the man.

But the real question for you is, however they may phrase it, had the witnesses any doubt in their own minds that the prisoner was the man whom they saw haunting the street outside the house, and leaving the house? The Lord Advocate has pointed out to you that, neither in regard to the crucial witnesses nor in regard to the witnesses who came into incidental contact with the man, have any of them expressed any positive doubt. By positive doubt, I mean what occurs every day in the criminal Courts. A witness brought up for identification says when asked, "Was that the man who robbed you?" — "Well, I think so, but I think he was taller than that man, or I think he had darker hair, or I think he had a mark on his face," and so on. The witness, although identifying the person, expresses a doubt. Now, the Lord Advocate quite properly stated that in this case not one of the witnesses has stated a doubt in that sense; they have not said that, while they think he is the man, there is a difference. A difference of dress amounts to nothing, because the way in which the prisoner is dressed now is not necessarily the way he was dressed at that time.

In considering the question of identification, you will also keep in view that the prisoner appears to have a distinct personality, a marked individuality — you have only to look at him to see that he has — because the most casual people, such as the Cunard office clerk, who only met him once or twice for a short time, have identified him in reference to occasions when the defence does not dispute that he was the man. It is suggested that there was failure of identification on the part of the telegraph clerk, who said she did not know who gave in a certain telegram sent by the prisoner. But we have no evidence that it was the prisoner who gave it in; the fact that the telegram was signed by him does not imply that he handed it in. It is, therefore, clear that the prisoner is not just the ordinary type of person of whom we say, "You cannot expect anybody to identify that man; he is like a hundred other persons." Instead of that, the prisoner impressed his individuality on every one he met under totally dissimilar circumstances.

In regard to the three crucial witnesses — Lambie, Adams, and Barrowman — Mr. M'Clure has properly said that you must not throw out of account what they said in New York. No doubt, as the Lord Advocate put it, they were there in difficult and unfamiliar circumstances, and perhaps methods were used there that would not be allowed here. Still we have their evidence recorded, and you have to consider the identification in New York as well as in the Glasgow Police Office and in this Court. The girl Lambie said three things in New York which are important for you to notice. First, she said, "One is very suspicious, if anything." It is a little difficult to know what she meant, because the sentence does not explain itself, and the reporter may not have caught the whole answer. Then she said, "I saw the walk. It is not the face I went by, but the walk." Third, she said, "I could nearly swear that was the man." You have heard her evidence here, and I do not go over it. Here she is positive that the prisoner is the man, but, again, I suggest to you that you should take that in connection with her identification of the coat, and you will probably hold that what she really means is, "So far as I can see, he resembles him in every particular." One witness will say, "I swear that is the man "; another, sensitive and timid, but meaning precisely the same thing, will say, "I will not swear it, but I believe that is the man." The question is, had they, when they were first examined, any doubt on the matter? If they had a doubt on the matter, then that will necessarily weigh with you in your opinion as to the weight of their evidence. Mr. Adams sums up his view by saying that he identifies the prisoner. He was asked by Mr. M'Clure, "You do not give an absolutely confident opinion that that was the man?" and he answers, "No, it is too serious a charge for me to say from a passing glance." Gentlemen, one cannot but regret — I do not blame Mr. Adams, the circumstances were very peculiar — that he did not slam that door. The man escaped, and Mr. Adams had only a passing glance at him, and Mr. M'Clure rightly tells you that it is for you to judge whether that passing glance in the case, on the one hand, of a man, who undoubtedly resembles the prisoner, and in the case, on the other hand, of a prisoner who has undoubtedly a strong personality, is or is not sufficient when taken along with other things.

Then as to the girl Barrowman. You will consider whether, young as she is, she was not a more impressive witness than Lambie. She showed no sign of want of mental capacity, or want of judgment and good sense, and she displayed no animus. She says she had no difficulty in telling that the prisoner was the man when she saw him in New York. You heard about the dramatic incident of the two girls pointing out the man when they were standing with Detective Pyper. Then you will remember that, on being confronted with him in the room at New York, she first said that he was something like, then that he was very like, and then that he was the man, and she has no doubt now that he is the man. It is for you to consider whether that sequence can be fairly founded on as weakening her evidence, or whether it has not the opposite effect, as indicating caution and discrimination — he is something like him; he is very like him; he is the very man! At the same time, you will not forget— what Mr. M'Clure strongly founded on — that she bases her opinion on what she calls the twist in the nose. Call it a twist in the nose, or a broken nose, or a peculiar nose, it is for you to judge whether the prisoner's face has not such personal peculiarity as makes all the difference in a question of identification by personal impression.

In addition to these, there are Mrs. Liddell and the other witnesses, eleven in all, who speak to a person haunting the part of the street opposite the house. Four of these witnesses say that they are positive that the prisoner is the man, viz., Mrs. M'Haffie, Police-Constable Walker, Euphemia Cunningham, and Bryson. The other witnesses — Margaret M'Haffie, Madge M'Haffie, Annie M'Haffie, Campbell, Nairn, and Gillies — say, generally — I can give it in detail if you like — that he resembles the man, but they will not swear it. Margaret M'Haffie says that she can identify him quite well, but she adds that at one time she was not quite sure; Madge M'Haffie says she is not quite sure; he is just like the man, but she cannot swear. Annie M'Haffie says that she is not quite certain, but he is like the man. William Campbell Bays that there is a general resemblance; he will not say more. Nairn says that he is certain he was the man he saw, but he will not go the length of being positive, which is an obvious contradiction in terms, although we may understand what he means. Gillies says that he resembles the man, but he cannot say that he is the same man. That leaves Mrs. Liddell, in regard to whom you have a very distinct remembrance, I am sure, of the way she gave her evidence, how she left the witness-box, got the prisoner to stand up, looked at him from the side, as she saw the man who haunted the street, and then said emphatically, "I believe the prisoner was the man standing at the railings."

The questions for you are — and they are purely jury questions — so far as identification is concerned, first, has the prisoner such a marked personality, and had the witnesses Lambie, Adams, and Barrowman such an opportunity to observe the man leaving Miss Gilchrist's house, and are they sufficiently credible witnesses to enable you to hold it proved that the prisoner is the same man? Second, has the prisoner such a marked personality, and had the eleven or twelve witnesses above referred to such opportunities for seeing the man who haunted the street, as to enable you to hold it proved that the prisoner is the same man? I assume — but again it is for you to say — that there can be no reasonable doubt as to the identity of the man haunting the street and the murderer. Lastly, is there corroboration, in other parts of the evidence, of the personal impression given you by these witnesses, assuming that they are strangers, and assuming that there is no such marked personality or personal peculiarity as would add weight to the mere personal impression?

Come, then, gentlemen, to the purely circumstantial evidence. You may think the direct evidence sufficient, and in that case the circumstantial evidence will only be of interest to you as confirming the view otherwise reached. If you do not, that may be either because you throw the direct evidence aside altogether and think, it of no value — which I do not think you will do — or because you think it not sufficient in itself. If you throw it aside altogether, there is in this case no such circumstantial evidence as would entitle you, taking that evidence by itself, to convict the prisoner. But if you are impressed by the direct evidence, although not satisfied that it is sufficient by itself, you will then proceed to consider anxiously the alleged circumstantial evidence. You have points both for and against the prisoner. In his possession nothing was found belonging to Miss Gilchrist. The police at first thought that the diamond brooch, which he had pawned on the 21st, had been part of Miss Gilchrist's belongings, but that turned out to be a mistake. In her premises nothing was found belonging to him. As you know, robberies and murders have often been traced by the offender having in his hurry left behind him a cap or other article belonging to him, which had been proved to be his, and which has convicted him. Then nothing was found in his possession on which you can rely as being connected necessarily with the murder. You have heard about the coat, and you have heard about the hammer. The doctors say that, while the stains on the coat and the marks on the top part of the hammer were thought by them to be due to mammalian blood, there was not enough material for them to apply confirmatory tests to show that the stains and marks were produced by mammalian blood, or even blood at all. The hammer in itself is a perfectly innocent weapon, but it is a weapon which might have been used to do the deed. If my suggestion to you at the beginning is correct, viz., that the person who went to get the jewels from Miss Gilchrist never thought that murder would be necessary, he would have a hammer with him not for a murderous purpose, but to break open any box in which Miss Gilchrist's jewels might be kept. These are strong points in favour of the prisoner, and you will give them due weight. Had the facts been the other way, there might have been enough in any of these points to convict the prisoner, taken along with the evidence of identification. If, the following day, he had pawned some jewel of Miss Gilchrist's, you would have convicted him, or if his cap had been found in her premises. There is nothing of that kind in the case.

Two points remain. What about his conduct after the murder? There is material there for your serious consideration. The incidents may be significant, although minute, such as the incident on the top of the tramway car.

Mr. M'Clure has put it to you that at 6.12 the prisoner is proved to have calmly taken a telegram to the post office, and to have sent it off, and signed it. Such conduct is said to be inconsistent with the idea of his then plotting murder within less than an hour of the murder. You will consider whether there is any evidence to support either of these suggestions. I have pointed out that probably the man who went to get the jewels never thought of murder being necessary. As to the telegram, there is no evidence that the prisoner sent off a telegram at 6.12. A telegram signed "Oscar Slater" was sent off, but the telegraph clerk cannot tell whether it was sent by a man or by a woman. Slater may have sent the telegram or he may not, but we do know that he was, according to the statement of his friends Aumann and Kattman, at Johnston's billiard rooms some time about five or six. The suggestion is that their evidence is inconsistent with his having committed the offence, because you cannot conceive a man plotting murder being in a billiard room within half an hour of the offence. If he was not plotting murder, but only plotting the getting of jewels from an unresisting old lady, there does not seem to be much in that. But, then, the second suggestion is that he had not time, after leaving the billiard room, to be at the place of the murder by the hour it was undoubtedly committed. You will consider whether, suppose he left at 6.30, and suppose he walked out to West Princes Street, he had not plenty of time to be there, and to see the servant girl leaving and to see that his opportunity had come. The servant girl talks about being usually out seven minutes. We know quite well how variable the time of her absence would be. He may have trusted to her being a good deal longer than that on this occasion, as she had no doubt been before. Suppose you are not to take Aumann 's evidence, which was that Slater was at the billiard room about 5.30 to sell the pawn ticket for the brooch, and did not stay long, suppose you prefer Rattman's statement that the prisoner left somewhere about 6.30, you will consider whether the prisoner would have had any difficulty in being at the scene of the murder by seven o'clock.

As to what happened after seven o'clock, you will remember what was said by Antoine — that poor, pathetic figure we saw yesterday — and by the servant Schmalz. They do not speak definitely about that particular occasion, but their evidence is that, during that week, Slater was always home for dinner by about seven o'clock. You will judge whether, in a disreputable house such as Slater's, we are, without evidence, to credit the statement that hours were so punctual and so regular that the inmates always dined at seven o'clock, or ten minutes afterwards. Schmalz admits that the dinner was sometimes as late as 7.30 or eight, so that there is nothing in her evidence to exclude the Crown's case that Slater left the billiard room at 6.30, committed the murder, fled from the house empty-handed, being surprised by Adams and Lambie, and was at home, say, by 7.30.

Gentlemen, the prisoner was not bound to prove that he was not the murderer. He was quite entitled to say, "I defy you, the Crown, to prove that I am the murderer." He was entitled to lead no evidence at all, and to rest his defence on the inadequacy of the Crown's case. But he has chosen, in accordance with the letter he wrote to Cameron, to bring evidence to show that at the time of the murder he was engaged elsewhere, and could not have committed the offence. You will judge whether or not he has done so satisfactorily to your mind. Suppose he has not, that would not entitle you to convict him. It is not for him to disprove the charge; it is for the Crown to prove it, and unless they prove it to your mind satisfactorily, then he is entitled to your verdict. As to the time immediately after the hour of the murder, you have heard how, at 9.45 that night, Slater went to the club and saw Gordon Henderson. Henderson says that Slater seemed excited, but his excitement did not connect itself in his mind with the commission of any crime. He thought he might have been losing money at cards. That exhausts the evidence so far as relating to the night in question.

Mr. M'Clure spoke of his witnesses as a credible body of witnesses. You have seen them. You know their occupation, you know how Antoine's fate is bound up with the prisoner's in the past and will be in the future, you know what kind of person the servant is, and in what employment she has been, and it is for you to say whether such witnesses form a credible body of evidence or not. But, even if you think they do not, still you have to come to a conclusion as to whether the Crown have proved the case on their own evidence.

With regard to the alleged flight from Glasgow, it is quite clear that Slater intended, at some time or other, to go to America. It may be doubtful what place he was going to in America, but I do not think it can be suggested that he was not intending to go abroad. It is for you to say whether, in the circumstances detailed to you, there was a hastening of that intention, which is suggestive, if it does not prove, that he had a new and very serious motive of expediting his going abroad. The realisation of the money, and the attempt to sell the pawn ticket, were all before the murder. The limit of £10 was given to Cameron, and afterwards, apparently, the prisoner was willing to take any money — he was willing to take £4 — but you will judge whether that was sufficient to show that there was, as the Lord Advocate called it, a flight from Glasgow, which could only be consistent with his desire to escape from the consequences of a crime of a serious nature. It is quite certain he was not back in the clubs after the 21st, and, although he was in Johnston's billiard rooms on the 23rd for the first time he did not play. Then you have got the incident connected with his being, or alleged to have been, on the top of the tramway car. The weight and effect of all that is eminently matter not for me to enlarge upon or discuss, but for you, as men of the world, to consider.

That is the whole case. Mr. M'Clure has made some observations on the Lord Advocate not having cross-examined Antoine. You will keep in view her position, and the weight to be given to a witness with such tremendous motives as she has for standing by the prisoner, and with the record that she has in the past. But you will also remember that, if you read the evidence as I do, her statements were not inconsistent with the Crown case. I noted that she did not say that the tickets were taken for Liverpool. There is a question there, which has not been cleared up, as to whether tickets were taken for London or Liverpool. She, who must know, did not say, and was not asked to say, that the tickets were not taken for London, but for Liverpool. If she had said that, and had not been cross-examined on it, the defence might have made a point which is not open to them.

Gentlemen, the case is entirely in your hands. If the whole matter is in the region of speculation or suspicion, then you cannot convict. Mr. M'Clure said that, if you had a doubt on the matter, you could not convict. One knows what he meant by that — he meant reasonable doubt, and the distinction is an important one. There is nothing almost in human affairs that does not admit of speculative doubt. Many eminent persons have doubted whether we really existed. A brilliantly satirical treatise was written to show that the great Napoleon never existed, but we do not look upon these as reasonable doubts. If you have a reasonable doubt on the matter, you will acquit in one form of verdict or another. It is a serious thing that a brutal offence of this kind, on an unoffending old lady, in a crowded part of a town alleged to be civilised, in an age alleged to be civilised, should go undiscovered and unpunished, but it is a much more serious thing to convict any prisoner on insufficient evidence.

Gentlemen, I suppose you all think that the prisoner possibly is the murderer; you may very likely all think that he probably is the murderer. That, however, will not entitle you to convict him. The Crown have undertaken to prove, not that he is possibly or probably the murderer, but that he is the murderer. That is the question you have to consider. If you think there is no reasonable doubt about it, you will do your duty and convict him; if you think there is, you will acquit him.

VERDICT AND SENTENCE

The jury retired to consider their verdict at five minutes to five o'clock, and returned in an hour and ten minutes.

CLERK OF COURT — What is your verdict, gentlemen?

FOREMAN OF THE JURY — The jury, by a majority, find the prisoner guilty as libelled.

THE PRISONER — My lord, may I say one word? Will you allow me to speak?

LORD GUTHRIE — Sit down just now.

THE CLERK — Then this is your verdict, "The jury, by a majority, find the panel guilty of murder as libelled"?

THE FOREMAN — Yes.

Mr. MORISON — I move for sentence.

While the verdict and sentence were being recorded.

THE PRISONER — My lord, my father and mother are poor old people. I came on my own account to this country, I came over to defend my right. I know nothing about the affair. You are convicting an innocent man.

LORD GUTHRIE (to Mr. M'Clure) — I think you ought to advise the prisoner to reserve anything he has got to say for the Crown authorities. If he insists on it, I shall not prevent him now — will you see what he says?

THE PRISONER — My lord, what shall I say? I came over from America, knowing nothing of the affair, to Scotland to get a fair judgment. I know nothing about the affair, absolutely nothing. I never heard the name. I know nothing about the affair. I do not know how I could be connected with the affair. I know nothing about it. I came from America on my own account. I can say no more.

Assuming the black cap, Lord Guthrie then pronounced sentence of death in the usual form, adjudging the panel to be executed in Glasgow prison on Thursday, 27th May.

Lord Guthrie thanked the jury for their attendance at that long and complicated trial, and said they would be excused from jury service during the next three years.

The prisoner was then removed, and the Court rose.

APPENDIX I

———

NOTICES ISSUED BY THE GLASGOW CITY POLICE WITH REFERENCE TO THE MURDER OF MISS GILCHRIST

———

(1)

GLASGOW CITY POLICE

———

MURDER

———

About 7 p.m. on Monday, 21st December current, an old lady named Marion Gilchrist was brutally murdered in a house at 15 Queen's Terrace, West Princes Street, where she lived, the only other occupant being a servant woman, who, about the hour mentioned, left the house to purchase an evening paper, and on her return in less than fifteen minutes afterwards found that her mistress had been brutally murdered in the room in which she had left her.

On her return with the paper the servant met the man first described leaving the house, and about the same time another man, second described, was seen descending the steps leading to the house, and running away.

———

DESCRIPTIONS.

(First) A man from twenty-five to thirty years of age, 5 feet 7 or 8 inches in height, thought to be clean shaven; wore a long grey overcoat and dark cap.

(Second) A man from twenty-eight to thirty years of age, tall and thin, clean shaven, nose slightly turned to one side (thought to be the right side); wore a fawn-coloured overcoat (believed to be a waterproof), dark trousers, tweed cloth hat of the latest make, and believed to be dark in colour, and brown boots.

Please have every possible inquiry made within your jurisdiction, and communicate any information that may be obtained to the Superintendent, Criminal Investigation Department, or to

J. V. Stevenson,
Chief Constable.
Police Headquarters, St. Andrew's Square, Glasgow, 25th December, 1908.

[Note. — This bill was issued to the police forces only.}

---

(2)

GLASGOW CITY POLICE.

£200 REWARD.

MURDER.

Whereas on Monday night, 21st December, 1908, Miss Marion Gilchrist, an old lady, was foully murdered in her house at 15 Queen's Terrace, West Princes Street, Glasgow, by some person or persons unknown.

Notice is hereby given that the above reward will be paid by the Chief Constable of Glasgow to any one giving such information as shall lead to the apprehension and conviction of the person or persons who committed the crime.

Such information may be given at any Police Office in the City, or to the Subscriber,

J. V. Stevenson,

Chief Constable.
Central Police Office,
Glasgow, 31st December, 1908.

APPENDIX II

EXCERPTS FROM PRINT OF PRODUCTIONS IN CAUSA HIS MAJESTY'S ADVOCATE AGAINST OSCAR SLATER.

No. 6.

List of Jewellery Belonging to Deceased, prepared by Mr. Dick, Auctioneer and Valuator, Glasgow.

Gold bracelet.

Silver card case.

Morocco manicure case.

Silver necklet, brooch and earrings.

Silver solitaires.

Pair gold eyeglasses and chain.

Brass button hook.

Lace pin.

Curb bangle.

Gold bangle with pendant.

Half hoop ring with 5 diamonds.

Half hoop ring with 6 emeralds.

Half hoop ring with 5 sapphires.

Half hoop ring with 5 rubies.

Scent bottle with silver top.

Silver guard and pencil case.

Pair gold spectacles.

Rope of pearls.

Set 3 diamond star brooches.

Gold onyx pearl and diamond brooch.

Gold onyx pearl and diamond bracelet.

Lace brooch and pair earrings with topaz.

Small ring with diamond and rubies, and gold enamelled ring.

Gold bangle with 3 rubies.

Gold watch with black dial, and albertina and seals.

Single stone gipsy ring with diamond.

Gold bangle, 9 carat.

Signet ring.

Two keeper rings.

Pair gold sleeve links.

Emerald and diamond ring.

Ruby and diamond ring.

Pair diamond earrings.

Circular diamond brooch pendant.

Diamond necklace.

Two pairs gold earrings.

Gold catch with diamonds.

Pair gold solitaires.

Thin gold eyeglass chain.

Two small plain gold rings.

Gold keeper ring.

Cameo brooch with gold mounts.

Two silver bracelets.

Silver pebble brooch.

Gent.'s gold watch with gold fob, seal, and key.

Florentine brooch with gold mounts.

Gold-mounted brooch with hair.

Pair gold eyeglasses.

Silver shaving brush holder.

Pair pearl and onyx earrings and small brooch.

Gold bangle with pearl and turquoise.

Garnet and ruby lace brooch, "arrow."

Pearl and ruby brooch.

Gold eyeglasses.

Gold necklet with onyx, pearl, and diamond pendant.

Pair cameo earrings with gold mounts...............£1132.12.0

Two diamond bracelets............................. 250. 0.0

£1382.12.0

————

No. 7.

LETTER, in German, Accused to Max Rattmann, dated 26th December, 1908 (in envelope), of which the following is translation:—

Oscar Slater,
c/o Caesar Café,
544 Broadway, San Francisco.

North Western Hotel,
Liverpool, 26/12/1908.

Dear Max, — Surprisingly leaving Glasgow. Forgot to say goodbye. Let me hear from you as you have my address. Freedman's girl took over my flat; keep yourself as well as your wife well, and remain. — Your friend, O. Slater.

My French girl leaves for Paris from here. I will inform you over certain matters regarding San Francisco later. Tell Carl Kunstler, Soldata, and Willy, and respectfully Beyer to write. You can also make enquiries whether Beyer has paid the £15. He looked very pale latterly.

Best wishes to Soldata, Kunstler, and Willy.

————

No. 8.

(a) LETTER, D. R. Jacobs to Accused, dated 28th December, 1908.

New York, Dec. 28th, 1908.
326 Third Avenue.

Dear Oscar, — Just a line to acknowledge the receipt of your letter, and pleased to know that you are well, also Mr. Rogers and my friend Arthur Playdell. As for sending you emeralds I would be only too pleased if you sent me the cash, but I cannot afford to send goods to Scotland and wait for months for the money. I get rid of all I have made and have to pay cash for them before my man makes them, and no sooner you send cash I can forward you anything you want, and if you want anything quick, communicate with Joseph Oesterman, 58 Trinity Square, Soho, S.E., London, England, who has got my code cable book and can communicate with me on all business matters. Mr. Rogers knows him and saw him when Wrone was in London. We all send our best respects to you, the wife, and Mr. Rogers. — Yours truly, D.R. JACOBS.

Buy (? or bring) all you can when you come over.

(b) ENVELOPE in which above letter was enclosed, with note on back thereof.

Oscar Slater, Esq.,
c/o Mr. Anderson,
69 St. George's Road,
Glasgow.
Scotland, Eng.

If not delivered return to

D. R. Jacobs,
326 Third Avenue,
New York, U.S.

———

No. 9.

(a) LETTER, Accused to Dent, London, dated 9th December, 1908.

Glasgow, 9/12, 1908.
69 St. George's Road,
c/o A. Anderson.

Dear Sir,— Enclosed you will find my watch you have delivered to 36 Albemarle Street, London. The watch is 15-20 minutes daily to slow in time.

Kindly put the watch in order, and return same till the 30th of December. Cr.— Yours truly, OSCAR SLATER.

J. Dent, Esq., London.

G. watch received. Must have had a fall or heavy blow. Bal. pivots are badly bent, and back cover strained. We will repair and send in 10 days.

(b) TELEGRAM, Accused to Dent, 21st December, 1908.

DECEMBER 21, 08.
DENT, WATCHMAKER, TRAFALGAR SQUARE, LONDON. IF POSSIBLE PLEASE SEND WATCH AT ONCE. OSCAR SLATER.

(c) TELEGRAM, Accused to Dent, 23rd December, 1908.

DECEMBER 23, 08.
DENT, 34 COCKSPUR STREET, LONDON. MUST HAVE WATCH. LEAVING TO-MORROW NIGHT FOR THE CONTINENT. OSCAR SLATER.
69 ST. GEORGE'S RD. C/O A ANDERSON.

(d) ACCUSED'S CARD with address.

Oscar Slater,
Dentist,
36 Albemarle Street, W.
Telephone 1624, Mayfair.

Address till 30th December—
69 St Georges Road,
c/o A. Anderson,
Glasgow.

———

No. 10.

**CARD bearing name and address, Oscar Slater,
Dealer in Diamonds and Precious Stones, &c., &c.**

Oscar Slater,
Dealer in Diamonds and Precious Stones,
33 Soho Square,
Oxford Street, W.

———

No. 11.

FILE OF LETTERS, &c., containing

(1) LETTER, Thos. Cook & Son to Cunard Line, Liverpool, 23rd December.

83 Buchanan Street,
Glasgow, 23 Decr., 1908.

Messrs. Cunard Line, Liverpool.

"Lusitania," 26 Decr., 1908.

Dear Sirs, — Kindly wire us to-morrow if you can offer married couple a second-class room at £24 (£12 each), per the above to New York, and oblige. — Yours truly, THOMAS COOK & SON, per J. B.

(2) TELEGRAM from Cunard Line to Messrs. Cook, 24th December.

TO COUPON, GLASGOW. SECONDS, "LUSITANIA." SATURDAY. OFFER COUPLE ROOM E76, TWELVE POUNDS RATE. — CUNARD.

(3) LETTER, Thos. Cook & Son, to Cunard Line, Liverpool, dated 24th December.

83 Buchanan Street,
Glasgow, 24th December, 1908.
Messrs. Cunard Line, Liverpool.

"Lusitania," 26th December.

Dear Sirs, — We beg to thank you for your wire of date, offering room E76 at the £12 rate in favour of Mr. and Mrs. Oscar Slater. This gentleman has called to-day, and is very much disappointed at not having an outside room. We, however, explained to him that the rate of £12 provided only for inside accommodation. He, however, replies that he could do better with you in Liverpool. We asked him if he would take out ticket for room E76 and endeavour to adjust with you in Liverpool on Saturday. He has promised to give us his decision to-morrow, on receipt of which we will advise you. — Yours truly,

Thos. Cook & Son,
Per W. Dalziel.

(4) LETTER from Messrs. Cook & Son to Cunard Line, dated 25th December, 1908.

83 Buchanan Street, Glasgow, 25 Decr., 1908.

Messrs. Cunard Line, Liverpool.

"Lusitania," 26.12.08 to New York.

With further reference to your wire of yesterday offering Cabin E76 per the above in favour of Mr. and Mrs. Slater, please note they have not called here to-day as promised, so we shall be glad if you will kindly release cabin.

We shall be glad to know if they book with you to-morrow. — Yours truly,

Thos. Cook & Son,
Per W. D.

(5) APPLICATION FORM to Cunard Co., for Contract Tickets.

Cunard Line.

(1) Steamer, "Lusitania," sailing from Liverpool on the 26.12.08; (2) Name in full, Otto Sando and Anna Sando; (3) Age 38 years; (4) Sex,_____; (5) Married or single, Married; (6) Calling or Occupation, Dentist: (7) Able to read and write. Yes; (8) Nationality (country owning political allegiance or of which citizen or subject), Germany, U.S. citizen, American address, Chicago, 30 Staate Street

CONTRACT TICKET for two Berths from Cunard Co. in name of Mr. and Mrs Otto Sando.

CUNARD LINE.

————

Second Cabin.

————

The Cunard Steamship Company, Limited,
Royal Mail Steamers.

Second Cabin Passenger's Contract Ticket.
Not Transferable.

————

British steamship "Lusitania," of tons _____ register, to take in passengers at Liverpool for New York on the 26th day of December, 1908.

Names	Ages	No. of Statute Adults
Mr. O. Sando, ... A		1
Mrs. " . . . . A	1	

Deposit - - £28 0 0

Balance - - 0 0 0

————————————

Total - - £28 0 0

_____

I engage that the person named in the margin hereof shall be provided with a second cabin passage to and shall be landed at the Port of New York in the United States of America, in the British steamship "Lusitania," with not less than 20 cubic feet for luggage for such statute adult, and shall be victualled during the voyage and the time of detention at any place before its termination according to the subjoined scale, for the sum of £28 including Government dues before embarkation and head-money, if any, at the place of landing, and every other charge except freight for excess of luggage beyond the quantity above specified, and I hereby acknowledge to have received the sum of £28 in full payment.

The luggage carried under this engagement, whether in excess of 20 cubic feet or not, shall be deemed to be of a value not exceeding £10, unless the value in excess of that sum be declared and paid for.

_____

[Bill of fare.]

_____

for and on behalf of the Cunard Steamship Company, Ltd.,

26th December, 1908.

ANDREW DANIEL MEARNS,
per J. FORSYTH.

On back of Ticket.

The following information is required for use of the United States authorities.

_____

Name, - - - - - | Mr. Otto Sando.

| Mrs. Otto Sando.

|

Age, - - - - - | 38.

| 27.

|

Married or single,   -   - | Married.

| "

|

Occupation, -   -   -   - | Dentist.

|

Country of birth,-   -   - | Germany.

| England.

|

Last legal residence, -   - | Scotland.

| Scotland.

|

Country claiming allegiance | U.S.A.

   (Nationality),   -   - | —

|

Final destination | Chicago.

   (Town),   -   -   - | Chicago.

|

If ticket to destination, - |

|

If in possession of $50 or less, | Yes.

|

If ever in the United States | Yes.

   before,   -   -   - | Yes.

|

No. of packages of luggage, | 9.

            (Hotel)Chicago.

            (in pencil)

Notice to Passengers.

. . . .

. . . .

For and on behalf of the Cunard Steamship Company, Ltd.,

ANDREW DANIEL MEARNS.

No. 12.

LETTER, Accused to Hugh Cameron, Glasgow, addressed from Tombs Prison, New York, dated 2nd February, 1909.

New York,
Centre Street,
Tombs, 2/2/1909.

Dear Friend Cameron, — To-day it is nearly five weeks I am kept here in prison for the Glasgow murder.

I am very down-hearted my dear Cameron to know that my friends in Glasgow like Gordon Henderson can tell such liars about me to the Glasgow police.

I have seen here his statements he made in Glasgow telling the police that a German came up to him and had told him Oscar Slater had committed the murder, and also that I have been on the night of the murder in his place asking him for mony, I was very excited and in hurry, I didn't think it was very clever from him, because he like to make himself a good name by the police to tell such liars.

I don't deney I have been in his place asking him for mony because I went brocke in the Sloper Club. Only I will fix Mr. Gordon Henderson I will prove with plenty of witnesses that I was playing there mucky, and I am entitled to ask a proprietor from a gambling house when I am broke for mony.

He would not mind to get me hangt and I will try to prove that from a gambling point, I am right to ask for some money. I hope nobody propper mindet will blame me for this.

The dirty caracter was trying to make the police believe I done the murder, was excitet, asking for mony to hop off.

I think you know different remember when have been in the Cunard Line office trying to change for a £5:0:0 note, we have been in three or four differend place after found some change in the Grosvenor have posted with you on Hope Street office a registered letter.

I shall go back to Glasgow with my free will, because you know so good than myselfs that I am not the murder.

I hope my dear Cameron that you will still be my friend in my troubel and tell the truth and stand on my side. You know the best reason I have left Glasgow because I have shown to you the letter from St Francisco from my friend, also I have left you my address from St Francisco.

I reely was surprised I don't have seen your statement because I think you was too strait forvard for them. They only have taken the statement against me and not for me. Likely I will be in Scotland in fourteen days and so quicke your hear that I am in prison in Glasgow send me the best criminal lawyer up you get recomendet in Glasgow I stand on your dear Cameron.

Keep all this quiet because the police is trying hard to make a frame up for me. I must have a good lawyer, and after I can proof my innocents befor having a trial, because I will prove with five people where I have been when the murder was committed.

Thanking you at present, and I hope to have a true friend on you, because every man is able to get put in such a affair and being innocent. My best regards to you and all my friends. — I am, your friend,

Oscar Slater,
Tombs, New York.

No. 13.

LETTER, Robert Rogers, London, to John S. Marr, Glasgow, dated 5th October, 1908.

36 Albemarle Street, W.
London, Oct. 5, 1908.

Dear Sir, — In reply to yours of the 4th inst. I beg to state that Mr. A. Anderson has been my tenant for over two years. He is a highly respectable gentleman, and has always been prompt in his payments. — Yours faithfully,

Robert Rogers.

No. 14.

LETTER, Davenport & Co., London, to John S. Marr, Glasgow, dated 5th November, 1908.

7 and 8 New Coventry Street,
Piccadilly,
London, W., Novr. 5, 1908.

The person referred to in your letter of yesterday's date was a tenant of a client of ours, and he always paid his rent regularly and left the place in good condition, and we have had no complaints, and as far as we know of him, should consider him a desirable. — Yours faithfully, Devonport & Co.

No. 15.

TORN PAPER wrapper of a Registered Parcel addressed to Accused, 23rd Dec 1909.

Registered Fragile with care
R. London W.C. 1

No. 1292
Fee paid.

Oscar Slater, Esq.,
c/o A. Anderson, Esq.,
69 St Georges Road, Glasgow.

Dent

No. 16.

MISSIVE of LET of house at 69 St. George's Road, to A. Anderson, with Visiting Card of A. Anderson attached.

(a) Missive.

Glasgow 6th Novr. 1908.

Mr. John S. Marr,
175 St. Vincent Street.

Sir,— I hereby take from you that house 3 up 1 situated at 69 St. Georges Road from 28th Novr. 1908 until 28 May 1910 at the rent of £42:-:-, say Forty two pounds stg. per annum Sterling payable quarterly in equal proportions at the usual terms.

I also agree to pay my proportion of stair lighting at each term of Martinmas.

I accept the premises in good tenantable condition, and will leave them in the same state (ordinary tear and wear excepted). I agree to replace any glass broken from within. I bind myself to observe all the usual regulations as to stair, close, and washing-house, and I will not keep any dog on the premises. I also bind myself to flit and remove, and deliver up all keys at the end of this lease without any warning or Process at Law, and not to assign the lease or let the whole or any part of said premises without your consent in writing.

I will not hold you liable for any damage done to my effects from any bursting of water pipes, or flooding from without or within; and I will at the letting season give every facility to show the premises to any intending future tenant until they are let or unoccupied by me.

Name, A. Anderson.
Occupation, Dentist.
Address, 136 Renfrew Street.

(b) Visiting Card with (2) addresses on the back thereof.

136 Renfrew Street, 2 up,
c/o Campbell.

A. Anderson,
Dentist.

Telephone.
1624, Mayfair.

Addresses on back.

35 Albemarle Street,
Piccadilly.

R. Rodgers, same address.

Devonport & Co.,
7 & 8 New Coventry Street,
London.

————————————

APPENDIX III

UNTO THE RIGHT HONOURABLE LORD PENTLAND, HIS MAJESTY'S SECRETARY OF STATE FOR SCOTLAND

MEMORIAL
ON BEHALF OF
OSCAR SLATER

THIS Memorial is humbly presented on behalf of Oscar Slater presently a Prisoner in the Prison of Glasgow, who was, in the High Court of Justiciary at Edinburgh, on Thursday, the sixth day of May, Nineteen hundred and nine, found guilty of the charge of murdering Miss Marion Gilchrist in her house in West Princes Street, Glasgow, and sentenced to death. The Prisoner is a Jew, and was born in Germany. He is 37 years of age.

The Jury returned a verdict of "Guilty" by a majority of nine to six, and the legal advisers of the condemned man hold a very strong opinion that the verdict of the majority of the Jury was not in accordance with the evidence led, and that this evidence was quite insufficient to identify the Prisoner with the murderer, and so to establish the Prisoner's guilt. This view, they believe, is shared by the general public of all classes in Scotland, and by the Glasgow press (*vide* leading article in The Glasgow Herald of 7th May, 1909, sent herewith).

Your Memorialist has endeavoured in this paper to deal with the matter as briefly and with as little argument as possible; but in view of the fact that the trial of the Prisoner occupied four days, it is inevitable that the Memorial should extend to some length.

It is common ground that the late Miss Gilchrist, a lady of about 82 years of age, resided alone with her domestic servant, Nellie Lambie, a girl of about 21 years of age.

According to the evidence of Lambie, the latter left Miss Gilchrist alone in the house at seven o'clock on the evening of 21st December, 1908, and went to purchase an evening paper. Lambie deponed that she securely shut the house door behind her, and also the door at the close, or street entry; that she was only absent about ten minutes; that on returning about ten minutes past seven o'clock she found the close door open; that upon ascending the stair she found Mr. Adams, a gentleman who resides in the flat below, standing at Miss Gilchrist's house door; that Adams informed her that he had gone up to Miss Gilchrist's door because he had heard knocking on the floor of Miss Gilchrist's house, and had rung the bell, but that he could obtain no admittance; that the lobby was lighted by one gas jet turned half up, but giving a good light; that Lambie thereupon opened the house door with her keys; that upon the door being opened a man came through the lobby or hall of Miss Gilchrist's house, passed Lambie and Adams, went downstairs, and disappeared; and that, upon Lambie and Adams entering the house, they found Miss Gilchrist lying on the dining-room floor dead, her head having been smashed.

Upon the Wednesday following the murder (23rd December, 1908), the Glasgow Police were informed by a message girl named Mary Barrowman (about 15 years of age), that she had seen a man wearing a Donegal hat and a light coat running out of the close which leads from the street to Miss Gilchrist's house shortly after seven o'clock on the night of the murder; that the man passed her, running at top speed; that she noticed that he was dark, and clean shaven, and that his nose was twisted towards the right side. The servant Lambie had also informed the Police that a gold crescent brooch, set in diamonds, had disappeared from Miss Gilchrist's house on the night of the murder, and that this was all of Miss Gilchrist's property that she missed. These statements were published in the Glasgow newspapers on Friday, 25th December, 1908, and following upon this the witness Allan Maclean, a member of a club to which Slater belonged, informed the Police that Slater's appearance somewhat corresponded with the description advertised, and that he had been trying to sell a pawn ticket for a diamond brooch. Following up this clue, the Police went to Slater's house at 69, St. George's Road, Glasgow, on the night of Friday, 25th December, and learned that he and Miss Andrée Antoine, with whom he had been cohabiting, had left Glasgow that night with their belongings. The Police thereafter ascertained that Slater had sailed on the "Lusitania " for New York from Liverpool on Saturday, 26th December, and cabled to the Authorities at New York to detain and search him on his arrival. This was done, and the pawn ticket, which he had been trying to sell, was found upon him, but turned out to be a pawn ticket for a brooch which belonged to Miss Antoine, had never belonged to Miss Gilchrist, and had been pawned a considerable time before the murder. Proceedings, however, were instituted for Slater's extradition. The witnesses Lambie, Adams, and Barrowman gave evidence in America, purporting to identify him as the man seen leaving Miss Gilchrist's house, and Slater was (he states of his own consent) extradited, and brought back to Scotland for trial.

An advertisement was published by the Authorities in Glasgow offering a reward of £200 for information which would lead to the arrest of the murderer.

The only evidence against Slater, which might be called direct evidence, was the evidence of the persons who saw a man walk out of the lobby or hall in Miss Gilchrist's house on the night of the murder (Lambie and Adams), or leaving the close leading therefrom, or running along the street (Barrowman).

At the trials Lambie professed to identify Slater, as the man whom she had seen leaving the house, by the side of his face. It was put to her, however, and clearly proved, that when she gave evidence in New York in the extradition proceedings she stated in Court there that she did not see the man's face, and professed to identify him by his walk. When Slater's own coat, the one found in his luggage, was shown to her at the trial, she at once remarked, even before it was unrolled, that it was not like the coat the man in the lobby wore—it was the coat. It was obviously impossible that she knew it to be the same coat. Lord Guthrie referred to this in his charge to the jury as a typical example of the nature of her evidence. With regard to the positive nature of her evidence generally, it is interesting to note that her first answer in America, when asked if she saw the man, was, "One is very suspicious, if anything." She stated that, when she saw Slater in the Central Police Office at Glasgow, she recognised him in his "own coat." It was proved that he was not then wearing his own coat, but one with which he had been dressed for identification purposes.

The witness only saw the man who was leaving the house for a moment or two. Adams and she contradicted each other as to where she was when the man walked across the lobby. Adams deponed that she was by the lobby clock and walking towards the kitchen. If so, she must practically have had her back to the man. She says she was on the threshold of the door. In any event, her view was momentary.

The witness Adams, who deponed that he had a better view of the man in the house than Lambie, stated at the trial that he, standing at the threshold, saw the man's face as he approached, that their eyes met, and that the man walked slowly towards him, face to face, but Adams would not go further than to say that Slater resembled the man very much. He is superior to Lambie and Barrowman in years, education and intelligence. Your Memorialist begs to emphasise the fact that this witness had a much better view of the man than any of the other witnesses.

The witness Barrowman stated at the trial that the man ran out of the close and rushed past her at top speed, brushing against her, and that he had his hat pulled well down over his forehead. The witness is a message girl, about 15 years of age. She also stated that the man had on brown boots, a Donegal hat, and a fawn coat, and that he was dark and clean shaven, and that his nose had a twist to the right. She professed to have noticed all these things as he rushed past her at top speed. At the trial this witness stated in cross-examination (i) that she was proceeding in the opposite direction from the man, to deliver a parcel, but that she turned and went some distance after him; that she thought he was probably going to catch a tramcar; but she could not explain why she should go out of her way to turn and follow a man running for a car in a busy city like Glasgow; and (2) that, although the girl Lambie and she had occupied the same cabin on the voyage to America, which lasted about twelve days, she had not once discussed the appearance of the man, and that no one had warned her not to do so. These two statements do not impress your Memorialist as bearing the stamp of truth. This girl started the description of the twisted nose. She is the only witness who refers to it. Her view of the man's face must necessarily have been momentary. Slater's nose cannot properly be described as "twisted to the right." It has a noticeable prominence in the centre.

All of these three witnesses had, as has been said, only a momentary view of the man, and it was proved that before Barrowman professed to identify Slater in New York she was shown his photograph, and that both she and Lambie, before attempting to identify him in New York, saw him being brought into Court by a Court official, wearing a badge. In her New York evidence she first said, "He is something like the man I saw." At the trial she stated that he was the man. These facts very much reduce, if they do not altogether vitiate, the value of the evidence of these identifying witnesses.

Another witness, Mrs. Liddell, who is a married sister of the witness Adams, stated that, at five minutes to seven on the evening of the murder, she saw a dark, clean-shaven man leaning against a railing at the street entry to Miss Gilchrist's house, but that this man wore a heavy brown tweed coat and a brown cap. It is to be observed that Constable Neil, who passed the house at ten minutes to seven, saw no one there; and Lambie, who left the house promptly at seven, or, as she said in America, "perhaps a few minutes before seven," saw no one there. Further, Mrs. Liddell did not observe where the man went to; according to her he merely glided away; and although she was in Miss Gilchrist's house that night and saw the body, and would naturally be greatly concerned over the murder, she did not recollect having seen this man until the Wednesday after the murder. Even taking her evidence as absolutely true and reliable, it provides an excellent object-lesson on the difficulty and responsibility of convicting on such evidence as this, because the man she saw was obviously dressed differently from the man seen by the other three witnesses. Her evidence does not, to any appreciable extent, further the case against Slater, as she stated that she thought this man was Slater, but admitted that she might be in error.

The other witness is a girl named Annie Armour, a ticket clerk in the Subway Station at Kelvinbridge, who says that between 7.30 and 8 that evening a man, whom she identified as Slater, rushed past her office without waiting for a ticket, and seemed excited. Lord Guthrie in his charge to the jury did not refer to this witness, and your Memorialist thinks advisedly. The mere question of time is sufficient to render her evidence valueless. She is sure the incident did not happen before 7.30. According to the other witnesses, the murderer must have run from the house by at least 7.15. It was proved that it would only take a man five or six minutes to run from the scene of the tragedy to this station, either by the most direct route or by the route which Barrowman's evidence suggests he took. Then it is impossible to suppose that she could get anything like a good view, even of the side face, of a man who rushed past her in the way she described.

All the witnesses who saw the man on the night of the murder (Monday) say that he was clean shaven. It was proved that on the next day or two after the murder Slater had a short, black, stubbly moustache.

These were the only witnesses called by the Crown to identify Slater with the murderer. Further circumstantial evidence, however, was led by the Crown to show that, on occasions before the day of the murder. Slater had been seen standing in or walking up and down West Princes Street—Mrs. M'Haffie, her daughters and niece, Campbell, Cunningham, Bryson, Nairn, and O'Brien and Walker (two policemen). It may be noted that Slater's house was situated about three minutes' walk from West Princes Street.

These witnesses did not all agree in their evidence. Some said that Slater was the man they had seen; others, equally or perhaps better able to judge, only said that he was very like him. The Memorialist does not propose in this paper to deal at length with this part of the evidence, except to point out that two witnesses (Nairn and Bryson) say they saw Slater in West Princes Street on the Sunday evening previous to the murder. Against this there is the evidence that Slater on this day, as usual, spent all Sunday (day and evening) in his house. Three witnesses from Paris, London, and Dublin spoke to this. Coming from different places, they had no chance to concoct a story.

At Slater's trial it was suggested that there were various circumstances tending to create an atmosphere of suspicion around him; but it is submitted that all these were capable of explanation, and in no way pointing to Slater's guilt as a murderer. Slater had written to Cameron that he could prove where he was on the evening of the murder "by five people." When this letter was written, he thought that the date of the murder was the Tuesday, the 22nd.

The evidence of his witnesses was to the effect that on the evening of the murder he was in a billiard room until 6.30 p. m., after which he went home for dinner.

It was shown that Slater dealt in diamonds. There was, however, no evidence of any dishonest dealing of any kind. The brooch said to have been missing from Miss Gilchrist's house has not been traced. There was no evidence of any kind led to show that Slater ever knew, or even heard of, Miss Gilchrist or her house, and the Memorialist would emphasise the fact that it was the missing brooch that put the Police on the track of Slater.

With reference to Slater's departure for America on 25th December, igo8, it was proved that he had formed the intention, some weeks before the murder, of going to America. Cameron, Rattman, and Aumann proved this. Slater had, in fact, tried to get the last named to take over his flat. The letter from Jacobs, of 28th December, and the card bearing the words "address till 30th December," produced by the Crown, also corroborate the evidence of this intention of leaving, which is further corroborated by the evidence of Nichols, the barber, a Crown witness.

On the morning of 21st December, 1908, Slater received two letters —one from London, stating that his wife was demanding his address, and the other from San Francisco, asking him to come over. These were spoken to by Schmalz, his servant girl, and Miss Antoine. Further corroboration of his intention to leave is (i) on the morning of 21st December he raised a further £30 from Mr. Liddell, pawnbroker, on his brooch, and on the same day tried to sell the ticket; (2) he wrote to the Post Office for payment of the money at his credit; (3) he wired to Dent, London, to send on his watch, which was being repaired, immediately; (4) on the Monday morning he gave notice to the servant girl that she would not be required after the following Saturday (these events all happened before the murder); (5) on the Tuesday morning he redeemed a pair of binoculars from another pawnbroker whose assistant, Kempton, proved this, and who stated that he was in no way excited; (6) on the 23rd and 24th December he made inquiries at Cook's Shipping Offices regarding berths, and betrayed no signs of any excitement; on the 23rd he was, in the evening, in Johnston's billiard room, which he used to frequent; and on the 24th he spent the afternoon about Glasgow with his friend Cameron, who gave evidence; (7) on Friday morning a Mrs. Freedman and her sister arrived from London to take over his flat, so that he and Miss Antoine left on Friday night.

A rumour got abroad at the time to the effect that he booked to London and left the train at Liverpool. This rumour was published in the various newspapers, to Slater's great prejudice, but nothing of the kind was proved at the trial. The Police were evidently misled by the fact that he went by a London train, but it was proved that there were two carriages in that train for Liverpool, and also that Slater's luggage, consisting of nine boxes, was labelled to Liverpool. The Porter who labelled the luggage was called, and stated that Slater told him that he was going to Liverpool, and entered a Liverpool carriage.

The point was also raised against Slater that he used various aliases. He had been staying apart from his wife for about four years, during which time he cohabited with Miss Antoine. She stated that Slater's wife was a drunken woman, and caused him a deal of trouble. At one time he adopted the name of "George," and when he came to Glasgow on the last occasion he took the name of "Anderson." On the voyage to America he took the name of Otto Sando, because his luggage was labelled O. S. At times he called himself a dentist. There was no evidence that he really was a dentist. Miss Antoine explained that he adopted the title of dentist, as he required a designation of some sort, although he was a gambler. A great deal was published in the newspapers about a hammer that had been found in one of his boxes. This turned out to be an ordinary small domestic nail hammer, purchased on a card containing several other tools, the lot costing only 2s. 6d. He, of course, took the hammer to America with him with all the rest of his belongings.

Nothing incriminating was found in any of his boxes.

No evidence whatever was led to show how the murderer gained access to the house.

It will be conceded that identification evidence, especially in a serious charge of this kind, must be examined very carefully, and should have little weight attached to it, unless it is very clear.

To sum up, the only real evidence in the case is that of those who saw a man running away on the night of the murder; and, as has been pointed out, these witnesses had only a momentary glance at him. Adams does not positively identify the prisoner as the man. He says he closely resembles him.

Lambie's New York evidence has already been referred to, and her evidence at the trial cannot be reconciled with it.

Lambie and Barrowman both saw him in custody before trying to identify him in New York, and the latter, before identifying him, was shown his photograph.

All the other identifying witnesses called to give evidence as to his having been seen in the vicinity on days previous to the murder were taken down to the General Police Office when Slater returned from America to identify him. They were shown into one room together, and then separately taken into a room in the Police Office, where Slater was amongst about a dozen men, none of whom were like him. (Cunningham says she could see that the other men were policemen in plain clothes.) All these witnesses knew that Slater had arrived from America, and was in the room. They had all read his description in the newspapers, or had seen his photograph. They all, therefore, looked for, and had no difficulty in pointing out, a dark, foreign-looking man, with a somewhat peculiarly shaped nose. It is submitted that this is not identification evidence in the proper sense at all. Had these people been able to pick out, as their man, from amongst several others, a man whose description they only knew from what they had previously seen of him, unassisted by description, and unassisted by a photograph, the value of their evidence would have been entirely different.

Some Crown witnesses identified him as the man they had seen and talked to (Shipping Clerk, Porter, &c.), but they, of course, were able to do so. None of the identifying witnesses had ever spoken to him.

Identification evidence is a class of evidence which the law distrusts. The most famous authority is the case of Adolf Beck. Beck was, in 1896, sentenced to seven years' penal servitude, on the evidence of ten women, who swore positively that he was a man whom they had each met on two occasions, and spent some time with in their own houses, and who had defrauded them, and on the evidence of two policemen, who swore positively that Beck was the man who had been previously convicted of similar crimes, taken along with certain circumstantial evidence—that he was known to frequent a hotel on the notepaper of which one of the women had received a letter. Again, in 1904, Beck was convicted of similar crimes on similar evidence. It was subsequently demonstrated that Beck committed none of the crimes, but that a man bearing a general similarity to him was the criminal.

In the report issued by the Commission appointed to investigate the matter, consisting of Lord Collins, Sir Spencer Walpole, and Sir John Edge, the following passage occurs:—"Evidence of identity, upon personal impression, however bona fide, is of all classes of evidence the least to be relied upon, and, unless supported by other evidence, an unsafe basis for the verdict of a Jury."

Now, the evidence in the Beck case was infinitely more overwhelming and consistent than in this case; and the report in the Beck case, and the report on which it followed, make it clear that on the evidence in this case the Jury had no right to bring in a verdict of "Guilty."

A good deal was said by the learned Lord-Advocate to the Jury about Slater's immoral character. It was not disputed that he was a gambler. It was also admitted that he had cohabited for about four years with Madame Antoine, who was of doubtful virtue, and who gave evidence. Yet the learned Lord Advocate addressed the Jury to the effect that the prisoner "had followed a life which descended to the very depth of human degradation, for, by the universal judgment of mankind, the man who lived upon the proceeds of prostitution has sunk to the lowest depth, and all moral sense in him had been destroyed." This he cited as proof of the disappearance of an obstacle which had previously been in his way, viz:—Whether it was conceivable that such a man as Slater could commit such an inhumanly brutal crime. The only evidence on that point was that of Cameron, Slater's friend, who, in cross-examination, said he had heard that Slater lived on the earnings of prostitution, but who did not say he knew. The Jury were distinctly told by the Lord Advocate, and by the prisoner's Counsel, and by the Judge, to banish from their minds anything they had heard regarding the man's character; but they had previously heard all about it, and the Memorialist feels strongly that they were evidently unable to do so.

Public feeling is also very strong on the point that the question of Slater's character should never have been brought before the Jury.

The Memorialist thinks it is only fair to prisoner to point out that he was all along anxious to give evidence on his own behalf. He was advised by his Counsel not to do so, but not from any knowledge of guilt. He had undergone the strain of a four days' trial. He speaks rather broken English—although quite intelligibly—with a foreign accent, and he had been in custody since January.

Apart from what has been set forth above, your Memorialist begs to draw attention to the fact that on the Crown list of witnesses is the name of a witness, Miss Agnes Brown (No. 46). This lady is 30 years of age, and a very intelligent school teacher. Your Memorialist is informed that she told the Police and Procurator-Fiscal that on the night of the murder, about ten minutes past seven o'clock, two men in company rushed along West Princes Street from the direction of Miss Gilchrist's house, and passed close to her at the corner of West Princes Street and West Cumberland Street; that one of them was dressed in a blue Melton coat with a dark velvet collar, black boots, and without a hat; that both men ran past the opening of West Cumberland Street, straight on along West Princes Street, crossed West Princes Street, and ran down Rupert Street, a street further west, and opening off the opposite side of West Princes Street. Your Memorialist understands that, in the identification proceedings before referred to, this witness pointed out Slater as the man in the Melton coat, as she thought. This witness's evidence is thus in sharp contradiction on material points to that of the message girl Barrowman (who had only a momentary glance at the man), but upon whose evidence so much weight has evidently been laid, and who says that Slater was dressed in a light coat, a Donegal hat, and brown boots, was alone, and ran down West Cumberland Street.

Your Memorialist respectfully submits that this illustrates the danger of convicting a man upon the kind of evidence given in this case. Miss Brown was in attendance at the trial, but was not called as a witness. Even on the evidence led, the votes of two more jurymen in his favour would have liberated the prisoner. In England the probability is that a conviction would never have been obtained.

Your Memorialist is authorised to state that Slater's Counsel agree that the evidence did not justify the conviction.

Your Memorialist, who has all along acted as Slater's Solicitor since he was brought back from America after the Extradition Proceedings, and who has had very many interviews with Slater, begs respectfully to state his absolute belief in Slater's innocence.

May it therefore please the Right Honourable the Secretary of State for Scotland to take this Memorial into his most favourable consideration, and thereafter to advise his Most Gracious Majesty to exercise his royal prerogative to the effect of commuting the sentence passed upon the prisoner, or to do otherwise as in the circumstances may seem just. And your Memorialist will ever pray.

EWING SPIERS, 190 West George Street, Glasgow, Oscar Slater's Solicitor.

Dated this seventeenth day of May, One thousand nine hundred and nine.

APPENDIX IV

DEPOSITION OF AGNES BROWN

At Glasgow, the thirty-first day of December, One thousand nine hundred and eight years.
In presence of Arthur Thomson Glegg, Esq., advocate, Sheriff-Substitute of Lanarkshire,
Compeared Agnes Brown, who, being solemnly sworn and examined,declares—

I am thirty years of age, a school teacher, and reside at 48 Grant Street, Glasgow.

On Monday, 21st December, 1908, about 7.8 p.m., I left the house there to attend evening classes in Dunard Street School. I went west along Grant Street to West Cumberland Street, and turned north along the east side of that street till I came to West Princes Street. I was in the act of stepping off the foot-pavement there to cross West Princes Street at an angle towards Carrington Street (a north-westerly direction) when two men came rushing past me from the direction of George's Road. They were on foot pavement (south foot pavement of West Princes Street). They were going very quickly, and the one nearest me came against me in passing; he merely touched me. He never spoke, however, and both continued running west along West Princes Street. They kept on the foot pavement for a little distance, and then they crossed to the centre of the street.

I stood for a moment at the corner of Carrington Street to see where they went, and they turned down Rupert Street towards Great Western Road. I then passed down Carrington Street to Great Western Road, but I saw no more of them. In crossing that road I saw the time on a clock in a chemist's shop — that it was then 7.12.

I returned home from my classes shortly after ten o'clock and then learnt of Miss Gilchrist's murder from my two sisters.

I did not at the time associate the two men with the murder, but next morning, after reading a description in the *Glasgow Herald* of a man who was said to have left deceased's house, I thought he might be one of the two men referred to.

I did not see the face of either man, but, so far as I could make out. they were each about thirty years of age, and about 5 feet 9 inches in height. The one next me was of medium build, with dark hair, and seemed to be clean shaven. He wore a three-quarter length grey-coloured overcoat — I think tweed — dark trousers, probably brown, dark tweed cap without flaps, and had both hands in his coat pockets as he ran away. I took no notice of his boots.

The man furthest from me was of medium build, but seemed to be squarer than the other man. He had very dark hair, probably jet black, well groomed and glossy, and was bareheaded.

He wore a navy blue overcoat with velvet collar, dark trousers, and black boots.

He had also a stand-up white collar, which seemed very clean, and carried something in his left hand, the one furthest from me.

I could not say what this was. It might have been a walking- stick, but I thought it looked clumsier than a walking-stick. _

I know the house which was occupied by Miss Gilchrist.

It is about 200 yards east from the corner of West Cumberland Street and Princes Street, where the two men ran past me.

All which I declare to be truth.

AGNES BROWN.
A. T. GLEGG.

———

Re-examined, says —

I adhere to the above statement as correct, and have to add that on Sunday, 21st February, I saw in the Central Police Office prisoner, Oscar Slater.

He was then dressed in a grey Melton overcoat with velvet collar, and was bareheaded.

I recognised him as one of the two men I had seen running away on the Monday night in question. He was bareheaded when I saw him running away, and the man who was with him was wearing a dark, close-fitting cap.

It is possible that Slater might be wearing another coat under the Melton overcoat, as the latter is large enough to cover another overcoat.

I also recognised Slater by his profile. I did not get a front view of his face, but I picked him out of a number of men, twelve to fourteen, as I think, in the police office, and I have not the slightest doubt about him.

It was not only by his profile and back view but the shape of his neck and ears and square shoulders.

I did not see Slater with a cap or hat when he was running away, but the man who was with him had a cap like the dark greenish cap shown me.

I think the second man resembles a man whom I had seen repeatedly in Grant Street, always between seven and eight. That street runs parallel with West Princes Street.

I have seen Miss Gilchrist frequently at her back bedroom window, and I have seen her lift the window. I cannot say that I saw her put anything out. These occasions were when she seemed to be dressing.

Also truth.

AGNES BROWN.

APPENDIX V

Act of Adjournal Relative to Capital Sentences.

At Edinburgh, the first day of June, Nineteen hundred and nine.

Present—

The Right Hon. the Lord Justice-General.
The Right Hon. the Lord Justice-Clerk.
The Right Hon. the Lord Kinnear.
The Hon. Lord Guthrie.

The Lord Justice-General, Lord Justice-Clerk, and Lords Commissioners of Justiciary, by virtue of the powers conferred upon the Court by an Act passed in the third session of the second Parliament of King Charles the Second, entituled "Act concerning the Regulations of Judicatories," and "The Criminal Procedure (Scotland) Act, 1887," 50 & 51 Vict. cap. 35, do hereby enact and declare that from and after the passing hereof the mode of pronouncing and recording the sentence of death shall be as follows, videlicit:—

1. After the verdict of the jury finding the pannel guilty has been recorded, the judge or judges present shall sign the sentence of death on a paper separate from the record, and immediately thereafter the presiding judge shall pronounce sentence. The said sentence may be wholly written or partly written and partly printed.

2. Immediately thereafter the clerk shall engross the said sentence in the record, and the judge or judges present shall sign the same.

3. It shall not be necessary that the pannel should be present in Court after the presiding judge shall have pronounced sentence.

4. The Court shall not proceed to other business until the said sentence has been engrossed in the record and signed as above provided.

The said Lords ordain this Act to be recorded in the Books of Adjournal and printed.

DUNEDIN, I.P.D.

APPENDIX VI

COPY of STATEMENTS submitted to the Secretary for Scotland, and of the Evidence taken at the Inquiry held by the Sheriff of Lanarkshire, on the 23rd, 24th, and 25th April, 1914.

Scottish Office,
Whitehall,
8th April, 1914.

Sir,—

As you are aware, the Secretary for Scotland has recently received through Mr. David Cook, Writer, Glasgow, certain information bearing upon the case of Oscar Slater, who was convicted of murder in the High Court, Edinburgh, on 6th]May, 1909, and sentenced to death, which sentence was afterwards commuted to penal servitude for life. The information in question is submitted by Detective Lieutenant Trench, of the Glasgow Police Force, and is of such a nature as in the Secretary for Scotland's opinion to call for full inquiry. Mr. M'Kinnon Wood understands with satisfaction that you are prepared to conduct an inquiry into these matters, and I am accordingly to transmit to you Mr. Trench's 'statement and relative documents, and to intimate to you that the Secretary for Scotland appoints you to inquire and report thereon for his consideration.

In the opinion of the Secretary for Scotland, as advised, the inquiry should be Conducted in private, should be limited to questions of fact, and should in no way relate to the conduct of the trial, a view in which he understands you concur, but subject to these limitations it is his desire that you should exercise your own discretion as to the conduct of the inquiry.

I am to add that the expenses of the inquiry will be defrayed from the Vote for Law Charges, &c., in Scotland.

Mr. M'Kinnon Wood will be glad to receive in due course your formal acceptance of the appointment herein intimated, and should there be any matters on which you desire further information or guidance he will be pleased to give them his consideration.

I am, &c.,

(Signed) John Lamb.
James G. Millar, Esq., K.C.,
Sheriff of Lanarkshire, Glasgow.

———————————————

Sheriff's Chambers,
County Buildings, Glasgow,
27th April, 1914.

Sir,—

In terms of your letter of the 8th instant, I received instructions to hold an inquiry into certain information bearing upon the case of Oscar Slater, who was convicted of murder in the High Court, Edinburgh, on 6th May, 1909, which was submitted to you by Detective Lieutenant Trench, of the Glasgow Police Force, through Mr. David Cook, Writer, Glasgow. The inquiry was to be conducted in private, limited to questions of fact, and should in no way relate to the conduct of the trial.

On receiving these instructions I communicated with Captain Stevenson, Chief Constable of the Glasgow Police, and Mr. J. N. Hart, Procurator-Fiscal. At interviews with these gentlemen they promised me every assistance.

The method of the inquiry was as follows:— As it was an extra- judicial one, the witnesses were not put on oath, but they were warned to tell the truth.

The only persons present were the witness, Mr. Andrew Sandilands, my clerk, and myself. I put questions to the witnesses and dictated the purport of the answers to Mr. Sandilands, who took it down in longhand. At the conclusion of the statement it was read over to the witness and signed by him as being true.

With regard to the manner of those making statements, I think it is enough to say that Miss Birrell and Miss Brown seemed to me to be very intelligent, careful, and trustworthy witnesses. Mrs. Gillon, Miss Mary Barrowman, and Mr. MacBrayne seemed to me to be honest and anxious to tell the truth. I should further say that Miss Birrell, Mrs. Gillon, and certain of the police witnesses exhibited signs of great surprise when Lieutenant Trench's statements were read to them.

With these explanations I beg humbly to report the statements made at the inquiry for your consideration.

I return Lieutenant Trench's precognition, with the accompanying papers which you sent to me.

I have, &c.,

(Signed) James G. Millar.

The Right Hon. T. M'Kinnon Wood, M.P., Secretary for Scotland,
Scottish Office, Whitehall, London,

Statement of Detective Lieutenant Trench Submitted to

John Thomson Trench (45), Detective Lieutenant Glasgow Police Force, Central Division, says:—

I joined the Glasgow Police Force as constable in May, 1893. I have been promoted from time to time. My last promotion was in November, 1912, when I received my commission as Lieutenant of Police.

The murder of Miss Gilchrist having taken place in the Western District, the police of that Division were first on the scene with regard to investigation. The matter being a grave one, the assistance of the Central Division was necessary. I was one of the officers deputed to make certain inquiries. Latterly the case was practically taken from the Western, and all investigations, &c., were made by officials of the Central Division. On the night of the murder. Superintendent Ord and Lieutenant Gordon visited Gilchrist's house. On their return to the Central, Gordon gave such information as he had gleaned. I was one of the officers present. Keith was another. Along with Keith I went to the door of the house. We did not enter. At this time the only description of the wanted man which we had to go upon was the description to be found in No. 1 of the Inventory herewith. (It will be noted that the description is meagre indeed.)

I am aware that on 22nd December, the day after the murder. Superintendent Douglas, along with Detectives Pyper and Dornan, drove in a taxi- cab to the house of A.B.* I am also aware that they did so in view of the information supplied by Nellie Lambie. I have endeavoured from time to time to elicit what took place in A.B.'s house, but I am without information.

*The letters A.B. are substituted for the name throughout. Certain passages in the statement relating to A.B. have been omitted, and these omissions are marked by asterisks.

On 23rd December I was instructed by Chief Superintendent Orr to visit and take a statement from Miss Birrell, 19 Blythswood Drive. I had particular instructions to question her with regard to A.B. and as to what Lambie said when she visited her house on the night of the murder. I visited Miss Birrell, and from her received the statement word for word as contained in her precognition No. 2 of the Inventory. On receiving the statement I returned to the Central Police Office. I told Superintendent Orr and Superintendent Ord what Miss Birrell had said. Chief Superintendent Orr seemed impressed with the statement, and remarked "This is the first real clue we have got." I was instructed to write out the statement. I did so. In handing that statement to Superintendent Ord, he said, "I have been ringing up Douglas (that is. Superintendent Douglas, of the Western), and he is convinced that A.B. had nothing to do with it."

Up to this point there had been no mention of a man with a peculiarly twisted nose, and no mention of a Donegal hat.

On Thursday, 4th December, the girl Barrowman came into the case. At that time she was living at 9 Seamore Street. At the same address there resided Detective M'Gimpsey of the Northern Division, now Lieutenant M'Gimpsey of the Central Division.

Reference is here made to No. 3 of the Inventory. For the first time a man with a nose slightly turned to the right comes into the case, but it will be noticed that the word "Donegal," somewhat glibly used by Lambie and Barrowman at the trial, has not come into any of the descriptions. I will deal with how the word "Donegal" came into the case.

A comparison of Lambie's description with Barrowman's description is significant.

A reference to No. 3 of the Inventory shows that the police evidently believed that the man whom Barrowman had seen was not the same man as had left the house when Lambie entered. In point of fact, the police first believed that there were two men connected with the crime. Latterly the two men became one — Oscar Slater. I particularly draw attention to page 299 of the book of the trial, and to the portion underlined.*

* This and subsequent similar reference.s are to the first edition of the present Report.— Ed.

On 25th December a man named Allan M'Lean, who was a witness at the trial, called at the Central Police Station and made the statement, a copy of which is No. 4 of Inventory. But for M'Lean's call. Slater's name would in my view never have been connected with the tragedy. The pawn ticket referred to in the statement was proved on inquiry to relate to a brooch which at no time was the property of Miss Gilchrist. The brooch was in pawn on the day of the murder. I wish particularly to draw attention to the fact that following

M'Lean's call the machinery was put in motion to find Slater in order to clear up the matter of the brooch. Of course every possible suggestion that might lead to a result was followed up.

Detective Inspector Powell was sent with Allan M'Lean to search for Slater, and it militated against Slater that Powell did not there and then interview him. M'Lean only knew Slater as "Oscar," and Powell was despatched to make inquiries with regard to a Mr. Oscar. In point of fact, had Powell been bold enough to have knocked at Slater's door, he would have seen Slater, and the matter could have been cleared up, at least so far as the brooch was concerned. I refer to No. 5 of Inventory — Powell's statement. He was not examined as a witness. In this connection I also refer to the evidence of the porters, John Cameron and John Mackay, No. 13 of Inventory. It will be seen that they were engaged on the 25th of December by Slater between the hours of six and seven o'clock. In other words, Slater made arrangements for his departure before M'Lean had been at the Central Police Office and before Powell had made such inquiries as he did.

Until 2 p.m. on Saturday, 26th December, no reference from any witness can be had relating to a man with a Donegal hat. The Donegal hat came info the case not from Barrowman, Adams, or Lambie, or from any other Crown witness, unless M'Lean mentioned that Slater was in the habit of wearing a Donegal hat. Further, by this time there was every opportunity to find out what manner of clothing and what particular manner of head covering Slater was in the habit of wearing. It is only too significant that the two vital witnesses, Lambie and Barrowman, had given their statements describing a man with a head covering entirely different to a Donegal hat. I refer to No. 6 of Inventory issued on Saturday, 26th December, from which it will be seen that by this date a fairly accurate description of Slater had been procured somewhere and somehow.

When it was learned by the police that Slater had fled, or rather believed by them that he had done so, it was assumed that he had gone to London. The only authority for such an assumption is to be found in the statement of Lieutenant Gordon, who had interviewed Slater's maid. Comparing the statement referred to with Gordon's evidence at the trial (page 176), underlined, discloses that Gordon materially altered the statement made to him by the maid. This point is of vital importance. Detective Anderson was on Saturday morning, 26th December, instructed to make inquiries at the various railway stations. Reference is made to his statement, No. 7 of Inventory. It will be seen that Anderson obtained information that two railway tickets to London for the 9.5 p.m. train on Friday night had been issued to a man 31 to 32 years of age, 5 feet 4 or 5 inches in height, dark hair and complexion, light dark moustache. This description was supplied by the witness Brown, the booking clerk who issued the tickets. No inquiry was made regarding Liverpool by the police. It will be noticed that the police did not direct their attention to passengers who might have booked for Liverpool.

It is now well known that on the night when Slater and his woman left Glasgow there was a through carriage to Liverpool attached to the 9.5 p.m. train. This was Christmas night, hence the unusual practice. I also know that when Slater's agent was making inquiries regarding the through carriage, he was told repeatedly by various officials in the Central Station that it was rubbish, there was no through carriage. In that connection it must be noted that Slater all along persisted that he travelled in a through carriage. Latterly an official was found who did remember that there was a through carriage on Christmas night. It is of the utmost importance to have regard to the fact that only two tickets were issued at the Central Station for Liverpool for the 9.5 train; that only two persons left the train at Liverpool (Slater and his woman). I refer to No. 8 of the Inventory, being telegram from Chief of Police, Liverpool, to Chief of Police, Glasgow; No. 9 of Inventory, telegram from Chief of Police, Liverpool, to Chief of Police, Glasgow; No.

10 of Inventory, being statements of Detective Chief Inspector Duckworth and Detective Sub-Inspector Bell, of the Liverpool City Police.

It is beyond doubt that if Slater and his woman travelled to Liverpool with London tickets, four people must have left the train at Liverpool — the persons who travelled to Liverpool with Liverpool tickets, and Slater and his woman, who are said to have travelled with London tickets. It is self- evident that only two persons travelled to Liverpool. These were Slater and his woman.

On arriving at Liverpool, Slater and his woman proceeded to the North Western Hotel. Reference is here made again to the telegram and statements, which disclose that Slater made no secret of who he was, where he was going, and where he had come from. Max Rattman produced at the trial a letter dated 26th December, 1908. The letter will be found on page 301 of the book. It will be noted that, with the exception of the letter to Rattman, all the other evidence was suppressed or at least not brought forward. Emphasis was laid by the prosecution on the fact that on the steamer Slater had changed his name to Otto Sando. It is worthy of comment that if he was changing his name with a purpose, he would not have used a name anything like Oscar. In fact, his baggage had the initials O.S. \Mien the baggage arrived at the Central Police Station each package bore labels, "Lime Street, Liverpool." I read the labels. There seems nothing peculiar in Slater changing his name on the steamer. He was known in Glasgow as Anderson, and in Edinburgh as Smitz. My experience as a detective warrants me in saying that men who, like Slater, live on their wits not infrequently change their names.

The result of my inquiries convince me that, so far from Slater absconding from justice, his departure for Liverpool to catch the "Lusitania" was as open as daylight. Slater's maid furnished Gordon with an address in London where she was going to reside. The Glasgow Police communicated with the London Police asking that inquiry should be made of the maid in the hope that a more definite statement as to where Slater had gone would be forthcoming. On 28th December a telegram was received that the maid had stated that Slater and his woman had gone to Liverpool and were travelling to America. The maid, it may be mentioned, is anything but a fluent English speaker. It was in this way that the Glasgow Police directed inquiry at Liverpool.

I refer to No. 11 of Inventory — statements by Mary Cooper and Catherine Fitzpatrick. These persons were not examined at the trial. They wore not even on the Crown List. Every one who has seen Slater is impressed with his distinct foreign appearance. I draw attention to the fact that no witness adduced at the trial who had seen the supposed murderer spoke of him as of foreign appearance. Cooper speaks of him as a German Jew.

On 3rd January, 1909, along with Detective Keith, I visited Nellie Lambie at 15 South Kinning Place, at the house of her aunt. She was lodging there. I had with me a sketch of Oscar Slater which I had received from Superintendent Ord. I showed the sketch to Lambie. She could not identify. She said she did not know him. The sketch was a fair representation of Slater, and had evidently been drawn by some one who knew him. Although I had not spoken to Lambie, I was aware, having taken Miss Birrell's statement, that she had declared that A.B. was the man. I touched on A.B., asking her if she really thought he was the man she saw. Her answer was, "It's gey funny if it wasn't him I saw."...My conclusion after meeting Lambie was that if she had had any one to support her she would have sworn to A.B. So much impressed was I that I mentioned the fact to Superintendent Ord next morning, asking if he thought that A.B. might not be the man. His only answer was, "Douglas has cleared up all that, what can we do?"

Compare Lambie's evidence, page 64 of the book (underlined), with the statement which she made on the night of the murder and which she persisted in on the 3rd of January. Her evidence cannot be characterised as a mistake. There is another word for it. Lambie knew A.B. as a visitor to the house. Her identification of him is more valuable because of that fact. If A.B. was the man whom Lambie saw leaving the house as she entered, the whole mystery {as yet unexplained) of how the murderer obtained access to the house is cleared up.

I am forced to the conclusion that Mary Barrowman was not at or near Miss Gilchrist's close at the time the murderer rushed therefrom. I have had from her employer and from his sister an emphatic statement. No. 15 of Inventory, that Barrowman did not deliver a message on the night of the 21st at Howitt's house. In the original statement supplied by Barrowman to the police. No. 12 of Inventory, she makes no mention of having been at a Band of Hope meeting. In the statement I find as follows, viz.: — "Shortly after 7 p.m. on Monday, 21st December, 1908, I was on my way from the shop with a message to Cleveland Street, and was passing along West Princes Street, and when near close No. 47 (where Mr. Adams resides) I saw a man running out of the close No. 49, and he looked towards St. George's Road and immediately turned westwards. I wondered what was wrong, and turned round and watched him, following him a few yards, and saw that he turned into West Cumberland Street, running all the time.

"I went and delivered my message and returned to the shop by Woodland Road, and after leaving our shop at 8 p.m. I went to my brother's shop at 480 St. Vincent Street, and while going there I again passed along West Princes Street, and saw a crowd opposite No. 49, and learned of the murder, and I then thought of the man I had seen running out of the close there. He was a man about 28 or 30 years of age, tall and slim build, no hair on face, long features, nose slightly turned to the right, dressed in a fawn overcoat like waterproof, dark trousers, brown boots, and tweed cloth hat of respectable appearance.

"I did not see any other person near the close or about, but I think I could recognise the man again, although I could not say that I ever saw him before."

I refer to Barrowman's evidence, pages 108 to 115 of the book, in particular the passages underlined. If one would put themselves to the trouble of comparing the statements, it cannot be doubted but that Barrowman either lied in Tier original statement or lied at the trial.

There is no reference in her original statement to any Band of Hope meeting, nor is there any reference to a man knocking up against her. The statement with regard to the knocking up against her is either of her own invention or must have been put into her mouth.

I have drawn in red ink on the plan at the end of the book the route which Barrowman swore she followed from her employer's shop at Barrington Drive to Howitt's house at Cleveland Street. A glance will suffice to let one understand that she chose a most roundabout and circuitous means of arriving at her destination. I have gone over the ground and, as near as may be, Barrowman added somewhere between 10 and 15 minutes to her journey. In short, if she had chosen the natural route she would not have been in West Princes Street at all, unless to cross the street, but not at a point near to Gilchrist's house.

Couple the circuitous route which undoubtedly Barrowman says she followed with the fact that she neither saw Adams, Lambie, Miss Adams nor Mrs. Liddell, the four people who rushed out hot haste upon the heels of the murderer. None of them saw Barrowman, notwithstanding the fact that you will find in her evidence that she was there for such a length of time as to enable her to follow the man for a certain distance, turn again, passing !Miss Gilchrist's close.

Instead of finding anything or any one to corroborate Barrowman that she was at or near the close when the murderer left the close, everything goes to prove that her story of having seen the man was a cock-and-bull story of a young girl who was somewhat late in getting home and who wished to take the edge off by a little sensationalism.

Slater on arriving in Glasgow had with him nine packages: a number of these were trunks, and had not been opened. They were sealed by the American police. I was present when the packages were opened. Every package and trunk was carefully and systematically packed. A very considerable amount of time must have been spent in the packing. The linen and fine underwear were folded with camphor interposing between the layers. In no sense did the trunks reveal a hurried departure.

From a trunk I lifted the hammer upon which the Crown built their theory of the commission of the crime. Alongside of the hammer were other tools which go to make up the card bought by Slater. The hammer weighed one-half pound. I saw nothing on the shaft to indicate to me that it had been either scraped or cleaned. For what it may be worth I look upon the hammer as a most unlikely instrument to have caused the injuries. Like Dr. Adams, who was not used as a witness although the first medical man on the scene, I lean to the view that Miss Gilchrist was done to death by a chair.

(Signed) John Thomson Trench.

Documents Produced by Detective Lieutenant Trench AND Referred to in his Statement.

No. (1).

9.40 p.m. An old lady was murdered in her house at 15 Queen's Terrace between 7 and 7.10 p.m. to-day by a man from 25 to 30, 5 feet 7 or 8, thinks clean shaven. Wore a long grey overcoat and dark cap.

Robbery appears to have been the object of the murderer, as a number of boxes in a bedroom were opened and left lying on the floor. A large-sized crescent-shaped gold brooch, set with diamonds, large diamonds in centre, graduating towards the points, is missing and may be in possession of the murderer. The diamonds are set in silver. No trace of the murderer has been got. Constables will please warn booking clerks at railway stations, as the murderer will have bloodstains on his clothing. Also warn Pawns on opening regarding brooch and keep a sharp look-out.

No. (2).

Margaret Birrell, late of 19 Blythswood Drive, now residing at 6 Kelvinside Terrace, or 275 Wilton Street, Glasgow:—

I am niece of the late Marion Gilchrist, who resided at 15 Queen's Terrace, West Princes Street. My mother was a sister of the deceased. Miss Gilchrist was not on good terms with her relations. Few, if any, visited her...I can never forget the night of the murder. Miss Gilchrist's servant, Nellie Lambie, came to my door about 7.15. She was excited. She pulled the bell violently. On the door being opened she rushed into the house and exclaimed, "Oh, Miss Birrell, Miss Birrell, Miss Gilchrist has been murdered, she is lying dead in the dining-room, and oh, Miss Birrell, I saw the man who did it." I replied, "My God, Nellie, this is awful. Who was it, do you know him?" Nellie replied, "Oh, Miss Birrell, I think it was A.B. I am sure that it was "A.B." I said to her, "My God, Nellie, don't say that...Unless you are very sure of it, Nellie, don't say that." She again repeated to me that she was sure it was A.B. The same evening Detectives Pyper and Dornan visited me, and I learned from them that she had told them that it was A.B. I told a number of my friends about it, including a member of the Glasgow Corporation, who communicated with Chief Superintendent Orr. On Wednesday afternoon, 23rd December, 1908, Detective Trench visited me, and I told him exactly what Lambie had told me.

No. (3).

Thursday, 24th December, 1908, 7 p.m.

Description of a man who was seen to leave the close leading to Miss Gilchrist's house at 15 Queen's Terrace, West Princes Street, shortly after 7 p.m. on 21st instant (the night of the murder), and run westwards and turn into West Cumberland Street.

A man 28 to 30 years, tall and thin, no hair on face, nose slightly turned to one side (thinks right), dressed in fawn-coloured overcoat (thinks waterproof), dark trousers, tweed cloth hat, latest make, and thinks of dark colour, brown boots.

This man may have some connection with the murder but he should not be confounded with the man seen to leave the house by the servant and Mr. Adams. If any of your officers or constables should recognise this man from description, send immediate information to Detective Department.

Remark by Detective Trench:

Note. — The above was circulated throughout the country from the description supplied by Mary Barrowman. It will be noted that it is slightly different from her description, viz., "long features" is omitted and never appears again. Instead of "nose slightly turned to right," it now reads "nose slightly turned "to one side, thinks right." Instead of "fawn overcoat" it now reads "fawn-coloured overcoat," &c., &c. The footnote clearly shows that, even allowing that Barrowman saw the man at the time and place stated, he was not thought to be the same man seen by Lambie and Adams.

No. (4).

From Copying Book No. 45, page 1, Headquarters, Glasgow City Police.

Murder of Marion Gilchrist.

Allan M'Lean, a cycle dealer of 100 Agnes Street, Maryhill, says: — I am a member of the Sloper Club, 24 India Street. During the past few weeks a man named Oscar Slater, a German Jew about 30 years of age, 5 feet 8 inches in height, clean shaven, nose slightly twisted to one side, has been frequenting the club and has latterly become a member of it. I noticed that after the murder of Miss Gilchrist on 21st instant he did not return to the club, and on hearing that he had been offering a pawn ticket for a valuable diamond brooch for sale which was alleged to have been pledged for £50 on the day of the murder, I, on Friday, 25th instant, went to the Detective Department, Central Police Office, and reported the matter. I didn't know the number of the close or the street where Slater resided, but I stated that I would be able to point them out.

Between 7 and 8 o'clock the same night I accompanied Detective Inspector Powell to 69 St. George's Road and pointed out that close as the one where Slater was residing under the name of Anderson. I know that when Slat«r was proposed as a member of the club that he gave his address as 136 Renfrew Street, though he had not left there for some time. I afterwards heard that Slater had left Glasgow a short time after I had pointed out the close where he lived to Inspector Powell.

No. (5).

William Powell, Detective Inspector, Central Police Office, says — I was instructed by Superintendent Ord to accompany the witness M'Lean on Friday, 25th December, and he would point out a close where a man Slater was residing. I accompanied him, and he pointed out 69, St. George's Road. He then left me. I went into the close and called at a Miss Bernstein's house, as I knew her well. I spoke to Miss Bernstein in her house and also to her maid, and the latter told me that she had seen a man answering the description of the man I gave them coming down from Anderson's house on the top flat. I returned to the Detective Department and reported to Superintendent Ord, who arranged for me to go to Slater's house at night in company with the night officers. About 11.30 p.m. Detectives Lyon and Millican came to my house, and I accompanied them to 69 St. George's Road. We went upstairs and knocked at the door of Anderson's house and asked to be admitted. After some time we gained admittance. I asked the servant where Oscar was, but she did not seem to understand what I said. I then asked her where the man of the house was, and she said "No man live here." I then asked where Madame was, and the servant replied, "Madame away for night." I asked her who was with her, and she (the servant) replied, "A gentleman." We closed the door of the house and commenced a search of same. We did not find any men's clothing in the house, but a wrapper for some small parcel bearing Slater's name on it. I asked the servant, showing her the wrapper, if she knew whom that was for, and she replied, "A friend of Madame's," and added that they were away together. We then went downstairs, and I made inquiries at White's house on the second flat. The servant there informed me that shortly after 8 o'clock that night luggage had been carried downstairs from Fowlis' house and from Anderson's house (both on top flat), and that Mrs. Bernstein's maid had seen the man Slater cross the road and join a woman, who was supposed to be "Madame," and go down the street together. I then sent Lyon and Millican to the Sloper Club in India Street, and they returned in about three-quarters of an hour and informed me that Slater had been introduced into the Sloper Club by a man named Cameron, who resided in Cambridge Street, and that Slater's address had been given as 136 Renfrew Street, c/o M'Donald. We proceeded to Mrs. M'Donald's house, but she informed us that she had no lodger residing there. We then proceeded to Cambridge Street, where we located Cameron, who informed me that he had called at Slater's house at 69 St. George's Road about 8.10 p.m. on Friday, 25th December, 1908, and was informed by the servant that a gentleman had called and taken him away. I then questioned Cameron about the pawn ticket for a brooch and he told me that he had no pawn ticket, but that Slater had given him a pawn ticket two or three days ago for a brooch that had been pledged in Liddell's pawn office to sell for him. He had been unable to sell it and had returned it to him.

No. (6).

Saturday, 26th December, 1908.

2 p.m. Wanted for identification for the murder at Queen's Terrace on 21st instant, "Oscar Slater," sometimes takes the name of Anderson, a German, 30 years of age, 5 feet 8, stout, square shouldered, dark hair, clean shaven, may have few days' growth of moustache. Nose has been broken and is marked. Dressed when last seen in dark jacket suit, cap with flaps fastening with button at top; sometimes wears a soft "Donegal" hat; has a light and a dark coloured overcoat, either of which he may be wearing.

May be accompanied by a woman about 30, tall, stout, good looking, dark hair, dressed usually in dark or blue costume, heavy set of furs, sable colour, and large blue or black hat with green feathers, residing till yesterday at 69 St. George's Road.

No. (7).

Thomas Anderson, Detective Officer, Central District, says — On making inquiry at the booking office of the Central Railway Station on Saturday, 26th December, 1908, the booking clerk informed me that he had issued two single tickets to London for the 9.5 p.m. train on Friday, 25th December, 1908, to a man (thinks) 31 to 32 years of age, 5 feet 4 or 5 inches in height, dark hair and complexion, and (he thought) slight dark moustache. He did not see the second passenger.

No. (8).

>

Handed in at Liverpool at 4.19 p.m., received here at 4.34 p.m.

To Chief Constable, Glasgow.

Be murder case. Oscar Slater and woman arrived North-Western Hotel early morning 26th instant, left 4 p.m. same day, saying they were sailing for America on "Lusitania." No trace since leaving hotel. Man and woman giving name Mr. and Mrs. Hughes, booked third-class passengers on "Lusitania" and embarked 4.40 p.m. 26th instant. So far failed to get further particulars about these people.

Inquiry being continued.

" Devoir, Liverpool."

No. (9).

Handed in at Liverpool at 6.10 p.m., received here at 6.17 p.m.

To Chief Constable, Glasgow.

Re murder case Two passengers giving names Mr. and Mrs. Otto Sando left Liverpool on 26th instant on "Lusitania" for New York. Sando, whose age and height agree with Slater's description, told shipping officials he was American

Oscar Slater.

citizen, had just come from Glasgow, and had been staying at North- Western Hotel, Liverpool.

Mr. and Mrs. Sando are berthed in second cabin.

"Devoir, Liverpool."

No. (10).

Detective Chief-Inspector Duckworth, Liverpool City Police, says — On receipt of the telegram from the Chief Constable of Glasgow I made inquiry and discovered that only two people came off the Glasgow train, arriving at Lime Street at 3.40 a.m. on 26th instant. They engaged a bedroom in the North- Western Hotel. The man gave the name of Oscar Slater, Glasgow, the woman was supposed to be his wife, but there is no mention in the books to that effect. The chamber-maid had a conversation with the woman, who told her that they were about to sail by the S.S. "Lusitania" for America.

She answered the description of the woman said to be with Slater. They left the hotel about 4 p.m. same day.

Detective Sub-Inspector Bell, Liverpool City Police, says — I beg to report that I have seen Mr. Forsyth, manager of the second-class passenger department for the Cunard Steamship Company, and he stated that he booked a man and woman by the s.s. "Lusitania" for New York. They gave the names of Mr. and Mrs. Otto Sando, and he said that he was an American citizen and had just come from Glasgow, and was staying at the North-Western Hotel. Sando paid £28 and insisted on having an inside* berth. They sailed on the "Lusitania" and are berthed in second cabin "C. 1." Mr. Forsyth cannot describe the man, but the age and height agree with that of Slater; the woman he did not see.

* Sic. Qy. outside.—Ed.

On 26th instant, about 3.50, John Williamson, driver of one of the station cabs, took a man and woman from the Great Western Hotel to the "Lusitania," but he cannot describe either of them, except that the man wore a soft felt hat and they had three pieces of luggage. He pointed out that the initials of Sando and Slater are the same.

No. (11).

Criminal Investigation Department, 7th January, 1909.

Mary Cooper (30), 19 Windsor Street, Glasgow, states—

I am shopwoman in the receiving shop of William Gardner & Company, Ltd., 26 St. George's Road, Glasgow (Holm Laundry, Paisley).

On 12th November, 1908, a man who gave his name and address, A. Anderson, 69 St. George's Road, opened an account with me, and on that date we received from him per our message girl, laundry work for which we charged 12s. 6d., which was paid on the goods being delivered. On 18th November, 1908, we received work value 5s. 8d., on 26th November, 1908, work value 5s. 8d., on 9th December, 1908, work value 6s. 8d., and on 17th December, 1908, work value 5s. 0d., which last item has not been paid.

In the last lot of laundry goods we received from the Anderson's house was six very fine men's shirts, which Anderson asked me to have sent him in a box. They were the best shirts I ever saw. These goods were delivered at his house by next witness on Saturday afternoon, 19th December, 1908, and on Monday, 21st December, 1908 (the date of the murder of Miss Gilchrist), between 3 and 4 p.m., Anderson called at the shop and said there was a shirt short in the laundry goods, that the shirt cost 16s. 6d., and as he was going out of town he must have the shirt. He was very haughty and abrupt in his manner, and I informed him that I would communicate at once with the laundry at Paisley regarding his shirt, and he left the shop.

Shortly afterwards Mr. Anderson's servant called at the shop with the same complaint, and she said Mr. Anderson was going to London and must have his shirt. The same evening the missing shirt arrived from Paisley, and I immediately sent the message girl up to Anderson's house with the shirt and our account for 5s. 0d. She returned and told me she was to call the following day (Tuesday, 22nd December, 1908) for the money and washing, which she did, and was then informed by the servant that they would have no laundry goods till after the holidays. As they were fairly good customers, I did not insist on payment of the 5s. 0d. at the time.

Anderson was very particular about the dressing of his shirts, and mentioned several times that they cost him 16s. 6d. each in London, that he could not get them dressed as well in Glasgow as he could in London, and would not grudge an extra penny to have them well dressed.

Anderson appeared to me to be a German Jew, and had a crooked or twisted nose and was clean shaven. He was always well dressed and of a dominant manner. I could identify him again,

———

Catherine Fitzpatrick (16), 28 Harlaw Street, Port Dundas, Glasgow, states—

I am a message girl in the employment of William Gardiner & Company, Limited, 26 St. George's Road, and I deliver and collect the laundry goods at the house of Anderson, 69 St. George's Road. All the dealings I had was with the servant, and I never saw Anderson himself.

No. (12).

Mary Barrowman (14), a message girl with Malcolm M'Callum, Boot and Shoe Maker, at 333 Great Western Road, and residing with her parents at No. 9 Seamore Street, says—

Shortly after 7 p.m. on Monday, 21st December, 1908, I was on my way from the shop with a message to Cleveland Street, and was passing along West Princes Street, and when near close No. 47 (where Mr. Adams lives), I saw a man running out of the close No. 49, and he looked towards St. George's Road and immediately turned westwards. I wondered what was wrong, and turned round and watched him, following a few yards, and saw that he turned into West Cumberland Street, running all the time.

I went and delivered my message and returned to the shop by Woodlands Road, and after leaving our shop at 8 p.m. I went to my brother's shop at 480 St. Vincent Street, and while going there I again passed along West Princes Street and saw a crowd opposite No. 49 and learned of the murder, and I then thought of the man I had seen running out of the close there. He was a man about 28 or 30 years of age, tall and slim build, no hair on face, long features, nose slightly turned to the right, dressed in a fawn overcoat like waterproof, dark trousers, brown boots, and tweed cloth hat of respectable appearance.

I did not see any other person near the close or about, but I think I could recognise the man again, although I could not say that I ever saw him before.

No. (13).

John Cameron, a city porter residing at 7 Park Place, Stockwell Street, Glasgow, says—

On Friday, 25th December, 1908, between the hours of 6 and 7 o'clock, a man whom he thinks he could recognise again, engaged him at Central Railway Station to remove luggage from Anderson's house at 69 St. George's Road to the Central Station for the 9.5 p.m. train going south.

I went to the above address at 8.15 p.m. There was two women and a man in the house. I received ten pieces of luggage not addressed. I conveyed these on a barrow to the Central Railway Station. I was not long there when the gentleman and one of the ladies whom I had seen at the house joined me and asked me to label the luggage: I think Liverpool.

One of the railway porters whose name I do not know assisted me to put the luggage into the luggage van attached to the 9.5 p.m. train going to England. The man paid me 4s. for the removal of his luggage.

John M'Kay, 22 James Watt Street, Glasgow, was along with me and can corroborate.

No. (14).

William Gordon, Detective Lieutenant, Central District, says—

On Saturday, between 11 and 12 o'clock midday, I called at the house at 69 St. George's Road, accompanied by Inspector Powell. When going upstairs we passed two foreign-looking ladies on the stair.

I interrogated the servant, a German girl, who gave her name as Catherine Smaltz. She told me that Anderson or Slater and Madame Junio had left the house the previous evening (Friday), 25th December, 1908, and she did not know where they were going to first — she thought London. While I was in the house, one of the foreign women returned to the house. I interrogated her and asked her what she was doing in the house and where and who the lady was who was with her. This woman said her name was "Hoppie," then said, "Do you want her?" I said, "Yes." She then ran downstairs and soon returned with the other woman, who gave the name of "Freedman," and said that Mrs. Anderson was her step- sister.

She said she and her friend had arrived from London two days ago and had been living in the Alexandra Hotel, where her sister had visited her. It had been arranged that she and her companion would take possession of Anderson's house, and that she and Anderson was going to Monte Carlo for three weeks. I asked if Anderson had given any address for them in Monte Carlo, and she replied "No," but she was promised a postcard from them, and if I called back on Monday she would be able to furnish me with the address. I received from Smaltz Anderson's address, viz., 36 Albemarle Street, Piccadilly, and that she, Smaltz, lived at 72 Charlotte Street, c/o Anstro.

I called on Monday, 28th December, 1908, in company of Detective Inspector Pyper, of the Western District. Freedman then told me that she had not got a postcard, but that a man had called after our visit and said to the servant that the detectives were after Anderson in reference to a brooch that had been pledged by him and supposed to have been stolen from a woman who had been murdered. I asked who the man was, and she could not tell me. I then pressed her for further particulars regarding Anderson. She told me that when she had called at the house, Anderson asked her to lend him something, as he didn't think he had quite sufficient money, and she gave him £25, and he told her she had the whole house as security except the £4 to some man she could not name. I asked her if she knew Anderson under any other name, and she informed me that Anderson's name was Oscar Slater, that she knew nothing further about him, and that she had met him in London. She said she saw the brooch referred to in possession of her step-sister in London. She said she herself had considerable business in Germany, but had not lived with her husband for two years.

No. (15).

Colin Maccallum (38), 1 Kennedy Drive, Partick.

In December, 1908, I carried on business as a boot. and shoe-maker under the name of N. Maccallum & Son. The firm's address was 333 Great Western Road. The shop is at the corner of Barrington Drive and Great Western Road. My sister, Mary D. Maccallum, assisted me in the shop. Mary Barrowman, who gave evidence in the Slater case, was our message girl. I had a customer named Howat who in December, 1908, resided at 36 Cleveland Street.

Barrowman had been despatched on several occasions with messages to Howitt's house, such as the taking home of repairs, &c.

I remember that some days after the murder of Miss Gilchrist, Barrowman's name was publicly mentioned as an important witness. I saw from the daily paper that the girl was figuring as having seen a man leave Miss Gilchrist's close. I also noticed her statement that she was delivering a pair of boots at Howat's house on the night of the murder. To the best of my knowledge my sister drew my attention to Barrowman's statement as appearing in the papers, and to the fact that Barrowman had not been sent to Howat's house on the night of the murder. I was and am still convinced that she was not sent that message on the night of the murder, but several nights before. To the best of my belief, she delivered the message on Friday, 18th December. I consulted with my sister about the matter at the time. We spoke to Barrowman on the subject. She insisted that she went the message on the night of the murder.

Some time after Barrowman appeared in the case I drew the attention of Detective Inspector Pyper, of the Western District, to the fact. I showed him my books in support of what I said. Mr. Pyper told us not to say anything about it, as it would upset the whole case, and he might get into trouble about it. He impressed upon me not to mention it to any one, as the girl had insisted that she had gone the message on the night of the murder. I am sure she did not go that message on the night of the murder, and the books bore me out.

I was not called to give evidence at the trial, neither was I precognosced by Slater's agent.

I have often spoken on the subject to my sister. I obeyed Detective Pyper's instructions until I had a visit from Mr. Trench. I told him the truth.

My books were in existence up to May, 1913, but were destroyed when we removed from Napiershall Street to my present address. I destroyed them.

———

Mary B. Maccallum (31), 1 Kennedy Drive, Partick.

Corroborates in detail the evidence of her brother, Colin Maccallum.

———

Statements taken from Witnesses at the Inquiry held by the Sheriff of Lanarkshire.

Glasgow, 23rd April, 1914.

Compeared John Thomson Trench (45), Detective Lieutenant, Glasgow Police Force, Central Division, who states — I joined the Glasgow Police Force in May, 1893, as constable, and have been promoted from time to time, and received my commission as Lieutenant of Police in November, 1912. My first information as to the murder of Miss Gilchrist was on the evening of 21st December, 1908. A description of it was given by Superintendent Ord and Lieutenant Gordon, who had visited the scene of the murder. There was a description given to us, which is the description No. 1 referred to in my precognition. The first direct piece of business I had with the inquiry was on Wednesday, 23rd December, 1908, when I was requested by Chief Superintendent Orr to go to 19 Blythswood Drive to see a lady. Miss Birrell, who could give information. I was particularly requested to make inquiry as to a statement which it was said Helen Lambie had made on the night of the murder. I went to Miss Birrell's house and saw her, and obtained a statement from her, and afterwards, when I returned to the Central Police Office, I reduced it to writing and handed it to Superintendent Ord. I have never seen that statement since. The statement No. 2 of the Appendix to my precognition is my recollection of what Miss Birrell said, and was drawn up by me in Mr. Cook's office in the month of February this year. I state positively that Miss Birrell said to me that Helen Lambie on the night of the murder told her that the man she saw leaving the house was A.B. Notwithstanding I am told that both Miss Birrell and Helen Lambie emphatically deny the whole story and express astonishment at it, I adhere to my statement that that was what Miss Birrell told me. I told Superintendent Ord what Miss Birrell had said in presence of Superintendent Orr, and Superintendent Orr remarked, "This is the first real clue we have got." I was instructed to write out the statement, and did so. When I handed the statement to Superintendent Orr he said, "I have been ringing up Douglas" (that is, Superintendent Douglas, of the Western) "and he is convinced that A.B. had nothing to do with it." I was put specially on the murder case on the 27th of December (Tuesday), as shown by my diary, as the case was taken over by the Central Division. Detective Cameron and I went along to Blythswood Drive on 9th January, 1909, by instructions of Superintendent Ord. I went to number 19 to warn Miss Birrell, and Cameron went to number 23 to warn another family of Birrells not to say anything about the story of A.B., as it would do him no good and there was nothing in it. On the 3rd of January, along with Detective Keith, I visited Helen Lambie, taking with me a sketch of Oscar Slater which I had received from Superintendent Ord as an excuse for visiting her. In the course of the talk we had I brought the subject round to A.B., and asked her if she really thought he was the man she saw, and her answer was: "It's gey funny if it was not him I saw." I was so much impressed with her statement that I mentioned the fact to Superintendent Ord next morning, asking if A.B. might not be the man, and his reply was: "Douglas has cleared all that up, and what can we do?" Detective Keith was present during the whole time and must have heard what Helen Lambie said. I have not spoken to him on the matter since. If Helen Lambie positively denies all this, I still adhere to my statement. I have never seen A.B. I did not make any statement previous to the trial, either to the Fiscal or the Agent for the defence, as to what I now say Miss Birrell and Helen Lambie had said to me. I said nothing at all after Slater was condemned to death until he was reprieved, and even then not for a considerable period, when I mentioned it to Mr. Shaughnessy, the agent for Oscar Slater. I did not think much of the incident by itself, and it was only when I discovered other facts that I brought this one up. On the 2nd of January, 1909, I searched Oscar Slater's house after he had left, and found no matches similar to the box of "Runaway" matches which were said to have been discovered in the bedroom in Miss Gilchrist's house subsequent to the murder. I made inquiry at grocers and found that "Runaway" matches are sold in bulk and not in single boxes.

This statement was read over to the witness, and was signed by him as being true.

(Signed)
JOHN T. TRENCH. JAMES G. MILLAR.

———

Glasgow, 23rd April, 1914.

Compeared Margaret Dawson Birrell (49), residing at 61 Rupert Street, Glasgow, who states — I was not called as a witness at the trial of Oscar Slater. At the time of Miss Gilchrist's death I resided at 19

Blythswood Drive, Glasgow. I was in the habit of visiting Miss Gilchrist very seldom. She was not on friendly terms with her relations, on account of an estrangement as to money affairs. I visited her the Saturday previous to her death. She was 83 years of age and quite intelligent, and quite able to look after her affairs. She was active and able to go about by herself. At my visit on Saturday she was praising Helen Lambie for keeping the house clean and tidy. She never remarked about Helen Lambie's visitors, except that she once remarked about Helen Lambie having a sweetheart, a collier. As far as she said anything to me, she seemed perfectly satisfied with Helen Lambie...On the night of the murder, after seven o'clock, Helen Lambie came to my door and rang the bell violently. The maid opened the door, and Nellie Lambie rushed in and screamed out that something dreadful had happened to Miss Gilchrist. She said that she had gone out to get a newspaper, and when she returned she found Mr. Adams at the door. He told her that his sister had heard a noise in Miss Gilchrist's house, and that Helen Lambie had said to him that she thought it might be the pulleys in the kitchen falling. She opened the door of the house and entered, and then she saw a man slip past her and Mr. Adams. She went into the kitchen and saw that there was nothing wrong with the pulleys, and afterwards went into the dining- room and saw Miss Gilchrist lying there on the floor as if she had been knocked down and seriously injured, and then she came along for me at once. I at once sent Helen Lambie back to the house, and followed. At that time there was a gentleman who occupied apartments in my house, named Mr. Charles Cowan. He afterwards left, but returned recently to occupy rooms in my house, and is there now. He heard all that Helen Lambie said, and after she left he accompanied me at once to Miss Gilchrist's house. When I arrived I heard that she was dead. I saw the body lying in the dining-room, but, on the advice of those present, I did not examine it, as the sight was unpleasant. I was directed to go into the bedroom, and there I saw a few small articles of jewellery, of no great value, lying on the dressing table, ranged, as it seemed to me, for the purpose of being speedily picked up after the search was made. I remained in the house a considerable time. I had some talk with Helen Lambie with regard to the arrangements, but as far as I can remember she said nothing further about the man whom she had seen leaving the house. Mr. Cowan accompanied me home, and thereafter returned and took Helen Lambie to the South Side to a house where she was staying that night. Helen Lambie did not say to me that she knew the man. She did not mention to me the name of A.B. when she came along to the house after the murder. At no time did she ever say to me that she thought the man who left the house was A.B. I remember two police officers called on me, I think the day after the murder, and I made a statement to them then. I cannot say when I saw Detective Lieutenant Trench, but I know I saw him. The statement in No. 2 of the Inventory attached to Detective Trench's precognition has been read over to me. It purports to be a statement made by me to Detective Lieutenant Trench on 23rd December, 190Q. I now solemnly declare that I never made such a statement, and all that is contained in it is absolutely false. I did make a statement to Mr. Hart. I cannot remember what was in it, but I am quite certain that I made no statement to him as to Helen Lambie saying to me that the man who left the house was A.B. I never heard of it being said that I had made such a statement until a few days ago, and it took me completely by surprise.

(Signed)
M. DAWSON BIRRELL.
> JAMES G. MILLAR.

———

Glasgow, 23rd April, 1914.

Compeared Charles Frederick Cowan (36), residing at 61 Rupert Street, Glasgow, who states — I lived in apartments in Miss Birrell's house at 19 Blythswood Drive in December, 1908. I was in the house when Helen Lambie came along and informed Miss Birrell of Miss Gilchrist's murder. I was shaving at the time when Helen Lambie came. I heard a violent ring of the bell, followed by another, and then I heard Helen Lambie say that her mistress had been murdered. That is what she said, to the best of my knowledge. Helen Lambie may have made a statement to Miss Birrell that I did not hear, but I certainly did not hear her say that A.B. was the man she met when she returned after the murder to Miss Gilchrist's house. Miss Birrell never said to me that Helen Lambie told her that A.B. was the man she saw. Helen Lambie was told to go back to Miss Gilchrist's house, and Miss Birrell and I followed very shortly afterwards. I saw A.B. at the house. It was finally arranged that Helen Lambie should go home to her aunt's at South Kinning Place. I saw Miss Birrell home, and afterwards accompanied Helen Lambie to her aunt's. During the evening I had a long talk with Helen Lambie, and she never suggested to me, so far as I can remember, that A.B. was the man she saw.

This statement was read over to the witness, and was signed by him as being true.

(Signed)
CHAS. FREDERIC COWAN.
JAMES G. MILLAR.

———

Glasgow, 23rd April, 1914.

Compeared Helen Lambie or Gillon (27), residing at 169 Shearer's Land, Holytown, who states — I was over three years with Miss Gilchrist as a maid-servant. Miss Gilchrist was an old lady, but quite intelligent and able to look after her own affairs. On the day of Miss Gilchrist's death, about five minutes to seven, she asked me to go for a newspaper, and after I got that I was to go out for some messages, and she gave me a penny and a half-sovereign. I went out, taking the penny and leaving the half-sovereign on the table. I had the keys with me, but I can't say that Miss Gilchrist saw them in my hand. On former occasions I have forgotten the keys and rung the bell, and Miss Gilchrist opened the door for me and waited for me at the door. I never saw her leave the door open and go into her room. On the 21st December I went out for the paper, spoke to a constable on the way, with whom I was acquainted. I don't think I was more than ten minutes away from the house. When I returned the lower door was open, which I know was closed when I left, for I banged it. I went up the stair, and on the way up I saw wet marks of footprints on it. I found Mr. Adams standing at the upper door, and he told me that his sisters had heard strange noises in the house and had asked him to go up, and I said to him that that was likely to be the pulleys in the kitchen falling. I opened the door with the two keys. I am quite clear I did not enter the house and was standing on the mat when I saw a man proceed from the direction of the spare bedroom towards the door. He passed me and then passed Mr. Adams. He walked quite calmly until he passed us — with his head down — and after he passed us he walked swiftly down the stair, but not excitedly so as to raise my suspicion. I did not know the man and never saw him before. Q. Why did you not ask him what he was doing there? A. I never suspected there was anything wrong. I did not see his face in the house, but I saw the side of it as he was going down stairs. He was dressed in a fawn-coloured rainproof coat and a dark cap. I did not tell the police that night that he was wearing a long grey overcoat and dark cap. It was like a Donegal cap. I think I mentioned the Donegal cap that night. I went into the kitchen and saw nothing wrong with the pulleys. I came out of the kitchen and went into the spare bedroom, where I saw a light. I did not see Miss Gilchrist in the bedroom, so I went towards the dining-room door and looked into the dining-room, with the handle of the door in my hand. I did not see Miss Gilchrist at first, but I looked round the table and I saw her lying on the floor with a fur rug on the top of her. I told Mr. Adams that man had done something to Miss Gilchrist, and I ran down the stair, along with Mr. Adams, and I saw Miss Adams then, and I afterwards saw a constable and I told him about it, and after that I ran along to Miss Birrell's house. I rang the bell, and my impression is that Miss Birrell opened the door. I told Miss Birrell that I had been out for a paper and that a man had come into the house and done something to]Miss Gilchrist. I did not say to her who the man was. She told me to go back to Miss Gilchrist's house and she would follow immediately, and I did that. The statement in Appendix No. 2 to Detective Inspector Trench's precognition being read over to Mrs. Gillon, she states that there is absolutely not one word of truth in it. She never said to Miss Birrell that it was A.B., and the whole story is absolutely false. I had seen A.B. in Miss Gilchrist's house on one occasion before....The man I saw leaving the house was not at all like, nor did I ever see A.B. dressed like the man I saw...A gentleman who had apartments in Miss Birrell's house took me to my aunt's house. I saw several policemen on the night of the murder. I don't remember saying that it was a Donegal cap the man had on, but it was in my mind all the same. I remember, on the Sunday night after the New Year of 1909 I had a visit from Detective Inspector Trench and Detective Keith. I don't remember them showing me a sketch of Oscar Slater on that occasion, and I was not asked to identify him. On that occasion neither Trench nor Keith referred to A.B. I did not say in answer to a question as to whether A.B. was the man I saw "It's gey funny if it wasn't him I saw."...The whole of that story is absolutely false. At the interview on the Sunday night after the New Year A.B.'s name was never mentioned. I did not know Oscar Slater before the night of the murder. I never saw him before that. I never saw him in company with a man named Nugent. I was not in Oscar Slater's house, I didn't even know where he lived. I had nothing whatever to do with Slater previous to the murder and knew nothing about him. I wish to make it quite clear that neither to the Procurator Fiscal nor to the police, nor to anyone else, did I make the statement that A.B. was the man I saw leaving the house. When the identification took place in America, Barrowman, Pyper, and I were standing in the hall of the police office when Slater passed. I was the first to identify him. I said, "There's the man coming," and Mary Barrowman said, "Oh, ay that's him." I identified him most of all by his walk and his make and his general appearance, but not by his face. When I saw the man in the house on the day of the murder I thought his face was bare by the side of it, but I could not say positively whether he had a moustache or not.

This statement was read over to the witness, and was signed by her as being true.

(Signed)
HELEN GILLON.
JAMES G. MILLAR.

———

Glasgow, 23rd April, 1914.

Compeared Andrew Nisbet Keith (36), Detective Inspector, Glasgow Police Central Division, who states — On 3rd January, 1909, I went, along with Detective Lieutenant Trench, to 15 South Kinning Place, Glasgow, the house of Helen Lambie's aunt. I don't remember Lieutenant Trench taking a pencil sketch of Oscar Slater out to Helen Lambie. I have no clear recollection of what occurred there. I have no recollection of Lieutenant Trench bringing the conversation, round to the question if she knew the man who left]Miss Gilchrist's house, although it was likely that was done. There was not such a word said in my presence as a suggestion from Lieutenant Trench that A.B. was the man that Helen Lambie saw leaving the house. If such a thing had been said I would have remembered it. It is not true that she replied: "It's gey funny if it wasn't him I saw."...Lieutenant Trench's statement, as contained on page 9* of his precognition, has been read over to me, and the whole thing is news to me, and I have no recollection of its having occurred. If A.B.'s name had been mentioned I think I would have remembered it. My recollection is that we went to the house of Helen Lambie's aunt on our own initiative, without being sent by anyone.

* I.e., As to what passed at the interview witness and Lieutenant Trench had with Miss Lambie on 3rd January, 1909.

This statement was read over to the witness, and was signed by him as being true.

(Signed)
ANDREW N. KEITH.
JAMES G. MILLAR.

———

Glasgow, 24th April, 1914.

Compeared Mary Barrowman (20), residing at 19 Windsor Street, Glasgow, who states: — I was employed by Mr. Maccallum, a bootmaker in Great Western Road, in December, 1908. I remember that I was sent out with a parcel about seven o'clock on the night of 21st December, 1908. The shop was kept by Mr. Maccallum and Miss Maccallum, and sometimes old Mr. Maccallum came in. These were the only people employed in the shop except myself. I cannot remember who gave me the parcel. I got parcels to deliver both from Mr. Maccallum and Miss Maccallum, and I cannot say who gave me the parcel that night. The parcel was addressed to Mr. Howat, 36 Cleveland Street; I was often down at Mr. Howat's house, but I could not say if I delivered another parcel to him shortly before the 21st of December. As far as I remember, I went up Barrington Drive and along West Princes Street to St. George's Road. I don't remember speaking to anyone on the way to West Princes Street. I went along Princes Street on the south side. It was dark at the time. As I came near the close of the house where !Miss Gilchrist lived, and when I was near a lamp, I saw a man running down the steps from her outside door. Without stopping he looked towards George's Road and then in my direction, and then he ran towards me, and as he came up to me he came up against me. I was on the pavement at this time. When he passed me he did not turn and look at me. As he passed me I was next the lamp and he was nearer the houses, and the light of the lamp shone down upon him. I had a good look at him. I saw his face. He had a Donegal hat on. I don't remember the colour of it or whether it was dark or light. He had a fawn overcoat on, and under the overcoat a dark suit of clothes. Now I don't remember what colour of boots he had on. His nose was twisted at the upper part of the bridge. I don't remember if he had a moustache or not. I knew what a Donegal hat was then, and my original description may have been a tweed cloth hat, but I would have called it a Donegal hat. The man passed me very quickly. I had a good look at him. I think I could have identified him again, although it was a very short look I had. He was alone. After he passed me I turned and looked at him, but I don't remember of walking after him. He ran along to the corner of West Cumberland Street, and then he turned down that street. As long as he was in my sight I did not see anyone join him. I did not see him take off his hat after he passed me. As far as I remember, he had his hands in the overcoat pockets. I am quite clear about all that. I did not see two men

run straight past West Cumberland Street. After the man went down West Cumberland Street I went on with the parcel. I did not see anyone come out of the door of Miss Gilchrist's house. I don't remember seeing any other body in West Princes Street at that time. I went right along to St. George's Road, and then to Mr. Howat's house, by what direction I could not say, but I think it would be down George's Road and then down North Street. I remember arriving at Mr. Howat's house. I think it was Mrs. Howat who took the parcel, but I am not quite sure. After delivering the parcel I went back to the shop, but I don't remember what road I went home. I don't remember passing along West Princes Street again. I left the shop at eight o'clock, so far as I remember, and I went to the Band of Hope in Walker Street, of which Mr. Barbour was then Superintendent. After the Band of Hope meeting I heard of the murder, and I and some of the other girls went down to West Princes Street. That was not in the direction of my home. I saw the crowd there and heard more about the murder, and afterwards went home. My mother was angry with me for being late, and I told her about the murder and about the man I had seen. A day or two afterwards — two days after my mother informed Detective M'Gimpsey and an officer of the police came and saw me. I think it was Detective Pyper to whom I first made a statement. I afterwards went out to America to identify Slater. I had not seen any portrait of him before that. I don't remember seeing any portrait of him before I went to the court house to identify him. When I was in the corridor of the court house I saw three men pass me. There were with me then Mr. Adams, Mr. Pyper, Mr. Warnock, and Miss Lambie. I am sure that I recognised the man first and said to Mr. Pyper: — "There's the man coming" before I heard Miss Lambie say anything about it. Then I went into the court room and identified him there, as I have described in my evidence at the trial. I am quite certain the night I went out to deliver the parcel was the night of the murder. Two detectives came with me afterwards to Mr. Howat's house to make sure that I had delivered the parcel. I think they were Detectives Trench and Cameron.

This statement was read over to the witness, and was signed by her as being true.

(Signed)
MARY BARROWMAN.
JAMES G. MILLAR.

———

Glasgow, 24th April, 1914.

Compeared Colin Gillies Maccallum (40), residing at 1 Kennedy Drive, Partick, who states: — In December, 1908, I was a boot- and shoe-maker at 333 Great Western Road, Glasgow. My father and sister were also employed along with me, and the only other person employed was Mary Barrowman. On the 21st of December, 1908, I am quite sure that Mary Barrowman went with a parcel with a pair of boots to Mr.

Howat, at 36 Cleveland Street. I cannot say whether there was an entry to that effect in my books. I have not got the books now, because since we have removed to another address they have gone amissing. I think Mary Barrowman was sent on another message to Mr. Howat a few days previous to 21st December. Although my books were here and showed no entry of a message to Mr. Howat's house, that would not necessarily mean that Mary Barrowman had not gone with such a message, as the boots might only be straightened, and there would be no charge for that. I have no reason to believe that Mary Barrowman did not go on that message that day, and I never said to anyone that I did not believe that Mary Barrowman had gone that message that day. As a matter of fact, I believed that she did go the message.

This statement was read over to the witness, and was signed by him as being true.

(Signed)
COLIN G. MACCALLUM.
JAMES G. MILLAR.

———

Further, on the same date, Colin Gillies Maccallum states that he did not make the statement to Lieutenant Trench that is contained in No. 15 of the Appendix annexed to Lieutenant Trench's precognition. I did meet Lieutenant Trench about the months of December or January last, in the entry leading up to our house, but as my mother was ill I did not take him in. I did not state to him that I was and still am convinced that Mary Barrowman was not sent that message on the night of the murder but several nights before. I never said that Mary Barrowman did not go the message on the night of the murder and that she insisted that she did. I never said to Inspector Pyper that Barrowman had not gone on the message to Mr. Howat on the night of the murder and showed him my books in support of that statement. I never said to Lieutenant Trench that I was sure that Barrowman did not go that message on the night of the murder and that my books bore me out. That statement is absolutely false.

The truth.

(Signed)
COLIN G. MACCALLUM.
JAMES G. MILLAR.

———

Glasgow, 24th April, 1914.

Compeared Mary B. Maccallum (39), residing at 1 Kennedy Drive, Partick. West, who states: — I assisted my father and brother in carrying on a boot and shoe maker's shop at 333 Great Western Road, Glasgow, in December, 1908. Mary Barrowman was employed as a message girl in the shop in December, 1908. I cannot say whether she was sent upon a message to Mr. Howat's, 36 Cleveland Street, on 21st December, 1908. The Howats were very good customers of ours and messages were frequently sent to them, and for aught I know Mary Barrowman may have gone with a message there on 21st December, 1908. Even if there was no entry in our books, it would not necessarily mean that she had not gone there. Our books have gone amissing since we were in that shop.

This statement was read over to the witness, and is signed by her as being true.

(Signed)
MARY BLAIR MACCALLUM.
JAMES G. MILLAR.

————

Glasgow, 24th April, 1914.

Compeared James Howat (32), residing at 36 Cleveland Street, Glasgow, who says: — I remember that on the evening of 21st December, 1908, between seven and eight o'clock, Mary Barrowman called at my parent's house and left a parcel containing shoes. I was in the lobby, and opened the door and took the parcel from the girl Mary Barrowman. I am quite sure that it was on the 21st December I got that parcel. I remember that, on the Monday before, the girl Barrowman came with a gift from my mother, as my birthday had been on the preceding day, Sunday. I am certain that Barrowman did deliver the parcel on the 21st.

This statement was read over to the witness, and was signed by him as being true.

(Signed)
JAMES HOWAT.
JAMES G. MILLAE.

————

Glasgow, 23rd April, 1914.

Compeared William Roxburgh Barbour (45), 82 Cambridge Street, Glasgow, who states; — I am the late Superintendent of the Band of Hope Mission, Lansdowne Mission Hall, Walker Street, off Hopehill Road, Glasgow. I was Superintendent of the Mission in 1908. The Band of Hope]Mission usually met from about a quarter to eight till about nine. I know that there was a meeting of the Mission on the evening of Monday, 21st December, 1908. Miss Mary Barrowman, whom I know very well, was a fairly regular attender at the Mission and used to aid by singing at the entertainments. The opinion I formed of her was that she was a respectable girl, straight and honest, but quick tempered and indifferent to other people's opinion. She seemed to be a smart girl. I cannot say if she was at the meeting on the 21st December, 1908, as we keep no record of attendances and I cannot trust my memory so far back. So far as I know there is no means of discovering whether she was there that night.

This statement was read over to the witness, and was signed by him as being true.

(Signed)
WM. R. BARBOUR.
JAMES G. MILLAR.

———

Glasgow, 23rd April, 1914.

Compeared Agnes Brown (37), residing at 5 Barrington Drive, Glasgow, who states: — I am a school teacher, and on 21st December, 1908, I resided at 48 Grant Street, Glasgow. The house was in the same block as Miss Gilchrist's house and the back windows looked in towards hers. I was cited as witness for the Crown, but was not called at the trial of Oscar Slater. When I went to Dunard Street School I went west along Grant Street to West Cumberland Street, and turned north along the east side of that street till I came to West Princes Street. On 21st December, 1908, I left my house about eight minutes past seven. Since the time of the trial I have tried to forget what occurred on the evening of 21st December, 1908, and I have only a vague recollection now of what occurred, but I am prepared to say that the statements in my precognition are absolutely true, as I had a clear recollection of the facts then. I can say distinctly that when I came to the corner of West Princes Street I saw two men running west, and that one of them jostled me. I can only say that previous to seeing these two men I did not see a single man running down West Cumberland Street. The two men did not turn down West Cuniberiand Street, but ran straight on in a westerly direction. I did not see them turn either north or south from West Princes Street. I could not now describe how they were dressed. A man was shown to me along with others, and I identified him as being one of the men I saw. I was afterwards informed that his name was Oscar Slater. I am quite unable now to speak to the clothes the men were wearing. I remember that in crossing Great Western Road I saw the time in a chemist's shop.

This statement was read over to the witness, and was signed by her as being true.

(Signed)
AGNES BROWN.
JAMES G. MILLAR.

———

At Glasgow, the 31st December, 1908, in presence of
Arthur Thomson Glegg, Esquire, Advocate, Sheriff Substitute of Lanarkshire.

Compeared Agnes Brown, who, being solemnly sworn and examined, declares: — I am 30 years of age, a school teacher, and reside at 48 Bank Street, Glasgow.

On Monday, 21st December, 1908, about 7.8 p.m., I left the house there to attend evening classes in Dunard Street School. I went west along Grant Street to West Cumberland Street, and turned north along the east side of that street till I came to West Princes Street. I was in the act of stepping off the foot-pavement there to cross West Princes Street at an angle towards Carrington Street (a north-westerly direction) when two men came running past me from the direction of George's Road. They were on the foot-pavement (south foot- pavement) off West Princes Street. They were going very quickly, and the one nearest me came against me in passing. He merely touched me. He never spoke, however, and both continued running west along West Princes Street. They kept on the foot-pavement for a little distance and then they crossed to the centre of the street.

I stood for a moment at the corner of Carrington Street to see where they went, and they turned down Rupert Street towards Great Western Road.

I then passed down Carrington Street to Great Western Road, but I saw no more of them. In crossing that road I saw the time on a clock in a chemist's shop that it was then 7.12.

I returned home from my classes shortly after 10 o'clock, and then learned of Miss Gilchrist's murder from my two sisters.

I did not at the time associate the two men with the murder, but next morning, after reading a description in the "Glasgow Herald" of a man who was said to have left deceased's house, I thought he might be one of the two men referred to.

I did not see the face of either man, but so far as I could make out they were each about 30 years of age and about 5 feet 9 inches in height. The one next me was of medium build, with dark hair, and seemed to be clean shaven. He wore a three-quarter length grey-coloured overcoat, I think tweed; dark trousers, probably brown; dark tweed cap without flaps, and had both hands in his coat pockets as he ran away. I took no notice of his boots. The man furthest from me was of medium build, but seemed to be squarer than the other man. He had very dark hair, probably jet black, well groomed and glossy, and was bareheaded He wore a navy blue overcoat with velvet collar, dark trousers, and black boots. He had also a stand-up white collar which seemed to be very clean, and carried something in his left hand — the one furthest from me.

I could not say what this was. It might have been a walking stick, but I thought it looked clumsier than a walking stick.

I know the house which was occupied by Miss Gilchrist.

It is about 200 yards east from the corner of West Cumberland Street and Princes Street, where the two men ran past me.

All which I declare to be truth.

(Signed)
AGNES BROWN. A. T. GLEGG.

———

23rd March, 1909.

Re-examined, says:—

I adhere to the above statements as correct, and have to add that on Sunday, 21st February, I saw in the Central Police Office prisoner Oscar Slater. He was then dressed in a grey Melton overcoat with velvet collar, and was bareheaded. I recognised him as one of the two men I had seen running away on the Monday night in question. He was bareheaded when I saw him running away, and the man who was with him was wearing a dark close-fitting cap.

It is possible that Slater might be wearing another coat under the Melton overcoat, as the latter is large enough to cover another overcoat.

I also recognise Slater by his profile. I did not get a front view of his face, but I picked him out from a number of men — 12 to 14 as I think — in the police office, and I have not the slightest doubt about him.

It was not only by his profile and back view, but the shape of his neck and ears and square shoulders.

I did not see Slater with a cap or hat when he was running away, but the man who was with him had a cap like the dark greenish cap shown me.

I think the second man resembles a man whom I had seen repeatedly in Grant Street, always between 7 and 8 p.m.; that street runs parallel with West Princes Street.

I have seen Miss Gilchrist recently at her back bedroom window, and I have seen her lift the window. I can't say I saw her put anything out. These occasions were when she seemed to be dressing.

Also truth.

AGNES BROWN.

———

Glasgow, 25th April, 1914.

Compeared Allan M'Lean (32), residing at Lambhill House, Lambhill, who states: — In December, 1908, I was a member of the Sloper Club, 24 India Street, Glasgow; I remember a man visited that club whom I only knew as Oscar. I did not know him at that time by the name Oscar Slater, but merely Oscar. I heard, in the month of December, that he was offering a pawn ticket for a brooch to a friend of mine named Anderson. I heard of the murder of Miss Gilchrist on the 21st December. I say in the original statement that "I noticed after the murder of Miss Gilchrist on 21st instant he did not return to the club, and on hearing that he had been offering a pawn ticket for a valuable diamond brooch for sale, which was alleged to have been pledged for £50 on the day of the murder, I on Friday, 25th instant, went to the Detective Department, Central Police Office, and reported the matter. It was not so much his absence from the club that directed my suspicion towards him as his offering the pawn ticket for sale. I had only seen him three times in the club, and I myself was not a regular attender I had formerly seen him. go up a close in St. George's Road which I thought led to his home. Between 7 and 8 o'clock p.m. on 25th December, 1908, I took Detective Inspector Powell to the close. I think I had told Inspector Powell by this time that his name was Slater. I remained on the other side of the street from the close, and the Inspector went up; he afterwards came down and told me that he had made inquiries and there was no one of that name there. I did not see Slater near the close on that occasion, nor did I know then which of the houses on the stair was his. The close seemed quite quiet when I was standing opposite it. I wish to explain that at the early times I saw the man in the club I understood his name was Oscar, but previous to the day of the murder I discovered his name to be Slater.

This statement was read over to the witness, and was signed by him as being true.

(Signed)
ALLAN M'LEAN.
JAMES G. MILLAR.

————

Glasgow Police. I was along with Superintendent Ord in Miss Gilchrist's house on the night of the murder on 21st December, 1908. I saw Helen Lambie in the house, and took her into a room and pressed her with questions as to the identity of the man whom she had seen coming out of the house. She told me she was quite unable to identify him. She did not give me a description of the man, as I understood the other officers had got it. I did not afterwards get a description of the man from Helen Lambie. On 26th December, 1908, I went to a house, 69 St. George's Road, which had been occupied by Slater under the name of Anderson. The door was opened by a maid-servant, who gave the name of Catherine Schmaltz. I asked if she was alone in the house, and she said "Yes." When I was coming away I passed two ladies on the stair—they were coming up—and I turned and followed them and went into the house and asked the maid if these two ladies lived there, and she said "Yes." When I went in first I asked Schmaltz where Anderson had gone to, and she said he had gone to London with "Madame." I asked the maid for Anderson's address in London, and she said 36 Albemarle Street. Schmaltz told me she was going to London that night, and I asked her if she was going to the same address, and she said "No, I am going "to 72 Charlotte Street, care of Ostraw. "When we came back to the house I asked the ladies their names, and they said Mrs. Freedman and Mrs. Hoppe. They said that they knew Anderson and Madame in London, and that Freedman was a half- sister of Madame's. They told me that they were living at the Alexandra Hotel, and that on Friday", the 25th December, Madame had asked Schmaltz to ask them to come down, and that they found them busy packing and asked them where they were going, and Anderson had said that he had got a wire and had to go to Monte Carlo, and that Anderson had got a loan of £25 from Mrs. Freedman, which he promised to repay when he came back. She further said that she and Mrs. Hoppe had arranged to take over the house, paying Stewart & Stewart £4 a month. Mrs. Freedman also said that they were to get a wire from Anderson and Madame when they arrived in Monte Carlo. I called at the house on several occasions afterwards, and on one occasion got a letter addressed to Oscar Slater, Esq., c/o Mr. Anderson, 69 St. George's Road, Glasgow, which bore an American postmark. The night after the murder (22nd December, 1908), I was in Miss Birrell's house, and took a statement from her which was afterwards handed to the Fiscal. In the course of that statement Miss Birrell did not say to me that Helen Lambie had told her that the man she had seen leaving the house on the 21st was A.B. I never heard until this moment that Helen Lambie was supposed to have made such a statement...and according to the information I got it was impossible that he could have anything to do with the murder.

This statement was read over to the witness and was signed by him as being true.

(Signed)
WILLIAM GORDON.
JAMES G. MILLAR.

————

Glasgow, 25th April, 1914.

Compeared James Dornan (38), Detective Inspector, Marine Division, Glasgow Police, who states: — In December, 1908, I was Detective Sergeant in the Western Division, Glasgow. I know this district well, and while it might have been shorter for Mary Barrowman to go from the boot shop down Barrington Drive towards Woodlands Road, nevertheless, the route she took is a more frequented one and a more likely one for her to take. I was present with Inspector Pyper at various interviews with Miss Birrell, and I never heard her make any statement throwing any suspicion whatever upon A.B. I was often present at interviews with Helen Lambie, and she never said anything that connected A.B. with the case. I never heard from her, or any other person, till this week that she had told Miss Birrell that the man she saw on the night of the murder was A.B. I never heard anything that would justify such a suggestion. I remember Helen Lambie telling me in the County Buildings, within a week after the murder, that she had noticed a peculiarity in the man's walk, in the way in which he brought round his foot when walking, and she showed it with her own foot. When I saw Oscar Slater I thought I saw the peculiarity that Helen Lambie had described to me. With regard to Helen Lambie, I made careful inquiries into her character, both at her neighbours, young men whom she knew, and shopkeepers in the locality, and I found that although she was fond of joking she was a perfectly respectable girl. I could find no trace of her ever being in Oscar Slater's house or having any acquaintance with him whatever. On 2nd January, 1909, I, along with other officers, searched Slater's house, and could find no Runaway matches similar to the matches found in the spare bedroom in Miss Gilchrist's house on the night of the murder. When Slater returned from America. I met him at Renfrew and brought him and his baggage up to Glasgow. The boxes were opened in Slater's presence in the Central Police Station, and the clothing seemed to be carefully packed. For anything I saw I could not say that the clothes had been thrown in preparatory to a hurried flight. I saw labels on the boxes, but I could not say what they were, and I could not say whether there were railway labels on them "Glasgow to Lime Street, Liverpool." On 22nd February, 1909, I was present at the Central Police Station when the witnesses were brought in to identify Slater, and I saw Duncan MacBrayne brought in, and I remember that he identified him quite clearly.

This statement was read over to the witness and was signed by him as being true.

(Signed)
JAMES DORNAN.
JAMES G. MILLAR.

APPENDIX VII

EXCERPT FROM MINUTES OF THE GLASGOW MAGISTRATES' COMMITTEE OF DATE 14TH SEPTEMBER, 1914.

The Town Clerk reported that the diet 12th ultimo fixed at last meeting for proceeding with the inquiry into the case of the suspension of Detective Lieutenant Trench had been unsuitable for one of his witnesses, and that in lieu thereof this meeting had been called on the instructions of the Senior Magistrate.

The Committee thereafter heard the Chief Constable as to the charge and also Detective Lieutenant Trench, together with Mr. David Cook, Writer, and Dr. Devon, who were produced as witnesses for the officer in question.

After full and careful consideration of the case, and having regard to the admission made by Detective Lieutenant Trench in his letter to the Chief Constable of date 21st July last, the Committee unanimously found him guilty of the charge on which he was suspended by the Chief Constable, viz.: — communicating to a person who is not a member of the Glasgow Police Force, namely, Mr. David Cook, Writer, Glasgow, information which he (Detective Lieutenant Trench) had acquired in the performance of his duty, and copies of documents from the official records in the case of Oscar Slater, convicted of the murder of Miss Gilchrist on 21st December, 1908, and the Committee, in respect of said finding, and in terms of Section 78 of the Glasgow Police Act, 1866, dismissed Detective Lieutenant Trench from the Police Force of the City.

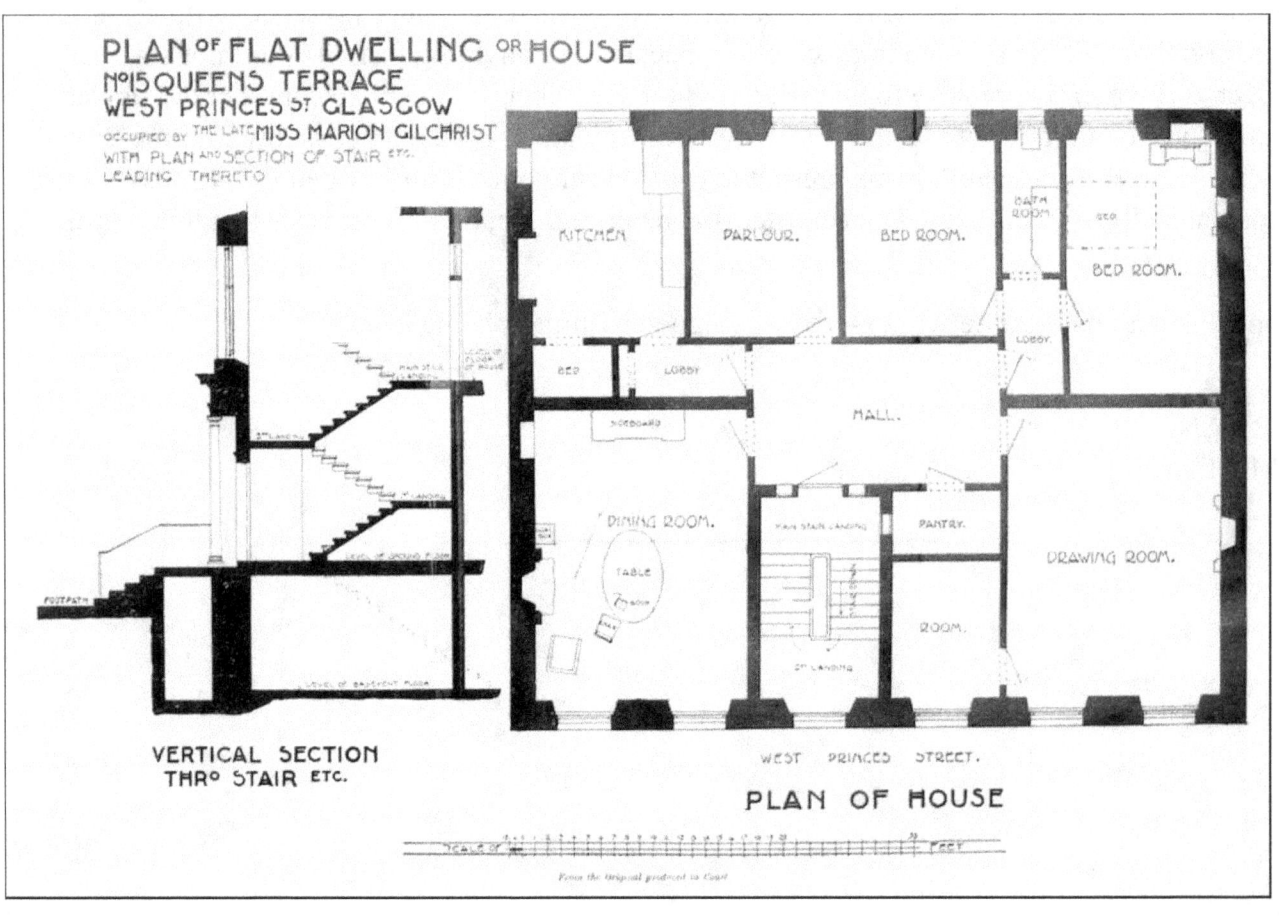

PLAN OF FLAT DWELLING OR HOUSE
Nº 15 QUEENS TERRACE
WEST PRINCES ST GLASGOW
OCCUPIED BY THE LATE MISS MARION GILCHRIST
WITH PLAN AND SECTION OF STAIR ETC.
LEADING THERETO

VERTICAL SECTION THRO STAIR ETC.

PLAN OF HOUSE

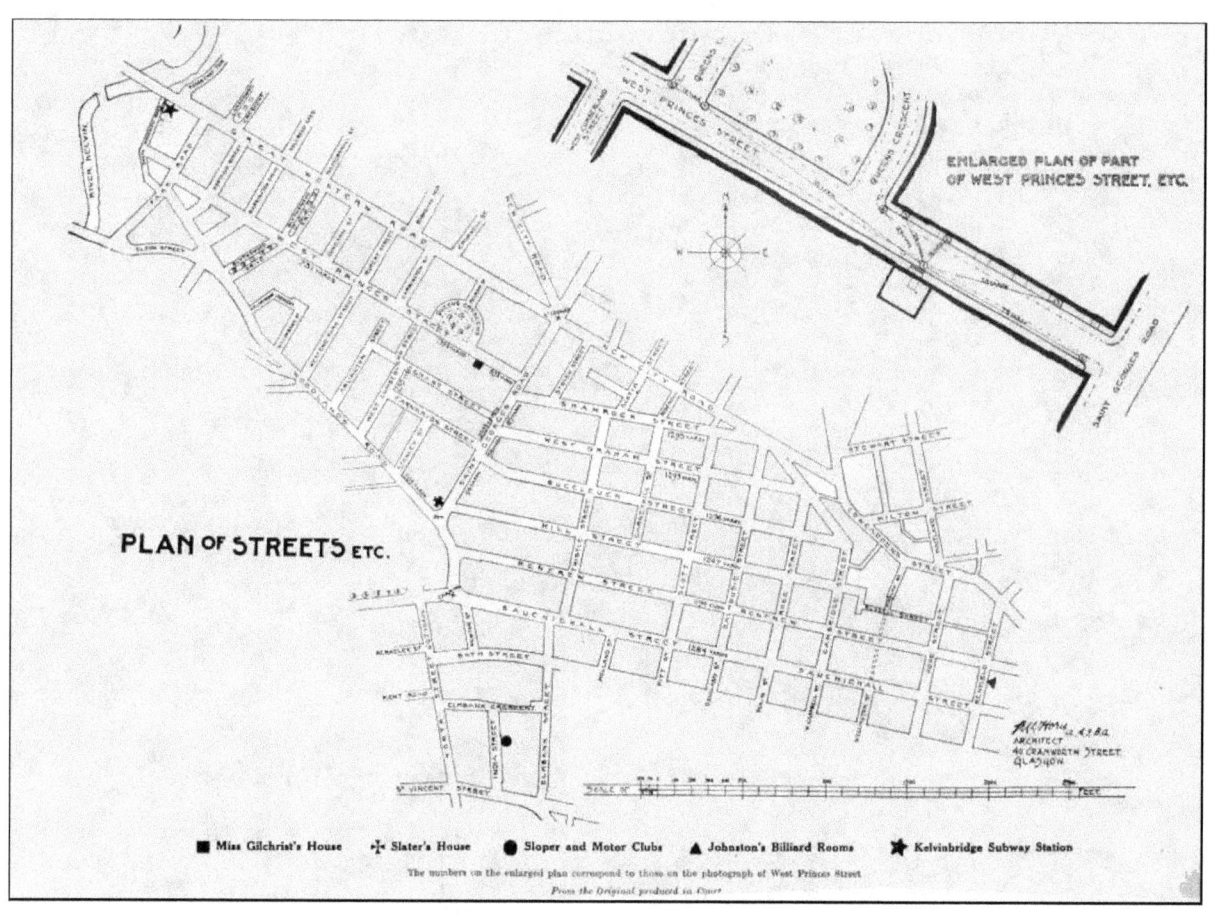

THE END